Shojo Beat

BE
EDGE

Vol. 4

Story & Art by
Io Sakisaka

STROBE EDGE

Volume 4
CONTENTS

Story Thus Far

Ninako is a down-to-earth high school girl who's in love for the first time—with Ren, the most popular boy in her grade. Even though she knows he has a girlfriend, she can't deny her feelings for him and tells him. She's not surprised when he turns her down and asks if they can still be friends.

During the new school year, Ninako meets Takumi Ando, a guy who doesn't seem to take anything seriously. But as they get to know each other, Ando sees how straightforward and good-hearted Ninako is, and he starts to get serious about *her*.

Ren's friend Manabu arranges for Ren, Ninako and Ando to all work part-time at his cousin's new café. One evening after work, Ren's girlfriend, Mayuka, joins the group. Despite having known about Ren and Mayuka's relationship all along, it's still hard for Ninako to see them together, and she makes her escape. Then, Ando tells Ninako that he'll make her forget Ren...

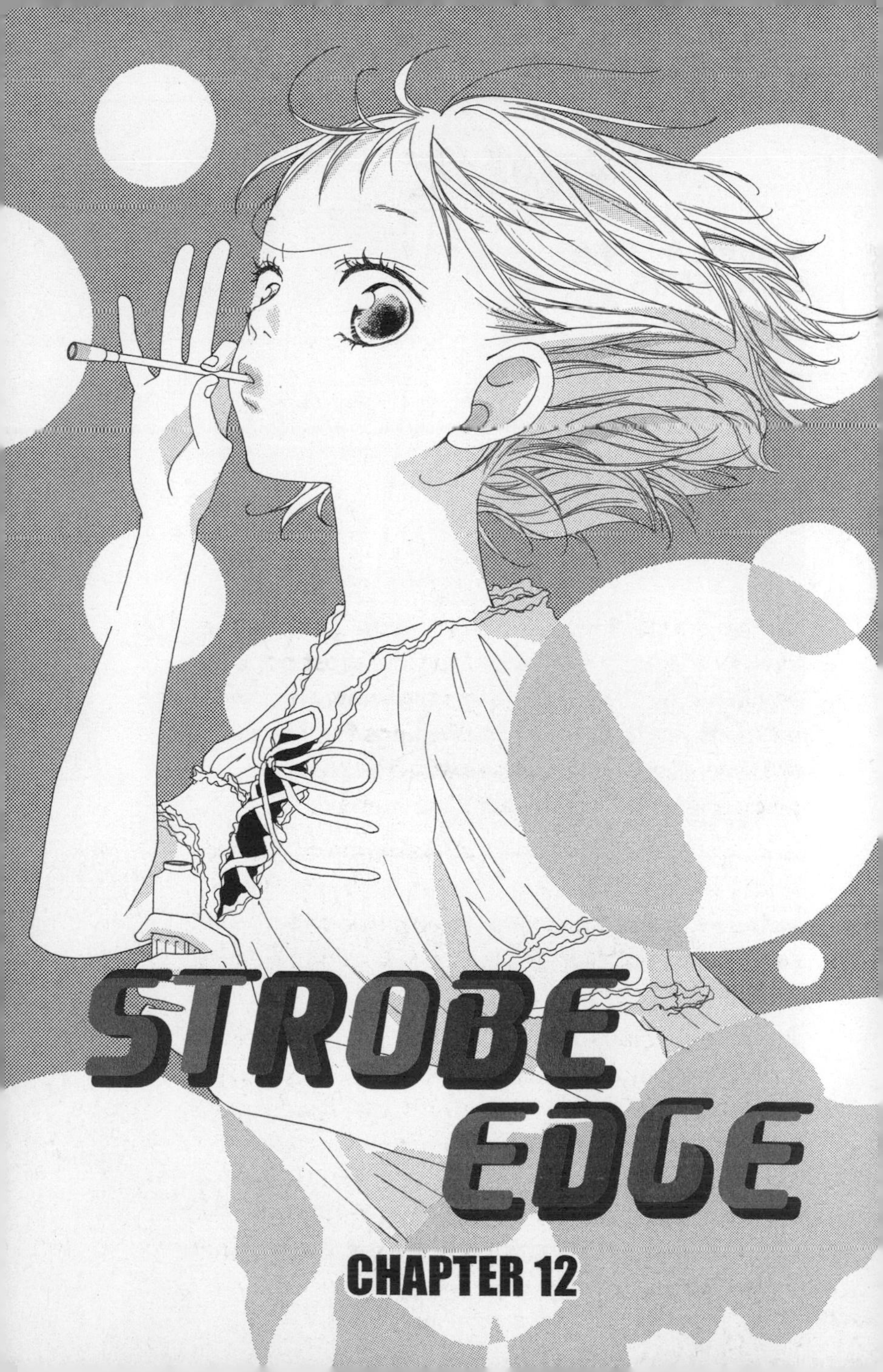
STROBE
EDGE
CHAPTER 12

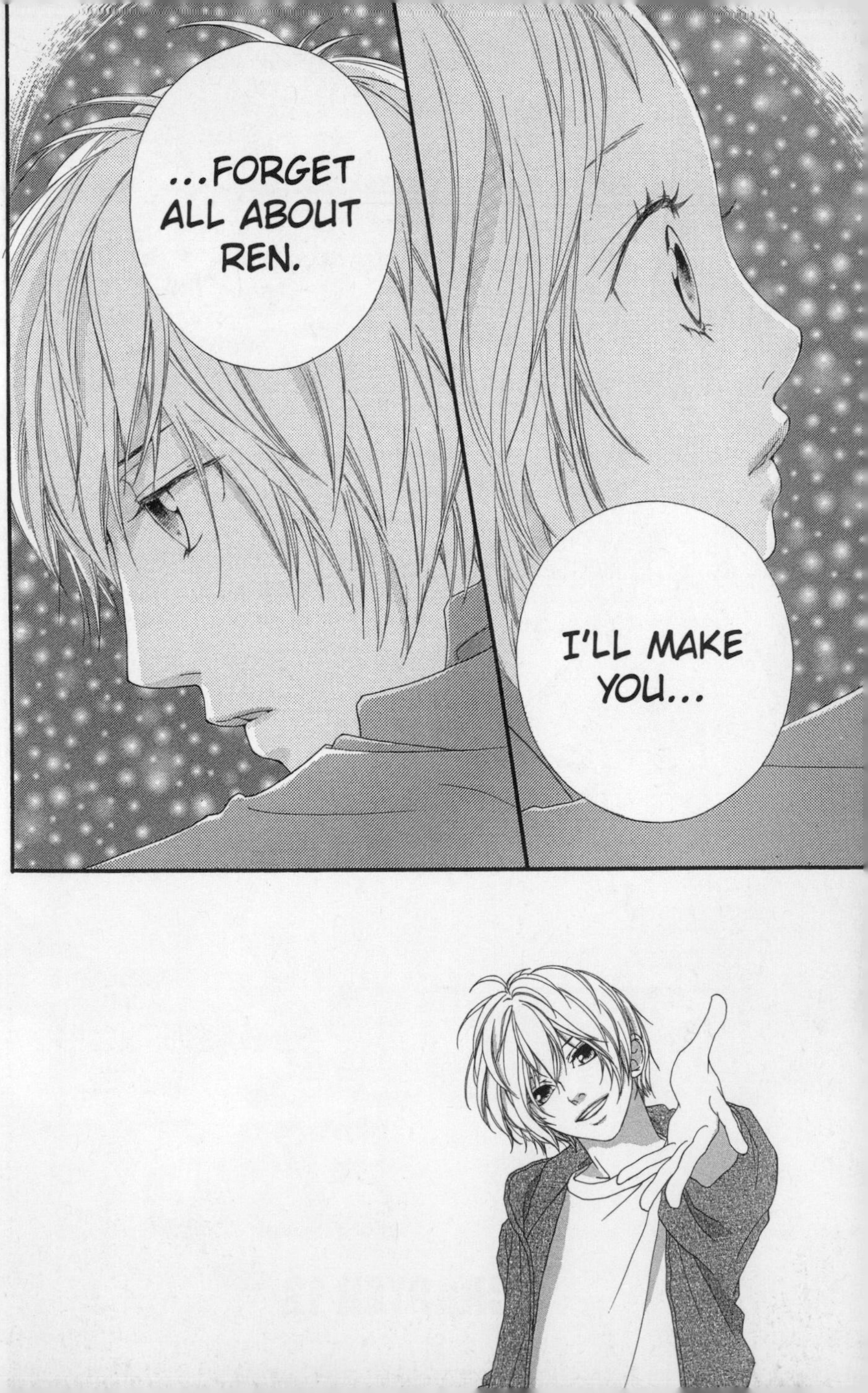
I'LL MAKE YOU...
...FORGET ALL ABOUT REN.

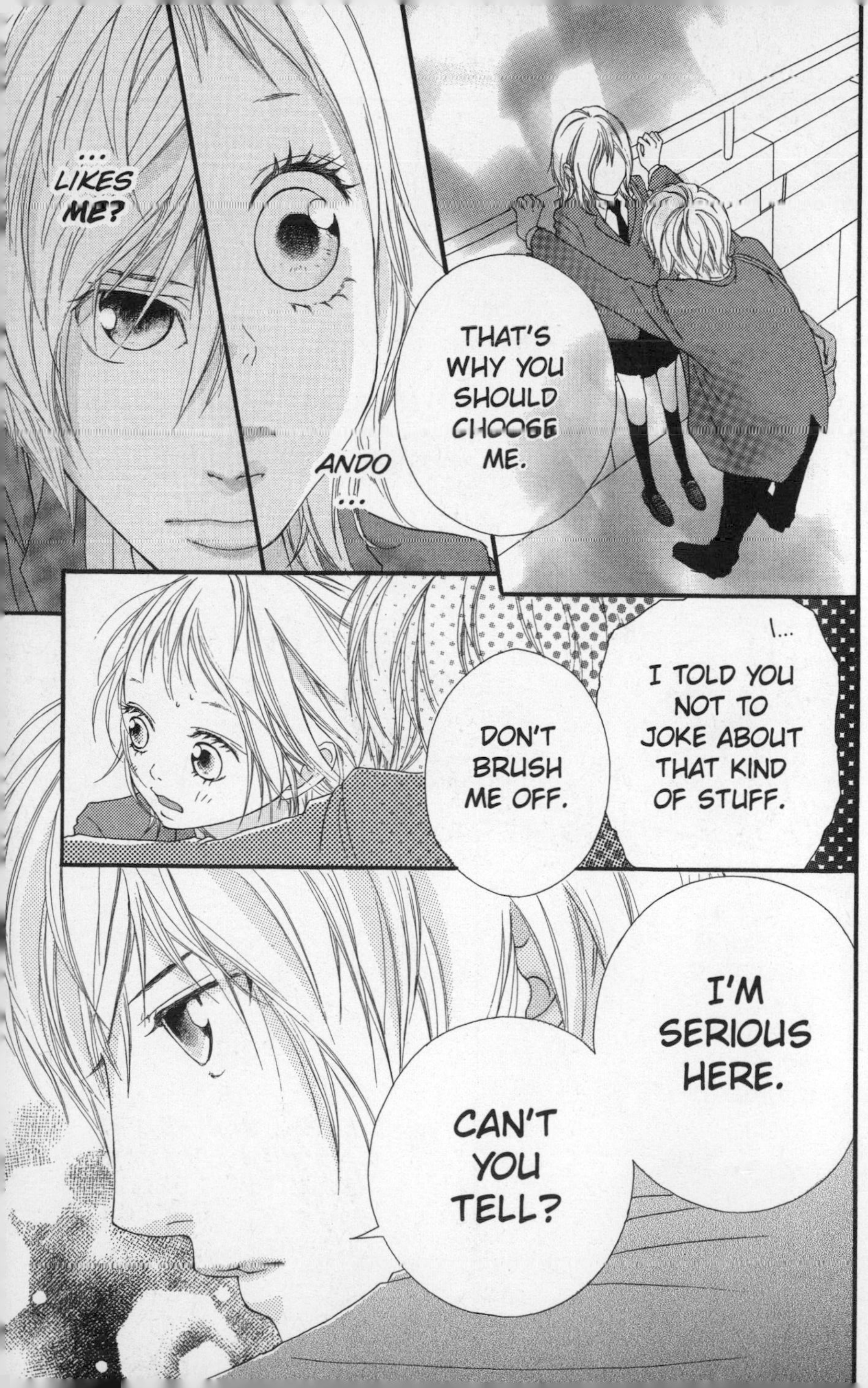
THAT'S WHY YOU SHOULD CHOOSE ME.
ANDO !! ...
... LIKES ME?
I...
I TOLD YOU NOT TO JOKE ABOUT THAT KIND OF STUFF.
DON'T BRUSH ME OFF.
I'M SERIOUS HERE.
CAN'T YOU TELL?

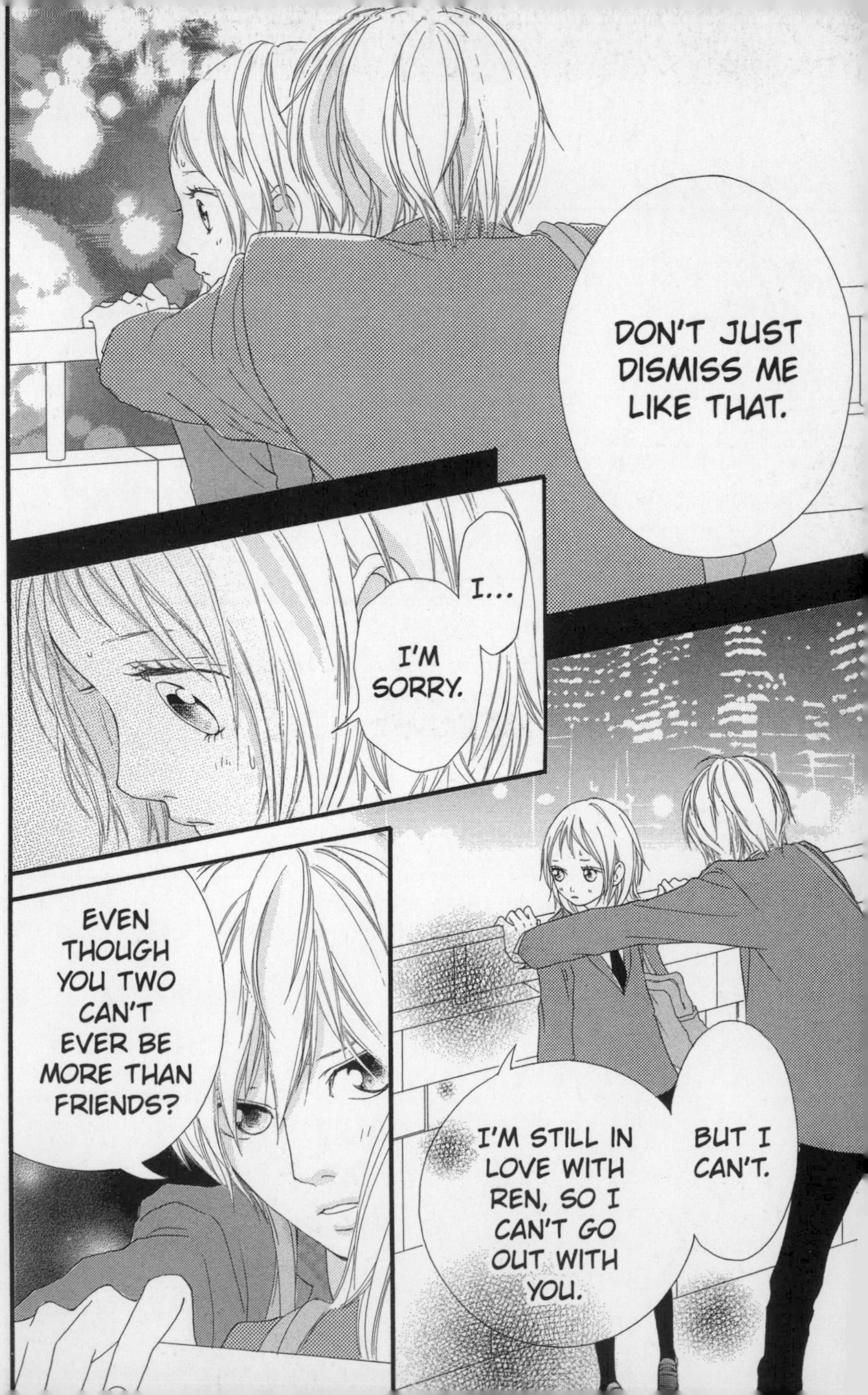
DON'T JUST DISMISS ME LIKE THAT.
I...
I'M SORRY.
EVEN THOUGH YOU TWO CAN'T EVER BE MORE THAN FRIENDS?
BUT I CAN'T.
I'M STILL IN LOVE WITH REN, SO I CAN'T GO OUT WITH YOU.

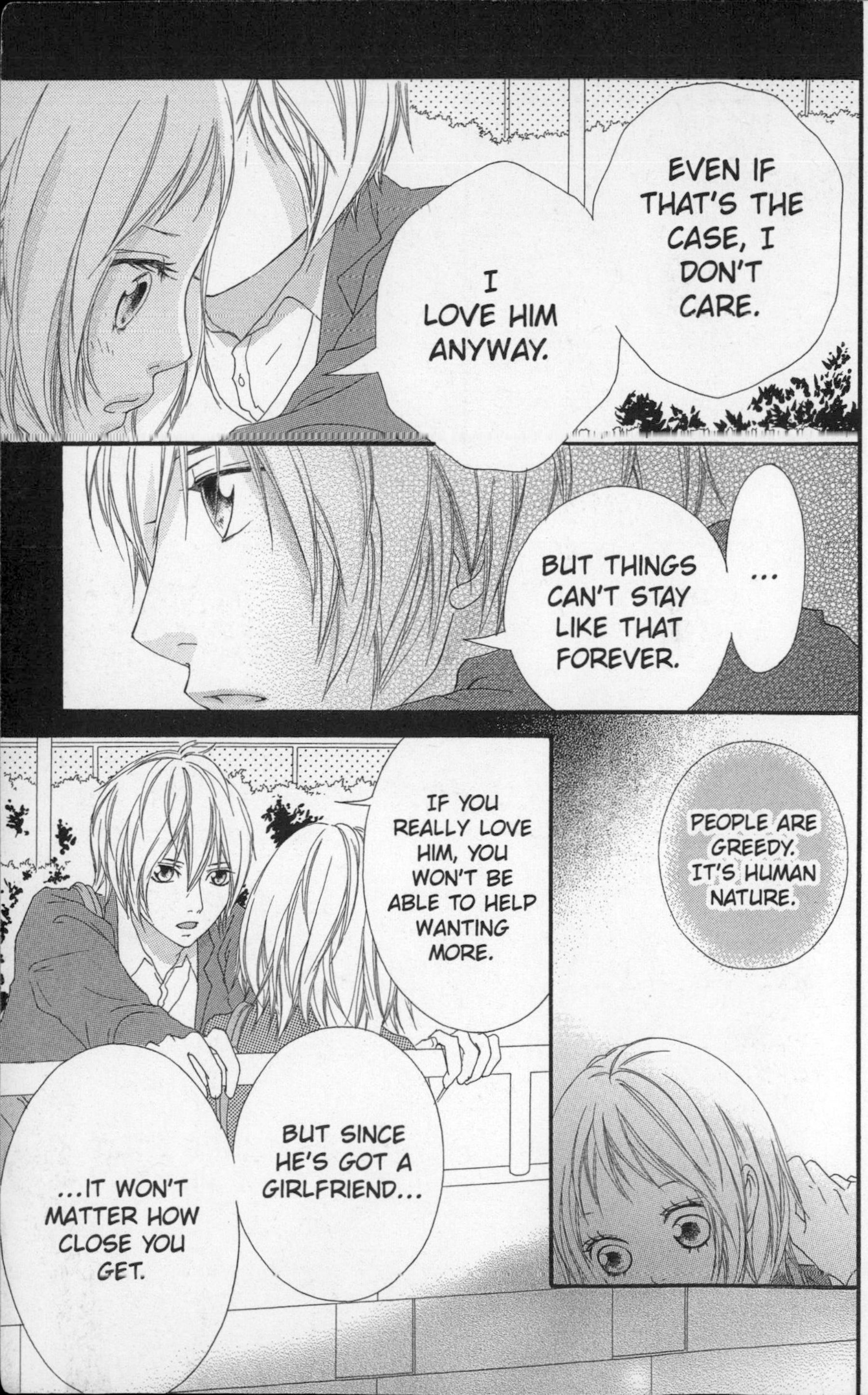
EVEN IF THAT'S THE CASE, I DON'T CARE.
I LOVE HIM ANYWAY.
...
BUT THINGS CAN'T STAY LIKE THAT FOREVER.
PEOPLE ARE GREEDY. IT'S HUMAN NATURE.
IF YOU REALLY LOVE HIM, YOU WON'T BE ABLE TO HELP WANTING MORE.
BUT SINCE HE'S GOT A GIRLFRIEND...
...IT WON'T MATTER HOW CLOSE YOU GET.

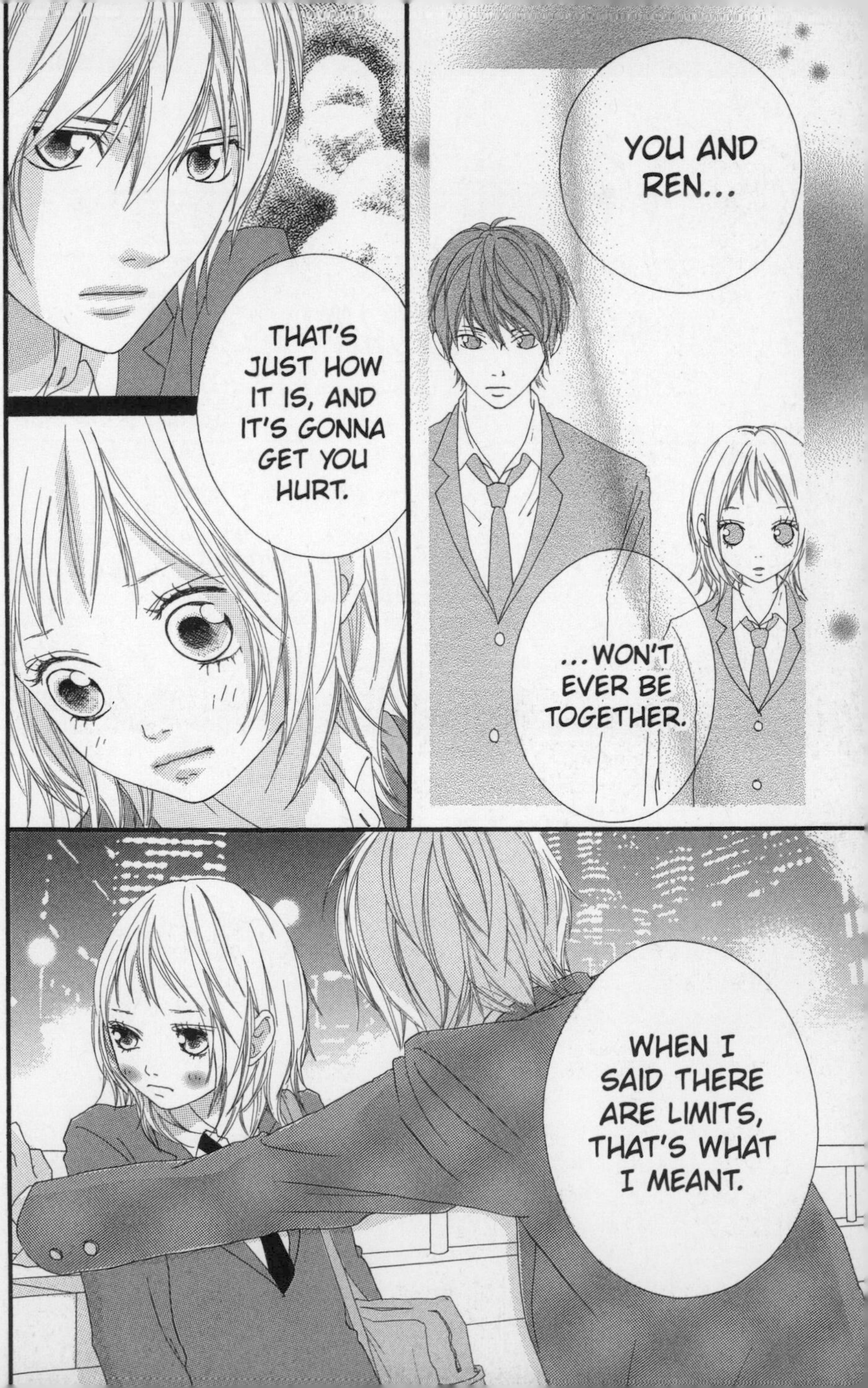
YOU AND REN...
...WON'T EVER BE TOGETHER.
THAT'S JUST HOW IT IS, AND IT'S GONNA GET YOU HURT.
WHEN I SAID THERE ARE LIMITS, THAT'S WHAT I MEANT.

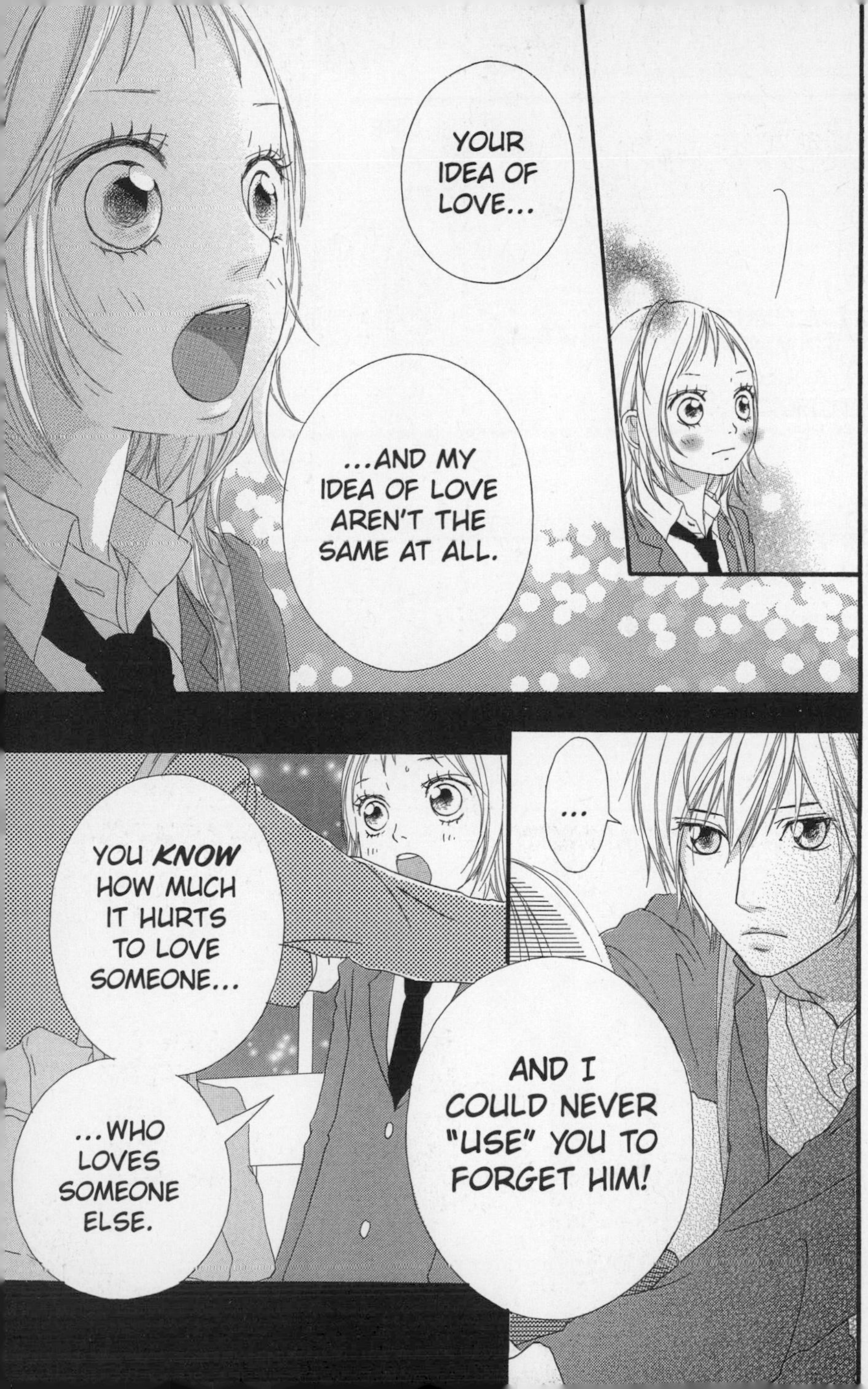
YOUR IDEA OF LOVE...
...AND MY IDEA OF LOVE AREN'T THE SAME AT ALL.
...
YOU **KNOW** HOW MUCH IT HURTS TO LOVE SOMEONE...
...WHO LOVES SOMEONE ELSE.
AND I COULD NEVER "USE" YOU TO FORGET HIM!

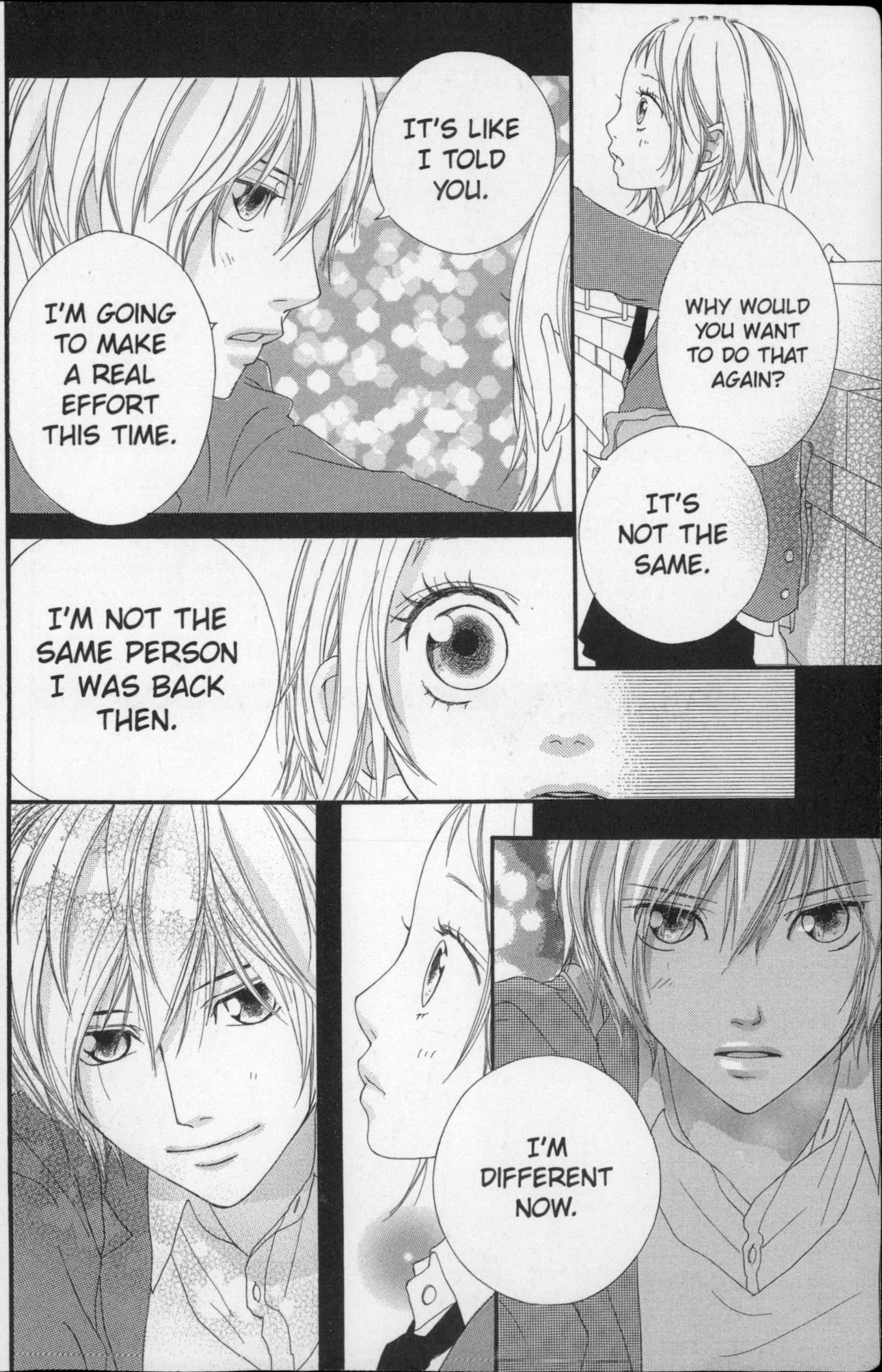
WHY WOULD YOU WANT TO DO THAT AGAIN?
IT'S NOT THE SAME.
IT'S LIKE I TOLD YOU.
I'M GOING TO MAKE A REAL EFFORT THIS TIME.
I'M NOT THE SAME PERSON I WAS BACK THEN.
I'M DIFFERENT NOW.

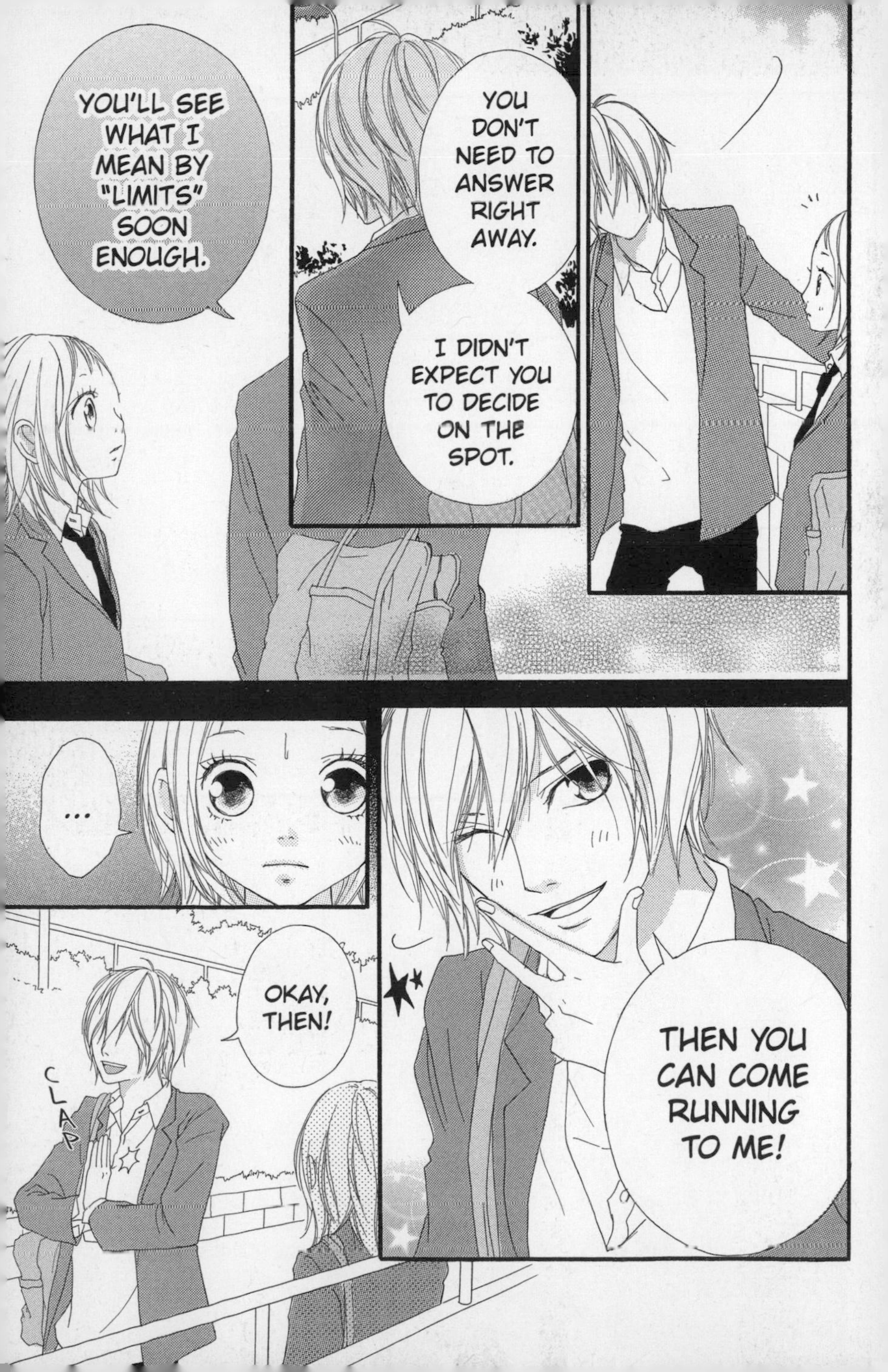
YOU DON'T NEED TO ANSWER RIGHT AWAY.
I DIDN'T EXPECT YOU TO DECIDE ON THE SPOT.
YOU'LL SEE WHAT I MEAN BY "LIMITS" SOON ENOUGH.
THEN YOU CAN COME RUNNING TO ME!
...
OKAY, THEN!
CLAP

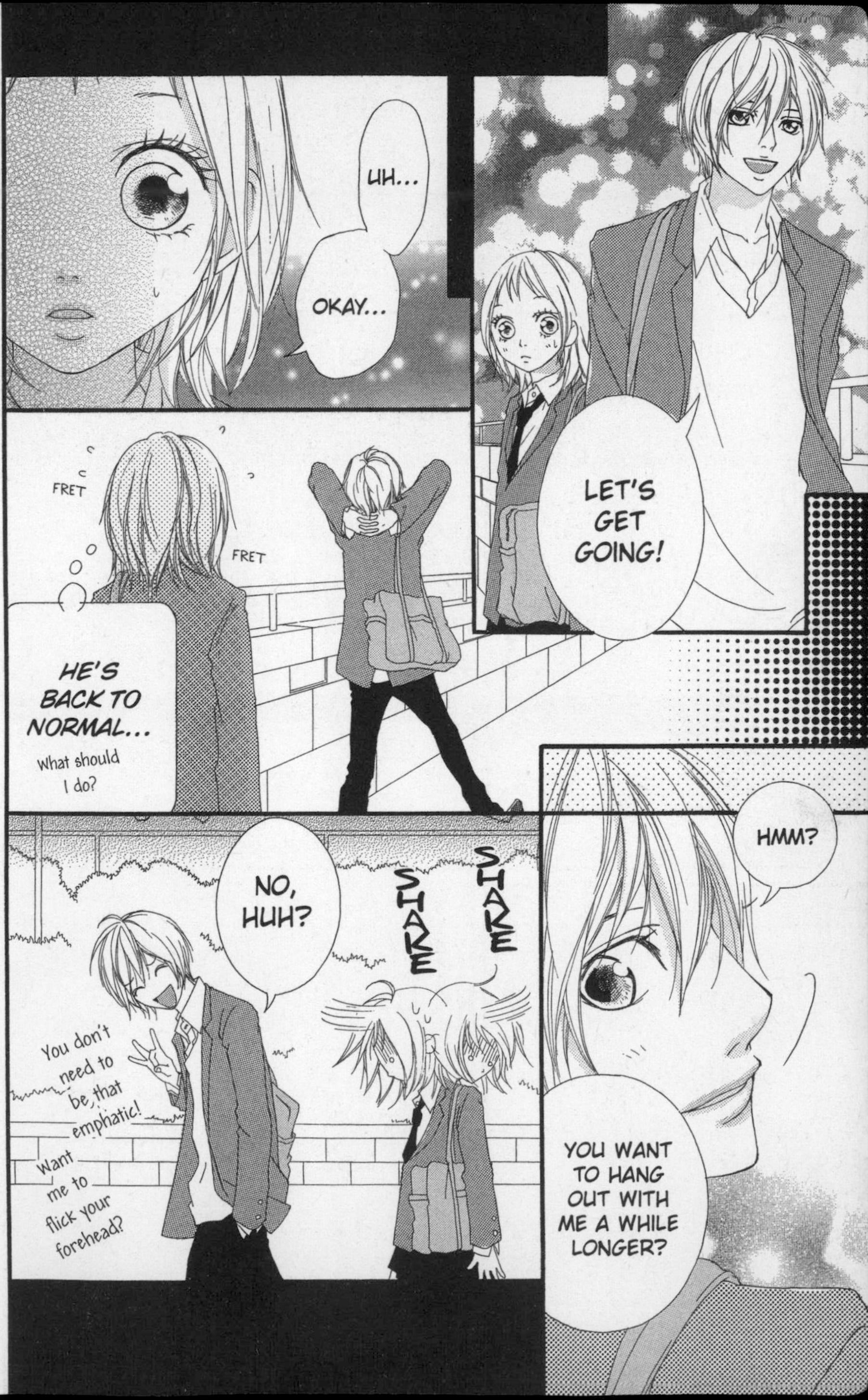
LET'S GET GOING!
UH...
OKAY...
FRET
FRET
HE'S BACK TO NORMAL...
What should I do?
HMM?
YOU WANT TO HANG OUT WITH ME A WHILE LONGER?
SHAKE
SHAKE
NO, HUH?
You don't need to be, that emphatic!
Want me to flick your forehead?

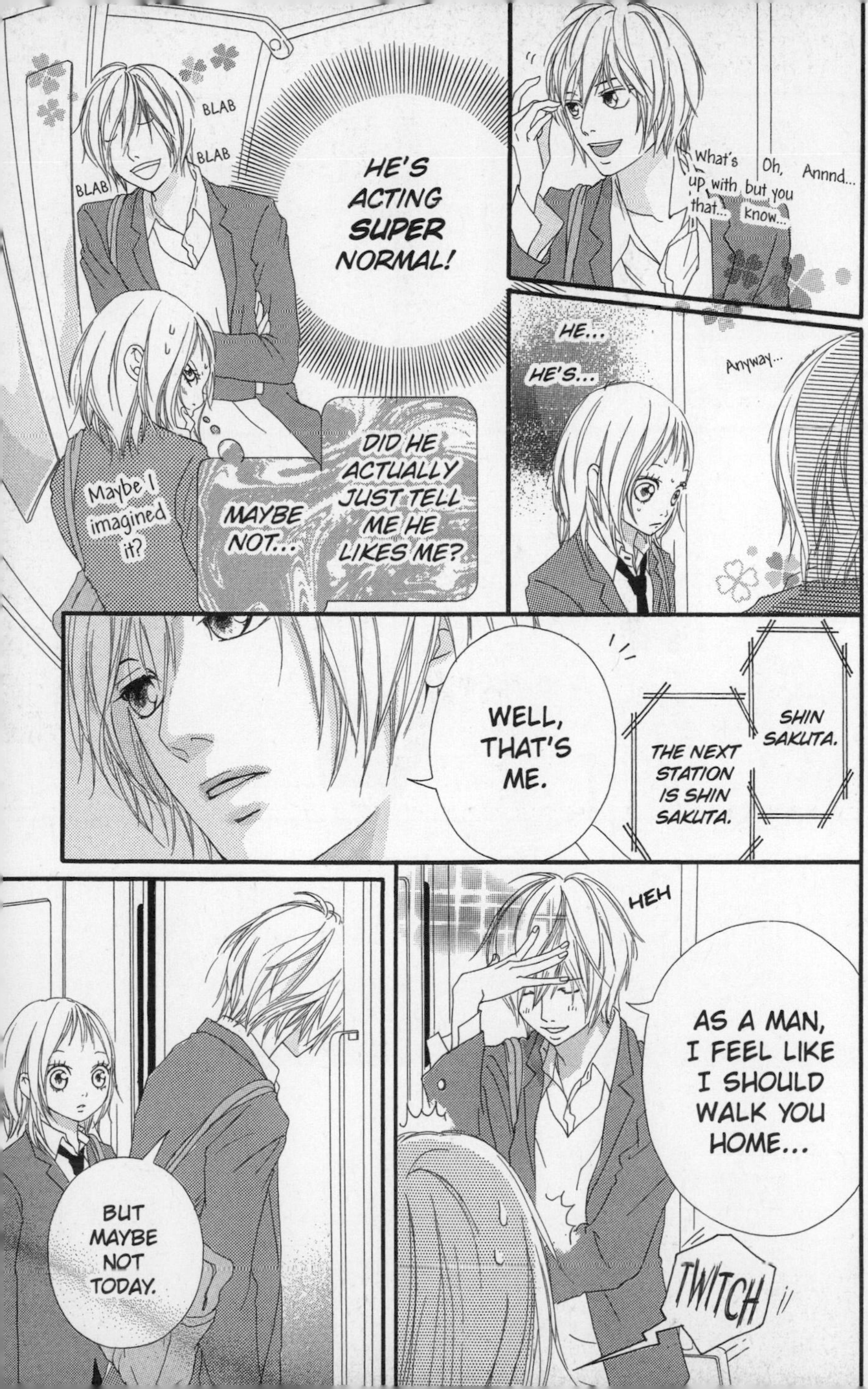
What's up with that...
Oh, but you know...
Annnd...
HE...
HE'S...
Anyway...
BLAB
BLAB
BLAB
HE'S ACTING SUPER NORMAL!
DID HE ACTUALLY JUST TELL ME HE LIKES ME?
MAYBE NOT...
Maybe I imagined it?
SHIN SAKUTA.
THE NEXT STATION IS SHIN SAKUTA.
WELL, THAT'S ME.
HEH
AS A MAN, I FEEL LIKE I SHOULD WALK YOU HOME...
TWITCH
BUT MAYBE NOT TODAY.

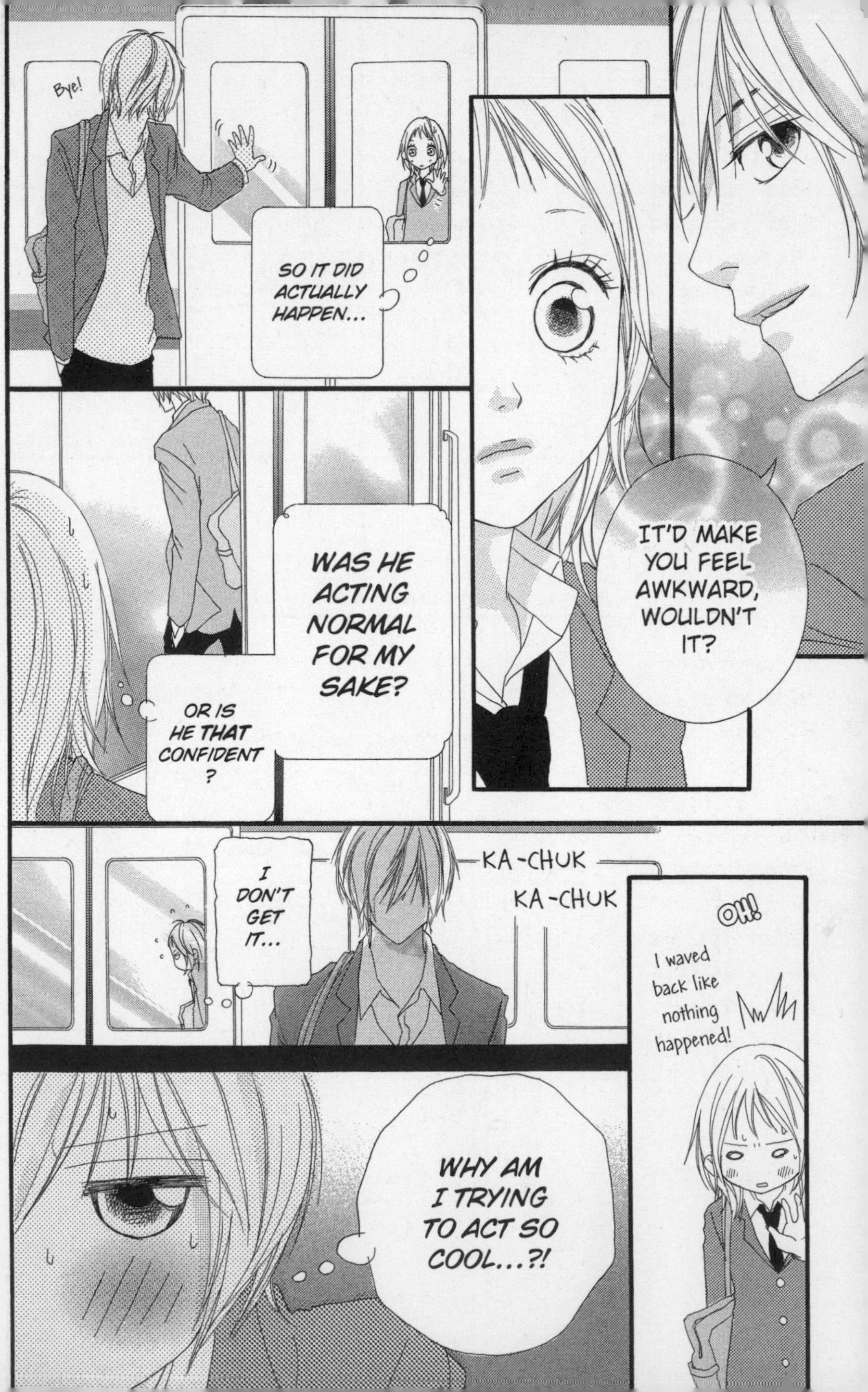
IT'D MAKE YOU FEEL AWKWARD, WOULDN'T IT?
Bye!
SO IT DID ACTUALLY HAPPEN...
WAS HE ACTING NORMAL FOR MY SAKE?
OR IS HE THAT CONFIDENT?
OH!
I waved back like nothing happened!
KA-CHUK
KA-CHUK
I DON'T GET IT...
WHY AM I TRYING TO ACT SO COOL...?!

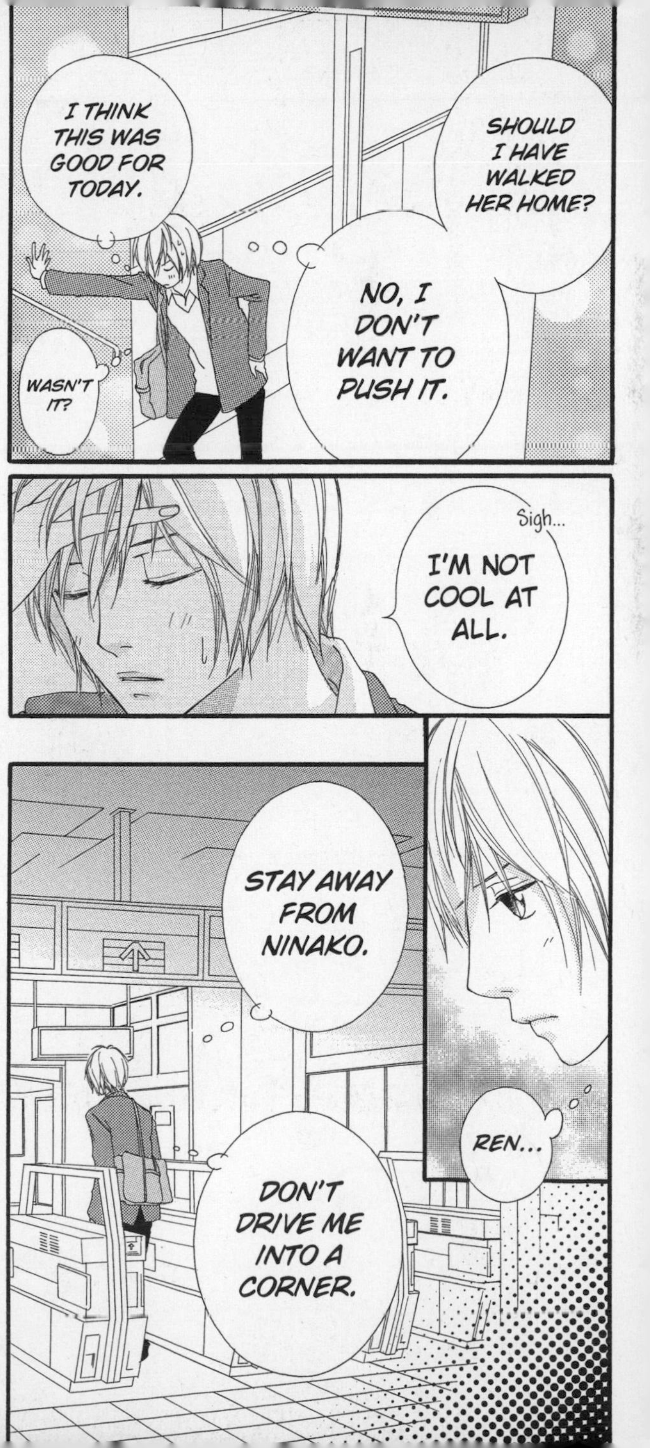
SHOULD I HAVE WALKED HER HOME?
I THINK THIS WAS GOOD FOR TODAY.
NO, I DON'T WANT TO PUSH IT.
WASN'T IT?
Sigh...
I'M NOT COOL AT ALL.
REN...
STAY AWAY FROM NINAKO.
DON'T DRIVE ME INTO A CORNER.

I won a fax machine a while ago, and it finally broke down. It had been acting up for a while, but I tried every trick in the book to keep it going. This time, it broke down for real, and I realized I had to buy a new one to avoid continuing to inconvenience my agent. I'm sorry for dragging my feet about it.

It's not just the fax machine. My policy is to never replace anything unless it's well and truly broken beyond repair. I won't let anything go until I'm 100 percent positive that it's kaput! It's a combination of laziness and frugality. My work chair is on its last legs too, but I'm going to push it as far as I can!

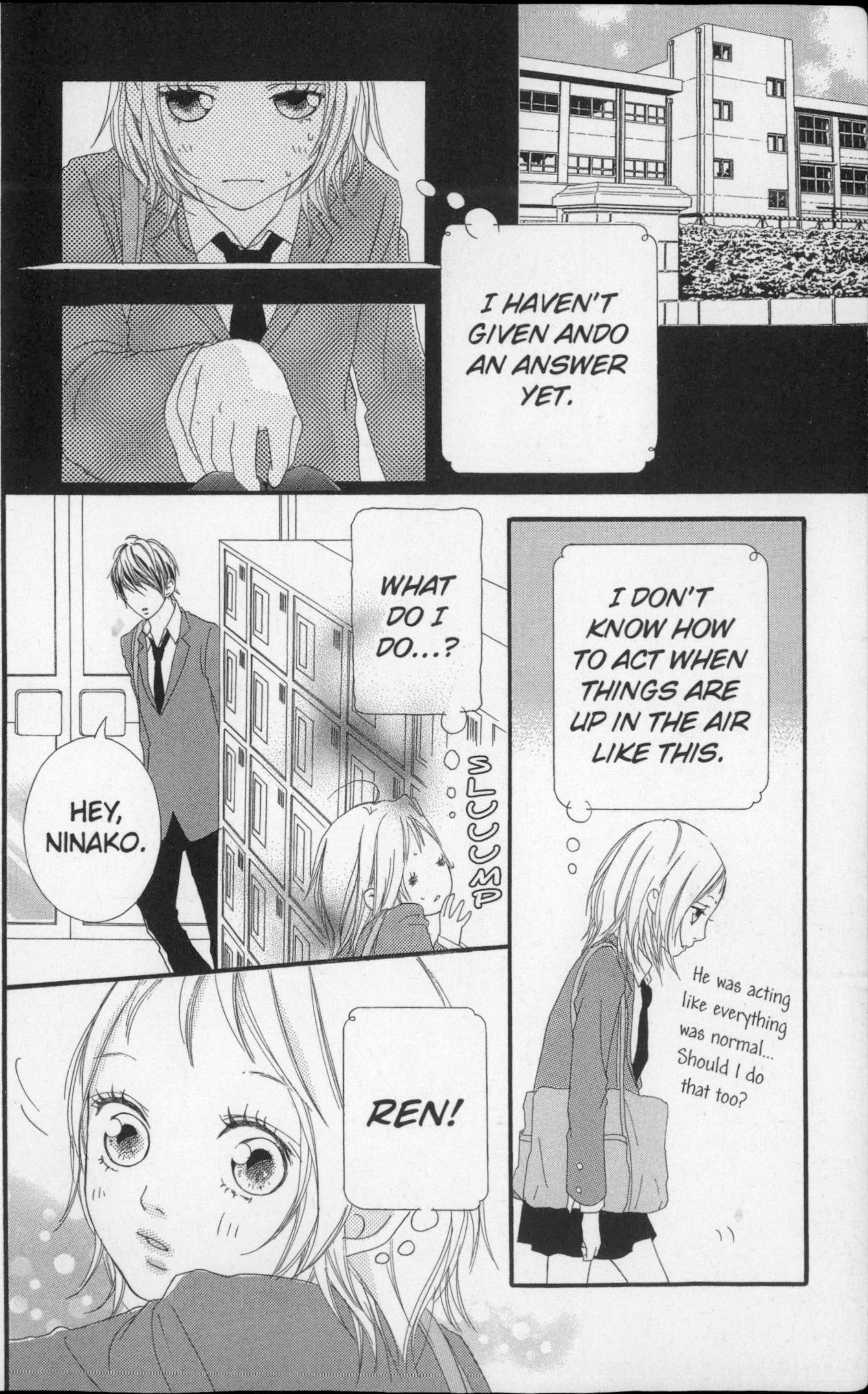
I HAVEN'T GIVEN ANDO AN ANSWER YET.
I DON'T KNOW HOW TO ACT WHEN THINGS ARE UP IN THE AIR LIKE THIS.
He was acting like everything was normal... Should I do that too?
WHAT DO I DO...?
SLUUUMP
HEY, NINAKO.
REN!

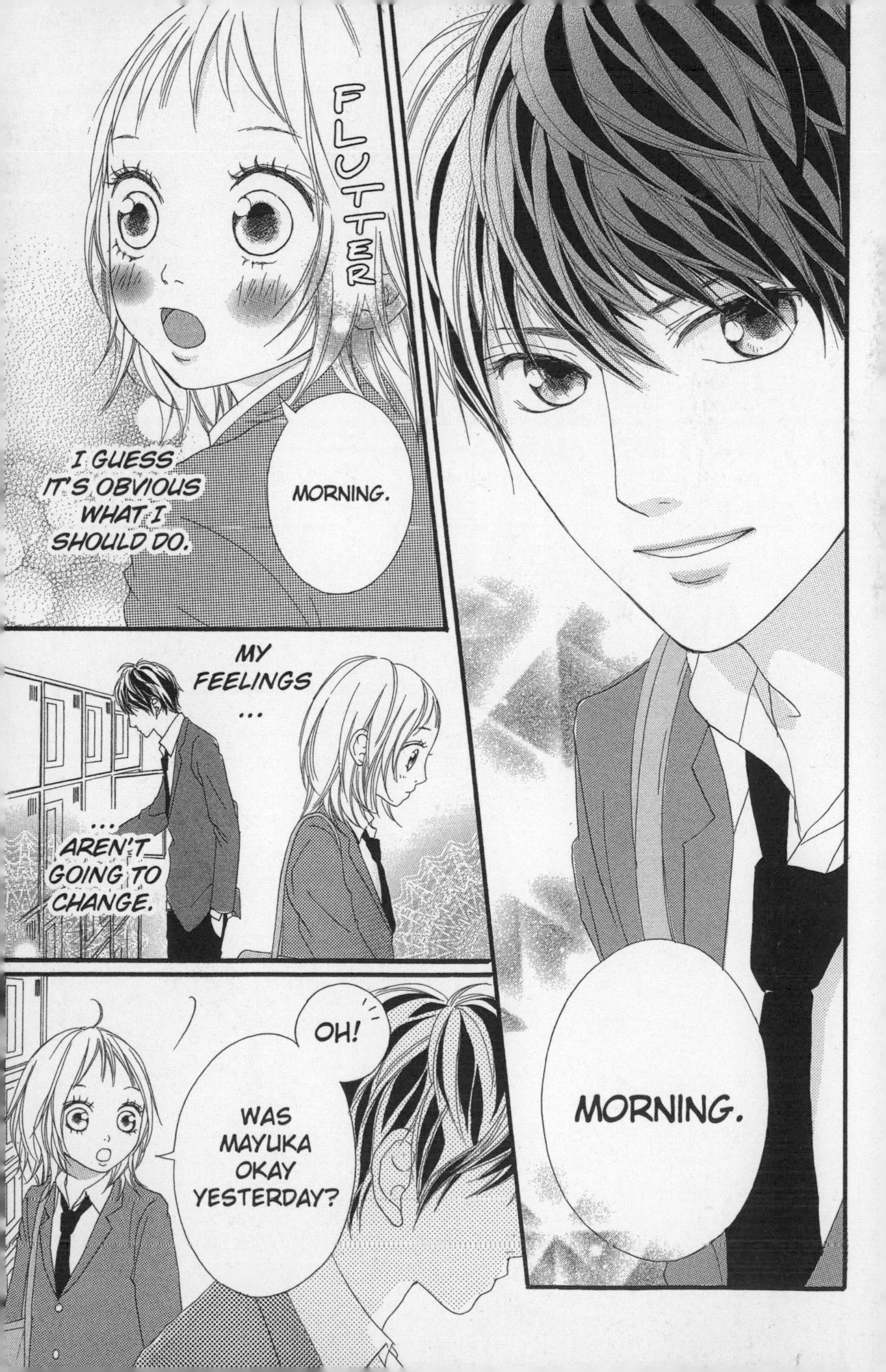
MORNING.
FLUTTER
MORNING.
I GUESS IT'S OBVIOUS WHAT I SHOULD DO.
MY FEELINGS ...
... AREN'T GOING TO CHANGE.
OH!
WAS MAYUKA OKAY YESTERDAY?

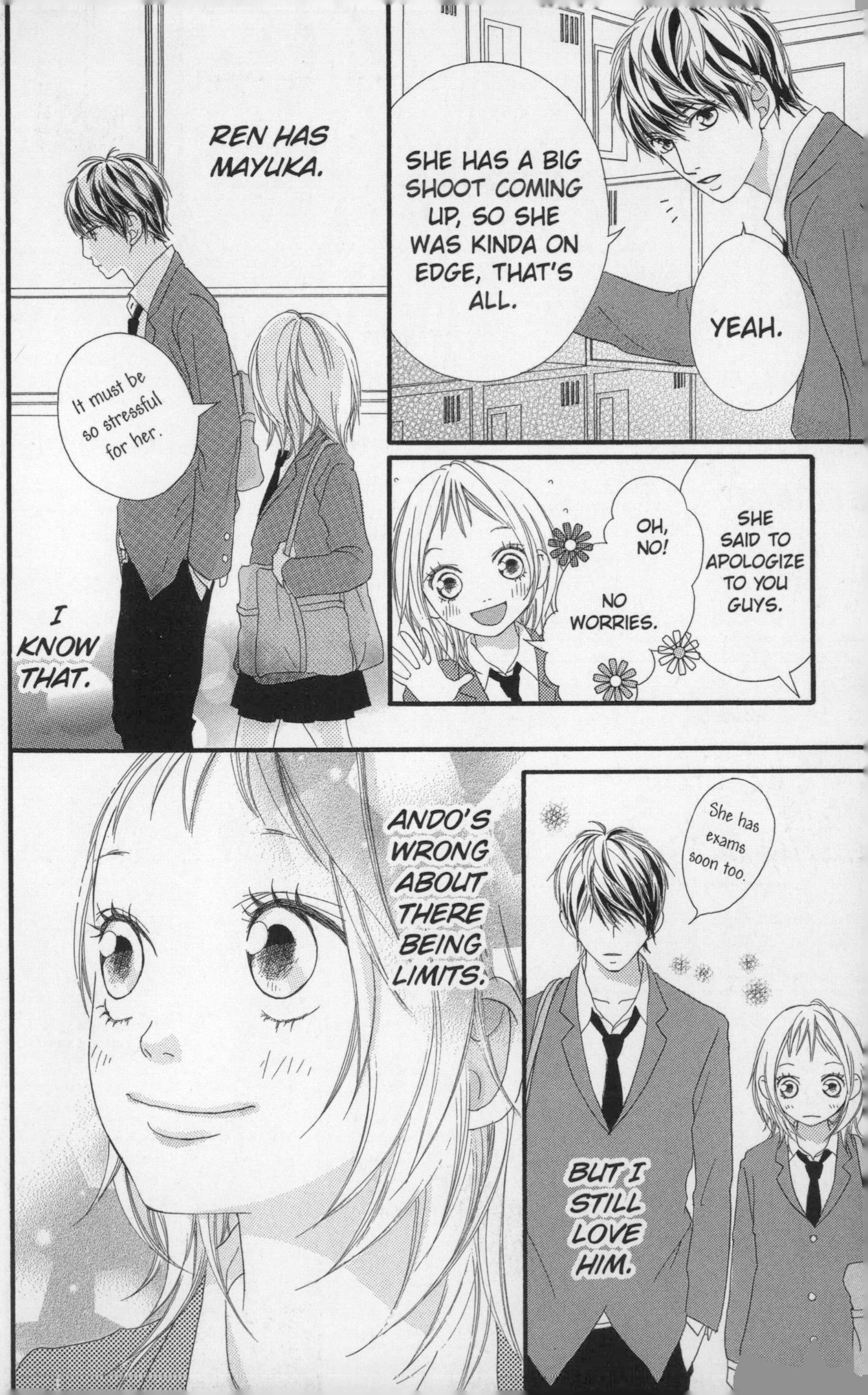
YEAH.
SHE HAS A BIG SHOOT COMING UP, SO SHE WAS KINDA ON EDGE, THAT'S ALL.
SHE SAID TO APOLOGIZE TO YOU GUYS.
OH, NO!
NO WORRIES.
REN HAS MAYUKA.
It must be so stressful for her.
I KNOW THAT.
She has exams soon too.
BUT I STILL LOVE HIM.
ANDO'S WRONG ABOUT THERE BEING LIMITS.

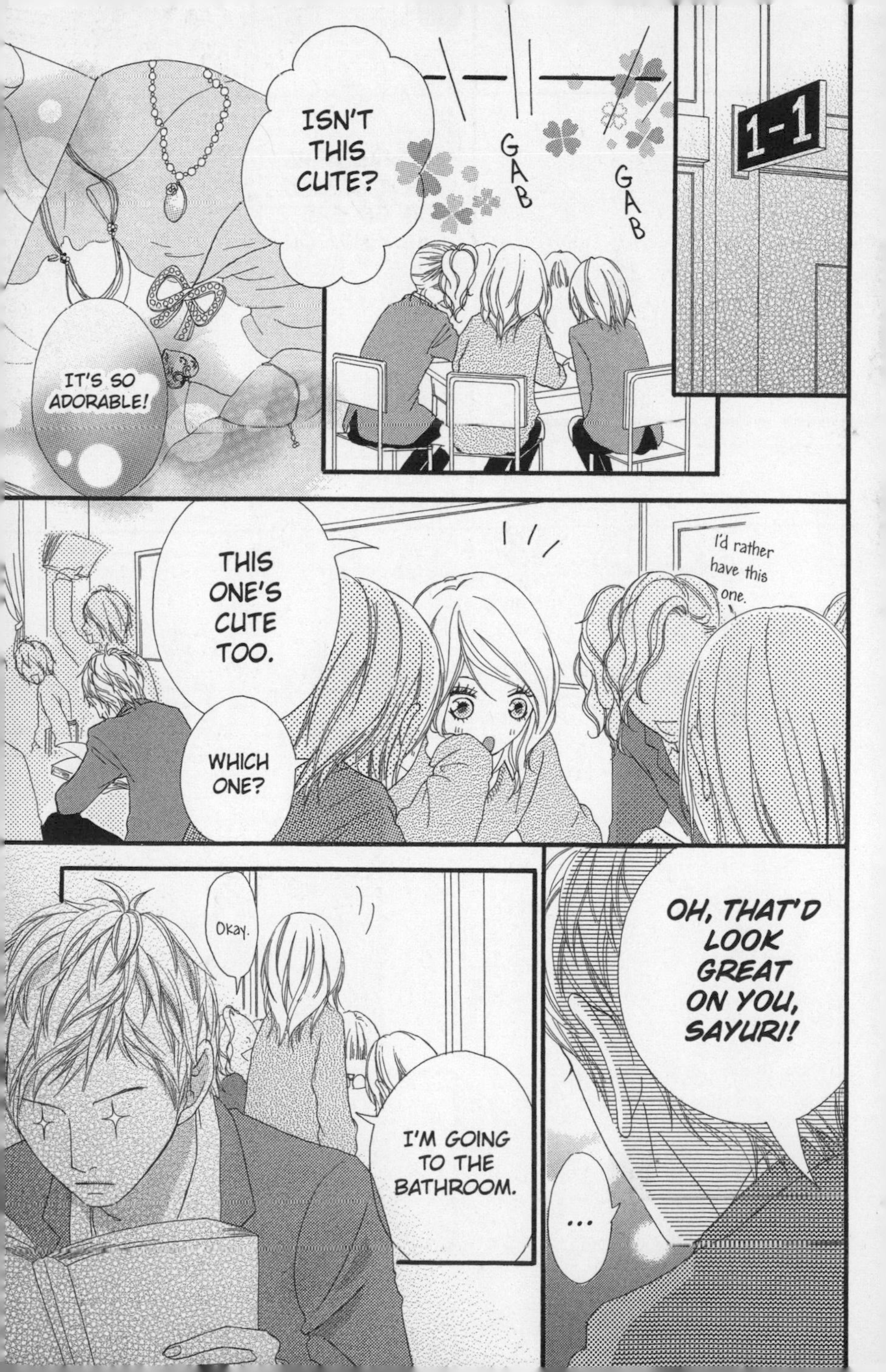
GAB GAB
ISN'T THIS CUTE?
IT'S SO ADORABLE!
I'd rather have this one.
THIS ONE'S CUTE TOO.
WHICH ONE?
OH, THAT'D LOOK GREAT ON YOU, SAYURI!
...
I'M GOING TO THE BATHROOM.
Okay.

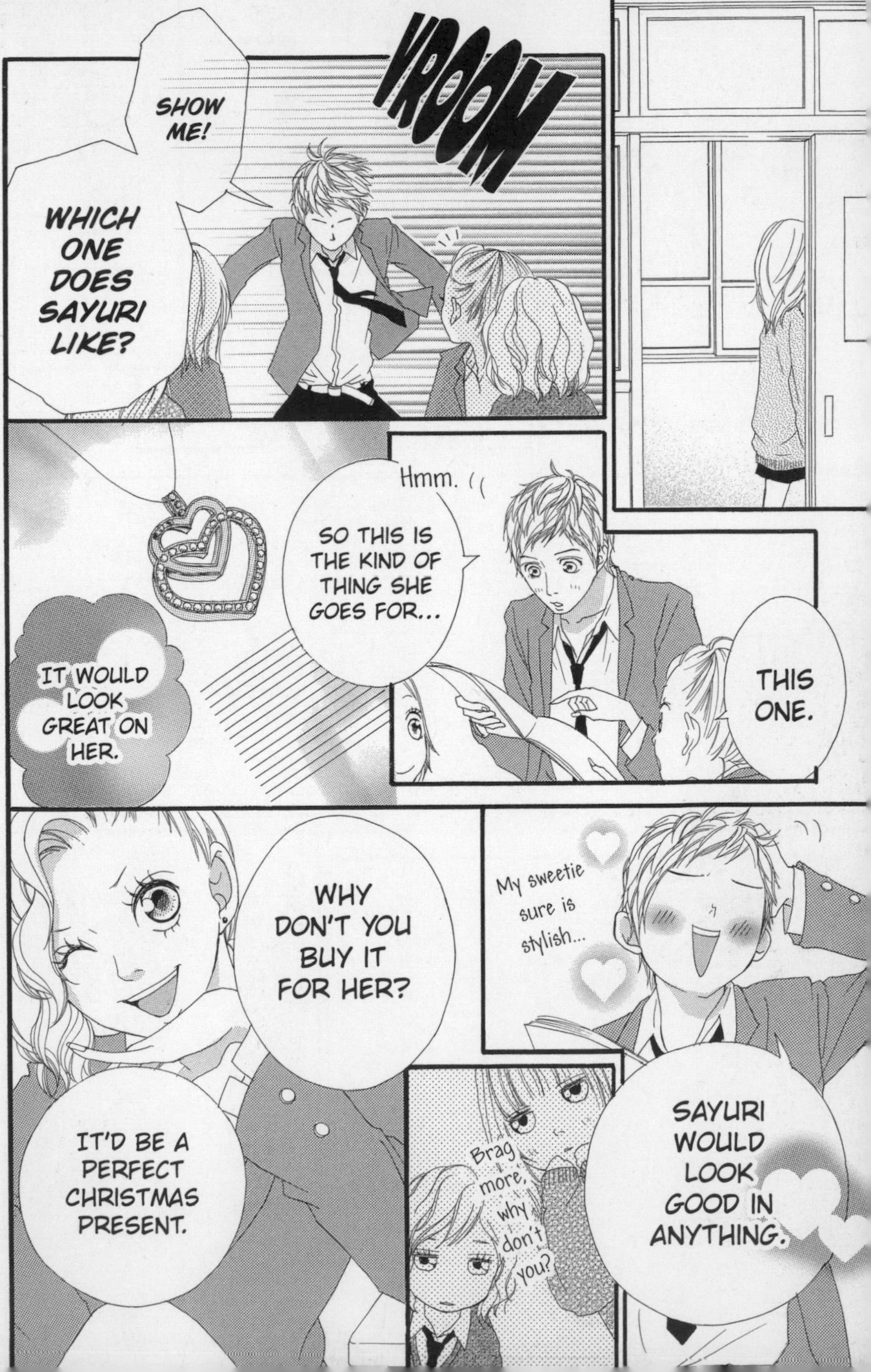
VROOM
SHOW ME!
WHICH ONE DOES SAYURI LIKE?
THIS ONE.
Hmm.
SO THIS IS THE KIND OF THING SHE GOES FOR...
IT WOULD LOOK GREAT ON HER.
My sweetie sure is stylish...
SAYURI WOULD LOOK GOOD IN ANYTHING.
Brag more, why don't you?
WHY DON'T YOU BUY IT FOR HER?
IT'D BE A PERFECT CHRISTMAS PRESENT.

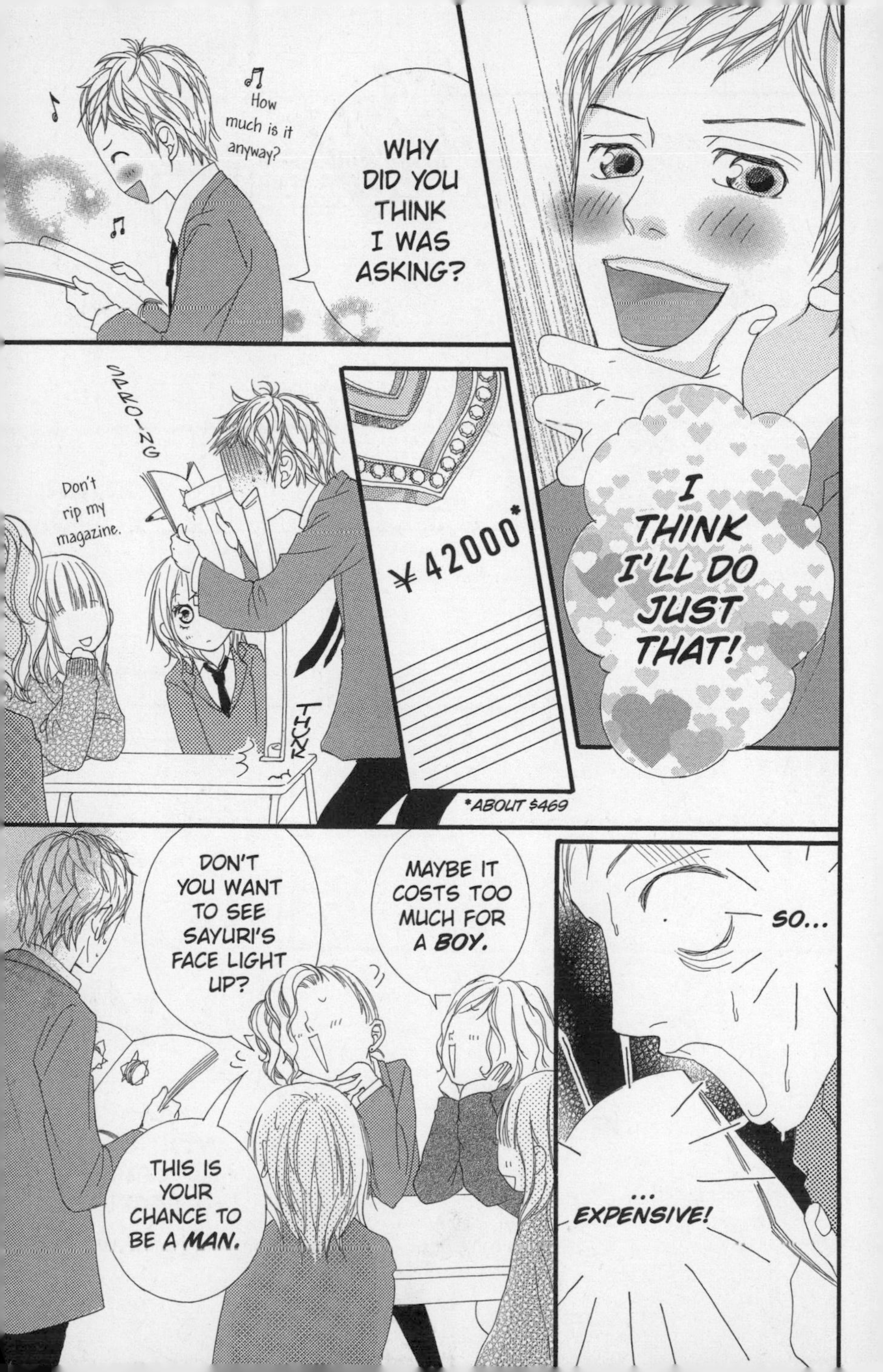
I THINK I'LL DO JUST THAT!
WHY DID YOU THINK I WAS ASKING?
How much is it anyway?
¥42000*
SPROING
THUNK
Don't rip my magazine.
*ABOUT $469
SO...
...EXPENSIVE!
MAYBE IT COSTS TOO MUCH FOR A **BOY**.
DON'T YOU WANT TO SEE SAYURI'S FACE LIGHT UP?
THIS IS YOUR CHANCE TO BE A **MAN**.

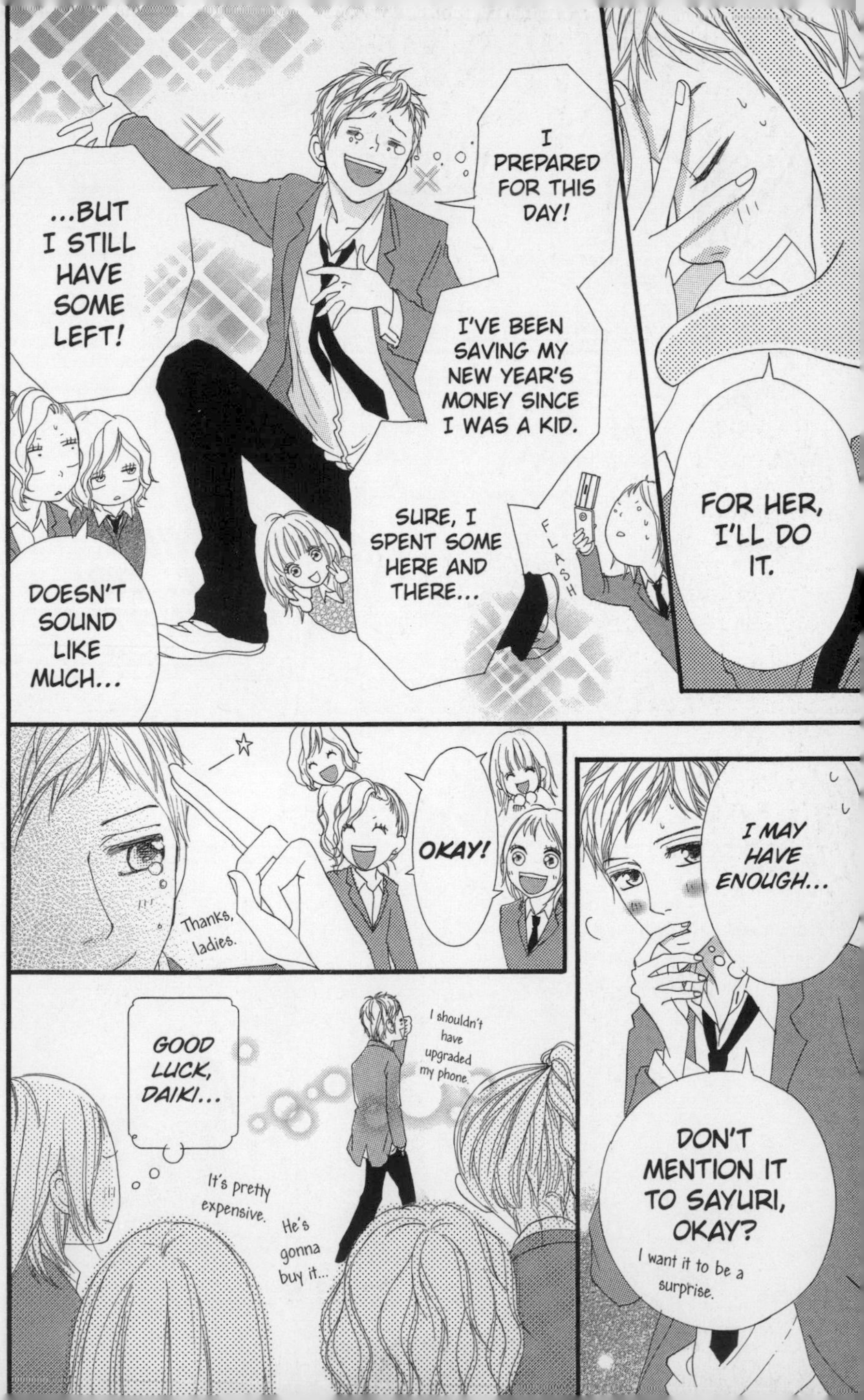
FOR HER, I'LL DO IT.
I PREPARED FOR THIS DAY!
I'VE BEEN SAVING MY NEW YEAR'S MONEY SINCE I WAS A KID.
SURE, I SPENT SOME HERE AND THERE...
FLASH
...BUT I STILL HAVE SOME LEFT!
DOESN'T SOUND LIKE MUCH...
I MAY HAVE ENOUGH...
DON'T MENTION IT TO SAYURI, OKAY?
I want it to be a surprise.
OKAY!
Thanks, ladies.
I shouldn't have upgraded my phone.
GOOD LUCK, DAIKI...
It's pretty expensive.
He's gonna buy it...

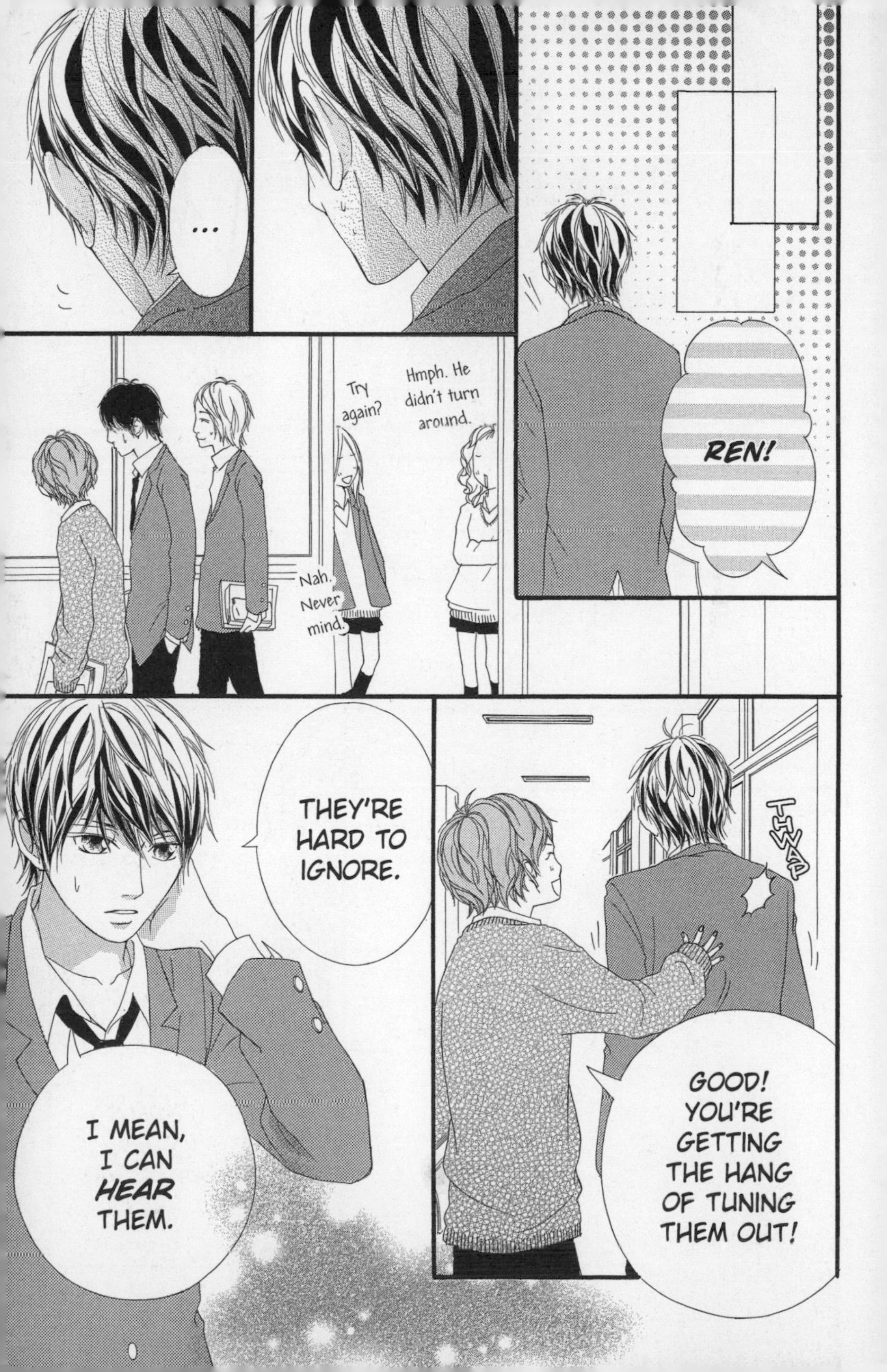
REN!
...
Hmph. He didn't turn around.
Try again?
Nah. Never mind.
THWAP
GOOD! YOU'RE GETTING THE HANG OF TUNING THEM OUT!
THEY'RE HARD TO IGNORE.
I MEAN, I CAN *HEAR* THEM.

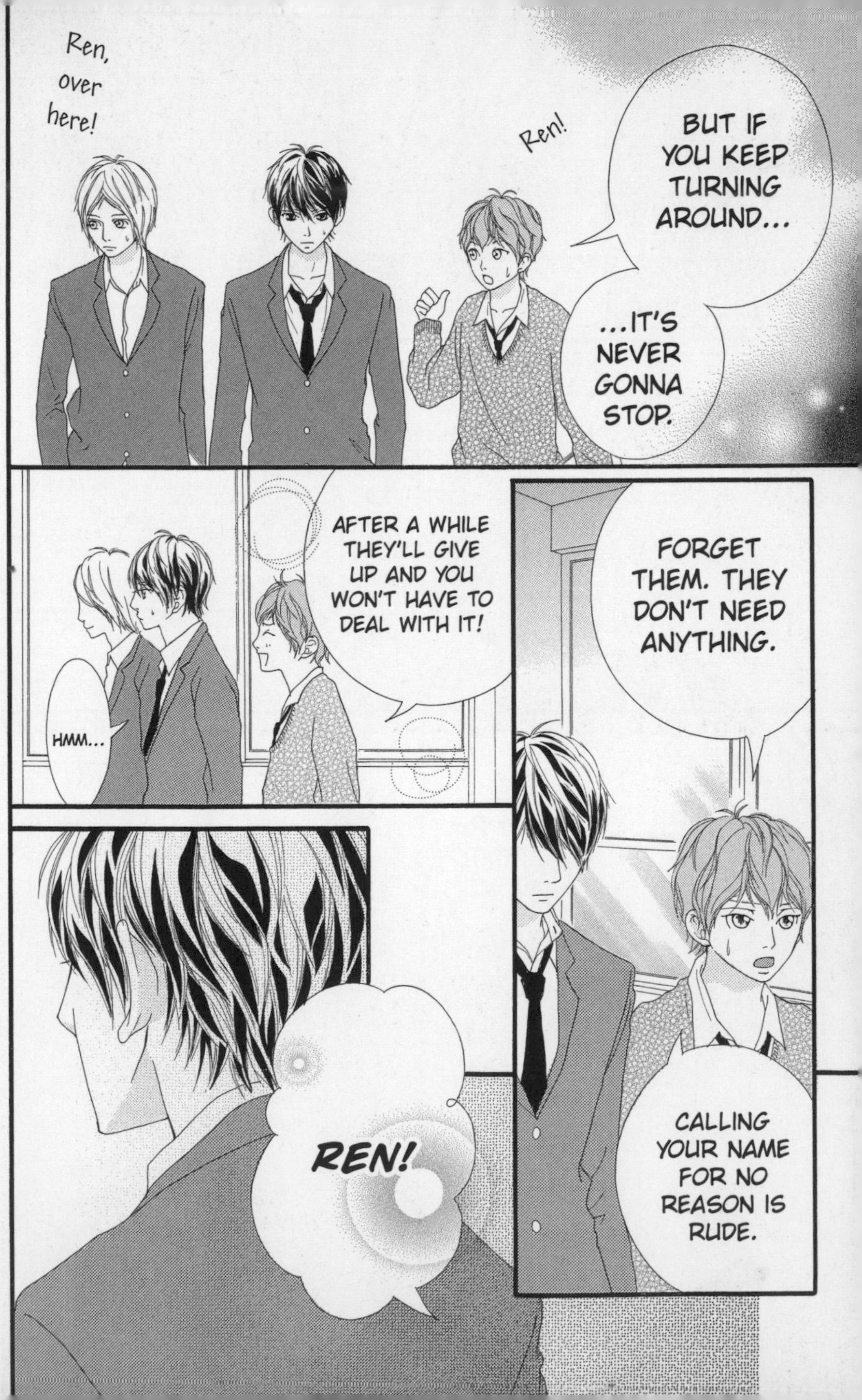
BUT IF YOU KEEP TURNING AROUND...
...IT'S NEVER GONNA STOP.
Ren!
Ren, over here!
FORGET THEM. THEY DON'T NEED ANYTHING.
CALLING YOUR NAME FOR NO REASON IS RUDE.
AFTER A WHILE THEY'LL GIVE UP AND YOU WON'T HAVE TO DEAL WITH IT!
HMM...
REN!

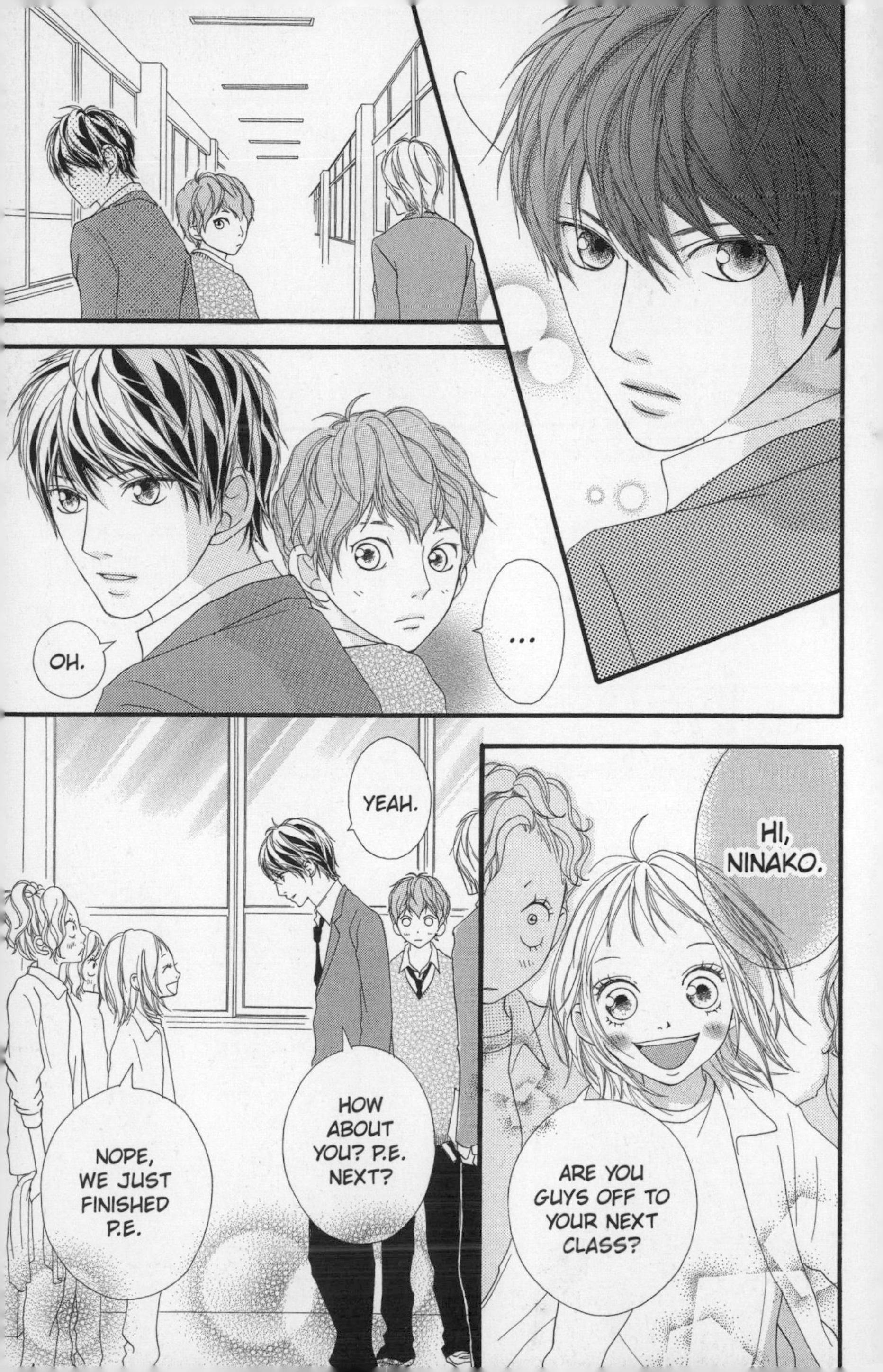
...
OH.
HI, NINAKO.
ARE YOU GUYS OFF TO YOUR NEXT CLASS?
YEAH.
HOW ABOUT YOU? P.E. NEXT?
NOPE, WE JUST FINISHED P.E.

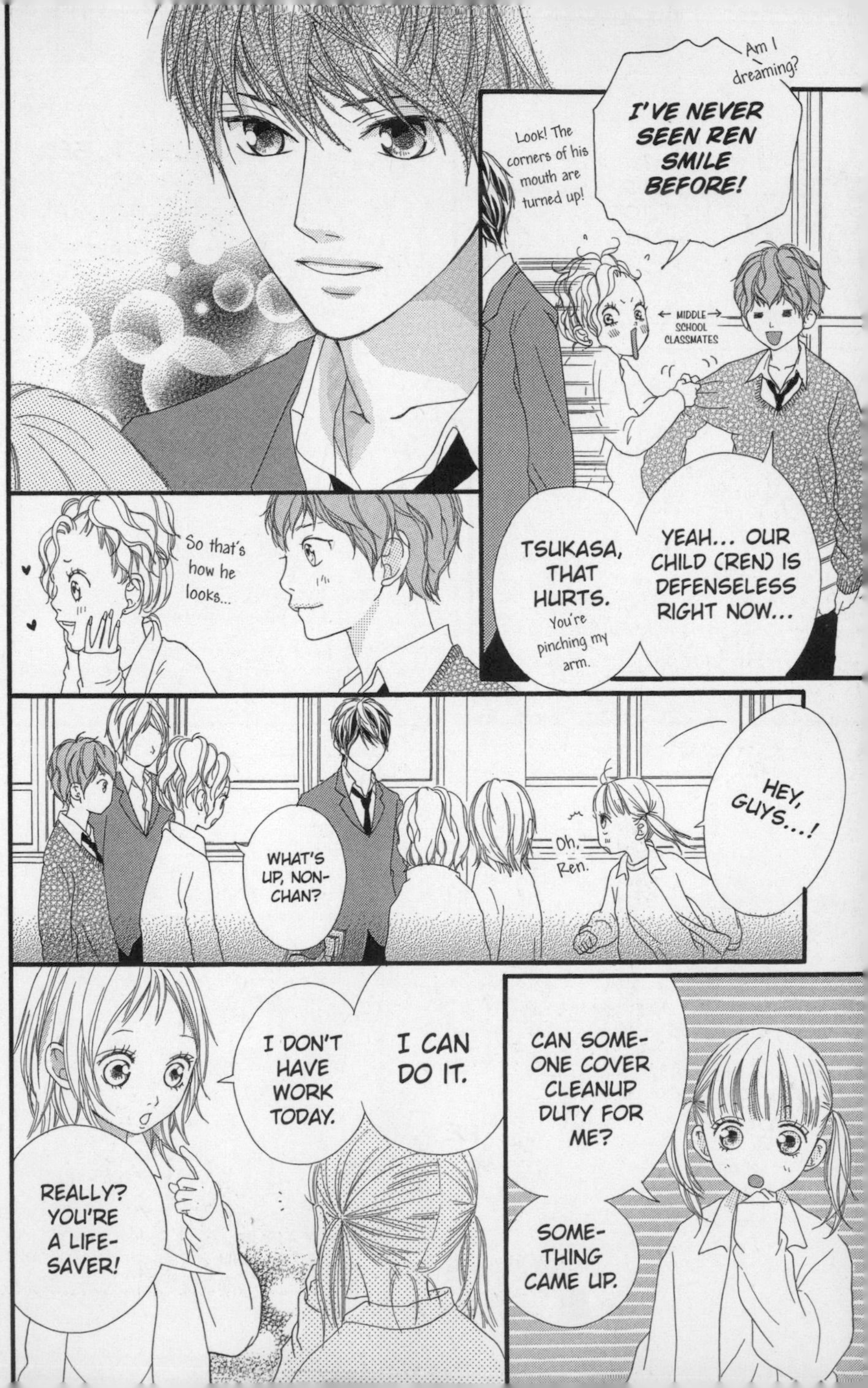
Am I dreaming?
I'VE NEVER SEEN REN SMILE BEFORE!
Look! The corners of his mouth are turned up!
MIDDLE SCHOOL CLASSMATES
YEAH... OUR CHILD (REN) IS DEFENSELESS RIGHT NOW...
TSUKASA, THAT HURTS.
You're pinching my arm.
So that's how he looks...
HEY, GUYS...!
Oh, Ren.
WHAT'S UP, NON-CHAN?
CAN SOME-ONE COVER CLEANUP DUTY FOR ME?
SOME-THING CAME UP.
I CAN DO IT.
I DON'T HAVE WORK TODAY.
REALLY? YOU'RE A LIFE-SAVER!

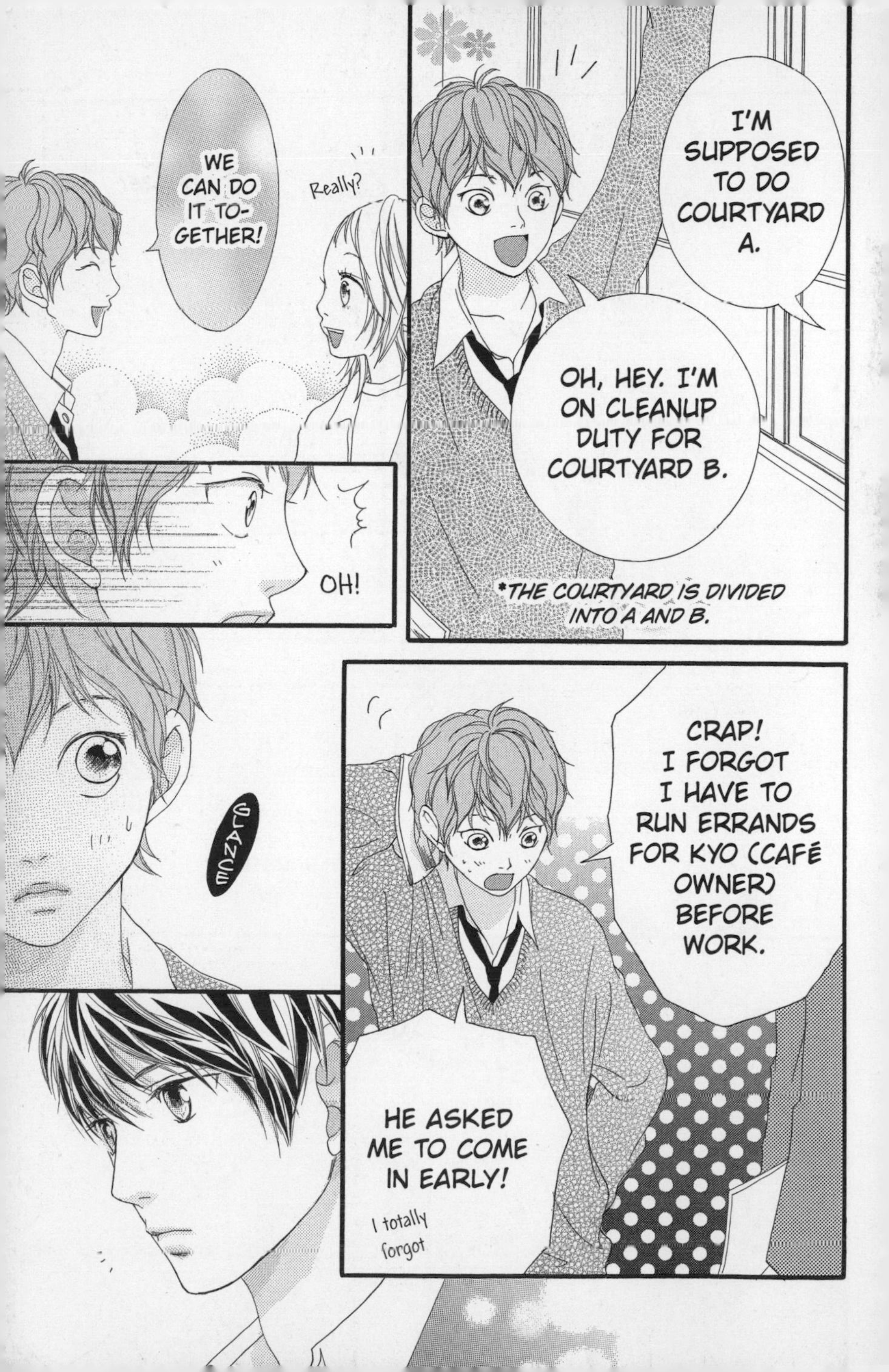
I'M SUPPOSED TO DO COURTYARD A.
OH, HEY. I'M ON CLEANUP DUTY FOR COURTYARD B.
*THE COURTYARD IS DIVIDED INTO A AND B.
WE CAN DO IT TO-GETHER!
Really?
OH!
CRAP! I FORGOT I HAVE TO RUN ERRANDS FOR KYO (CAFÉ OWNER) BEFORE WORK.
HE ASKED ME TO COME IN EARLY!
I totally forgot
GLANCE

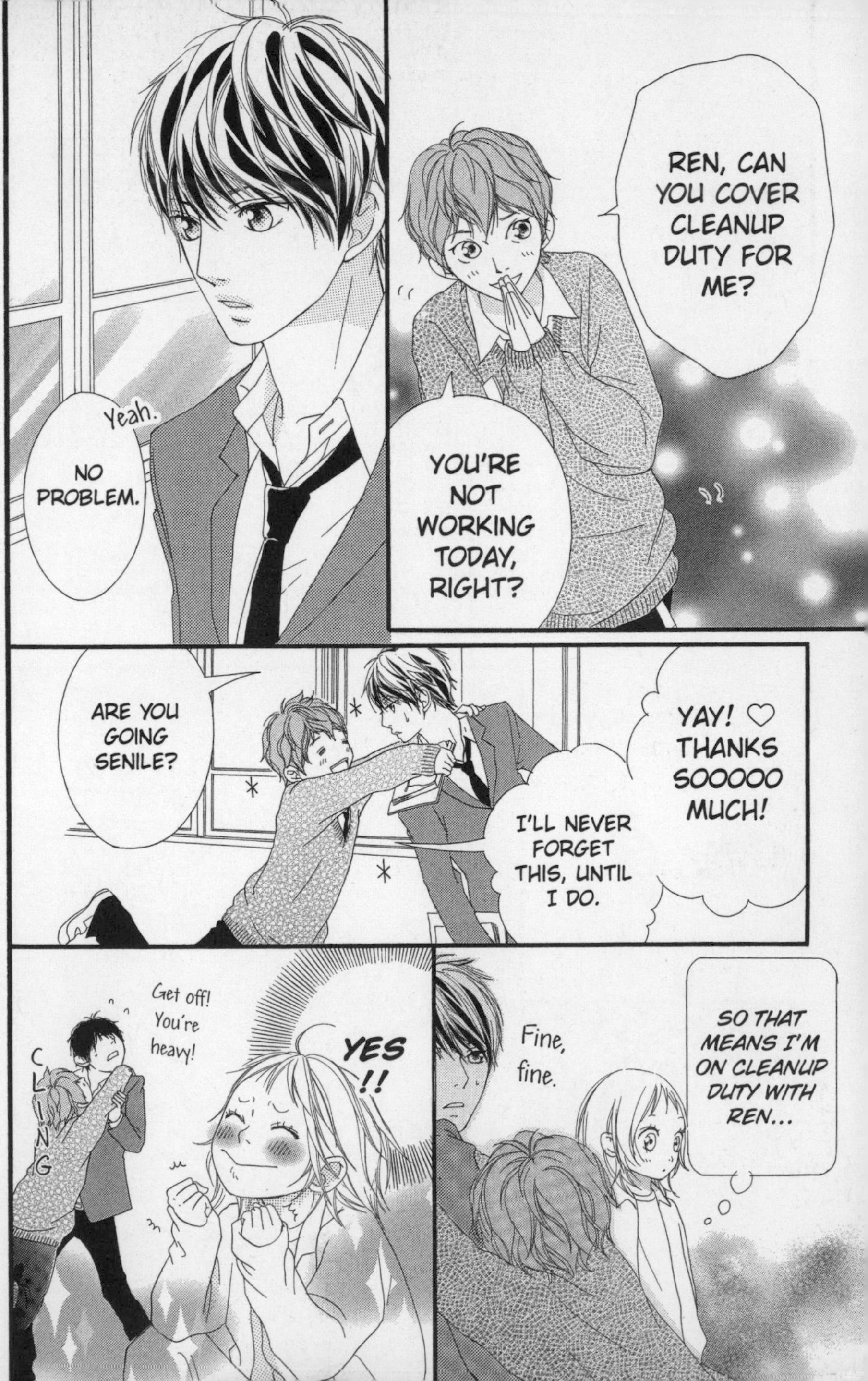
REN, CAN YOU COVER CLEANUP DUTY FOR ME?
YOU'RE NOT WORKING TODAY, RIGHT?
Yeah.
NO PROBLEM.
YAY! ♡ THANKS SOOOOO MUCH!
I'LL NEVER FORGET THIS, UNTIL I DO.
ARE YOU GOING SENILE?
SO THAT MEANS I'M ON CLEANUP DUTY WITH REN...
Fine, fine.
YES!!
Get off! You're heavy!
CLING

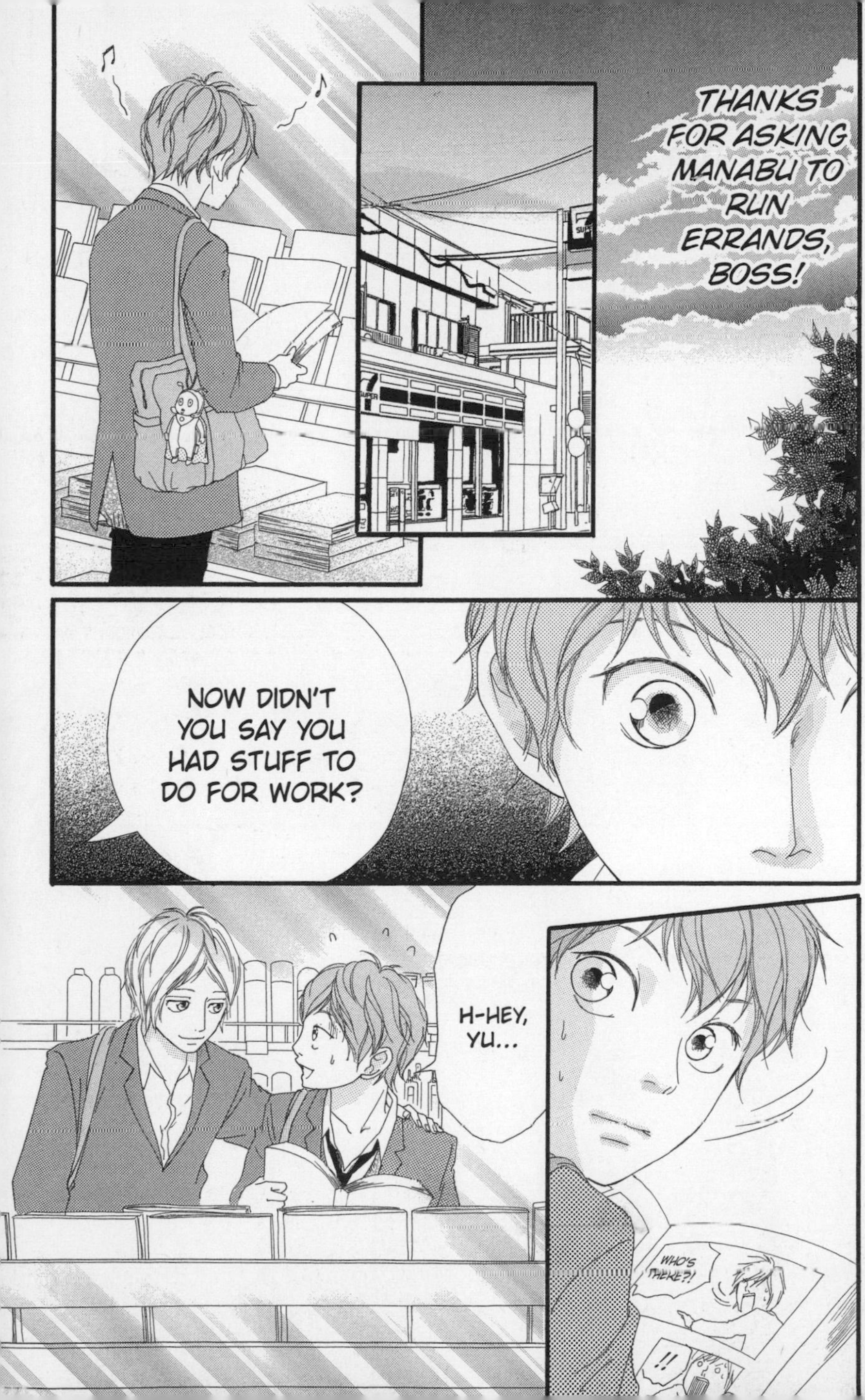
THANKS FOR ASKING MANABU TO RUN ERRANDS, BOSS!
SUPER
NOW DIDN'T YOU SAY YOU HAD STUFF TO DO FOR WORK?
WHO'S THERE?!
!!
H-HEY, YU...

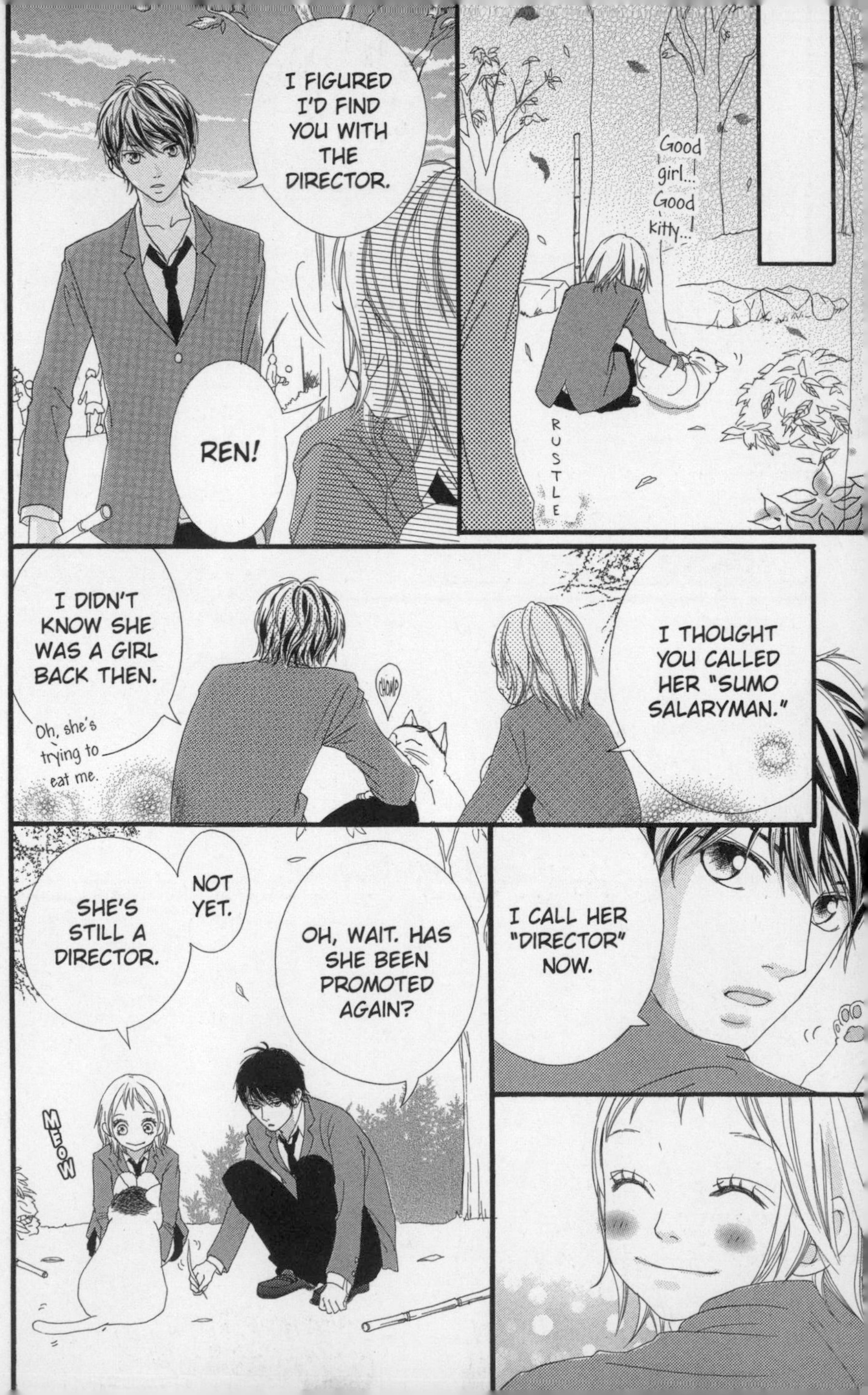
Good girl... Good kitty...
RUSTLE
I FIGURED I'D FIND YOU WITH THE DIRECTOR.
REN!
I THOUGHT YOU CALLED HER "SUMO SALARYMAN."
CHOMP
I DIDN'T KNOW SHE WAS A GIRL BACK THEN.
Oh, she's trying to eat me.
I CALL HER "DIRECTOR" NOW.
OH, WAIT. HAS SHE BEEN PROMOTED AGAIN?
NOT YET.
SHE'S STILL A DIRECTOR.
MEOW

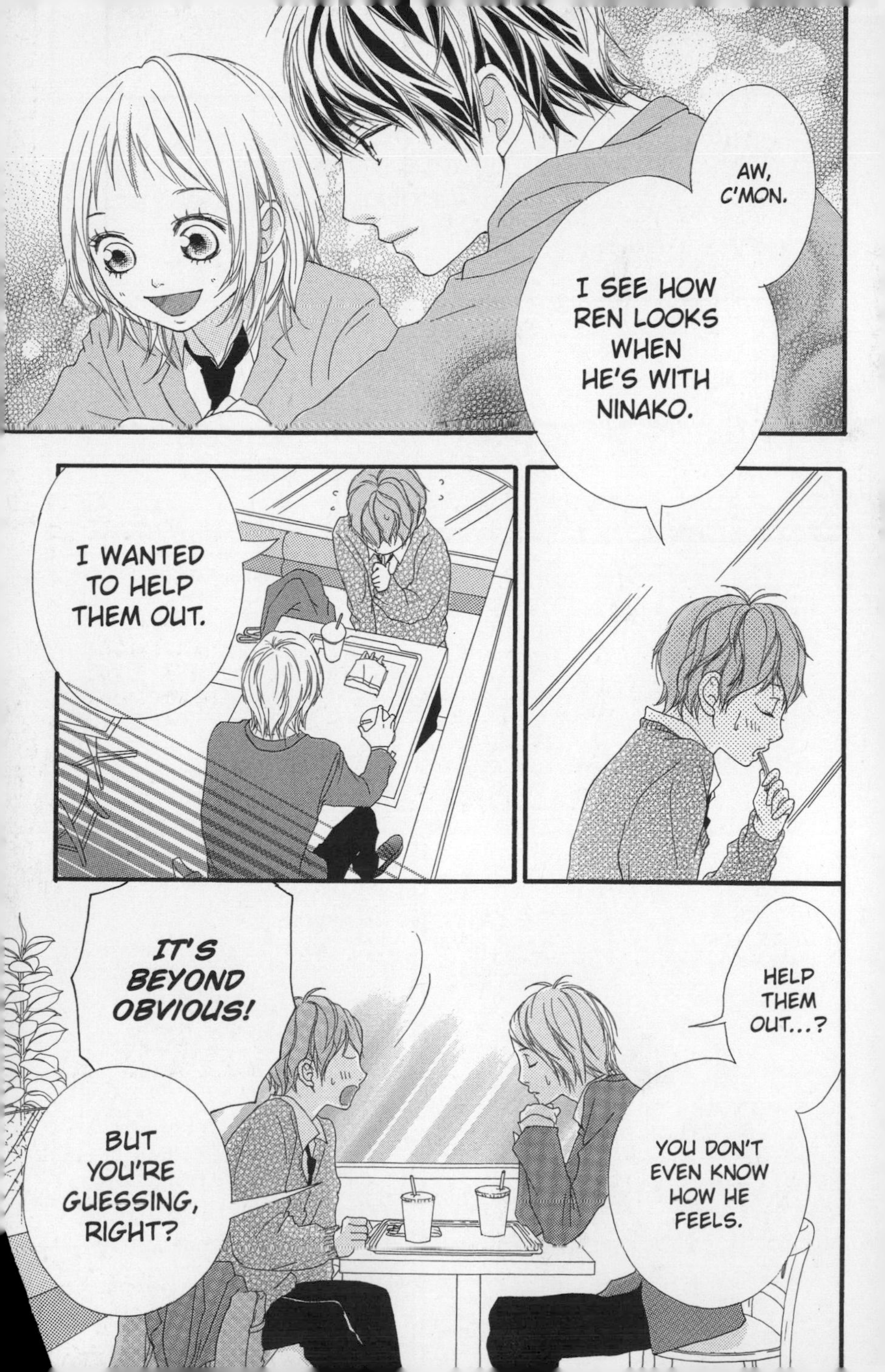
AW, C'MON.
I SEE HOW REN LOOKS WHEN HE'S WITH NINAKO.
I WANTED TO HELP THEM OUT.
HELP THEM OUT...?
YOU DON'T EVEN KNOW HOW HE FEELS.
IT'S BEYOND OBVIOUS!
BUT YOU'RE GUESSING, RIGHT?

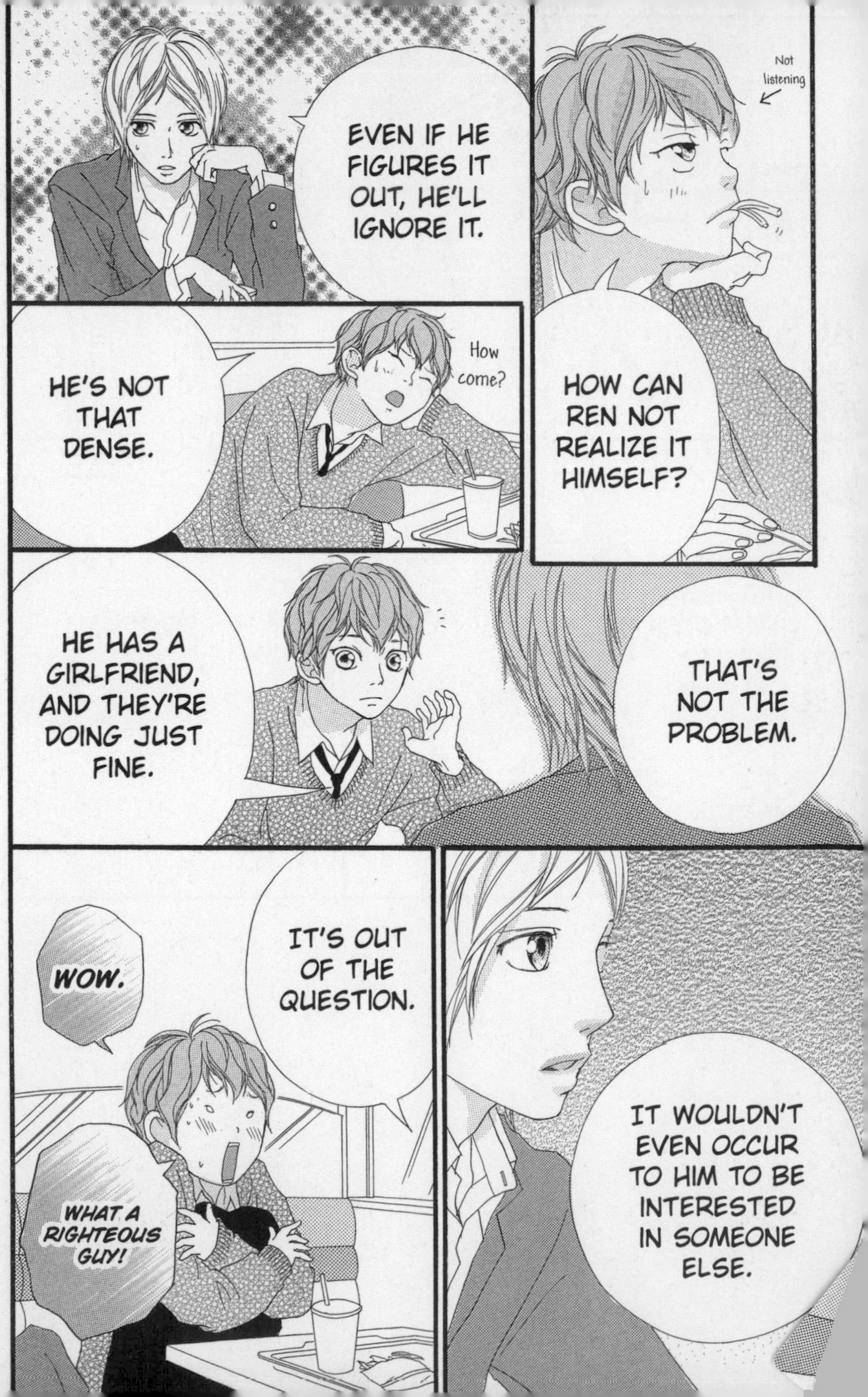
Not listening
HOW CAN REN NOT REALIZE IT HIMSELF?
EVEN IF HE FIGURES IT OUT, HE'LL IGNORE IT.
How come?
HE'S NOT THAT DENSE.
THAT'S NOT THE PROBLEM.
HE HAS A GIRLFRIEND, AND THEY'RE DOING JUST FINE.
IT WOULDN'T EVEN OCCUR TO HIM TO BE INTERESTED IN SOMEONE ELSE.
IT'S OUT OF THE QUESTION.
WOW.
WHAT A RIGHTEOUS GUY!

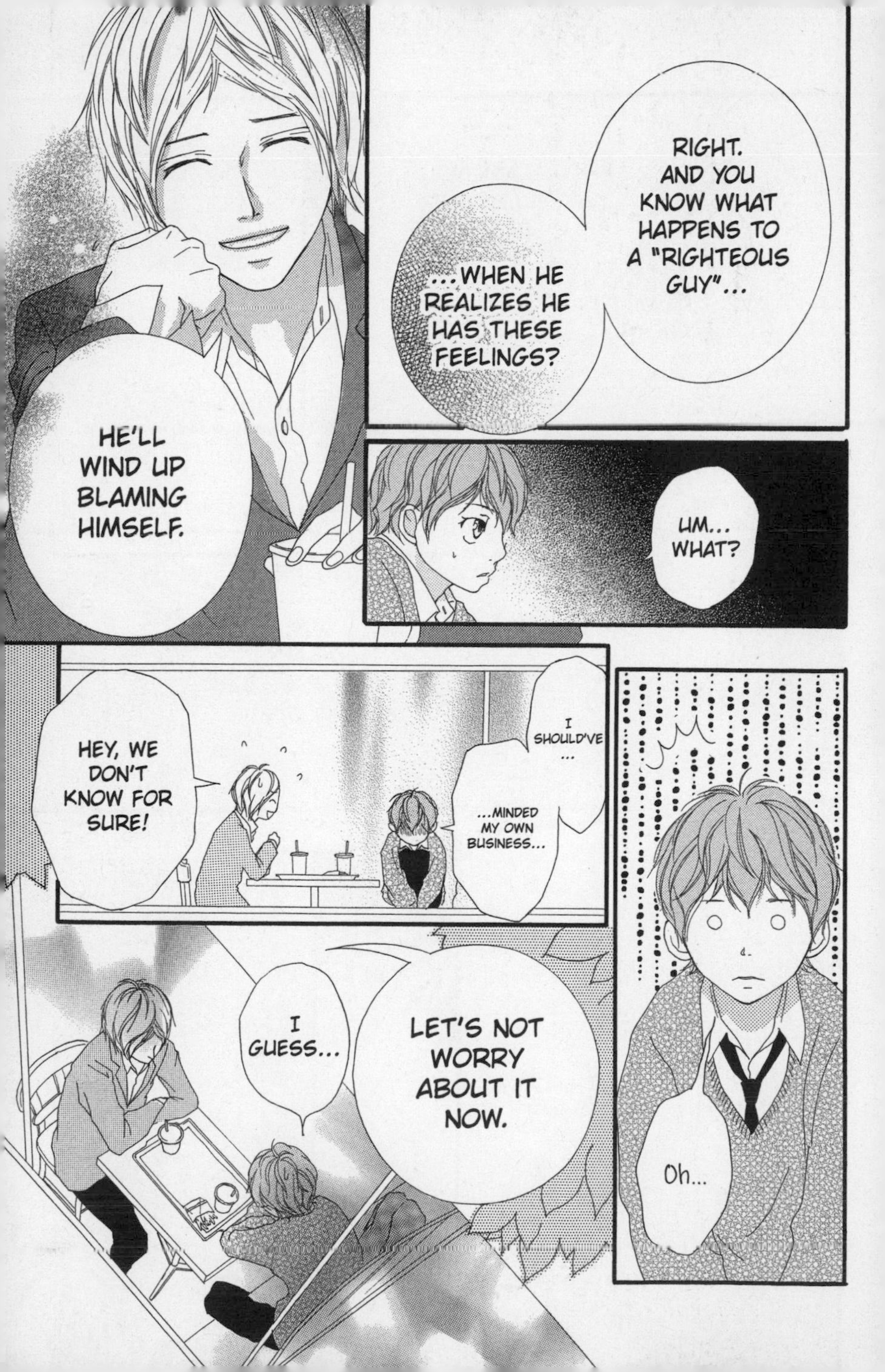
RIGHT. AND YOU KNOW WHAT HAPPENS TO A "RIGHTEOUS GUY"...
...WHEN HE REALIZES HE HAS THESE FEELINGS?
UM... WHAT?
HE'LL WIND UP BLAMING HIMSELF.
Oh...
I SHOULD'VE...
...MINDED MY OWN BUSINESS...
HEY, WE DON'T KNOW FOR SURE!
LET'S NOT WORRY ABOUT IT NOW.
I GUESS...

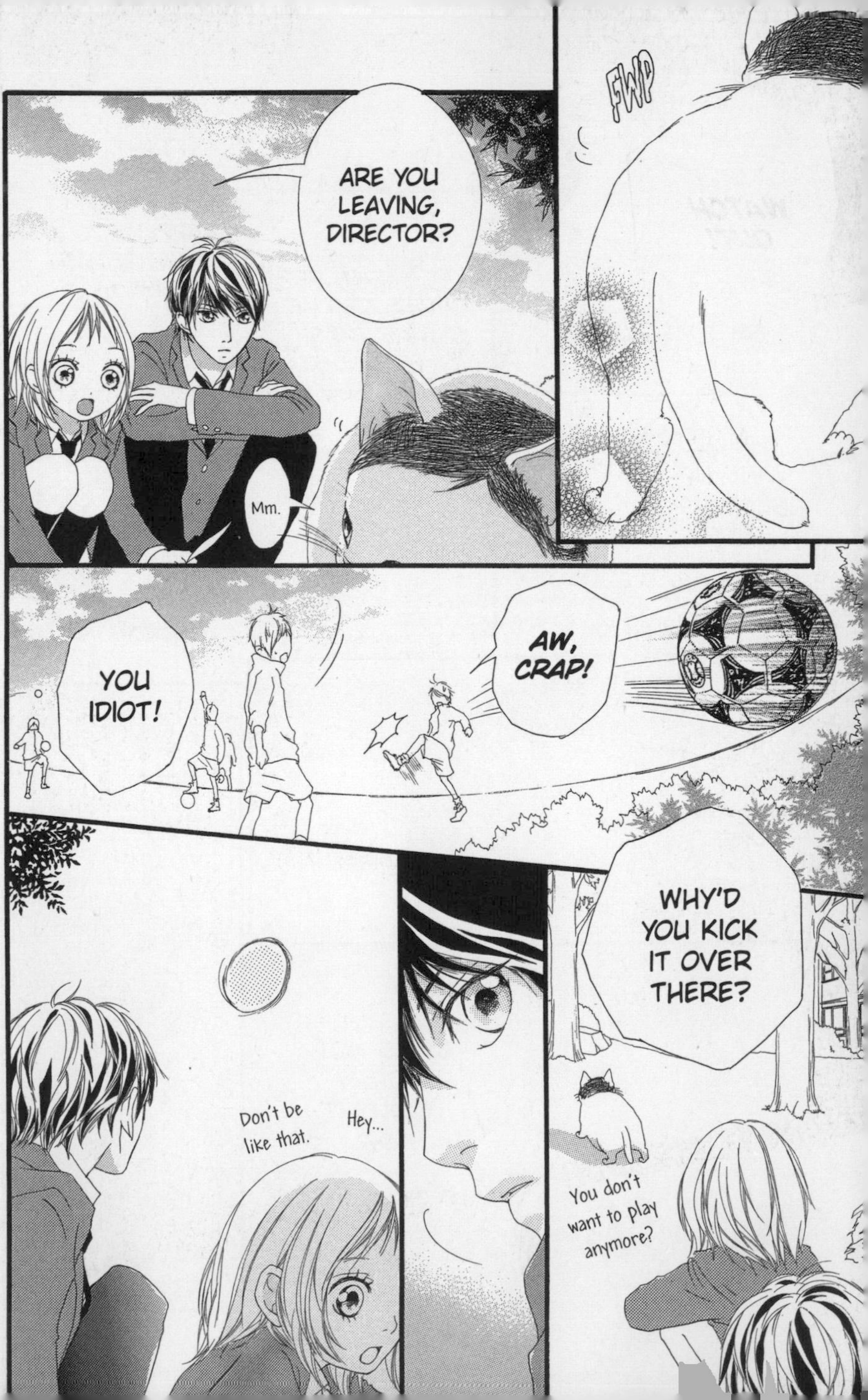
FWP
ARE YOU LEAVING, DIRECTOR?
Mm.
AW, CRAP!
YOU IDIOT!
WHY'D YOU KICK IT OVER THERE?
You don't want to play anymore?
Hey...
Don't be like that.

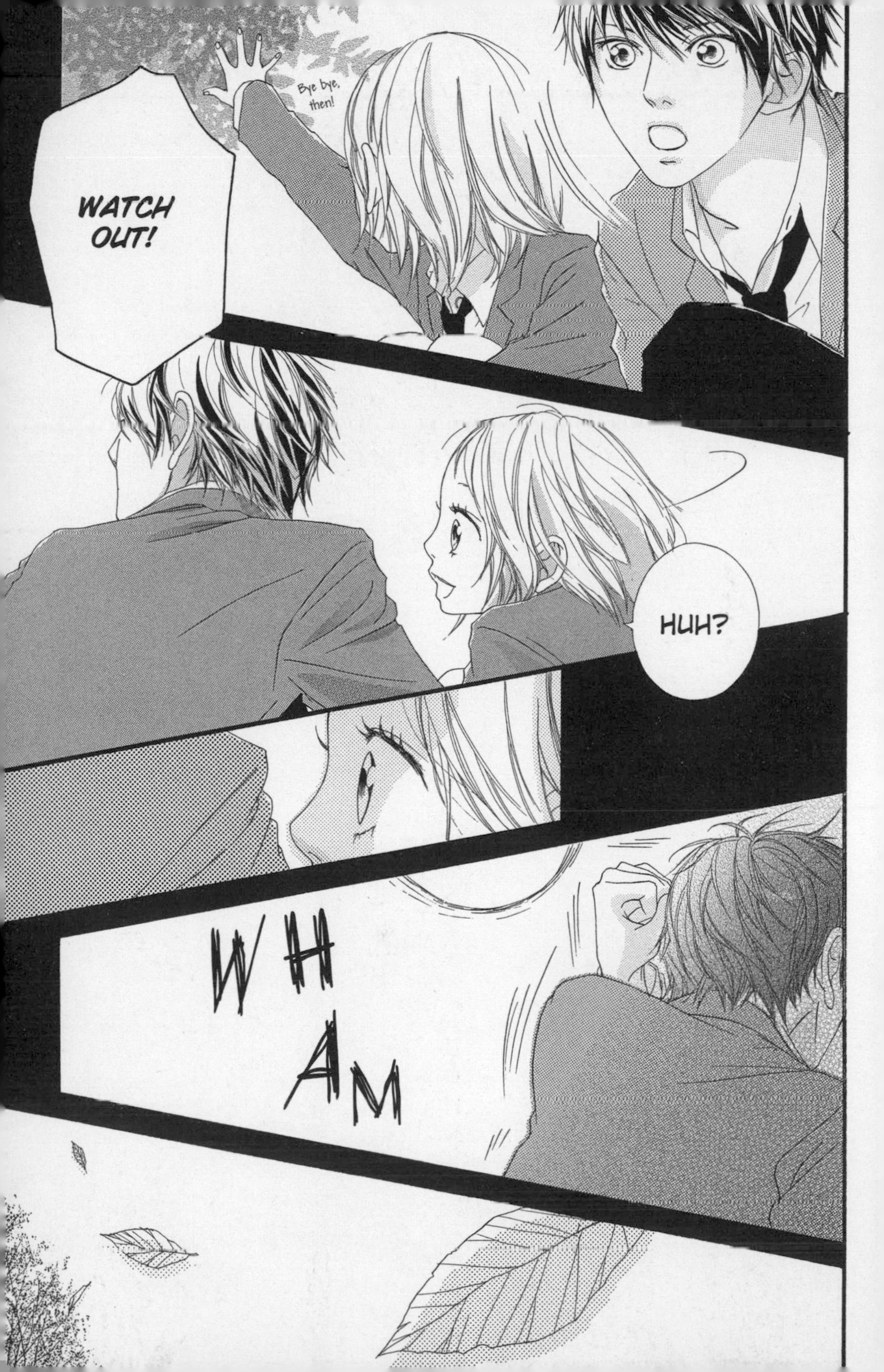
Bye bye, then!
WATCH OUT!
HUH?
WHAM

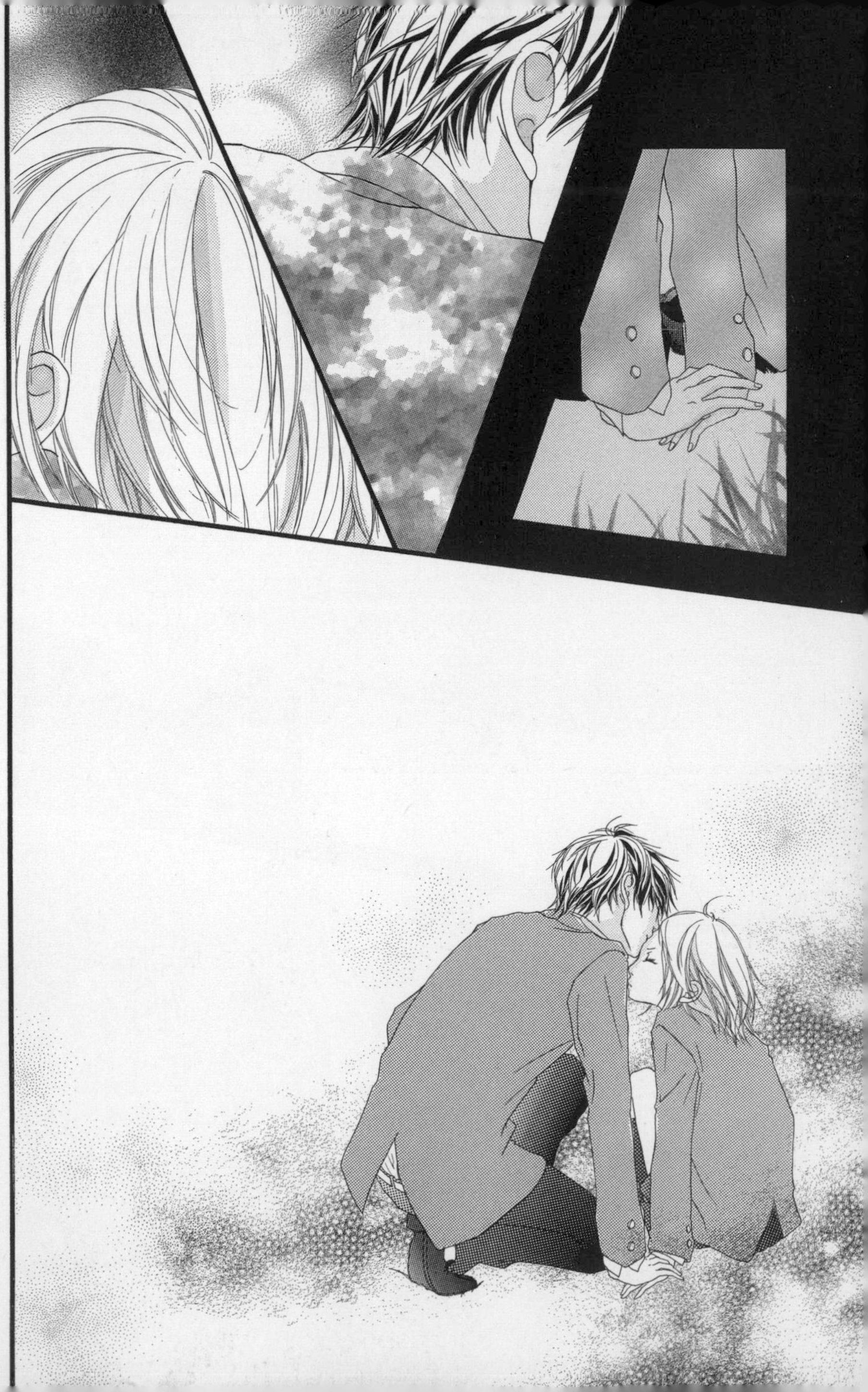

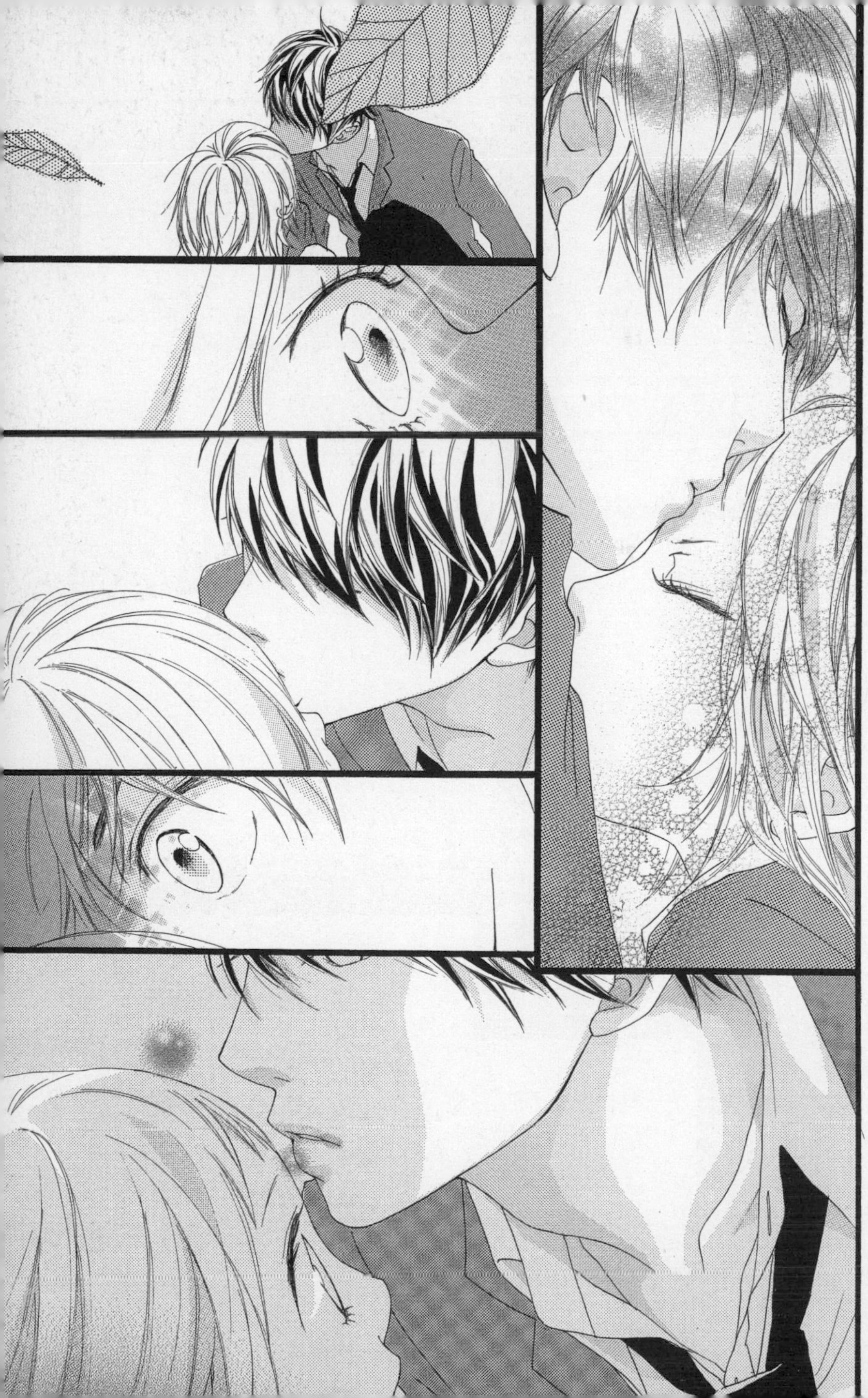

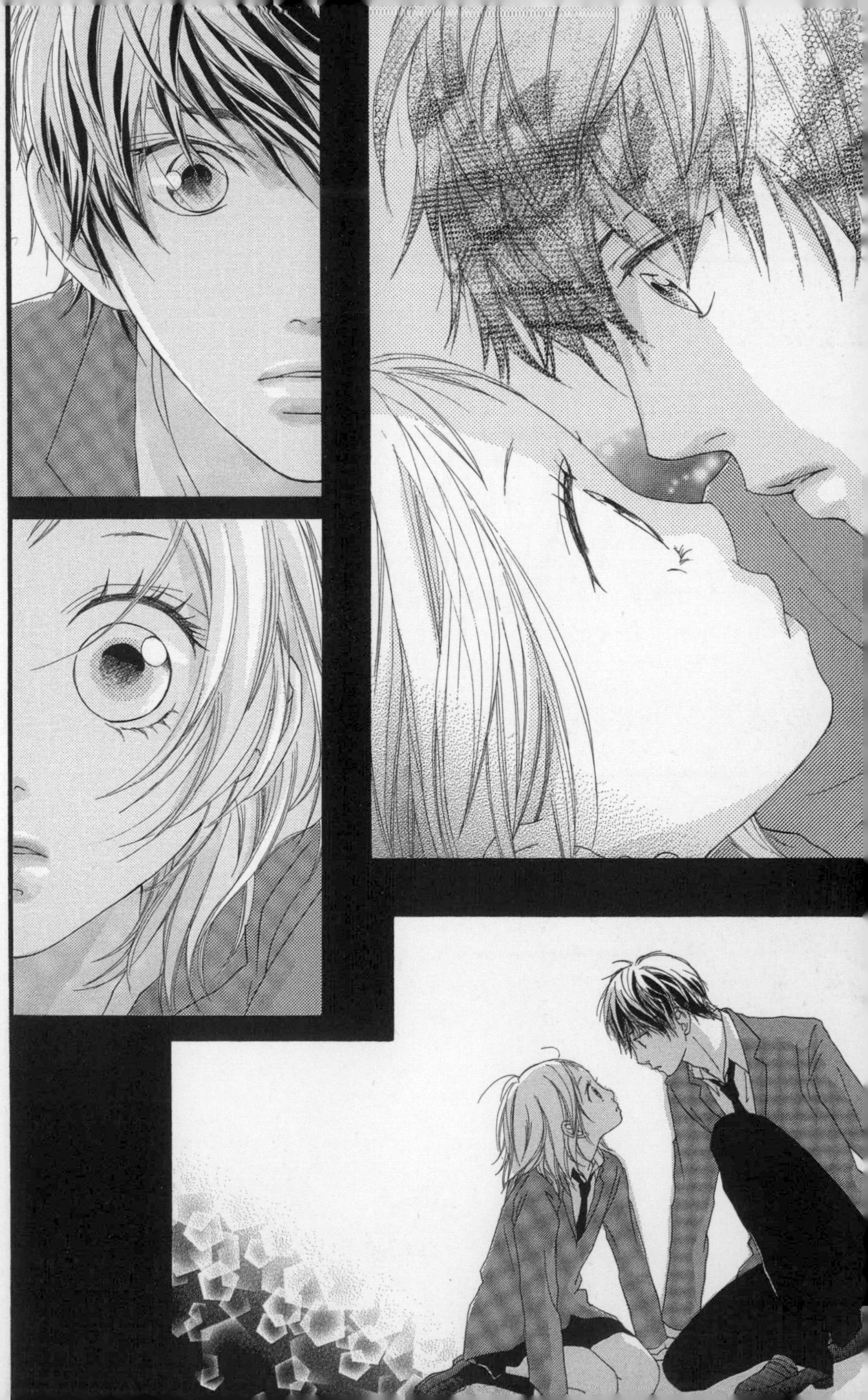

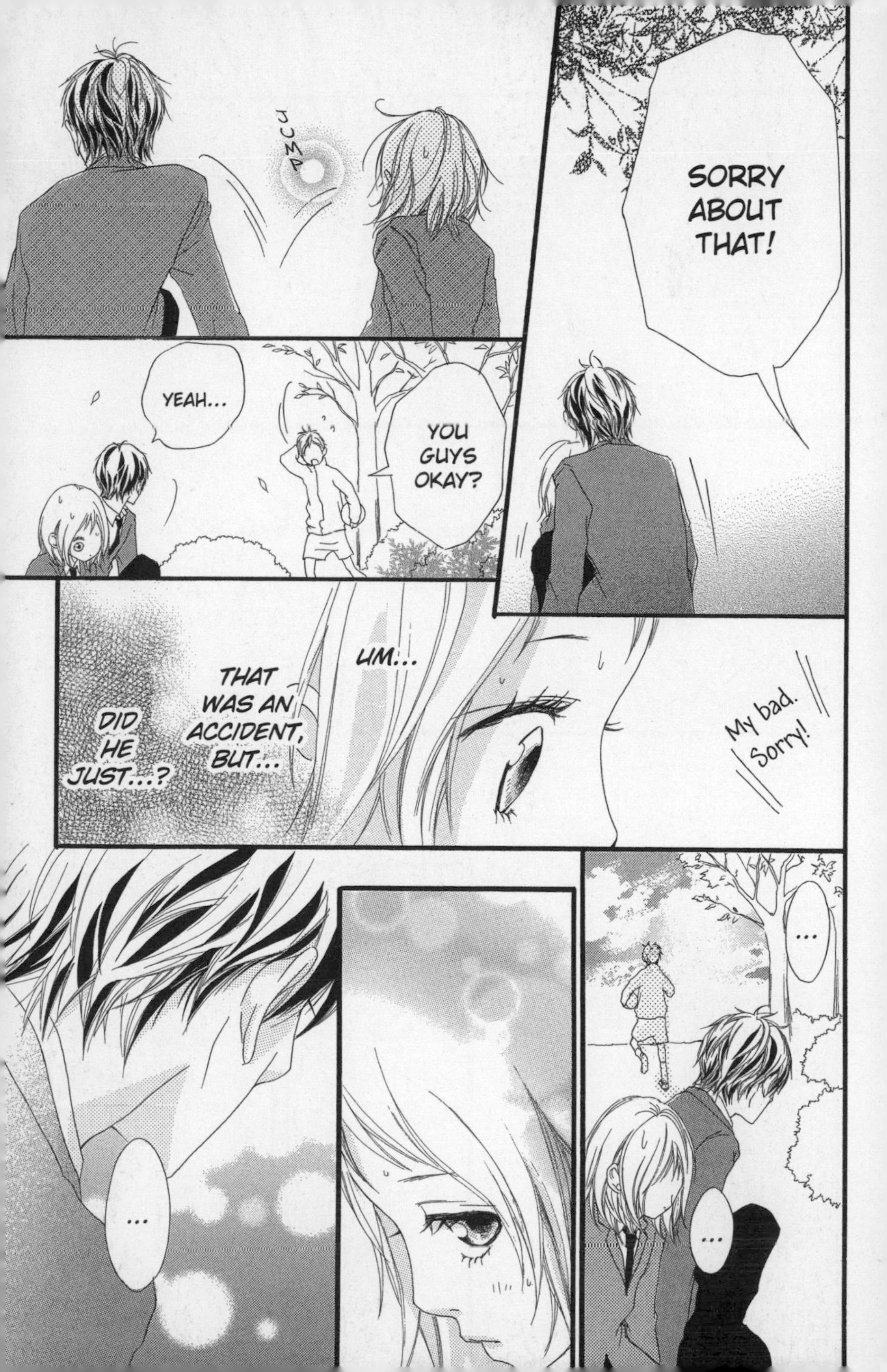
SORRY ABOUT THAT!
JUMP
YOU GUYS OKAY?
YEAH...
My bad. Sorry!
UM...
THAT WAS AN ACCIDENT, BUT...
DID HE JUST...?
...
...
...

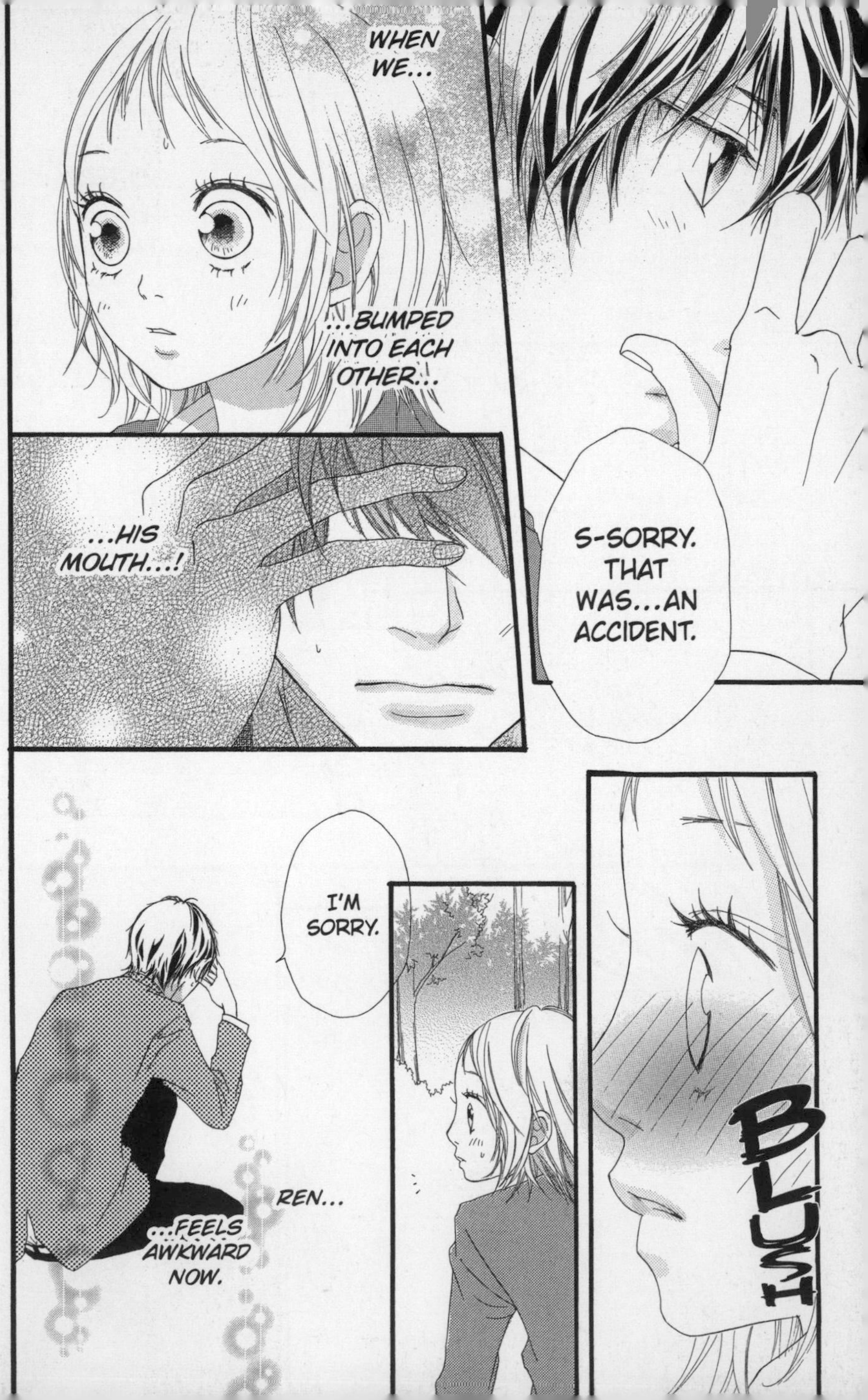
S-SORRY. THAT WAS...AN ACCIDENT.
WHEN WE...
...BUMPED INTO EACH OTHER...
...HIS MOUTH...!
BLUSH
I'M SORRY.
REN...
...FEELS AWKWARD NOW.

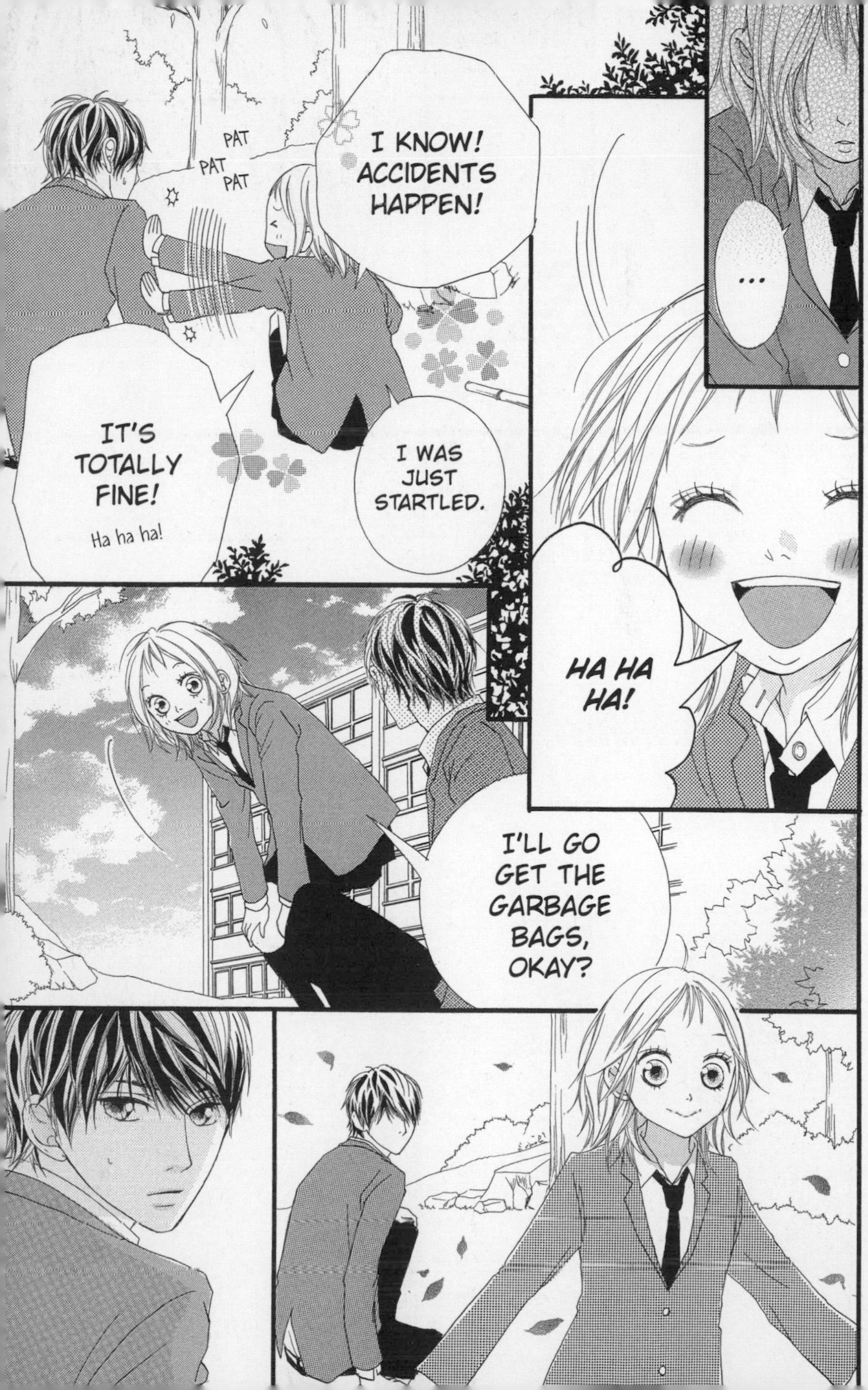
...
HA HA HA!
I KNOW! ACCIDENTS HAPPEN!
PAT PAT PAT
I WAS JUST STARTLED.
IT'S TOTALLY FINE!
Ha ha ha!
I'LL GO GET THE GARBAGE BAGS, OKAY?

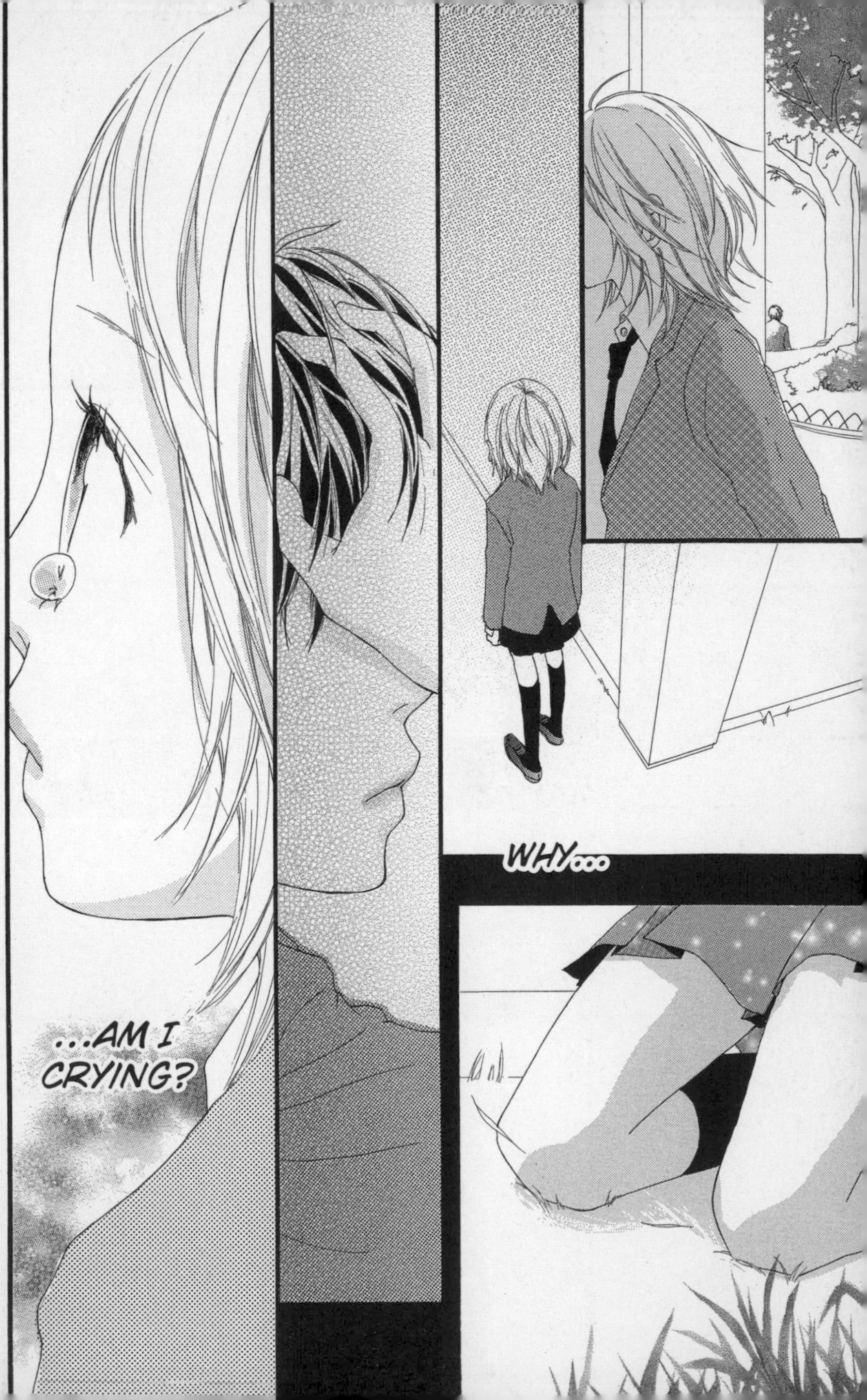
WHY...
...AM I CRYING?

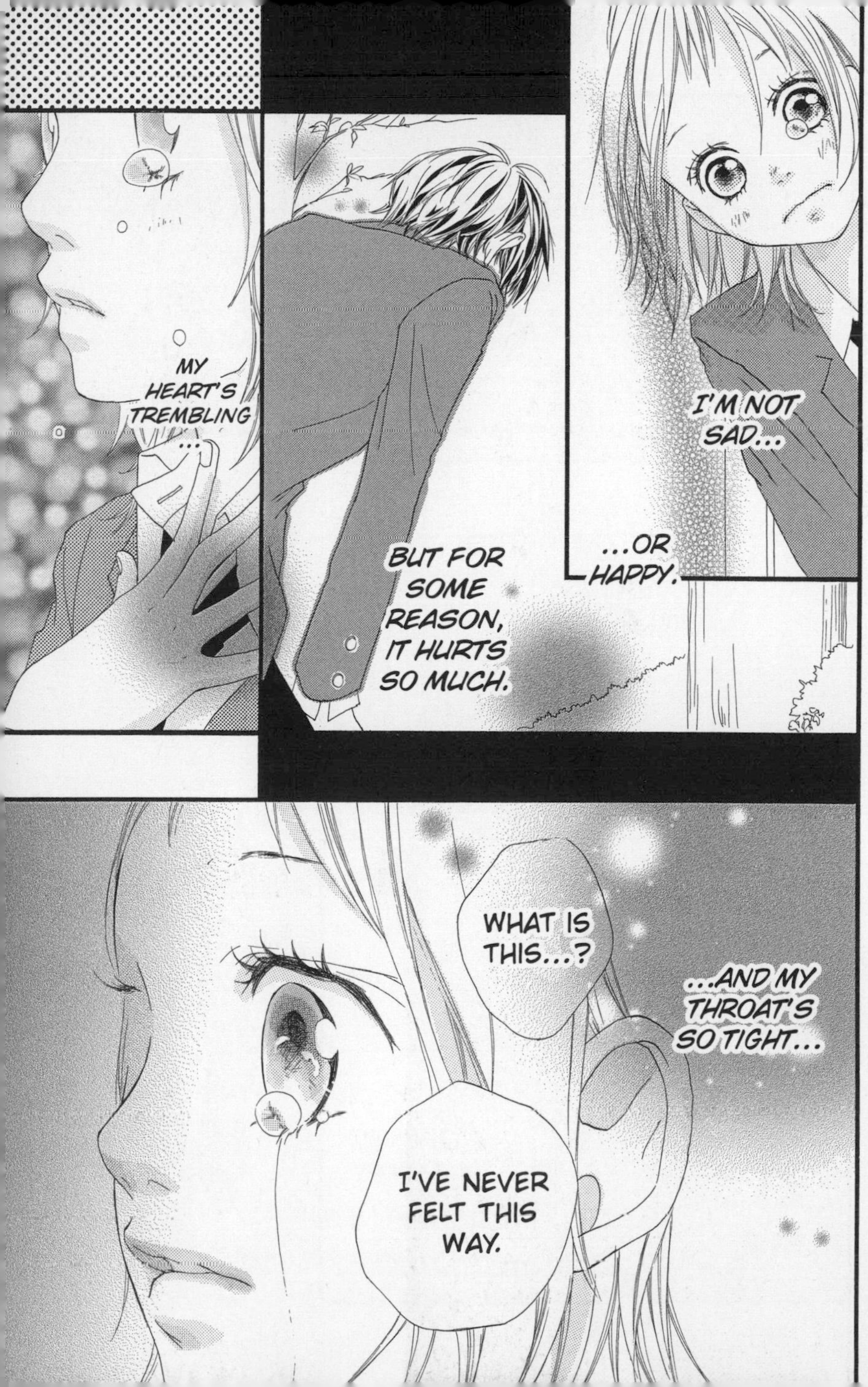
I'M NOT SAD...
...OR HAPPY.
BUT FOR SOME REASON, IT HURTS SO MUCH.
MY HEART'S TREMBLING...
...AND MY THROAT'S SO TIGHT...
WHAT IS THIS...?
I'VE NEVER FELT THIS WAY.

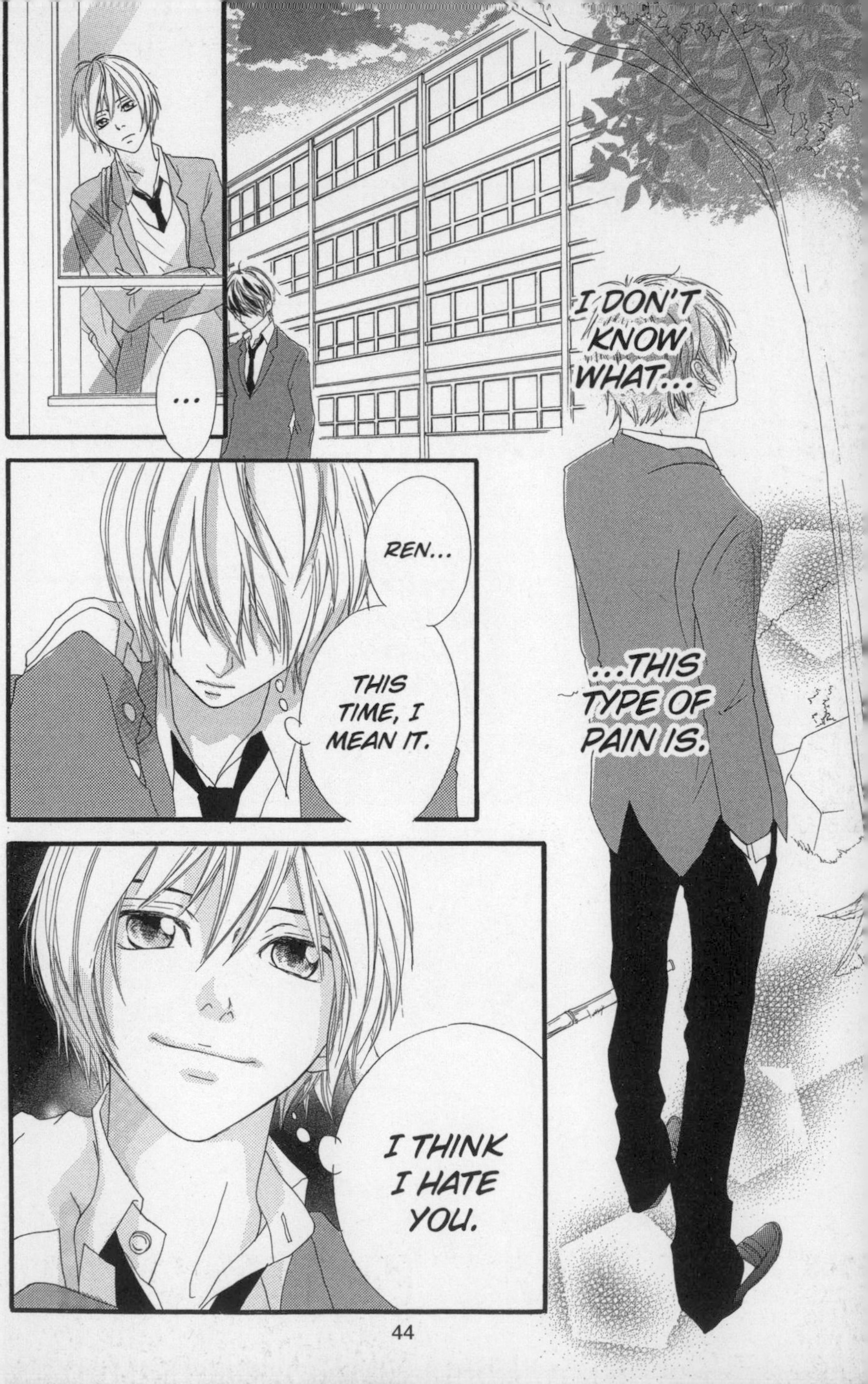
I DON'T KNOW WHAT...
...THIS TYPE OF PAIN IS.
...
REN...
THIS TIME, I MEAN IT.
I THINK I HATE YOU.

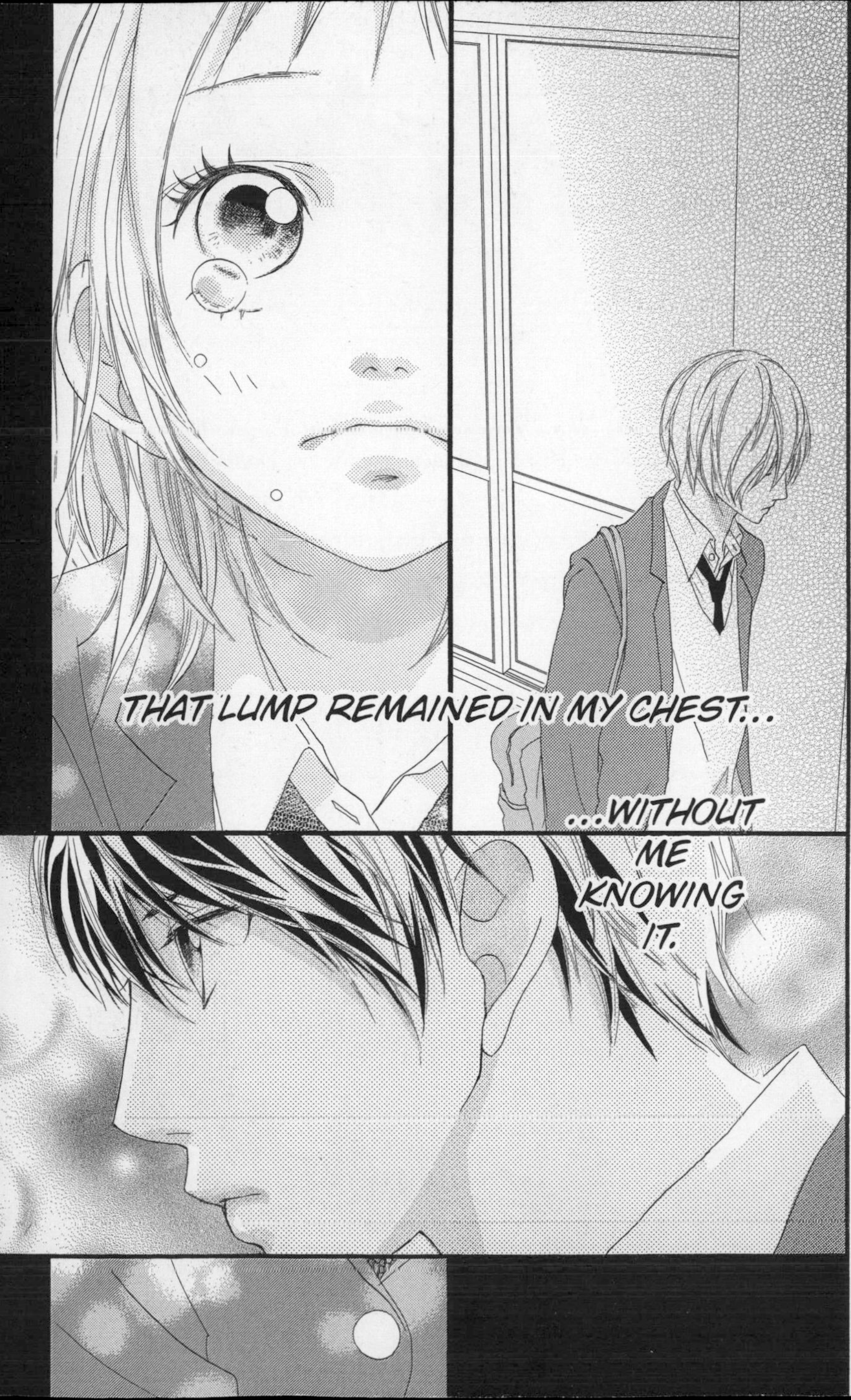
THAT LUMP REMAINED IN MY CHEST...
...WITHOUT ME KNOWING IT.

Hi! I'm Io Sakisaka. Thank you so much for reading
Strobe Edge 4!

I've been working on *Strobe Edge* for over a year now. That
year sure flew by...but my work is still so slow. I hate my right
hand—it refuses to adapt! But even when I'm struggling, I still
enjoy it so much. Working in this medium has allowed me to
establish bonds with complete strangers. This sensation of being
connected to my readers—whom I've never met—is totally
exciting.

I hope this book serves as a bridge between you and me
forever!

And, I hope you truly hear my prayer as you read the
rest of *Strobe Edge* 4.

Io Sakisaka

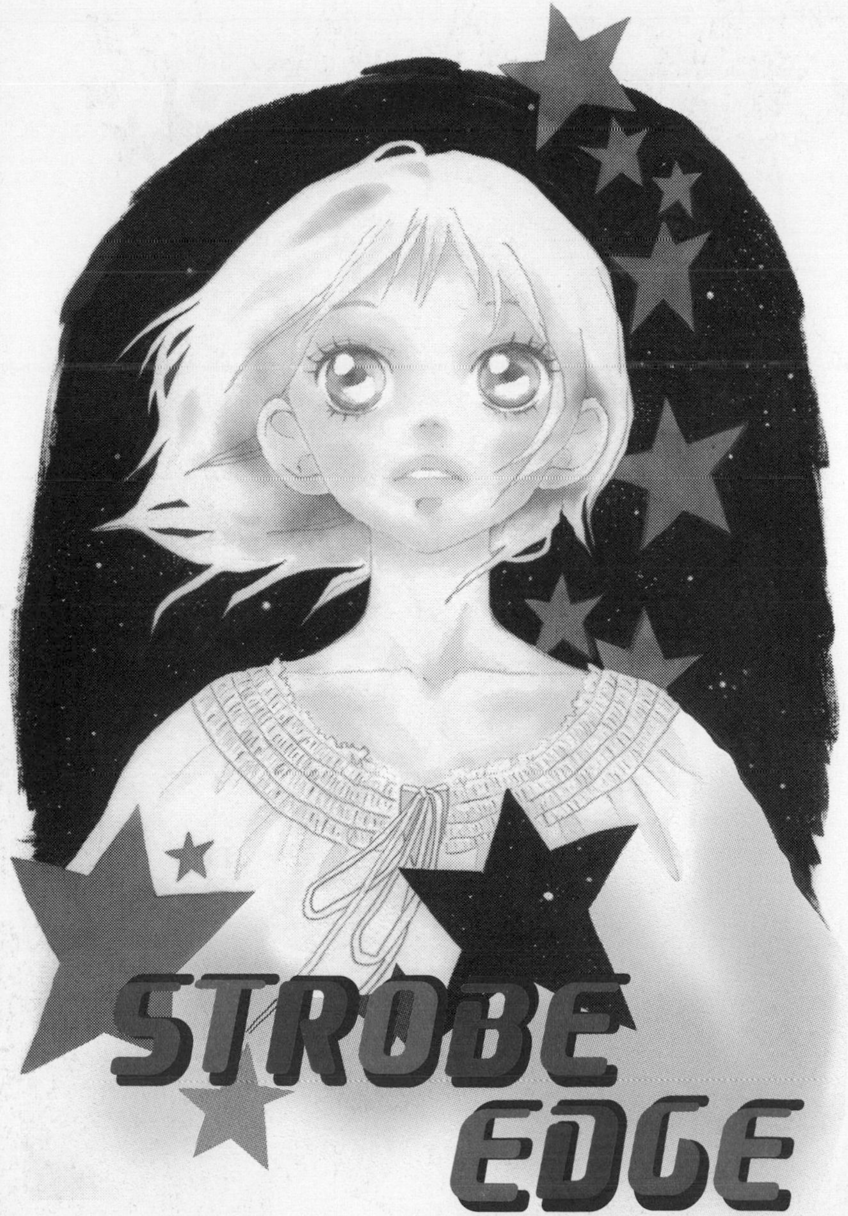
STROBE
EDGE

CHAPTER 13

The plushy that's hanging from Manabu's bag in chapter 12 is an actual promotional gift from *Bessatsu Margaret* magazine. Does that mean Manabu is a *Betsuma* fan? It's a mystery how he got ahold of one. I confess, I haven't really thought about it. It's pretty big, so the picture represents its actual size.

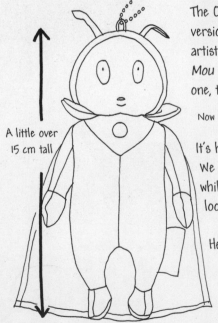

A little over 15 cm tall

The O-Kada Doll (normal version) is a creation of manga artist Fujimatsu, who's behind *Mou Kaette Kurenai Ka*. I have one, too. ♥♥♥

↖ Now I'm just bragging...

It's hanging from my desk lamp. We often exchange glances while I'm working, but I always look away. I wonder why?

He's always watching over me.

Thank you, O-Kada!

★ Sakisaka Hectopascal ★

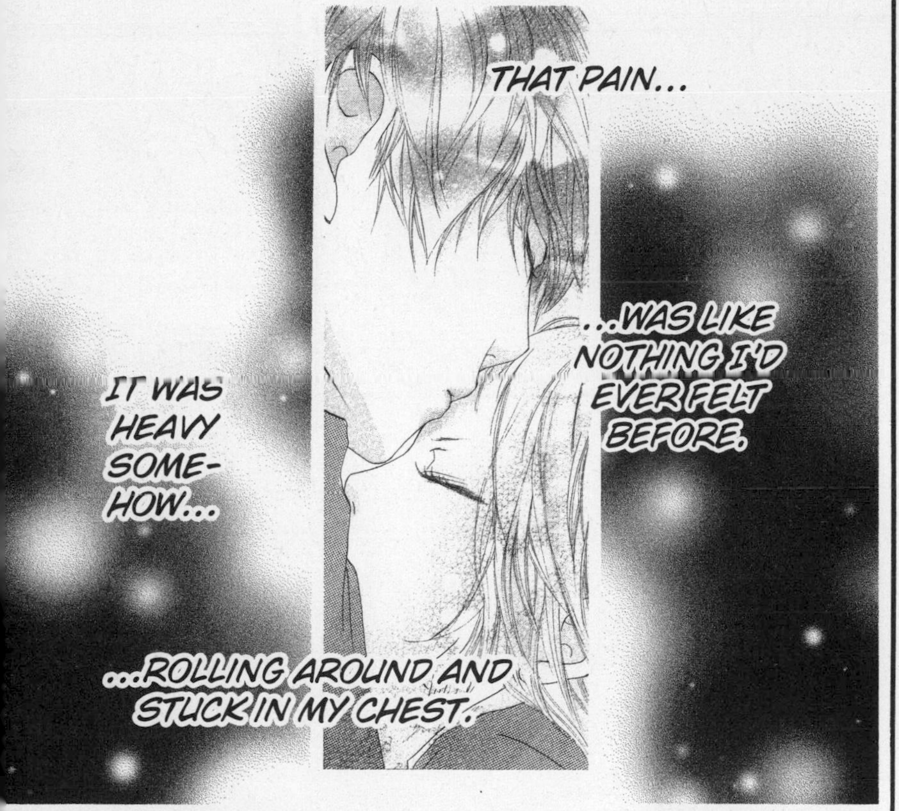
THAT PAIN...
...WAS LIKE NOTHING I'D EVER FELT BEFORE.
IT WAS HEAVY SOME-HOW...
...ROLLING AROUND AND STUCK IN MY CHEST.

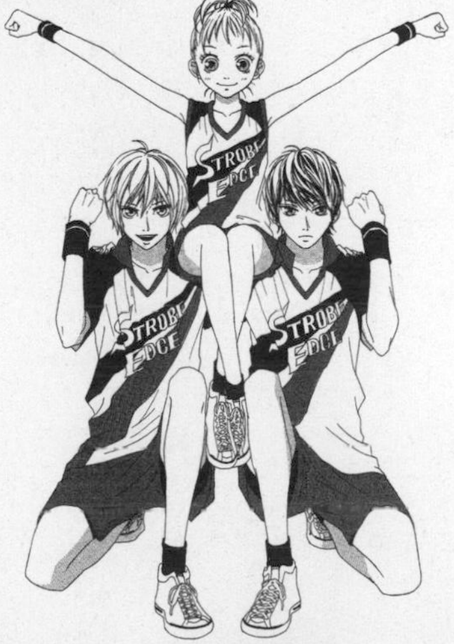

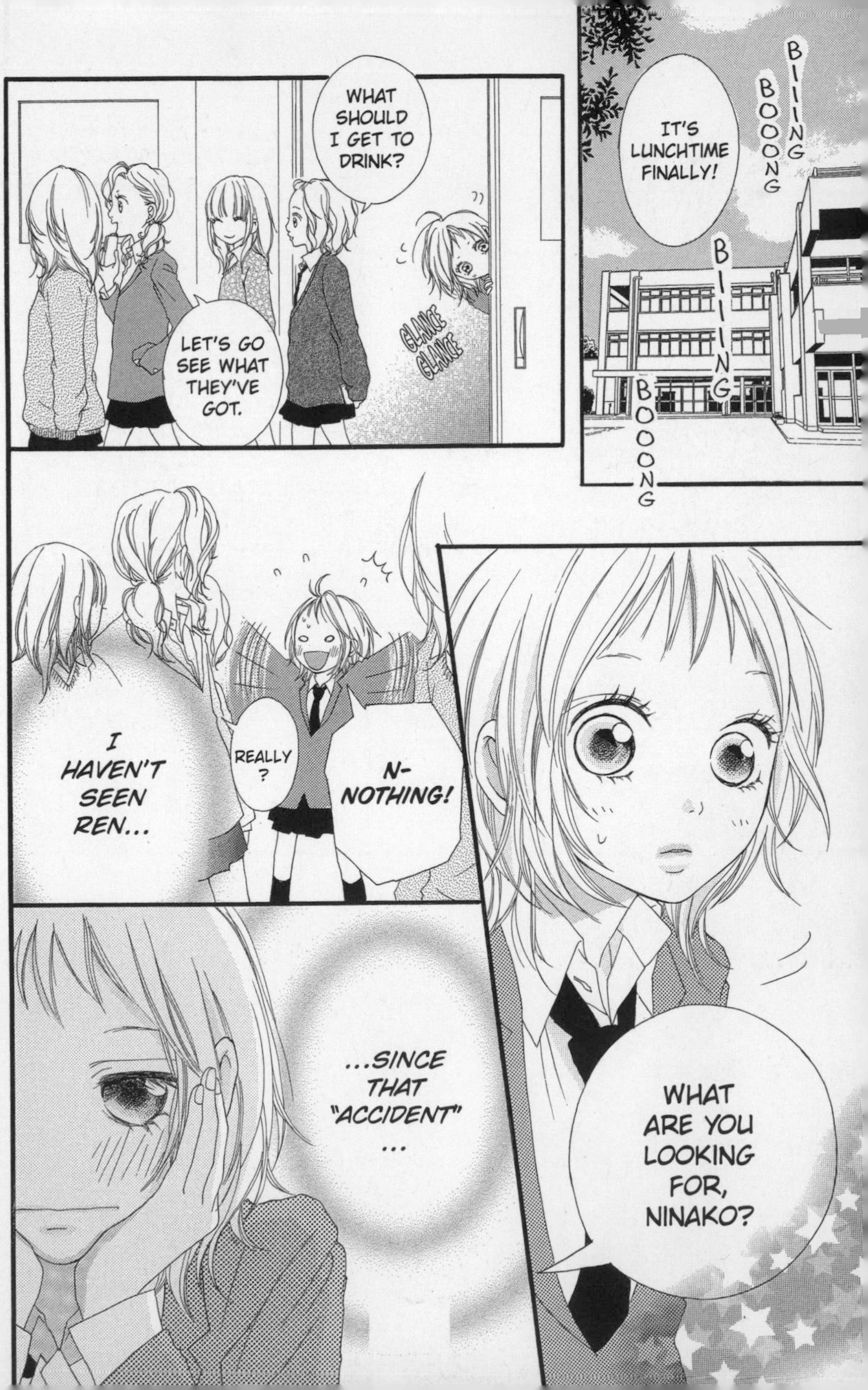
BIIING
BOOONG
IT'S LUNCHTIME FINALLY!
BIIING
BOOONG
WHAT SHOULD I GET TO DRINK?
GLANCE GLANCE
LET'S GO SEE WHAT THEY'VE GOT.
WHAT ARE YOU LOOKING FOR, NINAKO?
N-NOTHING!
REALLY?
I HAVEN'T SEEN REN...
...SINCE THAT "ACCIDENT"...

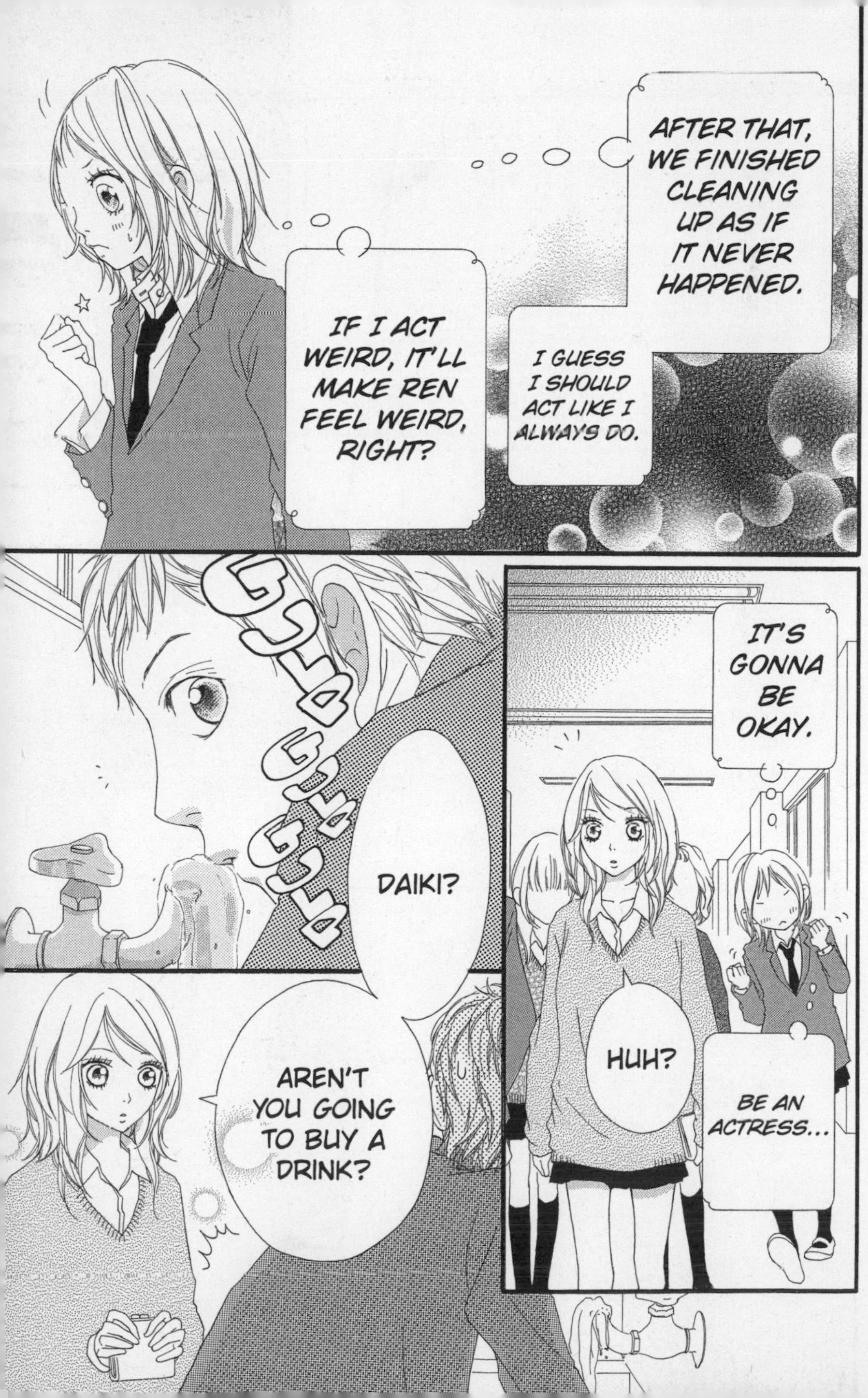
AFTER THAT, WE FINISHED CLEANING UP AS IF IT NEVER HAPPENED.
I GUESS I SHOULD ACT LIKE I ALWAYS DO.
IF I ACT WEIRD, IT'LL MAKE REN FEEL WEIRD, RIGHT?
IT'S GONNA BE OKAY.
BE AN ACTRESS...
HUH?
GULP GULP GULP
DAIKI?
AREN'T YOU GOING TO BUY A DRINK?

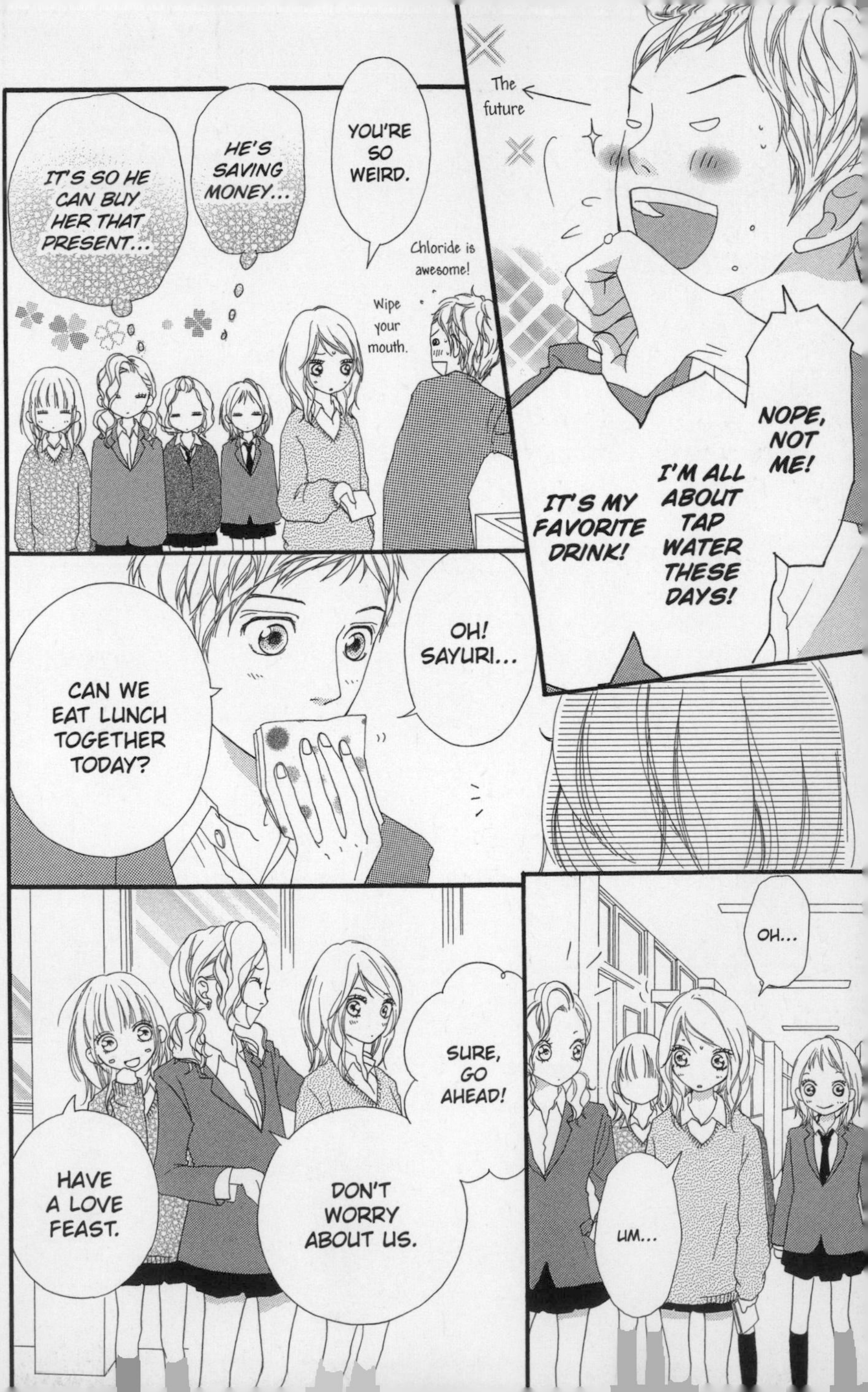
The future
NOPE, NOT ME!
I'M ALL ABOUT TAP WATER THESE DAYS!
IT'S MY FAVORITE DRINK!
YOU'RE SO WEIRD.
Chloride is awesome!
Wipe your mouth.
HE'S SAVING MONEY...
IT'S SO HE CAN BUY HER THAT PRESENT...
OH! SAYURI...
CAN WE EAT LUNCH TOGETHER TODAY?
OH...
UM...
SURE, GO AHEAD!
DON'T WORRY ABOUT US.
HAVE A LOVE FEAST.

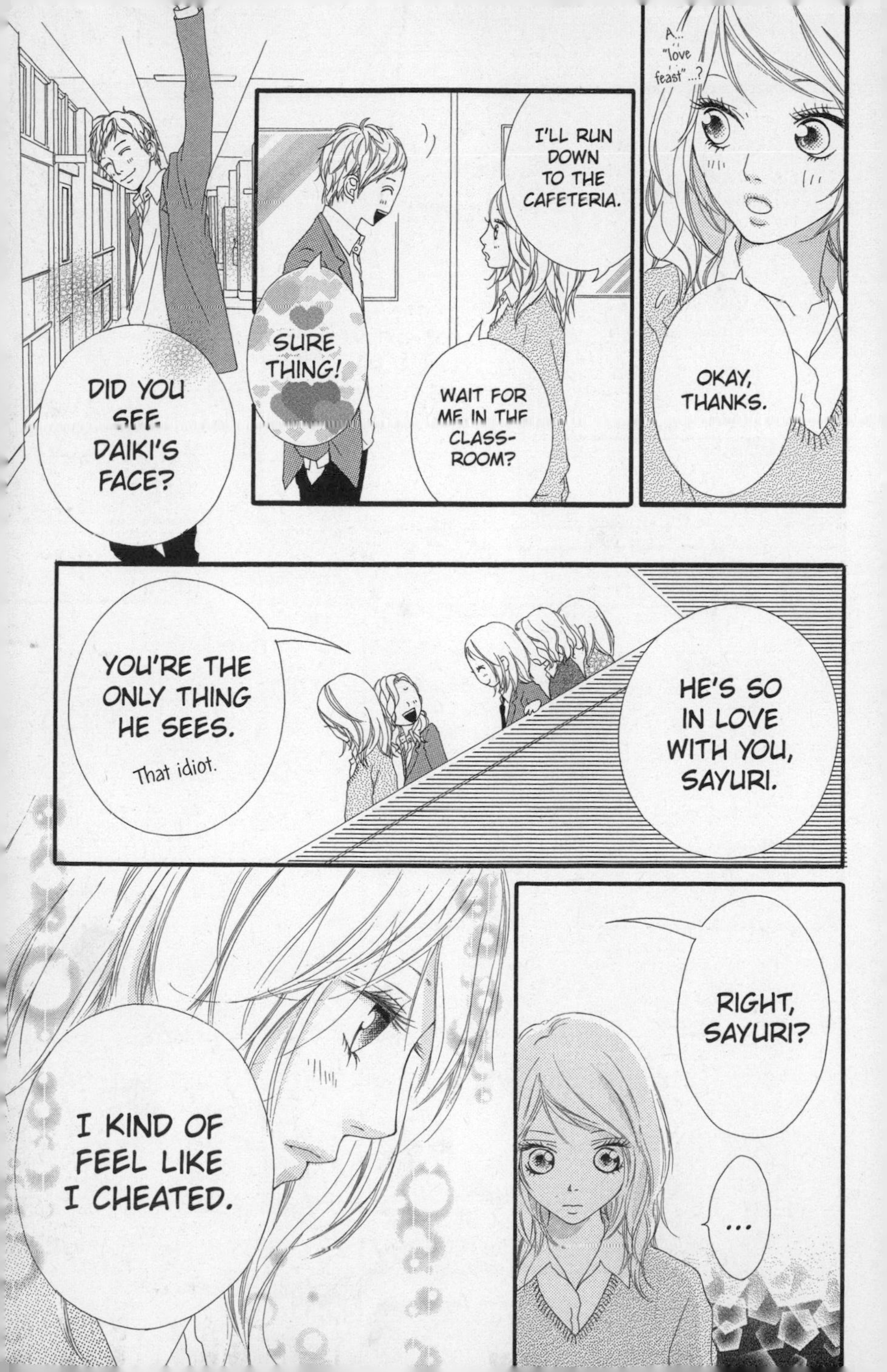
A... "love feast"...?
OKAY, THANKS.
I'LL RUN DOWN TO THE CAFETERIA.
WAIT FOR ME IN THE CLASS-ROOM?
SURE THING!
DID YOU SEE DAIKI'S FACE?
HE'S SO IN LOVE WITH YOU, SAYURI.
YOU'RE THE ONLY THING HE SEES.
That idiot.
RIGHT, SAYURI?
...
I KIND OF FEEL LIKE I CHEATED.

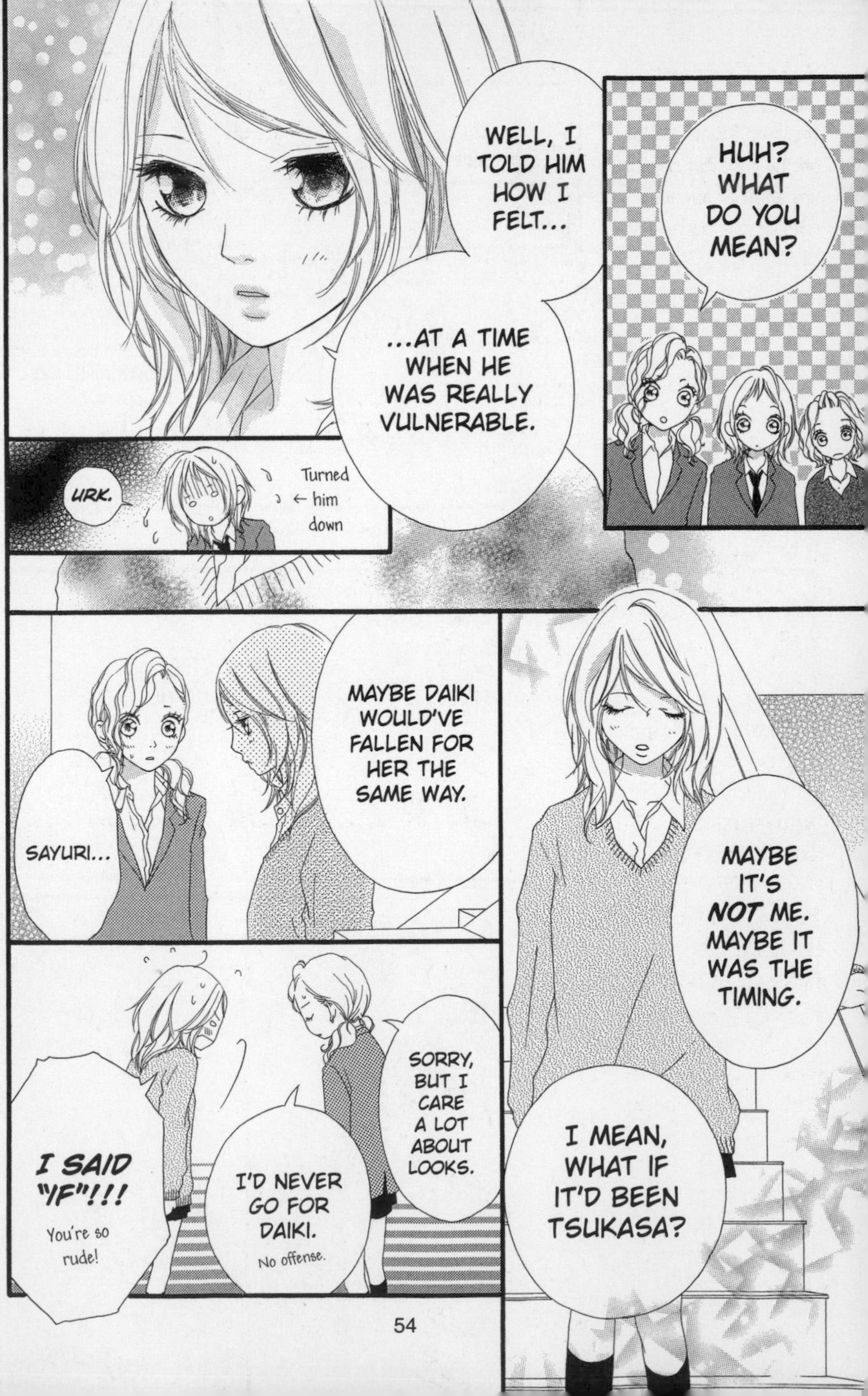
HUH? WHAT DO YOU MEAN?
WELL, I TOLD HIM HOW I FELT...
...AT A TIME WHEN HE WAS REALLY VULNERABLE.
URK.
Turned ← him down
MAYBE IT'S *NOT* ME. MAYBE IT WAS THE TIMING.
I MEAN, WHAT IF IT'D BEEN TSUKASA?
MAYBE DAIKI WOULD'VE FALLEN FOR HER THE SAME WAY.
SAYURI...
SORRY, BUT I CARE A LOT ABOUT LOOKS.
I'D NEVER GO FOR DAIKI.
No offense.
I SAID "IF"!!!
You're so rude!

My heart skips a beat whenever I see an adult (male or female!) eating on the run. But not just any adult at any time. Certain criteria have to be met:

* It has to be at night.
* They have to be alone.
* They have to be walking kind of fast.

If all of these criteria are met, my heart begins to flutter. The thing is, eating on the run is fundamentally bad manners.

Adults know that, but sometimes they do it in spite of themselves...on the sly. When I see this, my pulse speeds up. They must be so hungry! When I see an office lady on the way home from work, eating and walking at the same time, it brings tears to my eyes. In my mind, I yell, "Thanks for your hard work!" Even older men look cute when they are eating on the run.

Heart throb!

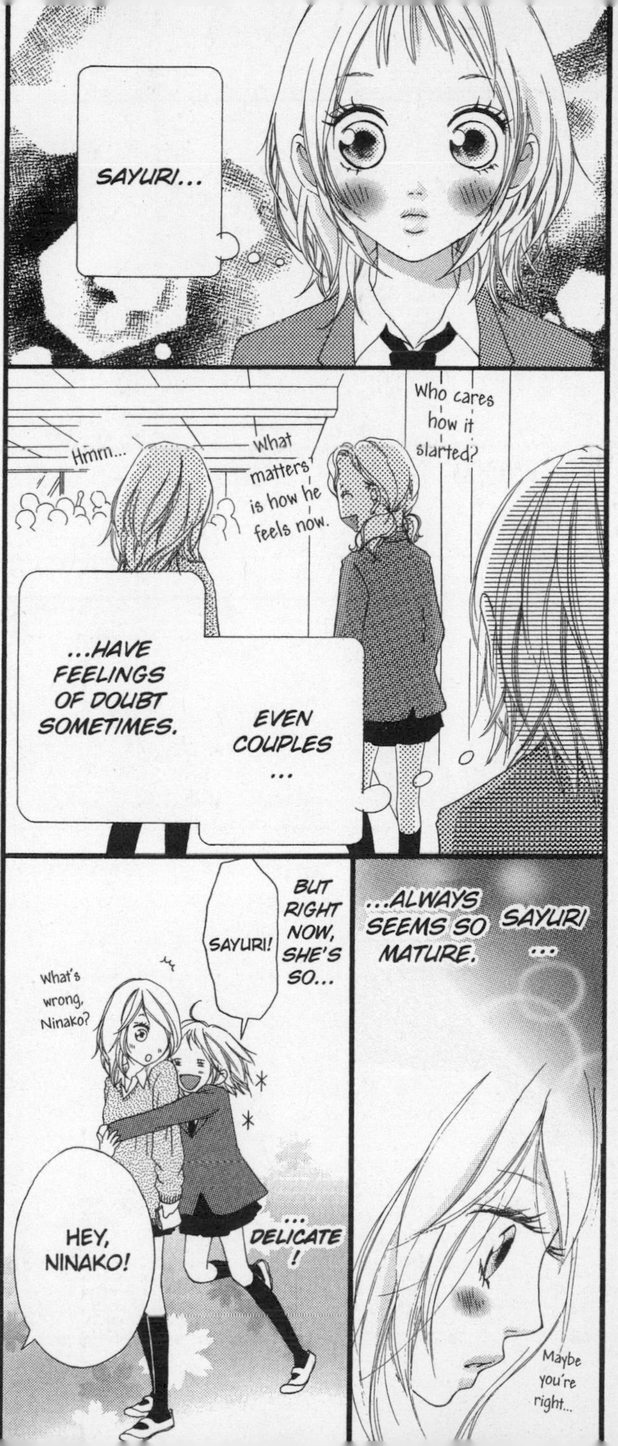
SAYURI...
Who cares how it started?
What matters is how he feels now.
Hmm...
EVEN COUPLES ...
...HAVE FEELINGS OF DOUBT SOMETIMES.
SAYURI ...
...ALWAYS SEEMS SO MATURE.
Maybe you're right...
BUT RIGHT NOW, SHE'S SO...
SAYURI!
... DELICATE !
What's wrong, Ninako?
HEY, NINAKO!

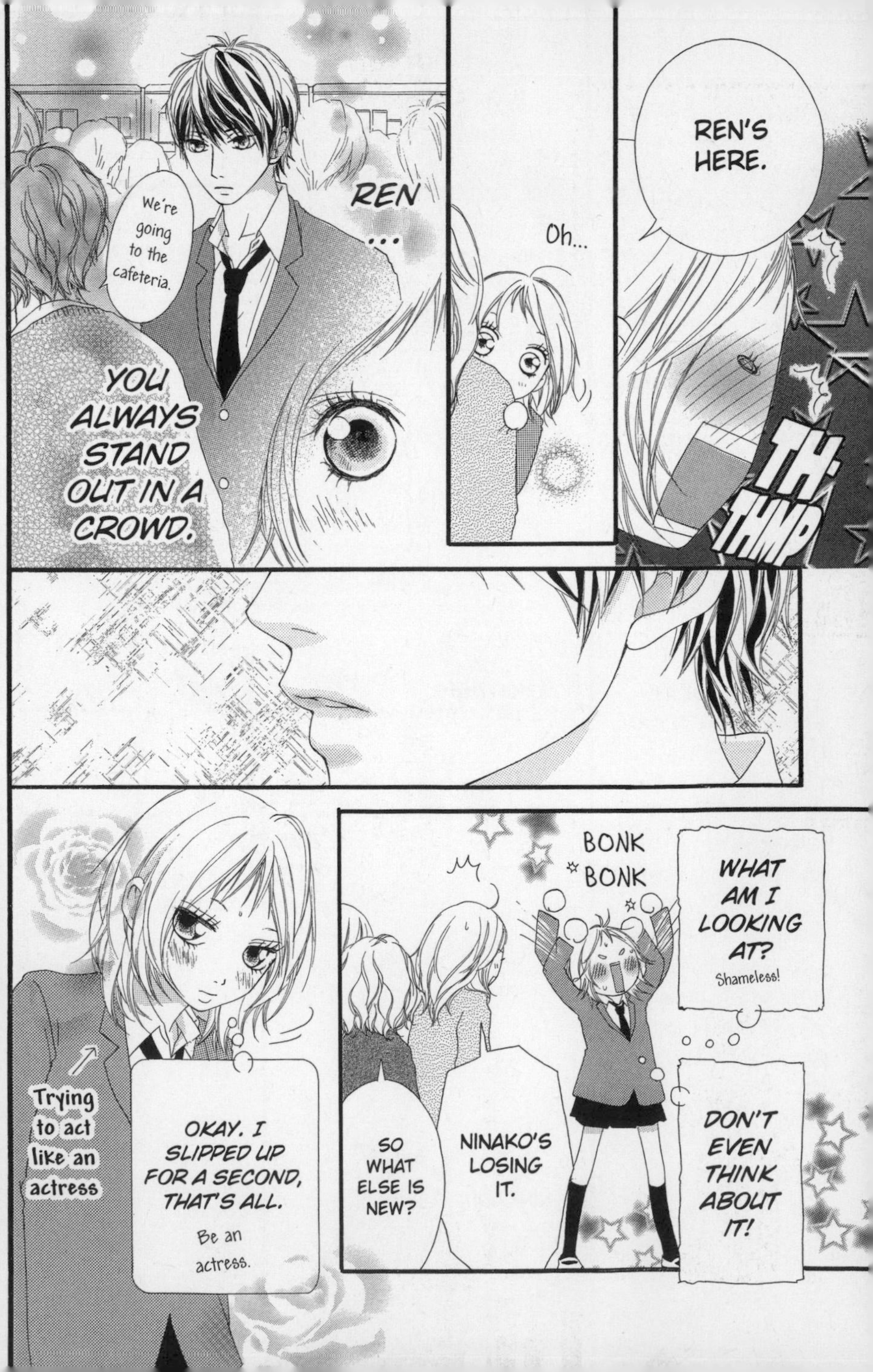
REN'S HERE.
TH-THUMP
Oh...
REN ...
We're going to the cafeteria.
YOU ALWAYS STAND OUT IN A CROWD.
WHAT AM I LOOKING AT?
Shameless!
BONK BONK
DON'T EVEN THINK ABOUT IT!
NINAKO'S LOSING IT.
SO WHAT ELSE IS NEW?
OKAY. I SLIPPED UP FOR A SECOND, THAT'S ALL.
Be an actress.
Trying to act like an actress

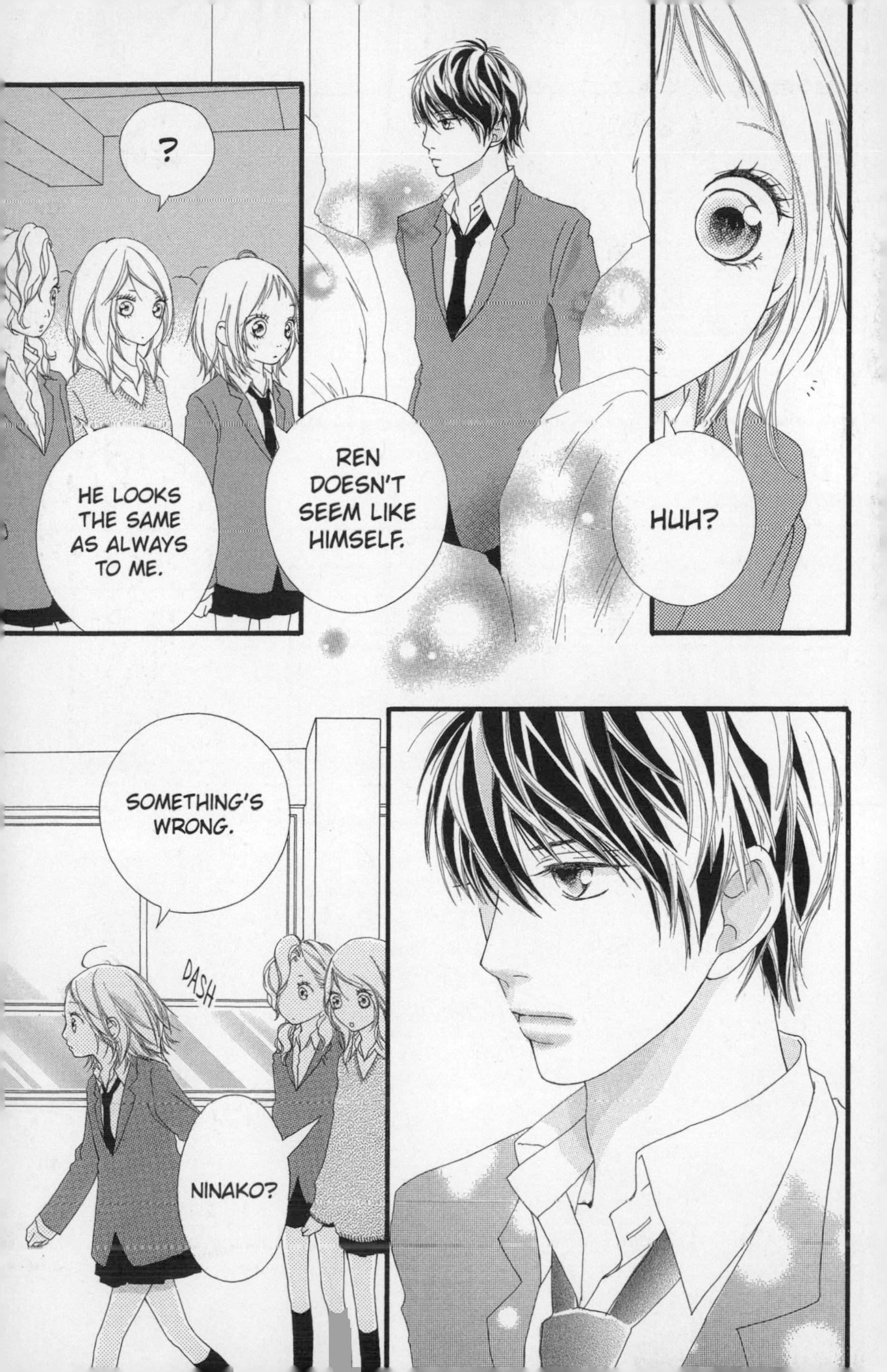
HUH?
REN DOESN'T SEEM LIKE HIMSELF.
?
HE LOOKS THE SAME AS ALWAYS TO ME.
SOMETHING'S WRONG.
DASH
NINAKO?

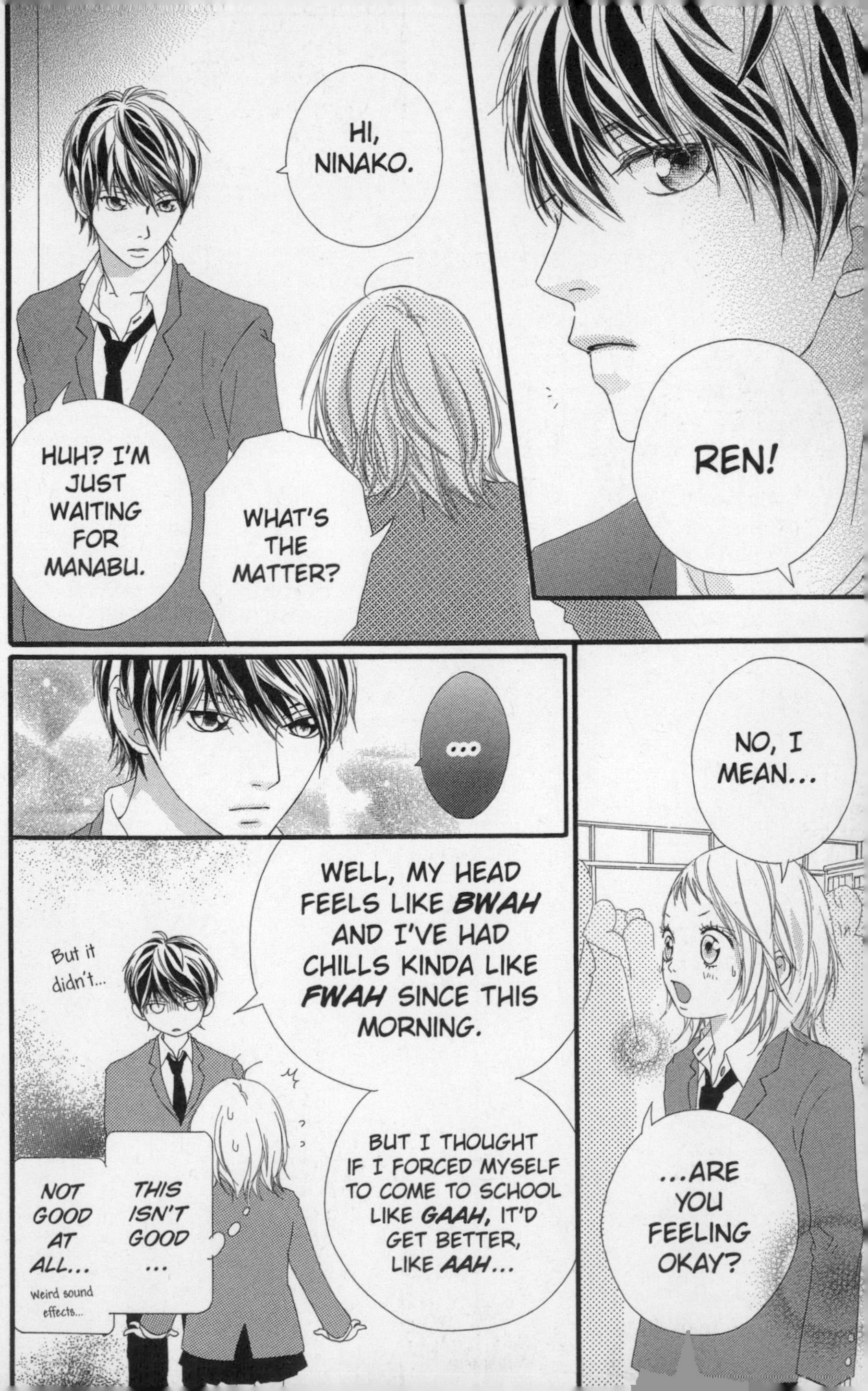
REN!
HI, NINAKO.
WHAT'S THE MATTER?
HUH? I'M JUST WAITING FOR MANABU.
NO, I MEAN...
...ARE YOU FEELING OKAY?
...
WELL, MY HEAD FEELS LIKE BWAH AND I'VE HAD CHILLS KINDA LIKE FWAH SINCE THIS MORNING.
BUT I THOUGHT IF I FORCED MYSELF TO COME TO SCHOOL LIKE GAAH, IT'D GET BETTER, LIKE AAH...
But it didn't...
THIS ISN'T GOOD...
NOT GOOD AT ALL...
Weird sound effects...

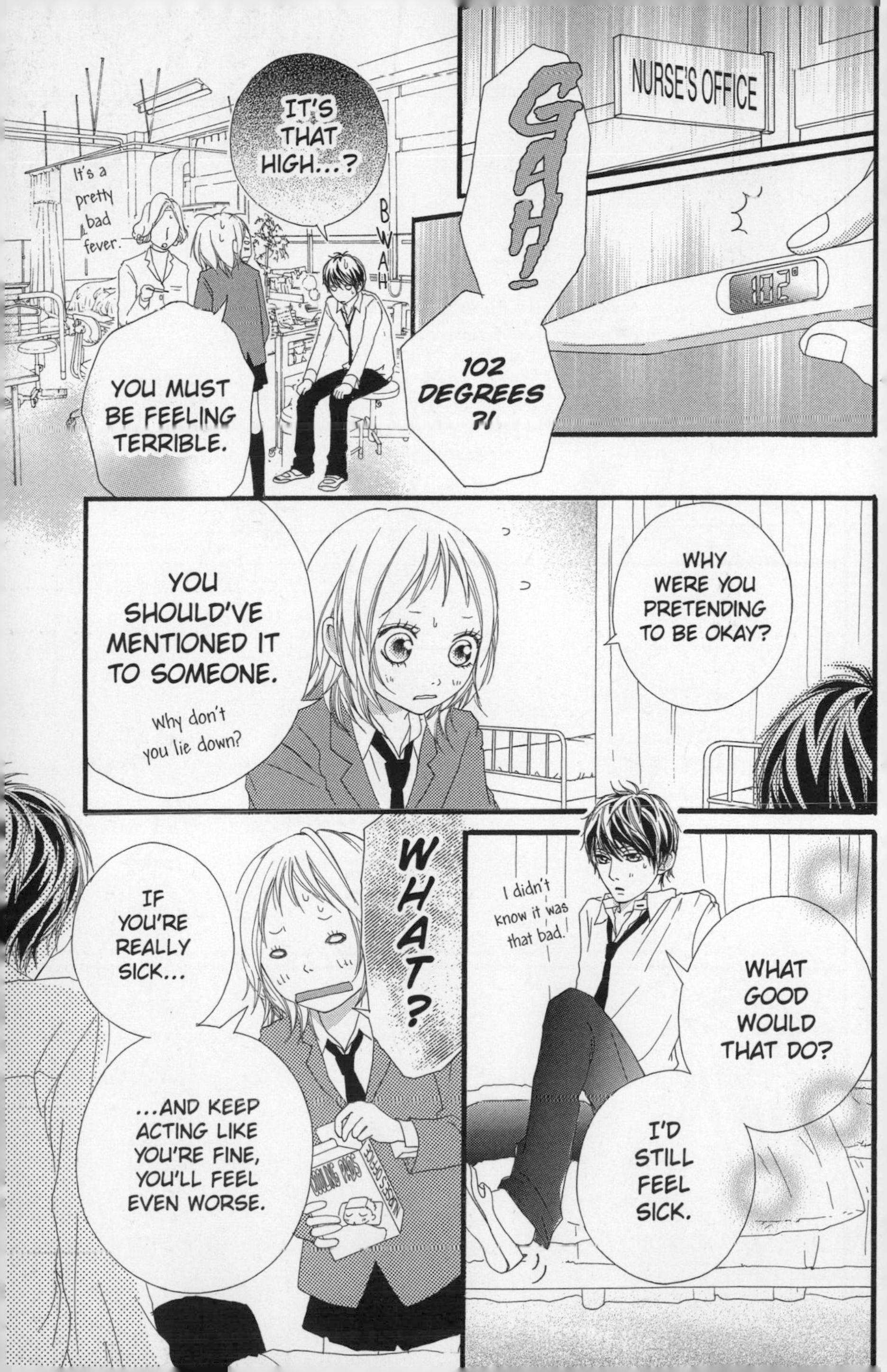
NURSE'S OFFICE
GAH!
102 DEGREES ?!
IT'S THAT HIGH...?
BWAH
It's a pretty bad fever.
YOU MUST BE FEELING TERRIBLE.
WHY WERE YOU PRETENDING TO BE OKAY?
YOU SHOULD'VE MENTIONED IT TO SOMEONE.
Why don't you lie down?
I didn't know it was that bad.
WHAT GOOD WOULD THAT DO?
I'D STILL FEEL SICK.
WHAT?
IF YOU'RE REALLY SICK...
...AND KEEP ACTING LIKE YOU'RE FINE, YOU'LL FEEL EVEN WORSE.
COOLING PADS
NURSE'S OFFICE

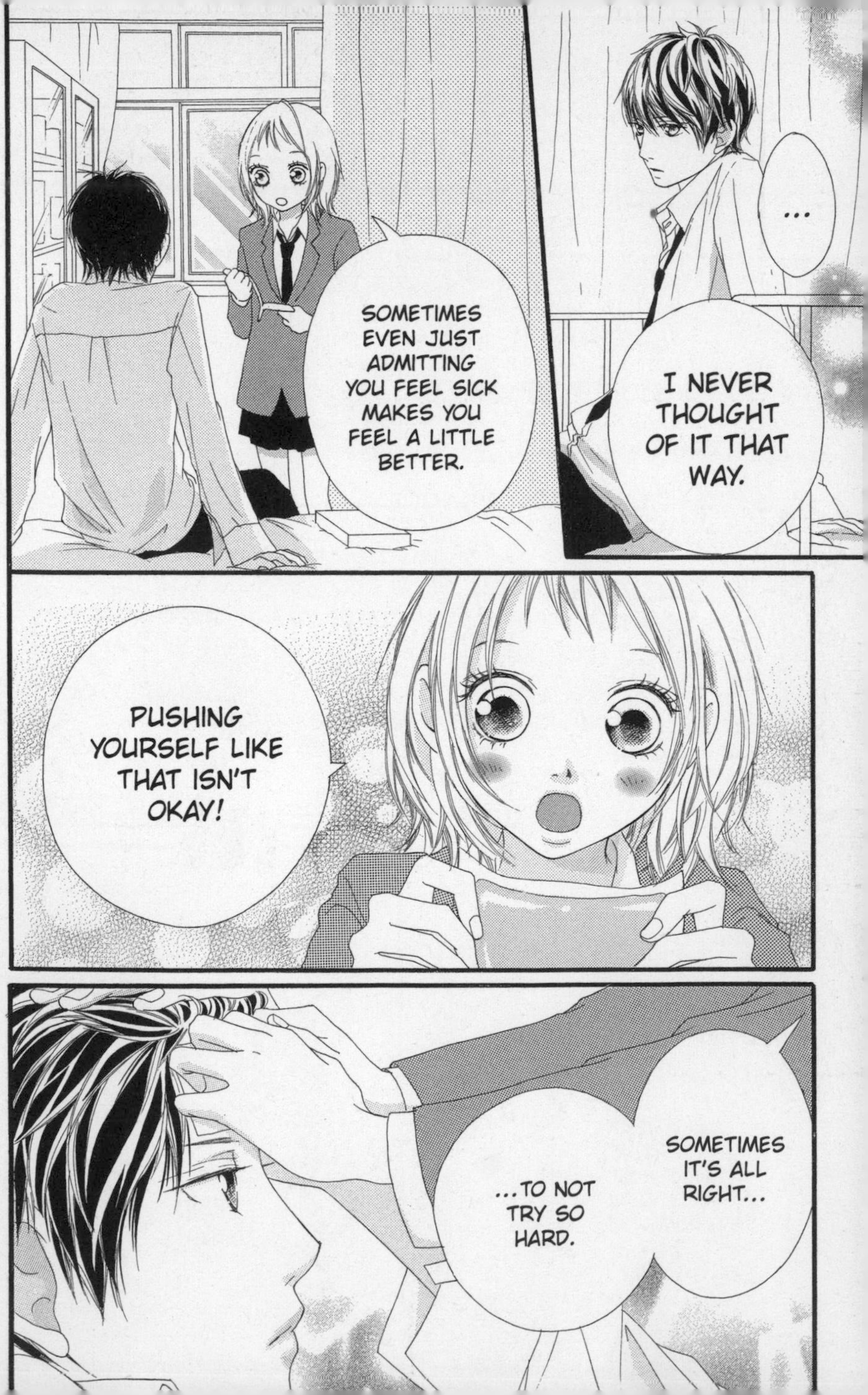
...
I NEVER THOUGHT OF IT THAT WAY.
SOMETIMES EVEN JUST ADMITTING YOU FEEL SICK MAKES YOU FEEL A LITTLE BETTER.
PUSHING YOURSELF LIKE THAT ISN'T OKAY!
SOMETIMES IT'S ALL RIGHT...
...TO NOT TRY SO HARD.

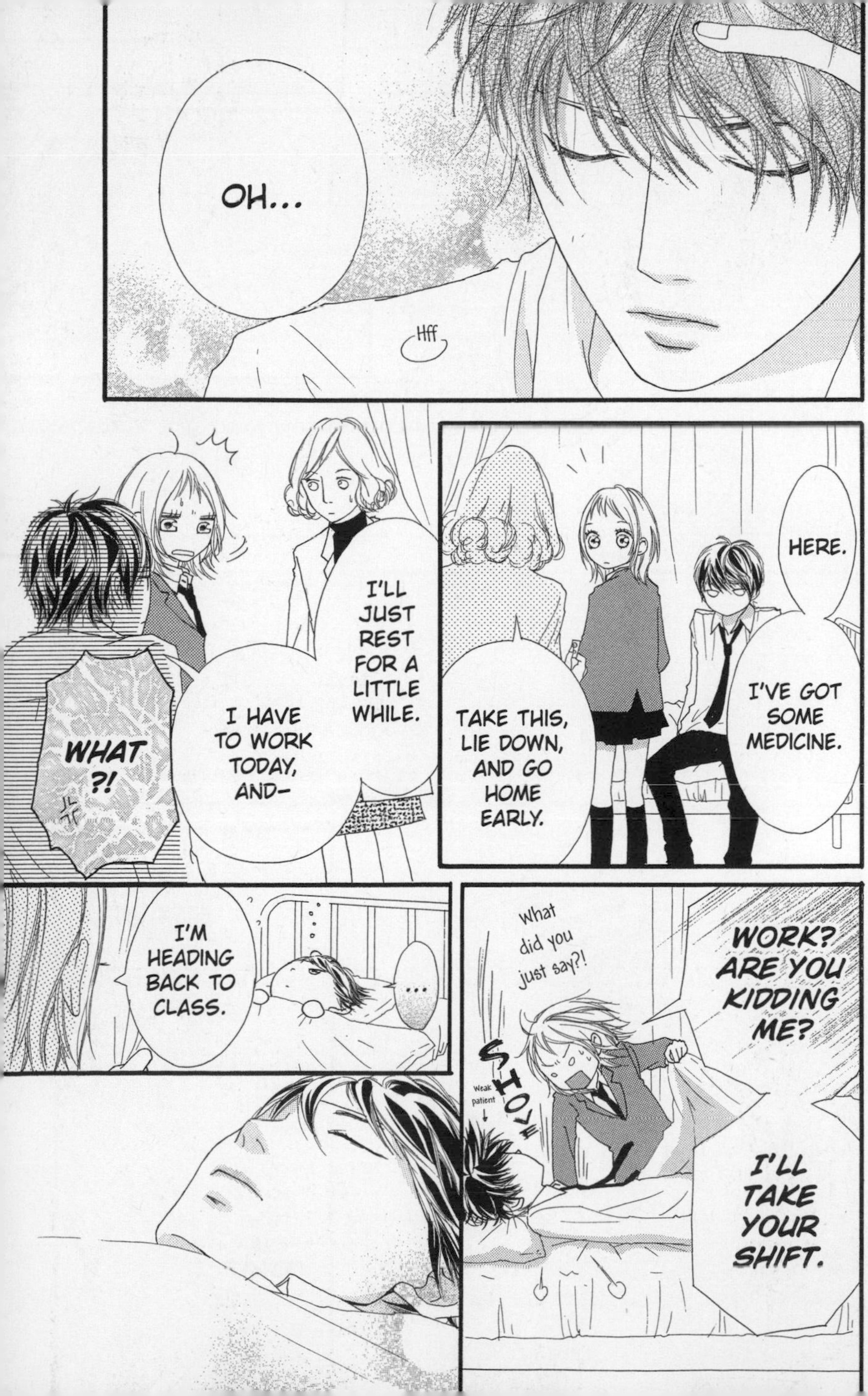
OH...
Hff
HERE.
I'VE GOT SOME MEDICINE.
TAKE THIS, LIE DOWN, AND GO HOME EARLY.
I'LL JUST REST FOR A LITTLE WHILE.
I HAVE TO WORK TODAY, AND-
WHAT?!
WORK? ARE YOU KIDDING ME?
What did you just say?!
SHOVE
Weak patient
I'LL TAKE YOUR SHIFT.
I'M HEADING BACK TO CLASS.
...

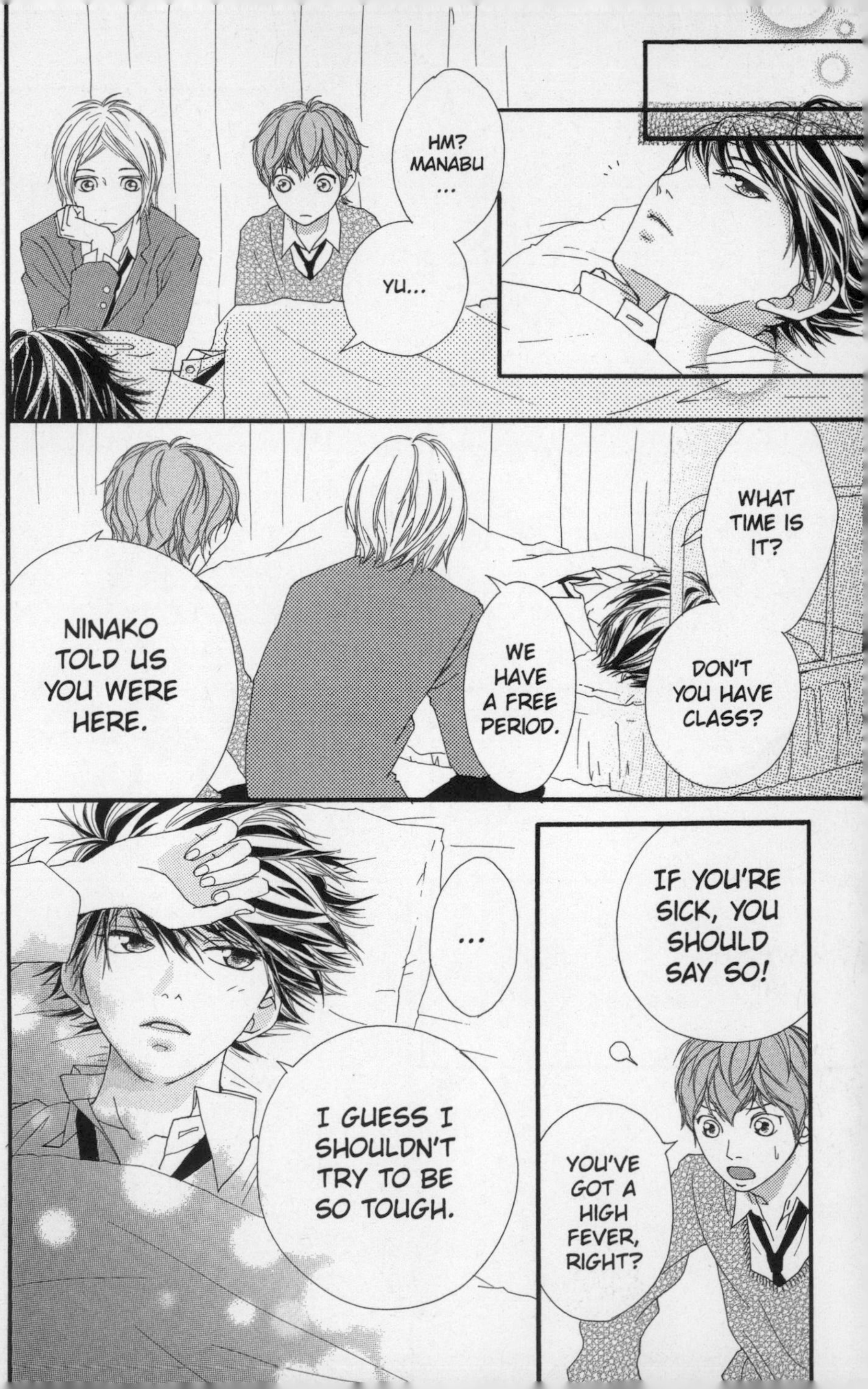
HM? MANABU ...
YU...
WHAT TIME IS IT?
DON'T YOU HAVE CLASS?
WE HAVE A FREE PERIOD.
NINAKO TOLD US YOU WERE HERE.
IF YOU'RE SICK, YOU SHOULD SAY SO!
YOU'VE GOT A HIGH FEVER, RIGHT?
...
I GUESS I SHOULDN'T TRY TO BE SO TOUGH.

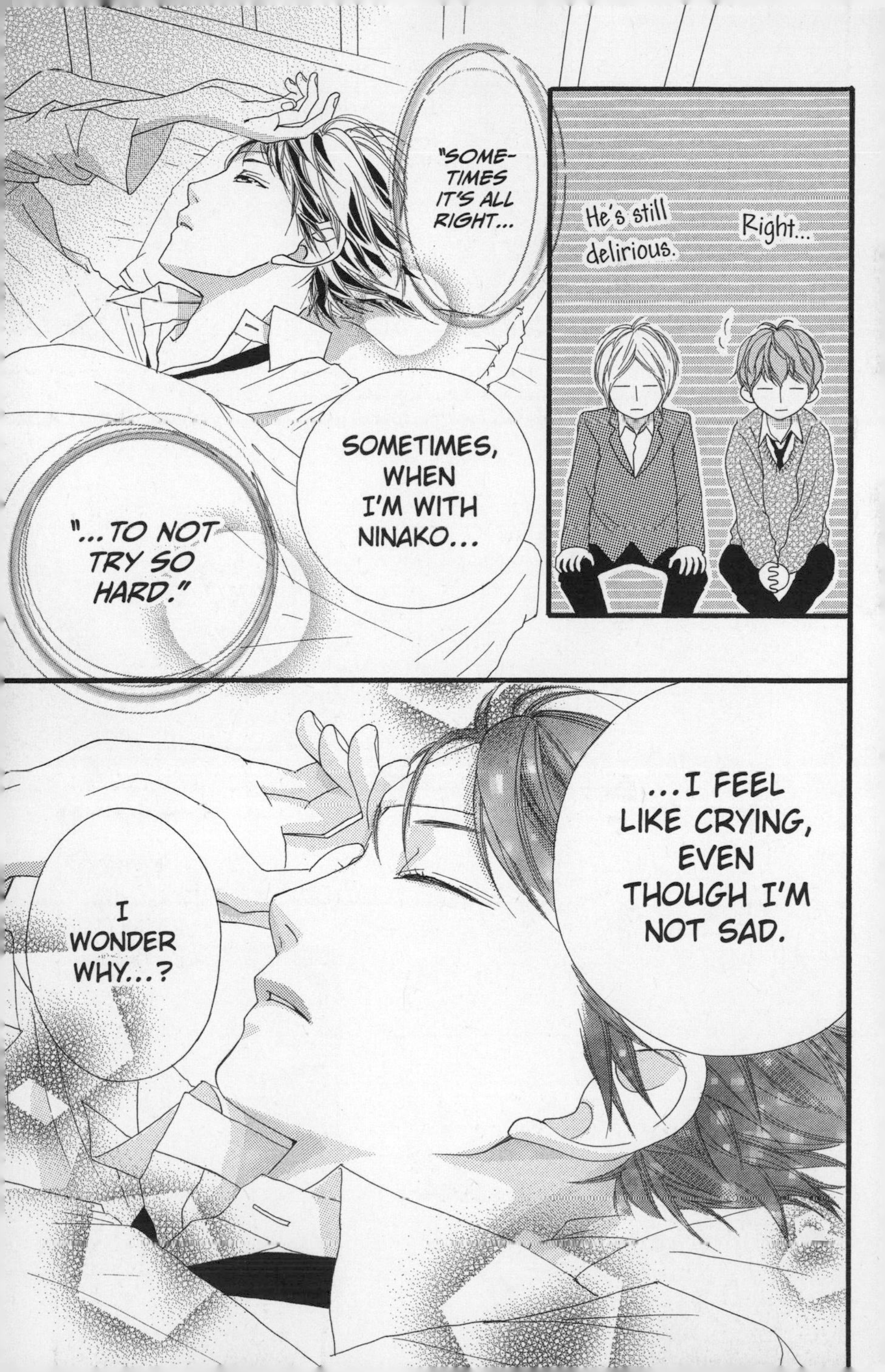
He's still delirious.
Right...
"SOME-TIMES IT'S ALL RIGHT...
SOMETIMES, WHEN I'M WITH NINAKO...
"...TO NOT TRY SO HARD."
...I FEEL LIKE CRYING, EVEN THOUGH I'M NOT SAD.
I WONDER WHY...?

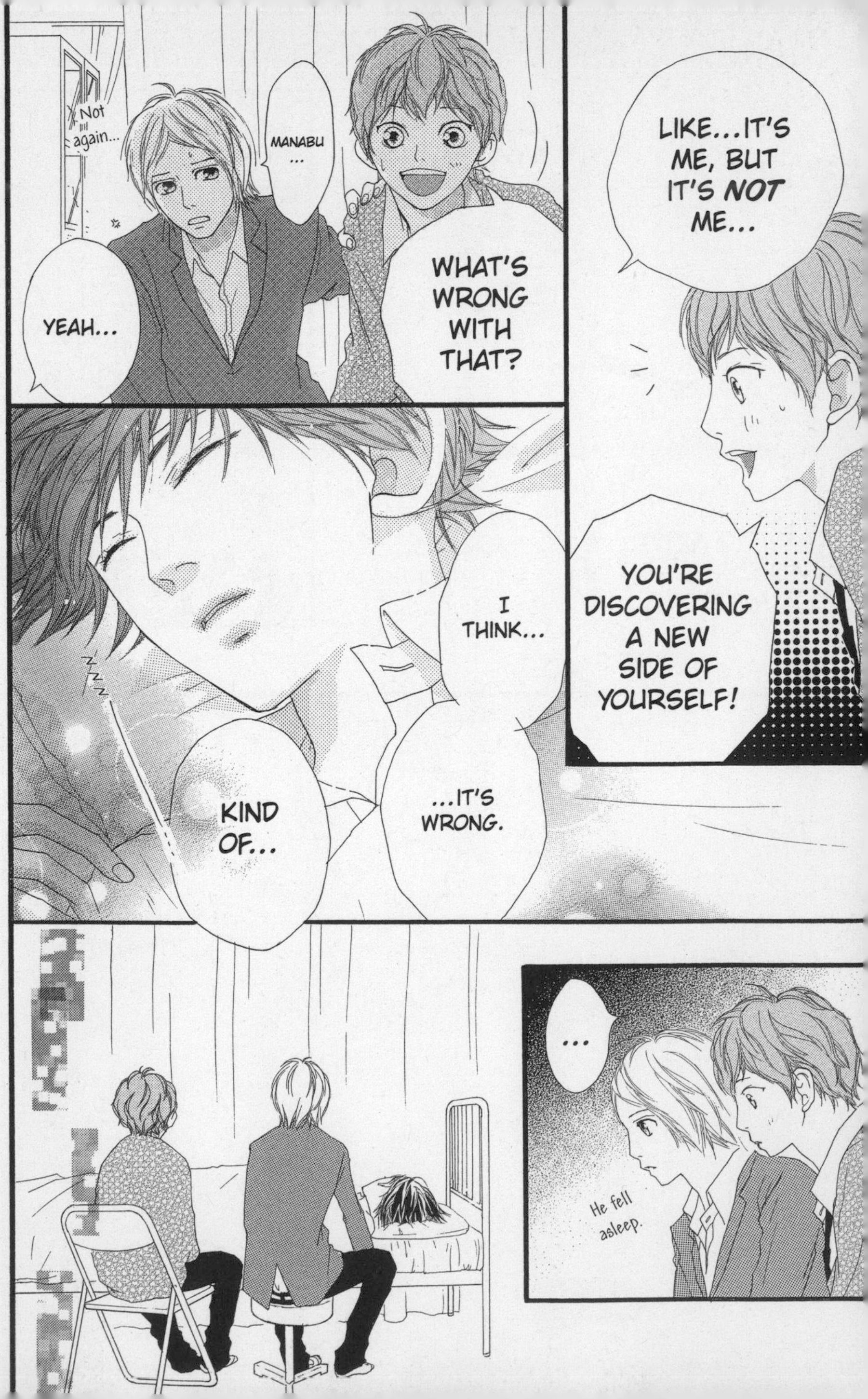
LIKE...IT'S ME, BUT IT'S *NOT* ME...
YOU'RE DISCOVERING A NEW SIDE OF YOURSELF!
WHAT'S WRONG WITH THAT?
MANABU ...
Not again...
YEAH...
I THINK...
...IT'S WRONG.
KIND OF...
...
He fell asleep.

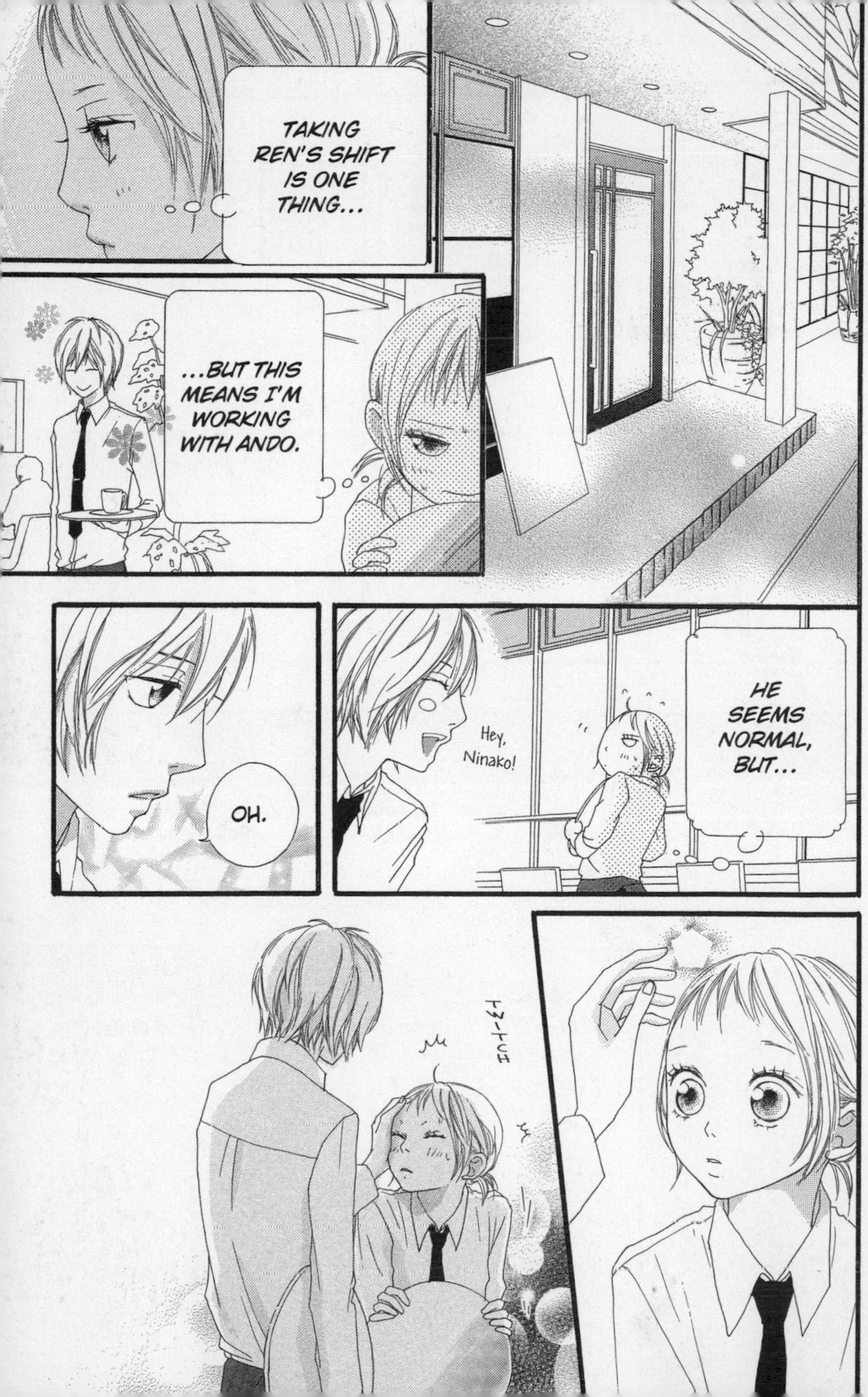
TAKING REN'S SHIFT IS ONE THING...
...BUT THIS MEANS I'M WORKING WITH ANDO.
HE SEEMS NORMAL, BUT...
Hey, Ninako!
OH.
TWITCH

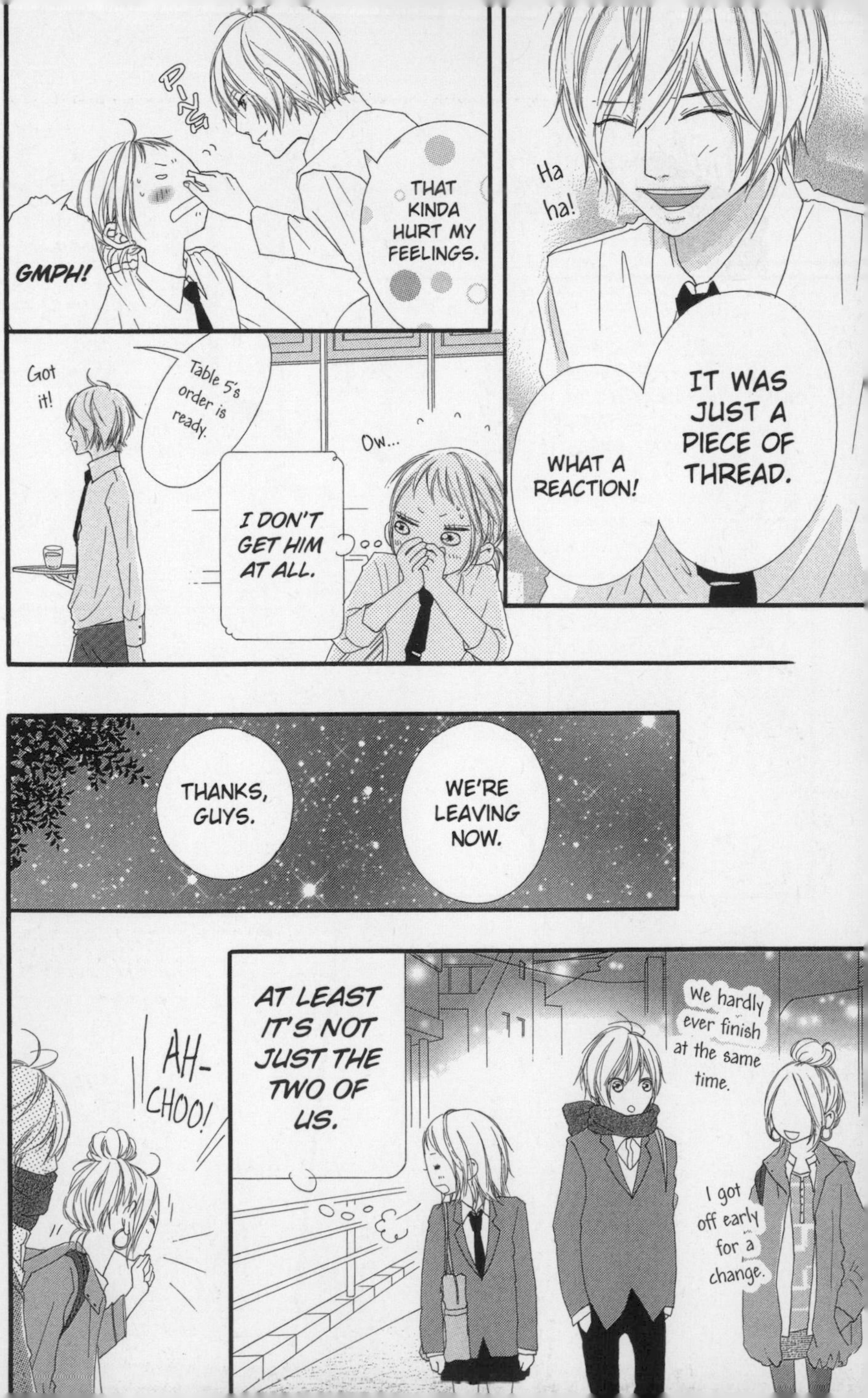
Ha ha!
IT WAS JUST A PIECE OF THREAD.
WHAT A REACTION!
THAT KINDA HURT MY FEELINGS.
GMPH!
Table 5's order is ready.
Got it!
Ow...
I DON'T GET HIM AT ALL.
WE'RE LEAVING NOW.
THANKS, GUYS.
We hardly ever finish at the same time.
I got off early for a change.
AT LEAST IT'S NOT JUST THE TWO OF US.
AH-CHOO!

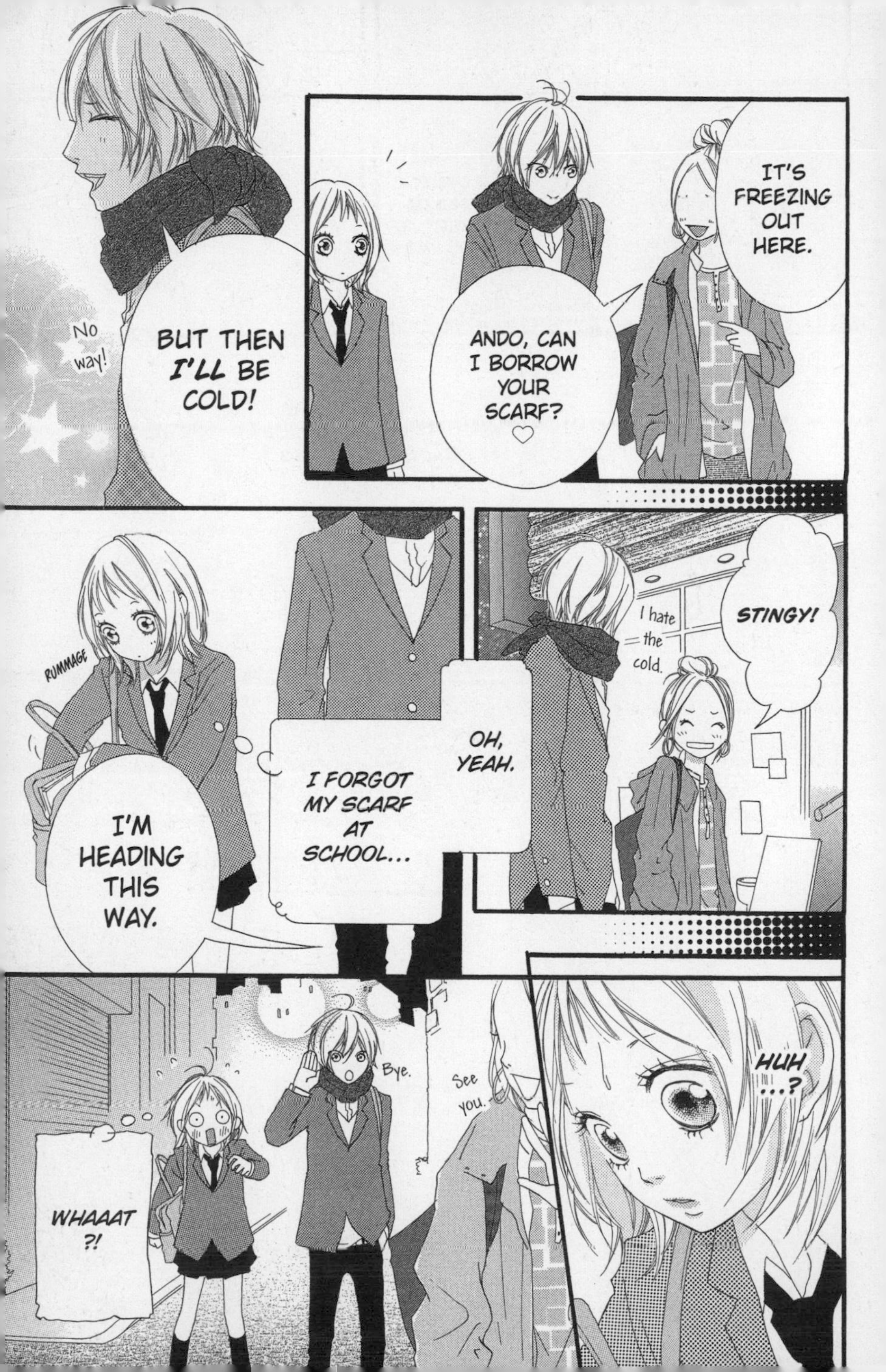
IT'S FREEZING OUT HERE.
ANDO, CAN I BORROW YOUR SCARF? ♡
BUT THEN I'LL BE COLD!
No way!
STINGY!
I hate the cold.
OH, YEAH.
I FORGOT MY SCARF AT SCHOOL...
RUMMAGE
I'M HEADING THIS WAY.
HUH ...?
See you.
Bye.
WHAAAT ?!

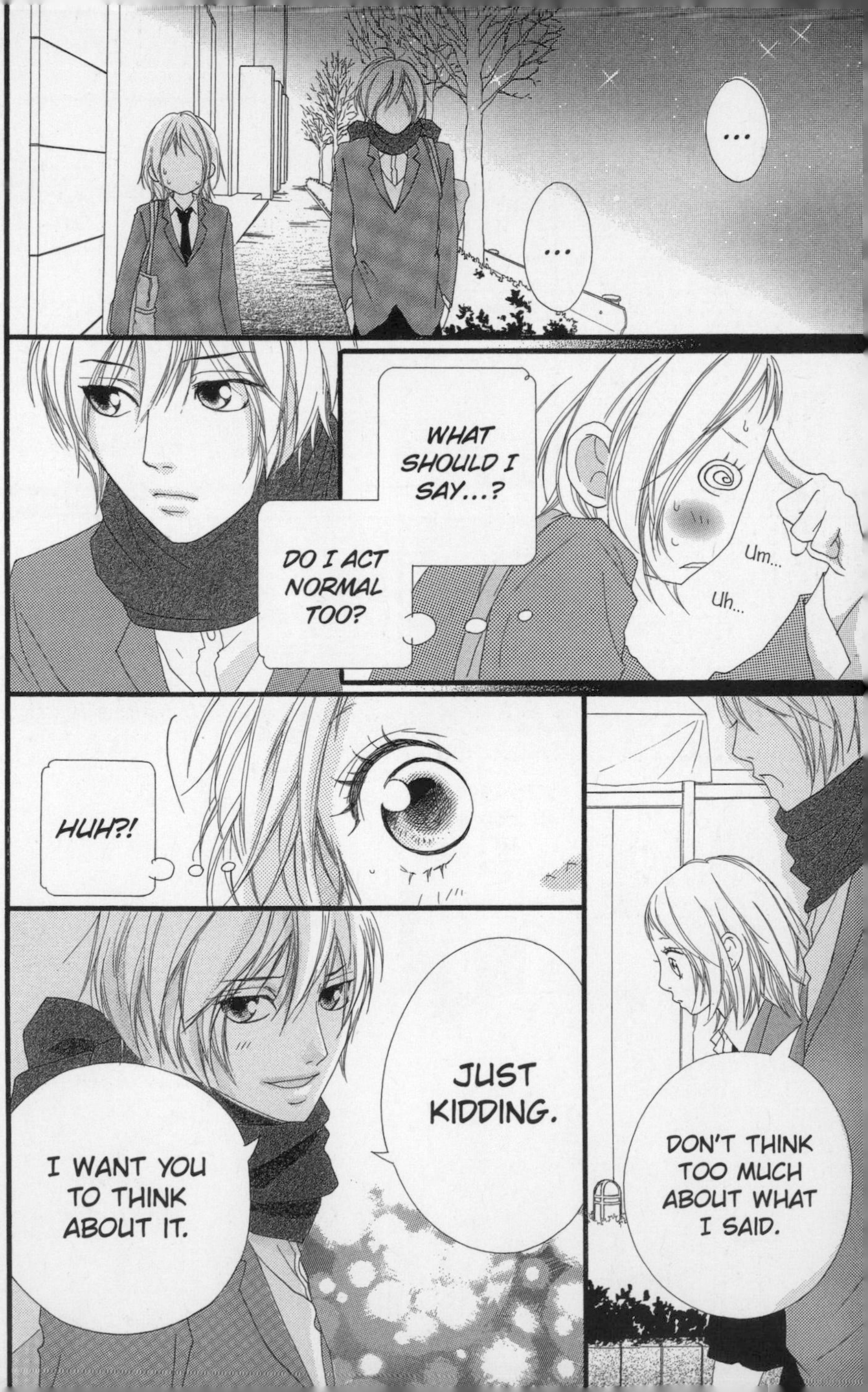
...
...
WHAT SHOULD I SAY...?
DO I ACT NORMAL TOO?
Um...
Uh...
DON'T THINK TOO MUCH ABOUT WHAT I SAID.
HUH?!
JUST KIDDING.
I WANT YOU TO THINK ABOUT IT.

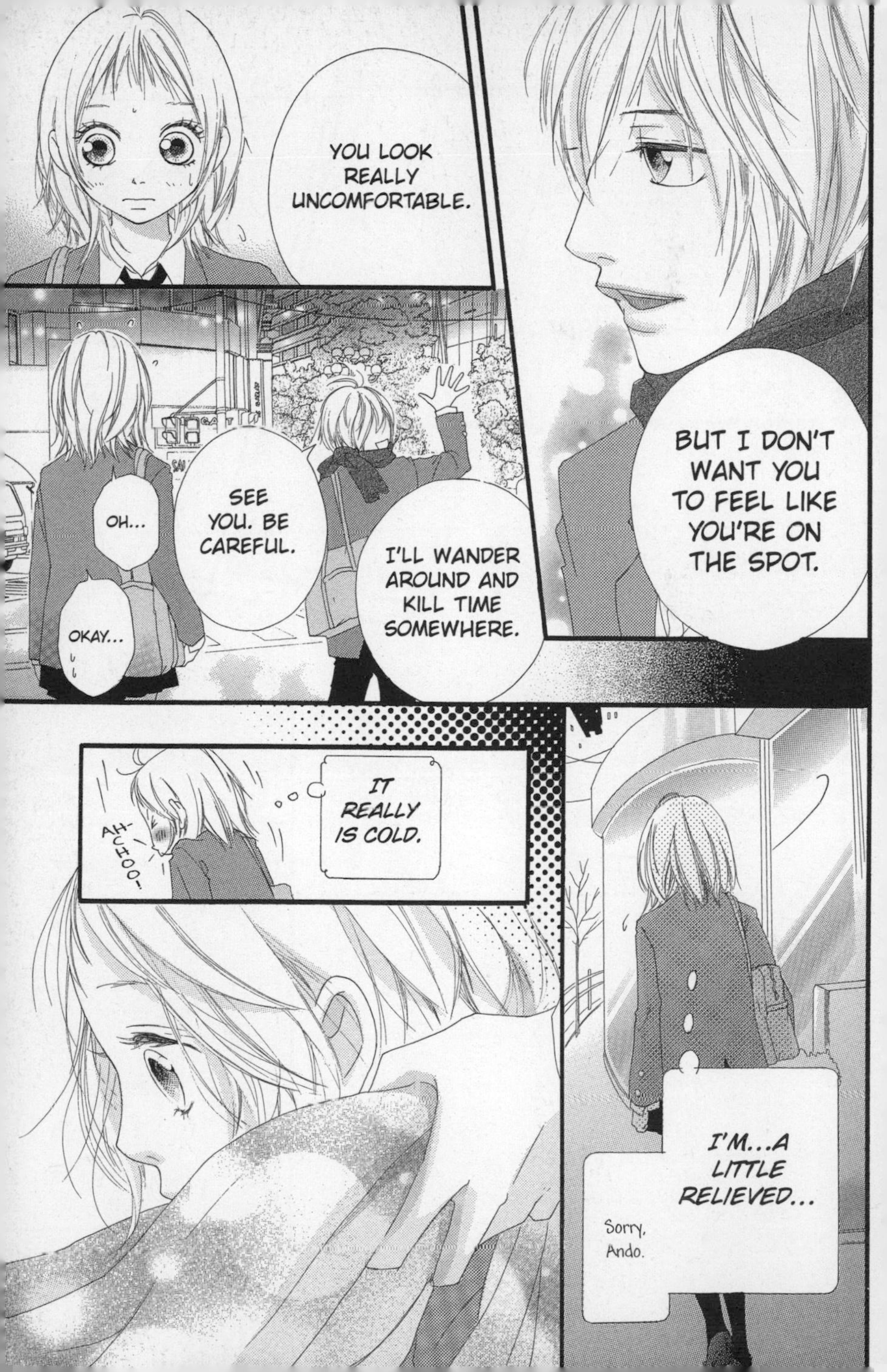
BUT I DON'T WANT YOU TO FEEL LIKE YOU'RE ON THE SPOT.
YOU LOOK REALLY UNCOMFORTABLE.
I'LL WANDER AROUND AND KILL TIME SOMEWHERE.
SEE YOU. BE CAREFUL.
OH...
OKAY...
I'M...A LITTLE RELIEVED...
Sorry, Ando.
IT REALLY IS COLD.
AH-CHOO!

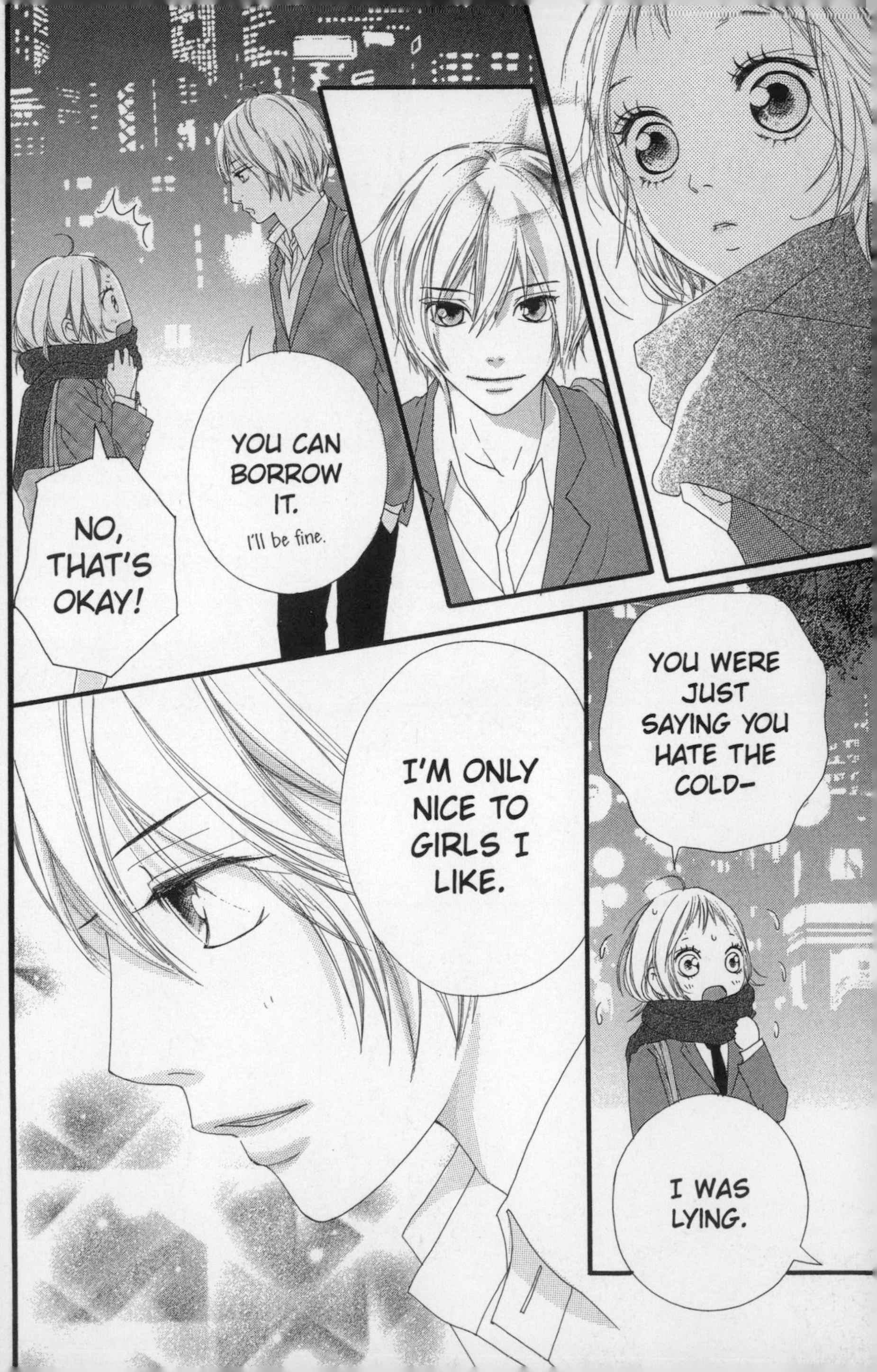
YOU CAN BORROW IT.
I'll be fine.
NO, THAT'S OKAY!
YOU WERE JUST SAYING YOU HATE THE COLD-
I WAS LYING.
I'M ONLY NICE TO GIRLS I LIKE.

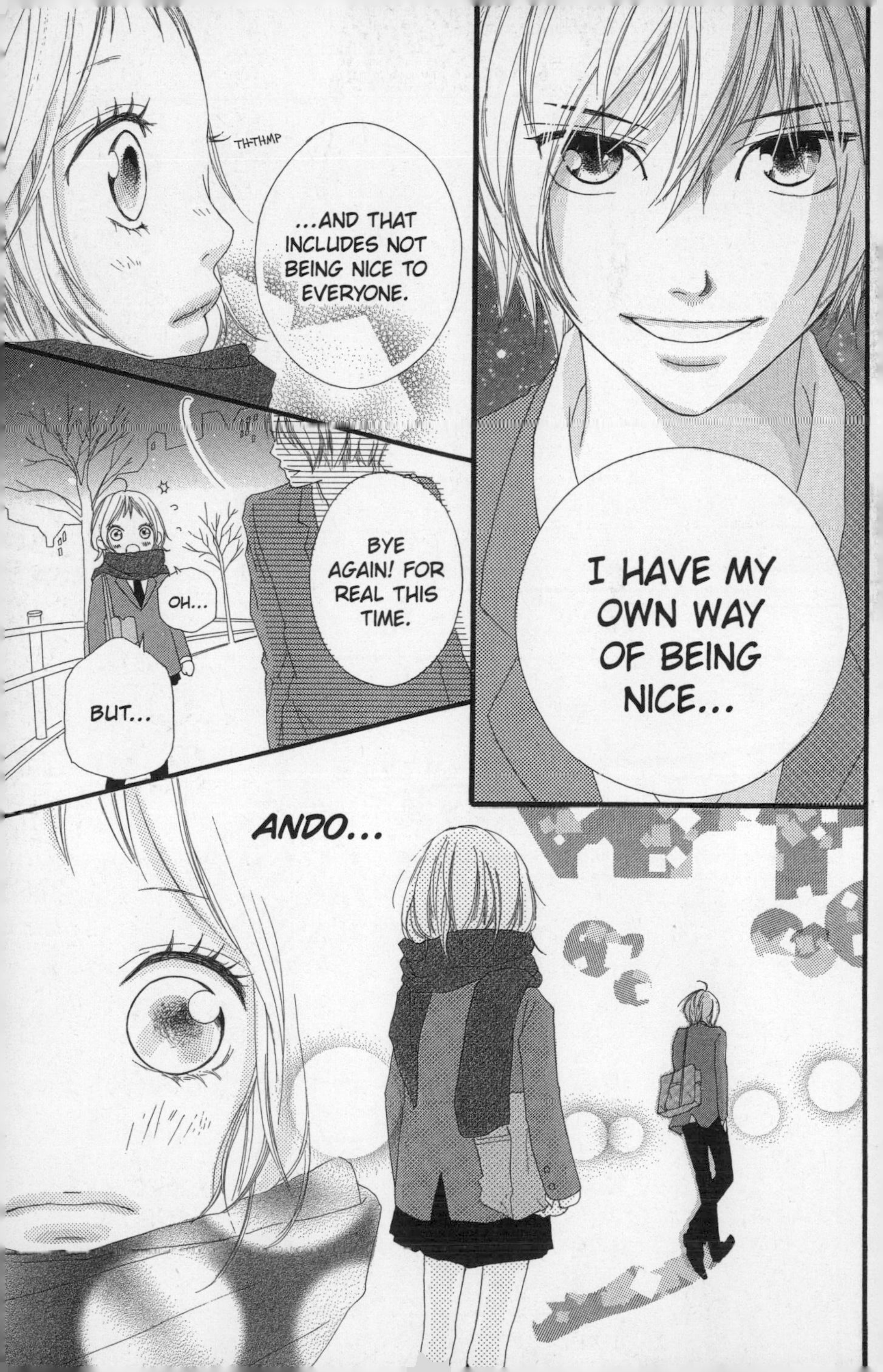
I HAVE MY OWN WAY OF BEING NICE...
TH-THMP
...AND THAT INCLUDES NOT BEING NICE TO EVERYONE.
BYE AGAIN! FOR REAL THIS TIME.
OH...
BUT...
ANDO...

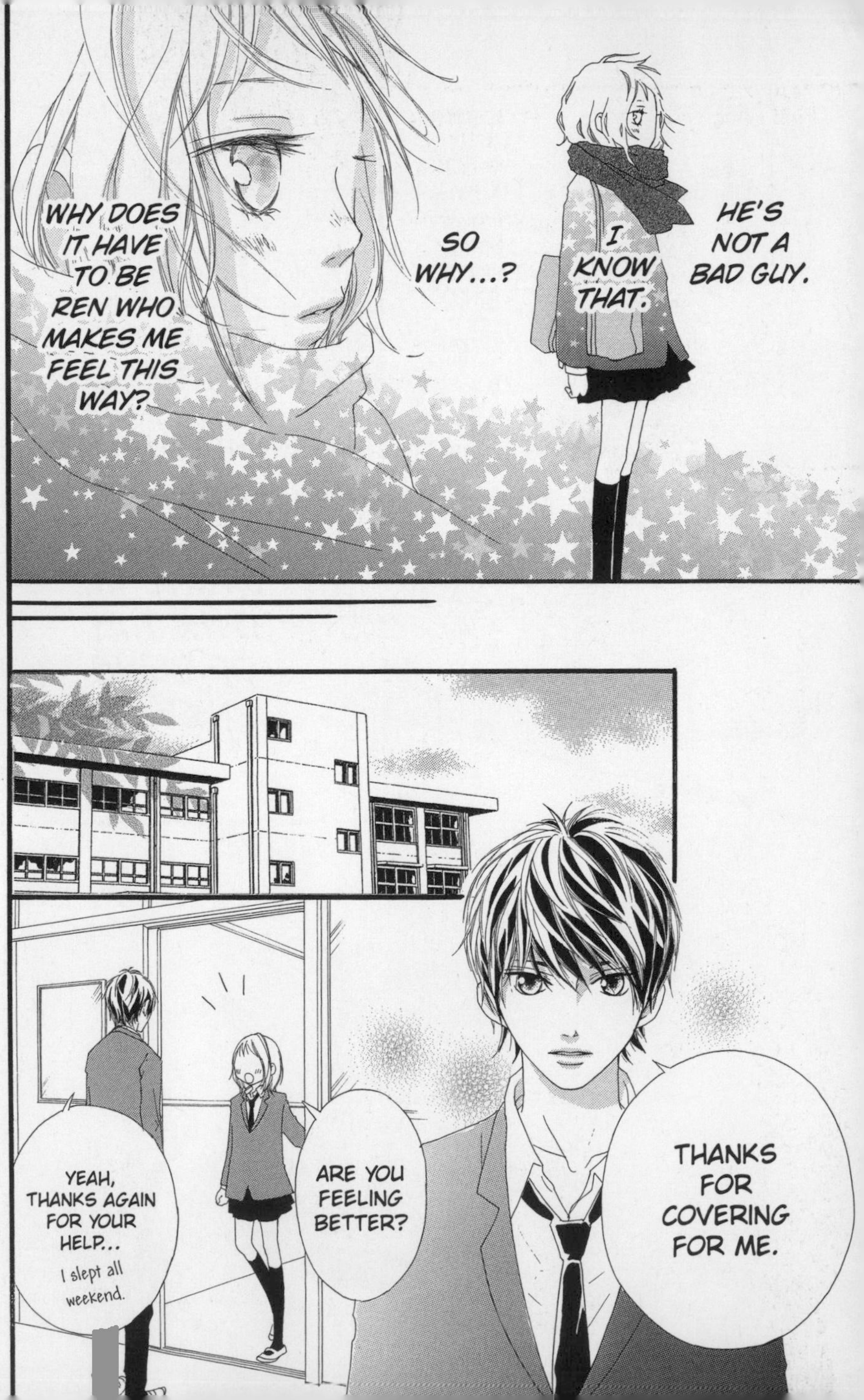
HE'S NOT A BAD GUY.
I KNOW THAT.
SO WHY...?
WHY DOES IT HAVE TO BE REN WHO MAKES ME FEEL THIS WAY?
THANKS FOR COVERING FOR ME.
ARE YOU FEELING BETTER?
YEAH, THANKS AGAIN FOR YOUR HELP...
I slept all weekend.

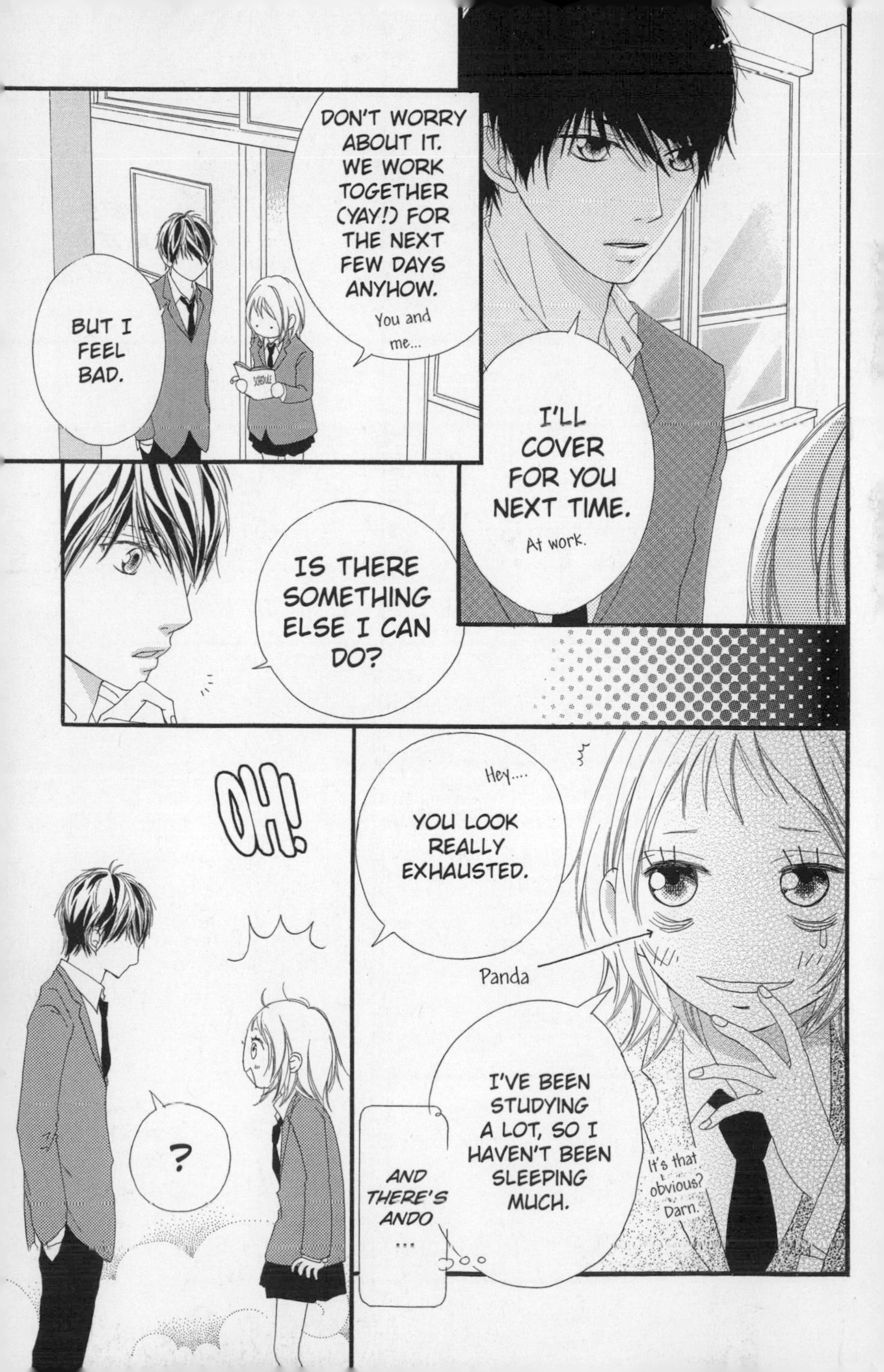
I'LL COVER FOR YOU NEXT TIME.
At work.
DON'T WORRY ABOUT IT. WE WORK TOGETHER (YAY!) FOR THE NEXT FEW DAYS ANYHOW.
You and me...
SCHEDULE
BUT I FEEL BAD.
IS THERE SOMETHING ELSE I CAN DO?
Hey....
YOU LOOK REALLY EXHAUSTED.
Panda
I'VE BEEN STUDYING A LOT, SO I HAVEN'T BEEN SLEEPING MUCH.
It's that obvious? Darn.
AND THERE'S ANDO ...
OH!
?

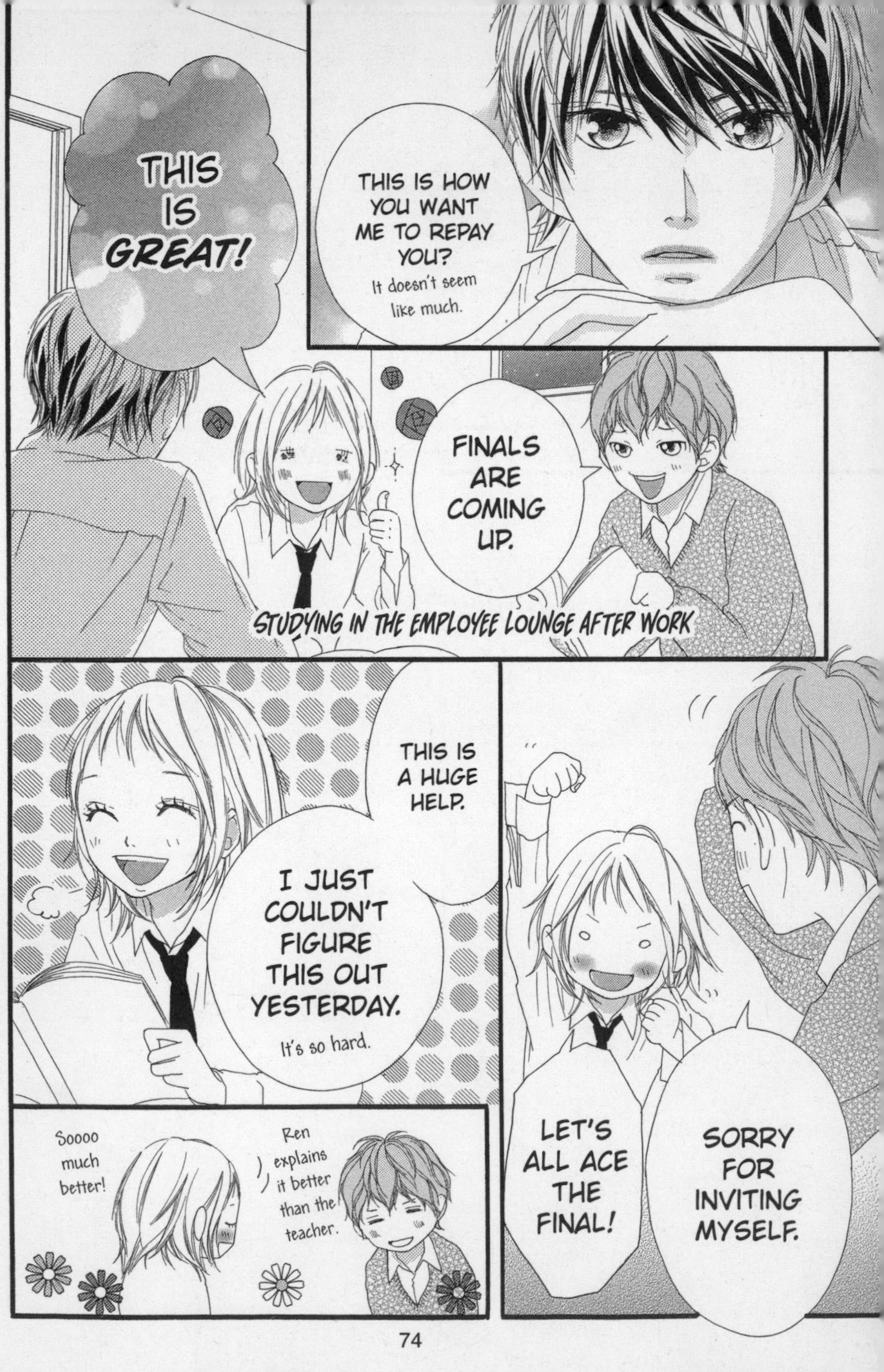
THIS IS HOW YOU WANT ME TO REPAY YOU?
It doesn't seem like much.
THIS IS GREAT!
FINALS ARE COMING UP.
STUDYING IN THE EMPLOYEE LOUNGE AFTER WORK
SORRY FOR INVITING MYSELF.
LET'S ALL ACE THE FINAL!
THIS IS A HUGE HELP.
I JUST COULDN'T FIGURE THIS OUT YESTERDAY.
It's so hard.
Ren explains it better than the teacher.
Soooo much better!

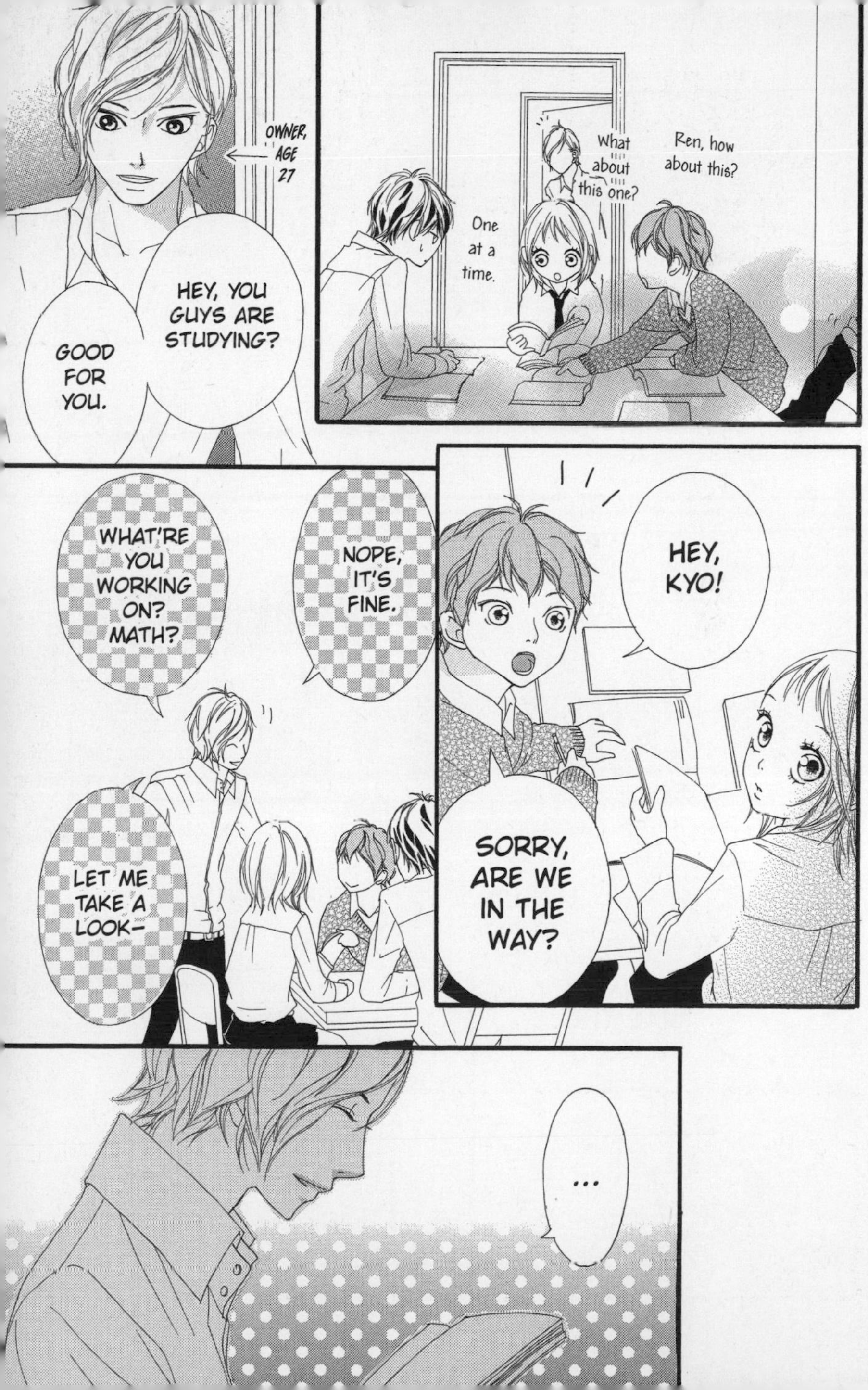
Ren, how about this?
What about this one?
One at a time.
OWNER, AGE 27
HEY, YOU GUYS ARE STUDYING?
GOOD FOR YOU.
HEY, KYO!
SORRY, ARE WE IN THE WAY?
NOPE, IT'S FINE.
WHAT'RE YOU WORKING ON? MATH?
LET ME TAKE A LOOK–
...

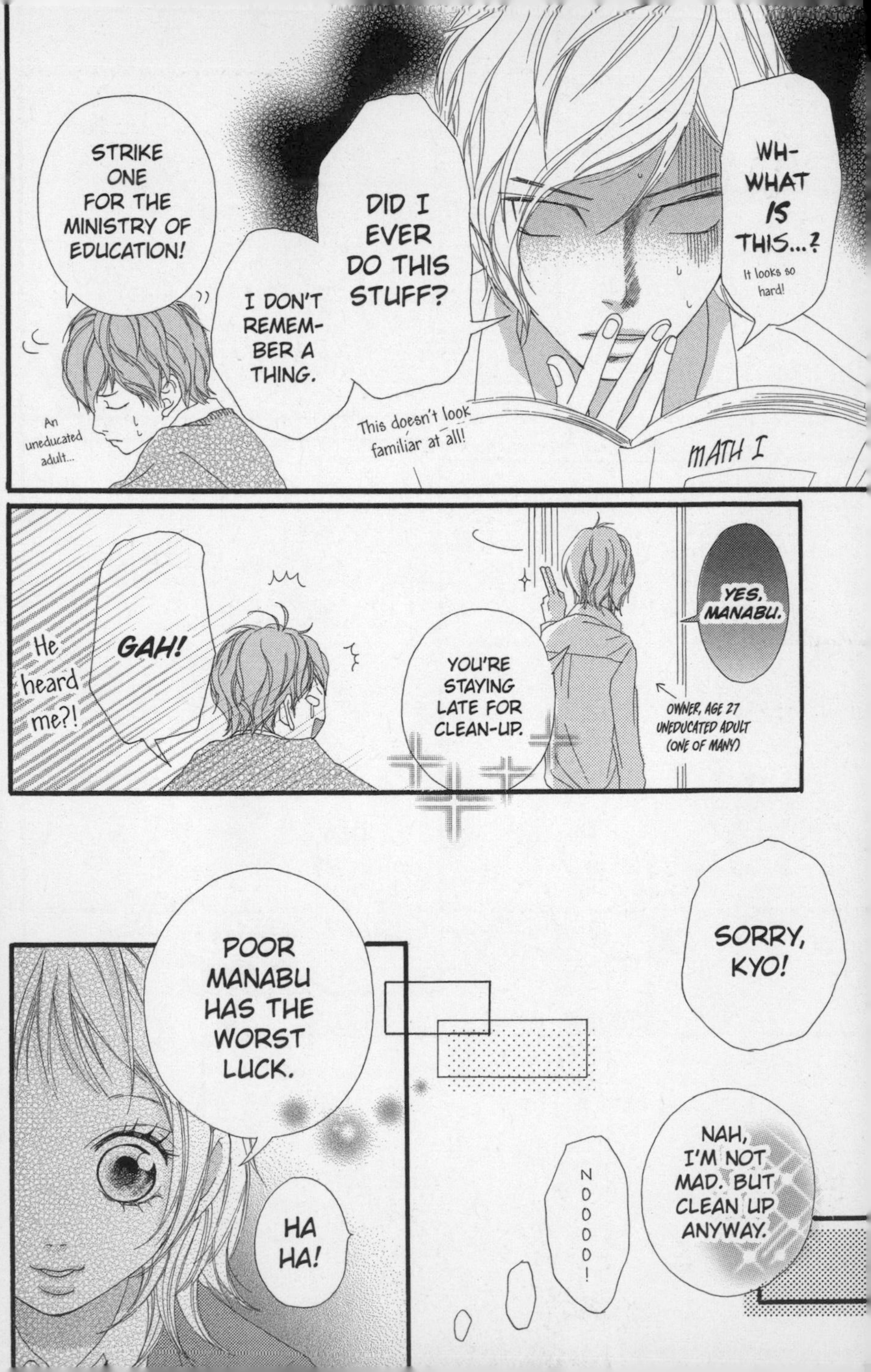
WH- WHAT IS THIS...?
It looks so hard!
DID I EVER DO THIS STUFF?
I DON'T REMEMBER A THING.
This doesn't look familiar at all!
MATH I
STRIKE ONE FOR THE MINISTRY OF EDUCATION!
An uneducated adult...
YES, MANABU.
OWNER, AGE 27 UNEDUCATED ADULT (ONE OF MANY)
YOU'RE STAYING LATE FOR CLEAN-UP.
GAH!
He heard me?!
SORRY, KYO!
NAH, I'M NOT MAD. BUT CLEAN UP ANYWAY.
NOOOO!
POOR MANABU HAS THE WORST LUCK.
HA HA!

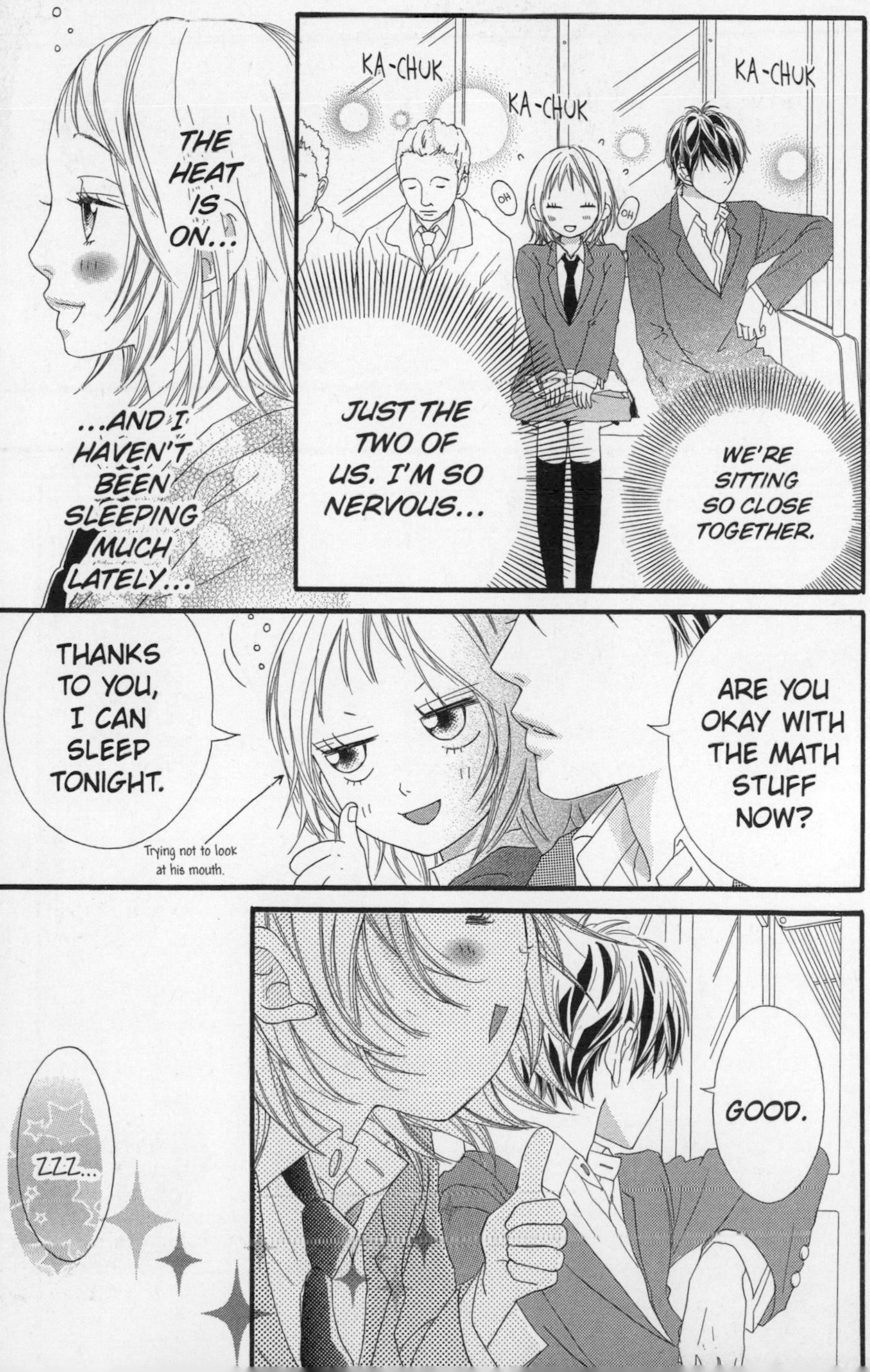
KA-CHUK
KA-CHUK
KA-CHUK
OH
OH
WE'RE SITTING SO CLOSE TOGETHER.
JUST THE TWO OF US. I'M SO NERVOUS...
THE HEAT IS ON...
...AND I HAVEN'T BEEN SLEEPING MUCH LATELY...
ARE YOU OKAY WITH THE MATH STUFF NOW?
THANKS TO YOU, I CAN SLEEP TONIGHT.
Trying not to look at his mouth.
GOOD.
ZZZ...

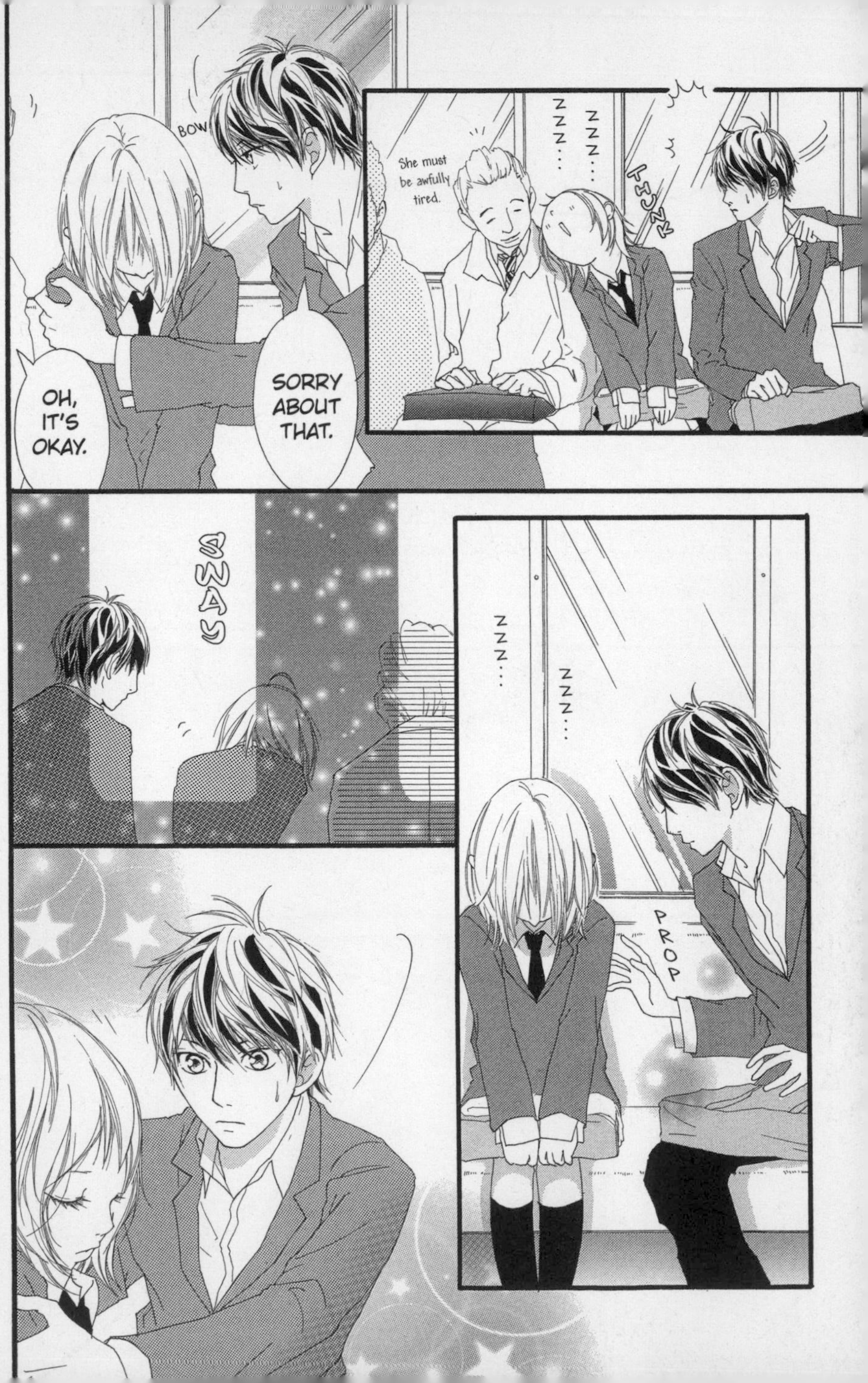
THUNK
ZZZ...
ZZZ...
She must be awfully tired.
BOW
SORRY ABOUT THAT.
OH, IT'S OKAY.
ZZZ...
ZZZ...
PROP
SWAY

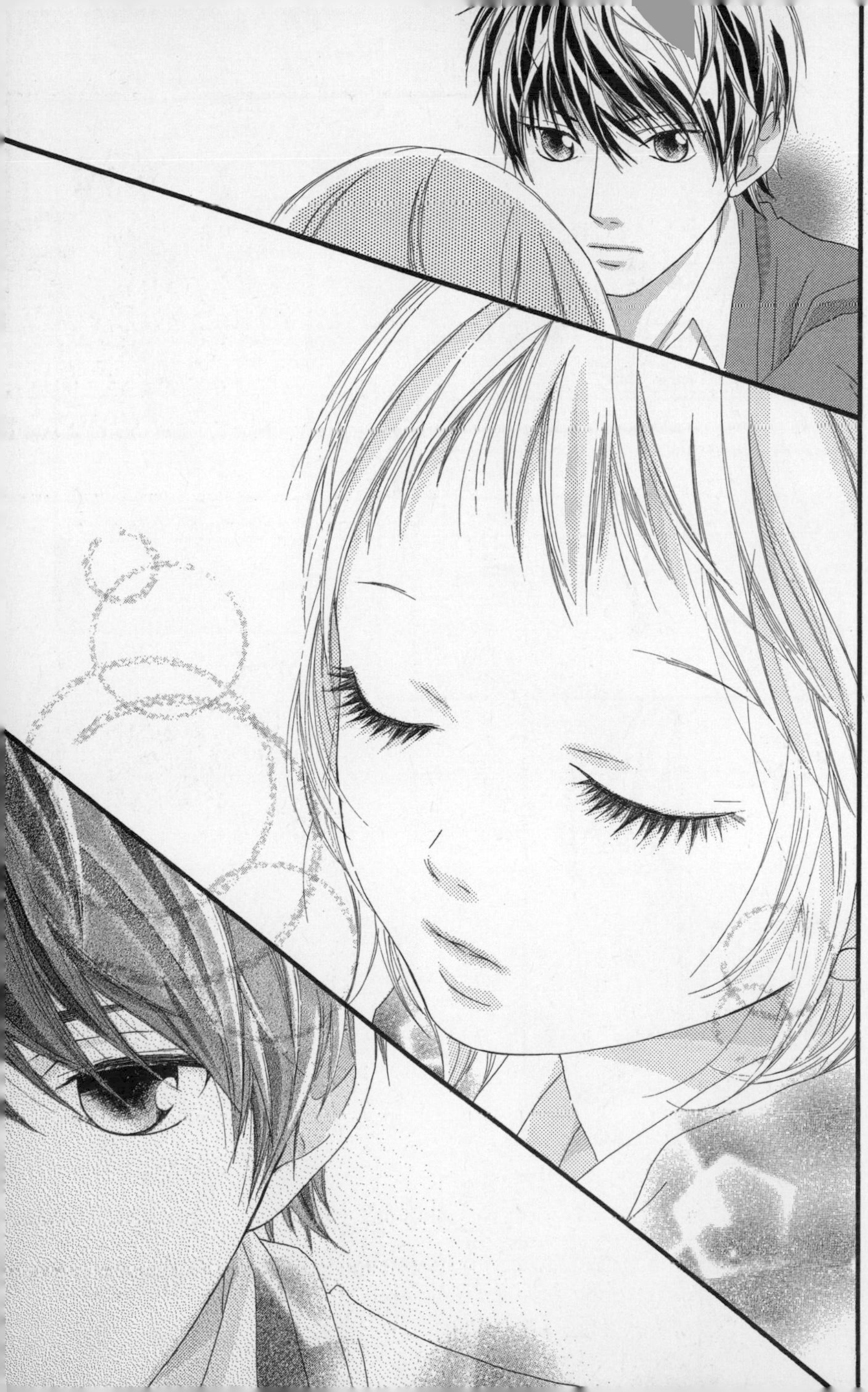

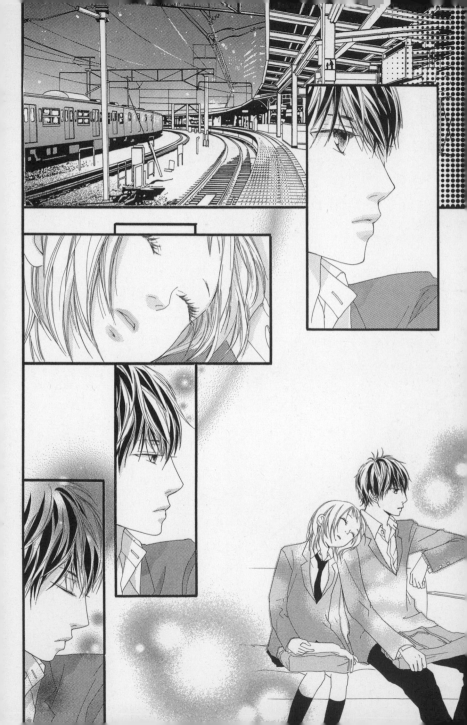

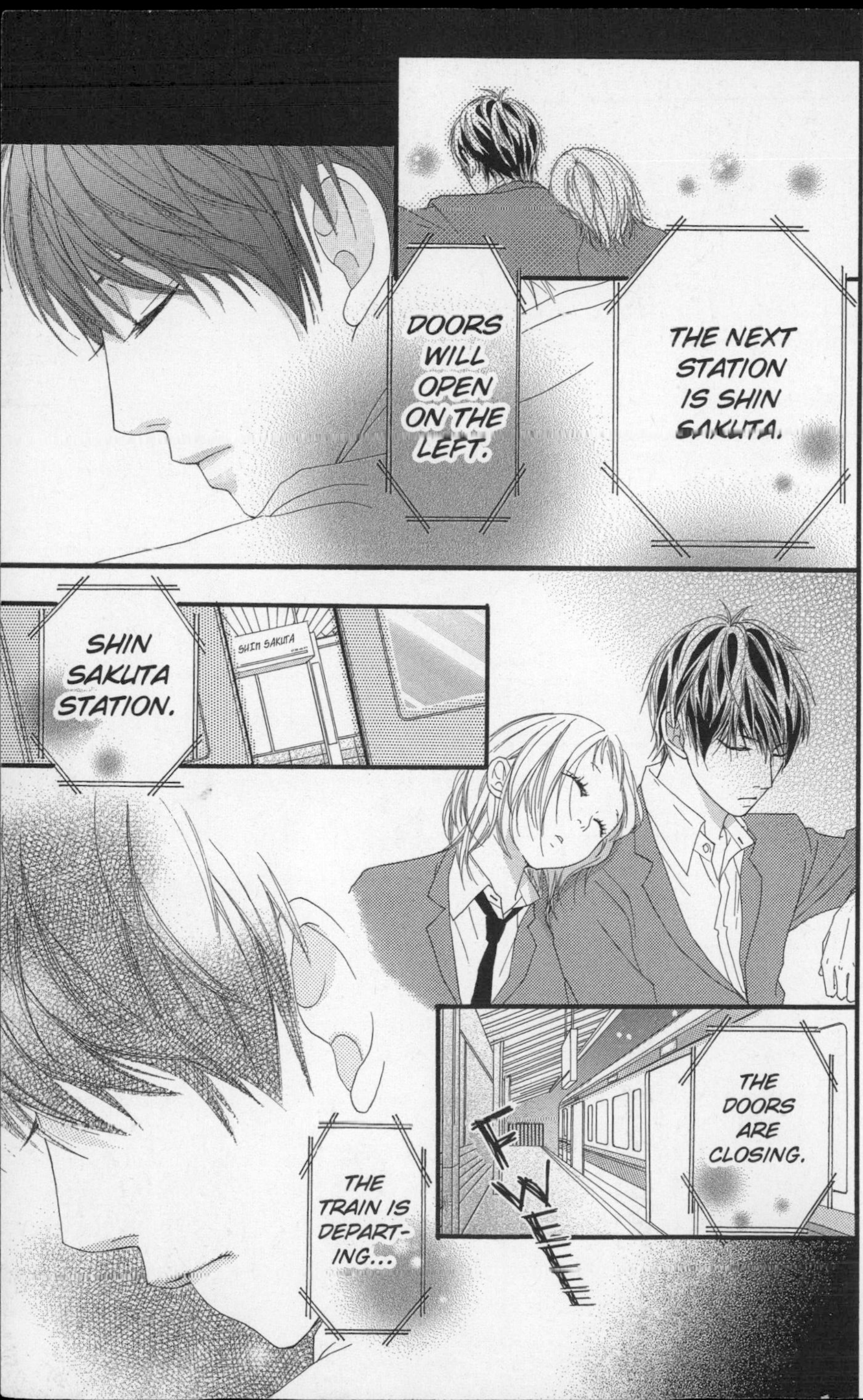
THE NEXT STATION IS SHIN SAKUTA.
DOORS WILL OPEN ON THE LEFT.
SHIN SAKUTA
SHIN SAKUTA STATION.
THE DOORS ARE CLOSING.
FWEEE
THE TRAIN IS DEPART-ING...

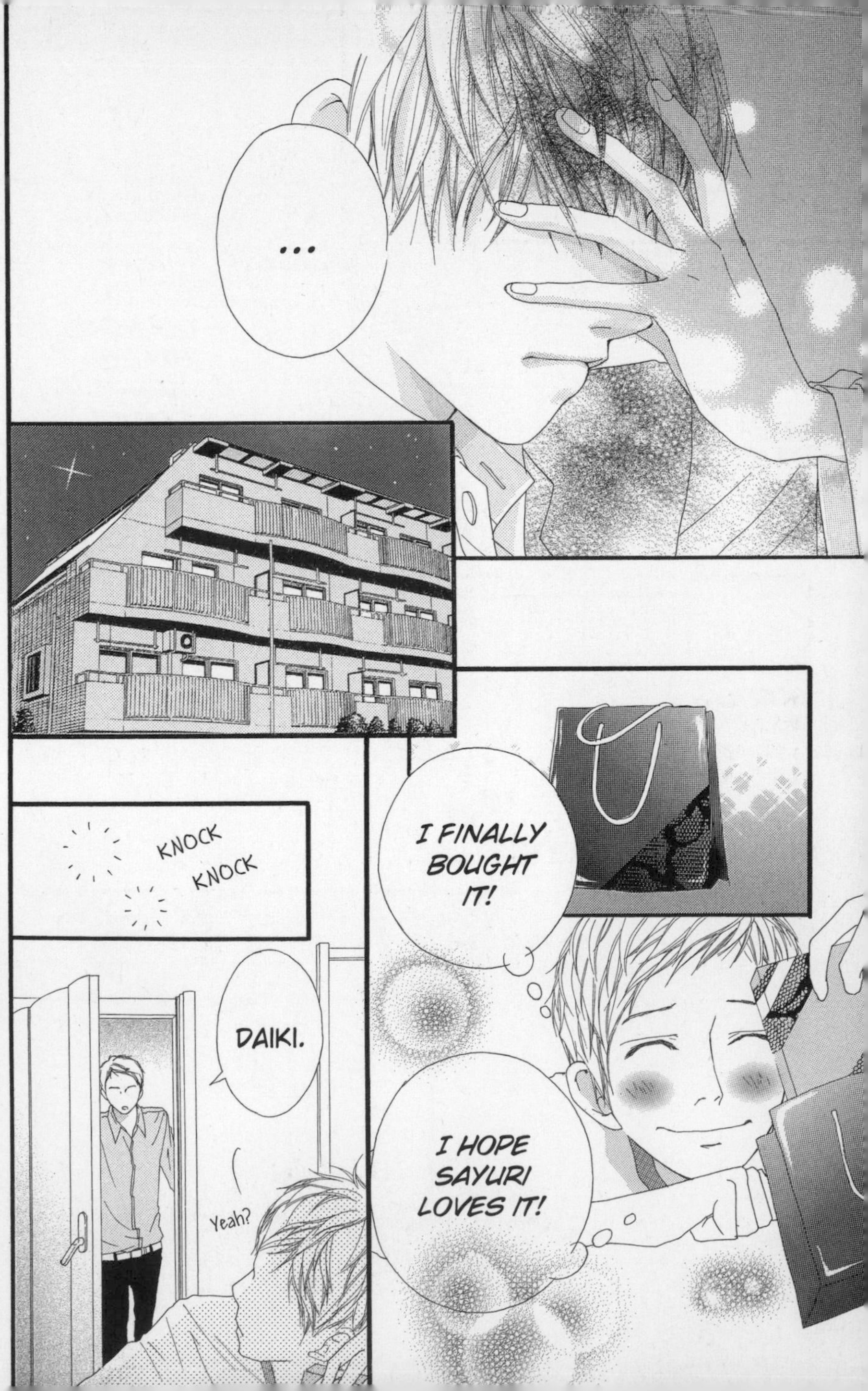
...
I FINALLY BOUGHT IT!
I HOPE SAYURI LOVES IT!
KNOCK KNOCK
DAIKI.
Yeah?

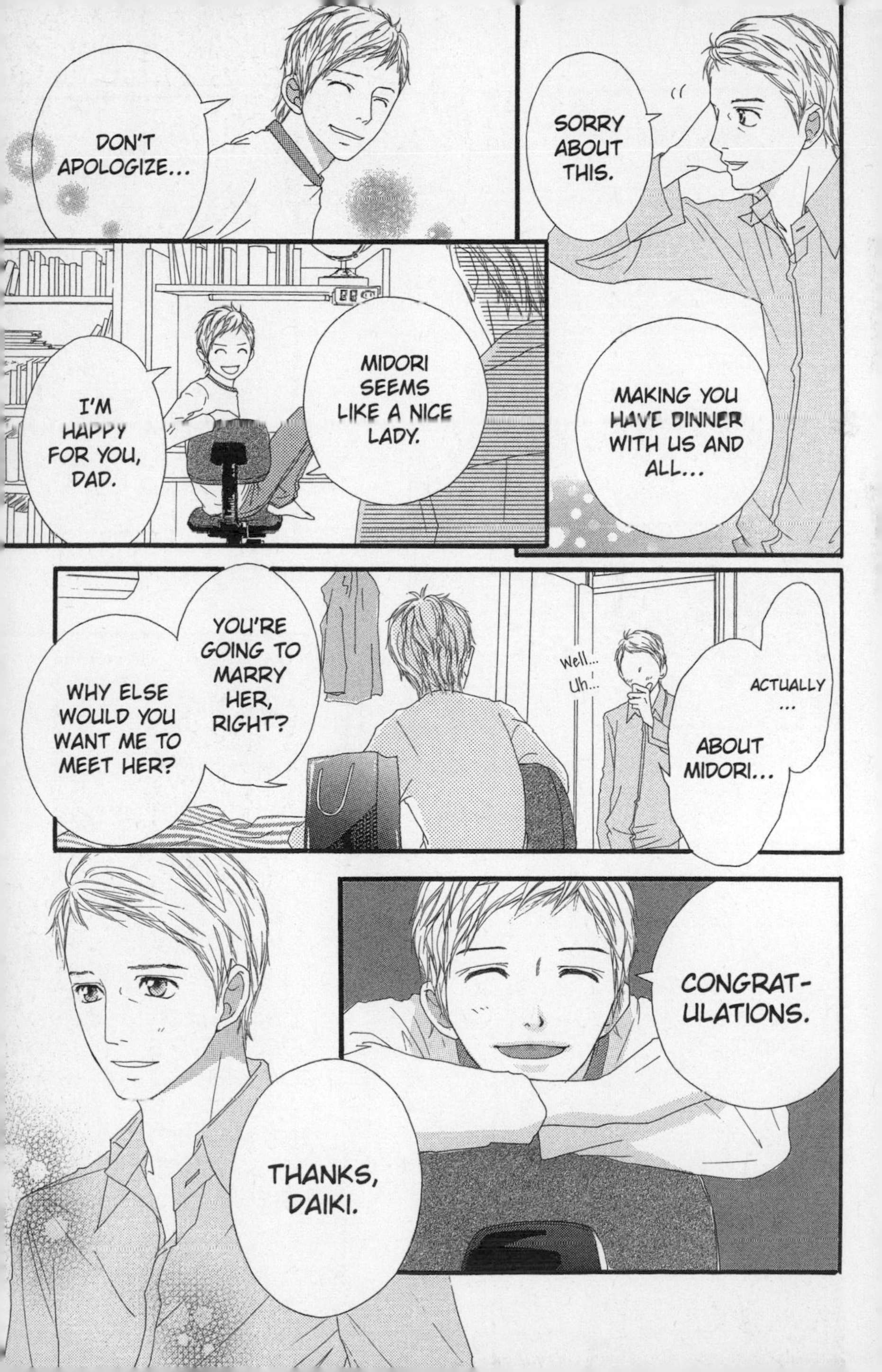
SORRY ABOUT THIS.
MAKING YOU HAVE DINNER WITH US AND ALL...
DON'T APOLOGIZE...
MIDORI SEEMS LIKE A NICE LADY.
I'M HAPPY FOR YOU, DAD.
ACTUALLY... ABOUT MIDORI...
Well... Uh...
YOU'RE GOING TO MARRY HER, RIGHT?
WHY ELSE WOULD YOU WANT ME TO MEET HER?
CONGRAT-ULATIONS.
THANKS, DAIKI.

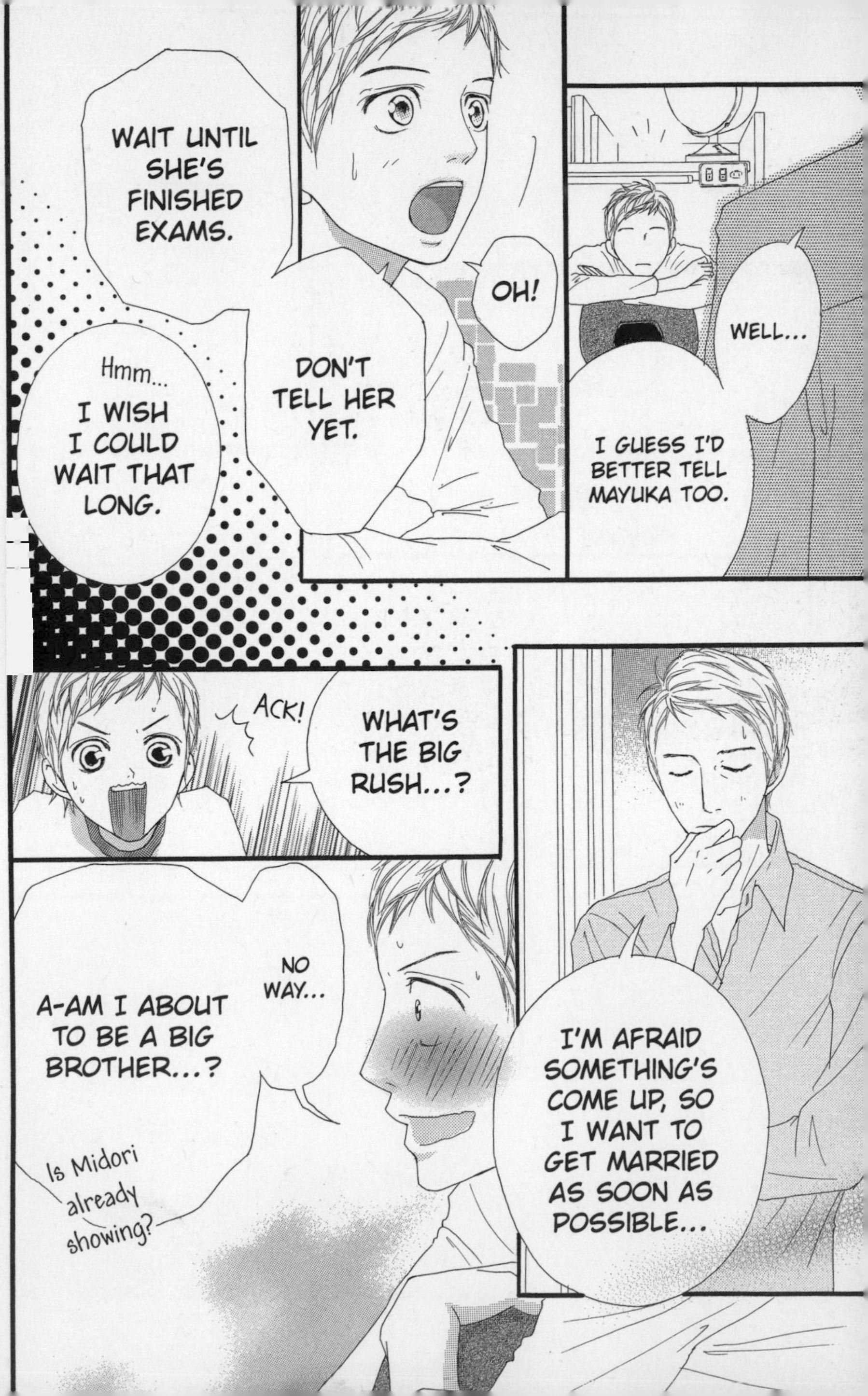
WELL...
I GUESS I'D BETTER TELL MAYUKA TOO.
OH!
DON'T TELL HER YET.
WAIT UNTIL SHE'S FINISHED EXAMS.
Hmm... I WISH I COULD WAIT THAT LONG.
I'M AFRAID SOMETHING'S COME UP, SO I WANT TO GET MARRIED AS SOON AS POSSIBLE...
WHAT'S THE BIG RUSH...?
ACK!
NO WAY...
A-AM I ABOUT TO BE A BIG BROTHER...?
Is Midori already showing?

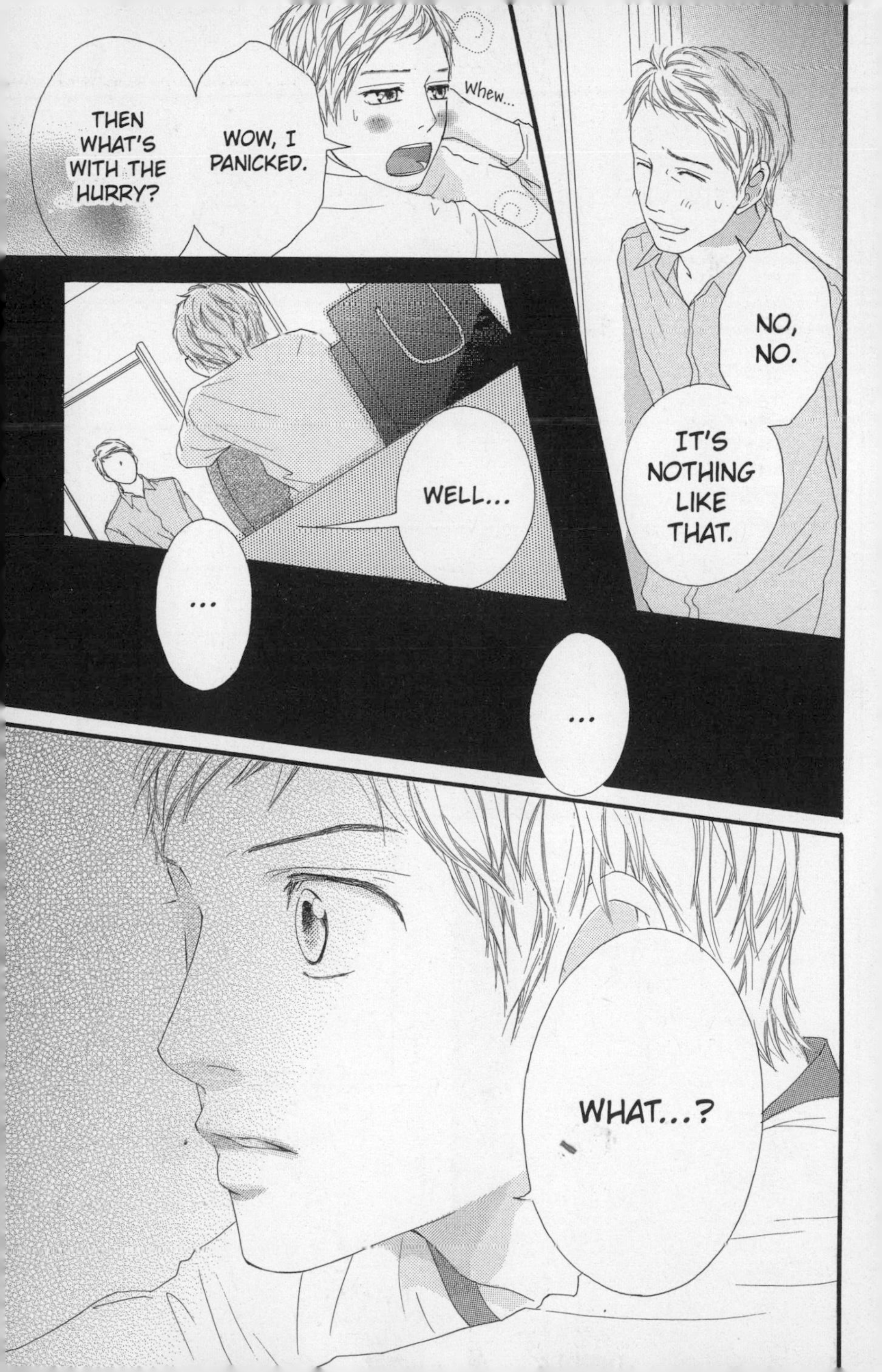
NO, NO.
IT'S NOTHING LIKE THAT.
Whew...
WOW, I PANICKED.
THEN WHAT'S WITH THE HURRY?
WELL...
...
...
WHAT...?

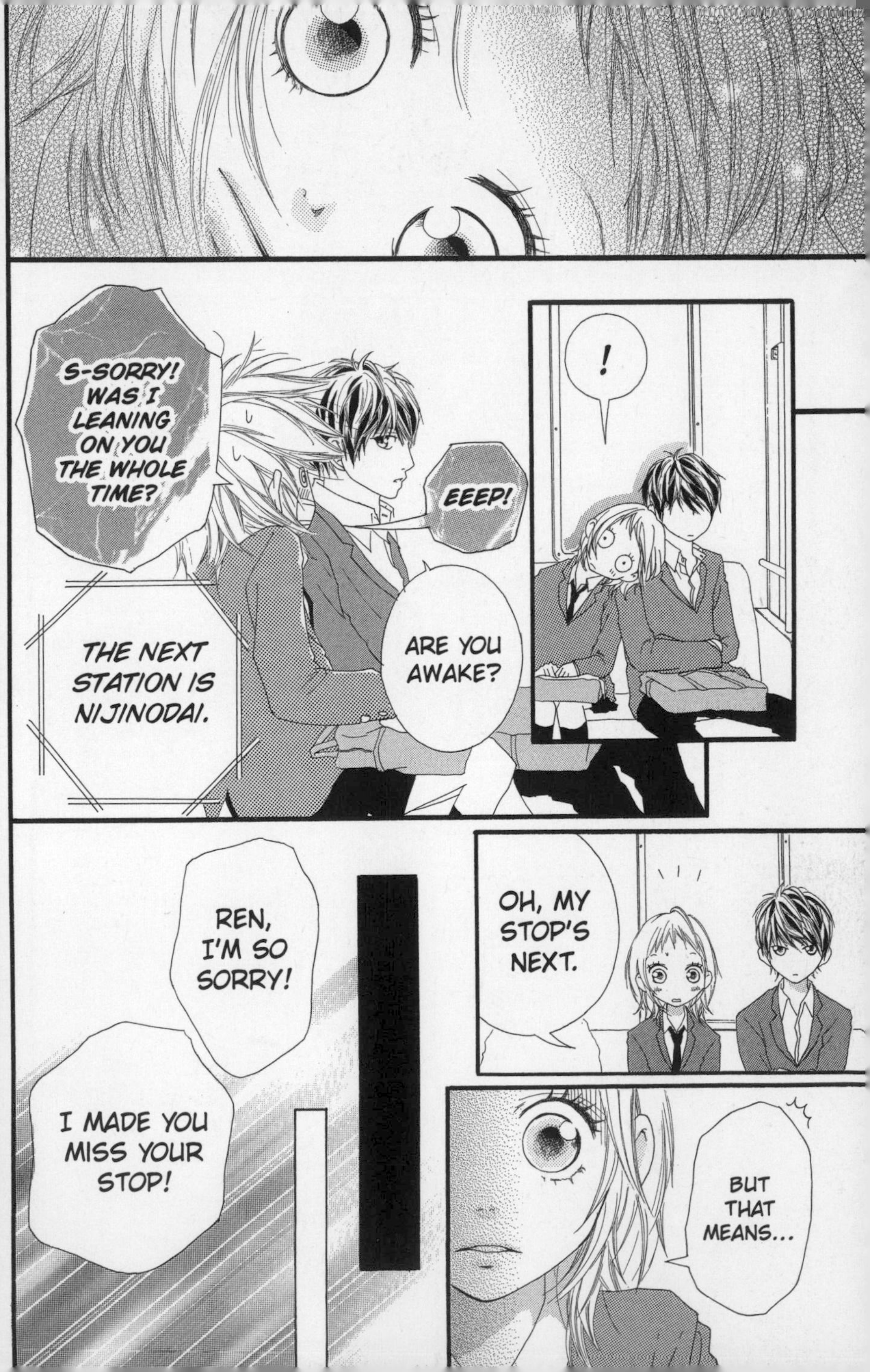
!
EEEP!
S-SORRY! WAS I LEANING ON YOU THE WHOLE TIME?
ARE YOU AWAKE?
THE NEXT STATION IS NIJINODAI.
OH, MY STOP'S NEXT.
BUT THAT MEANS...
REN, I'M SO SORRY!
I MADE YOU MISS YOUR STOP!

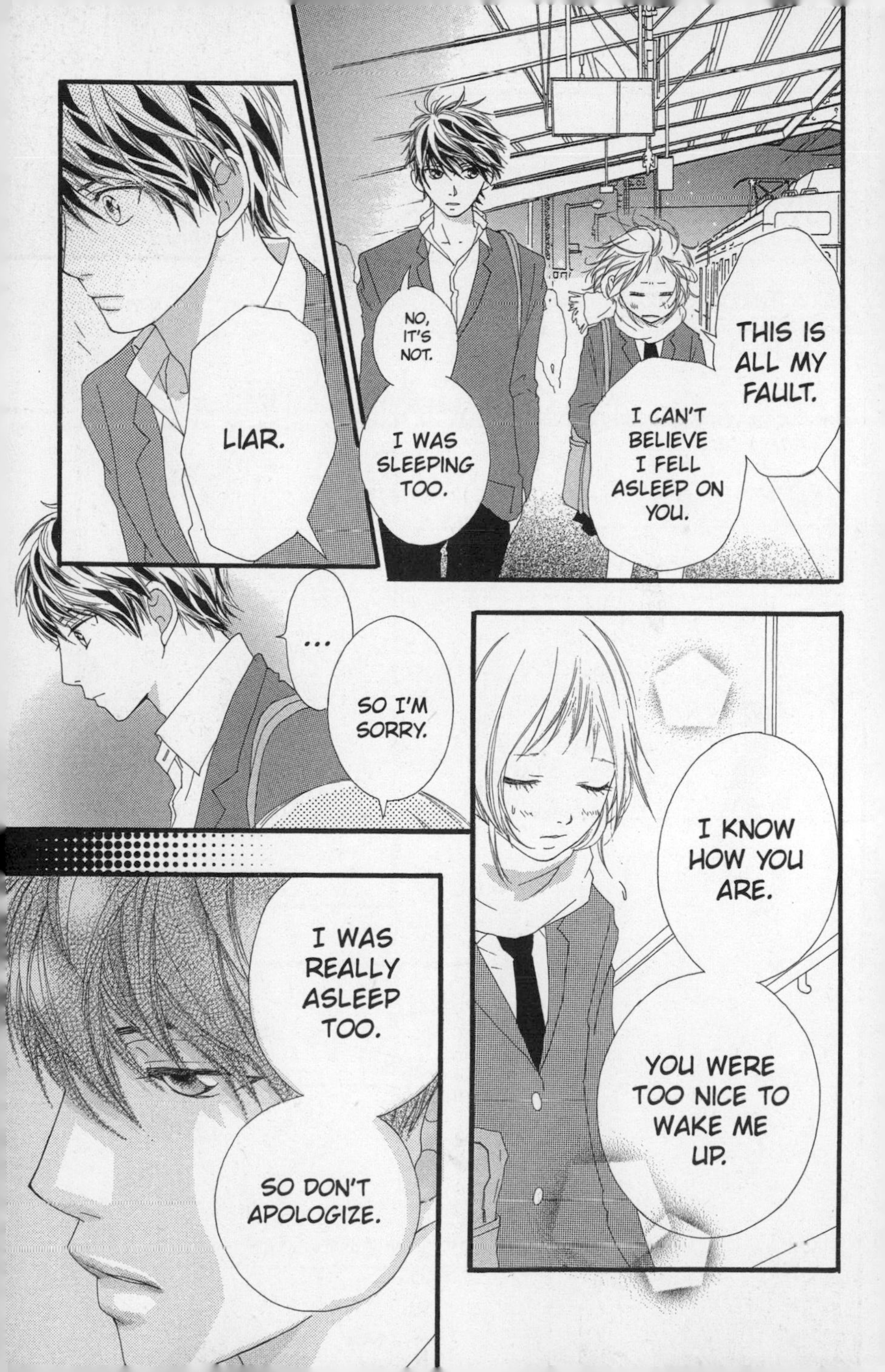
THIS IS ALL MY FAULT.
I CAN'T BELIEVE I FELL ASLEEP ON YOU.
NO, IT'S NOT.
I WAS SLEEPING TOO.
LIAR.
I KNOW HOW YOU ARE.
YOU WERE TOO NICE TO WAKE ME UP.
...
SO I'M SORRY.
I WAS REALLY ASLEEP TOO.
SO DON'T APOLOGIZE.

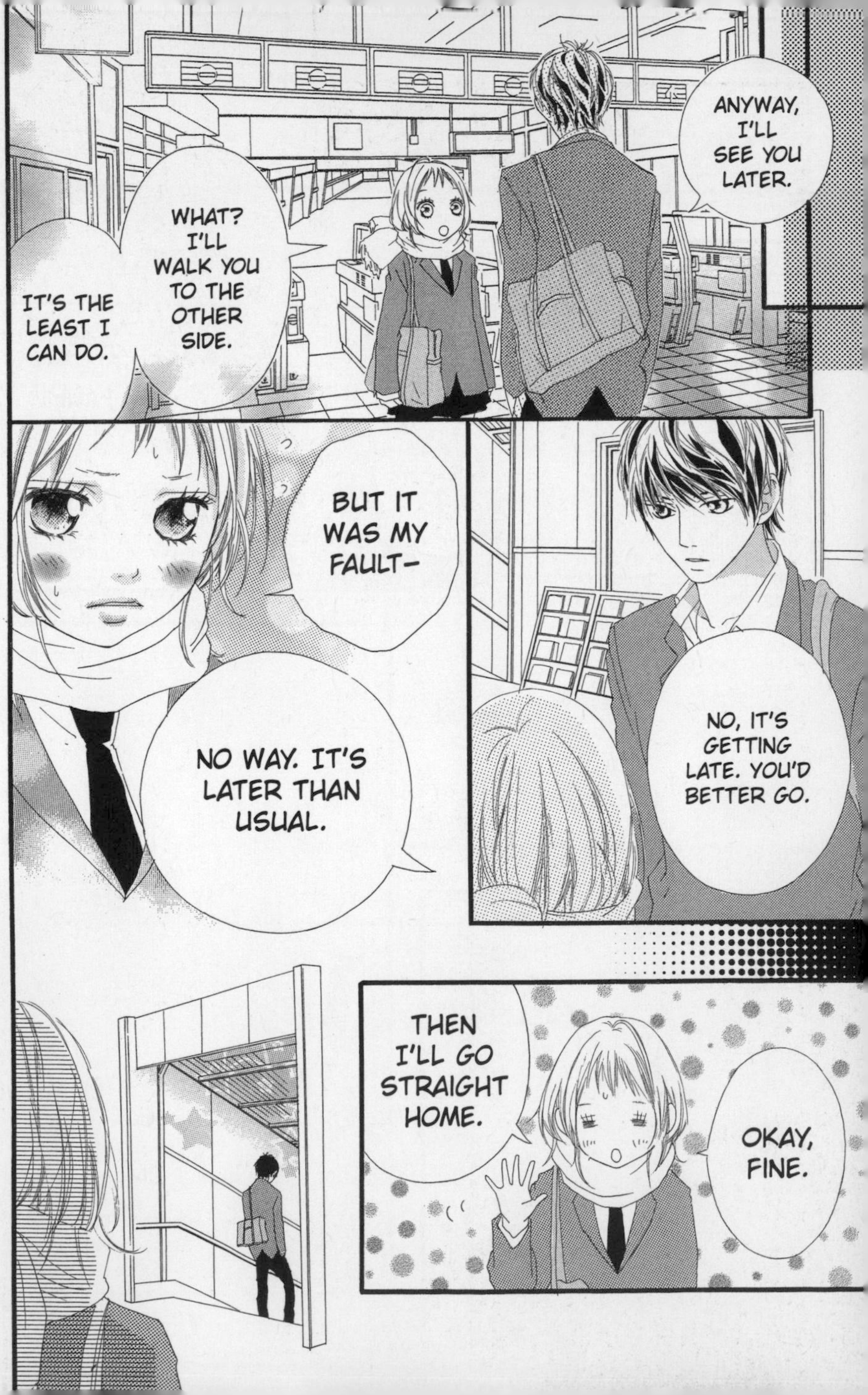
ANYWAY, I'LL SEE YOU LATER.
WHAT? I'LL WALK YOU TO THE OTHER SIDE.
IT'S THE LEAST I CAN DO.
NO, IT'S GETTING LATE. YOU'D BETTER GO.
BUT IT WAS MY FAULT–
NO WAY. IT'S LATER THAN USUAL.
OKAY, FINE.
THEN I'LL GO STRAIGHT HOME.

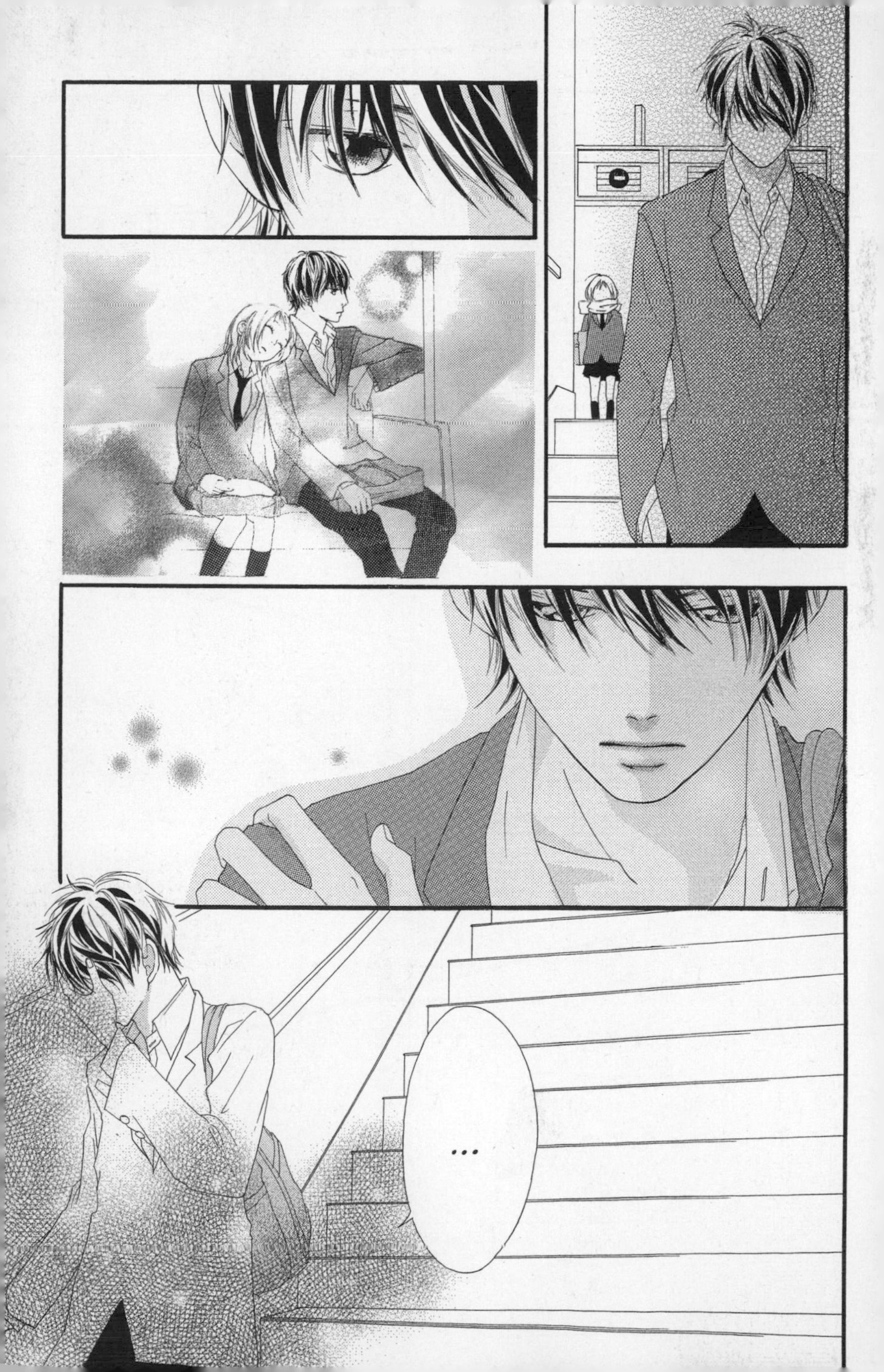
...

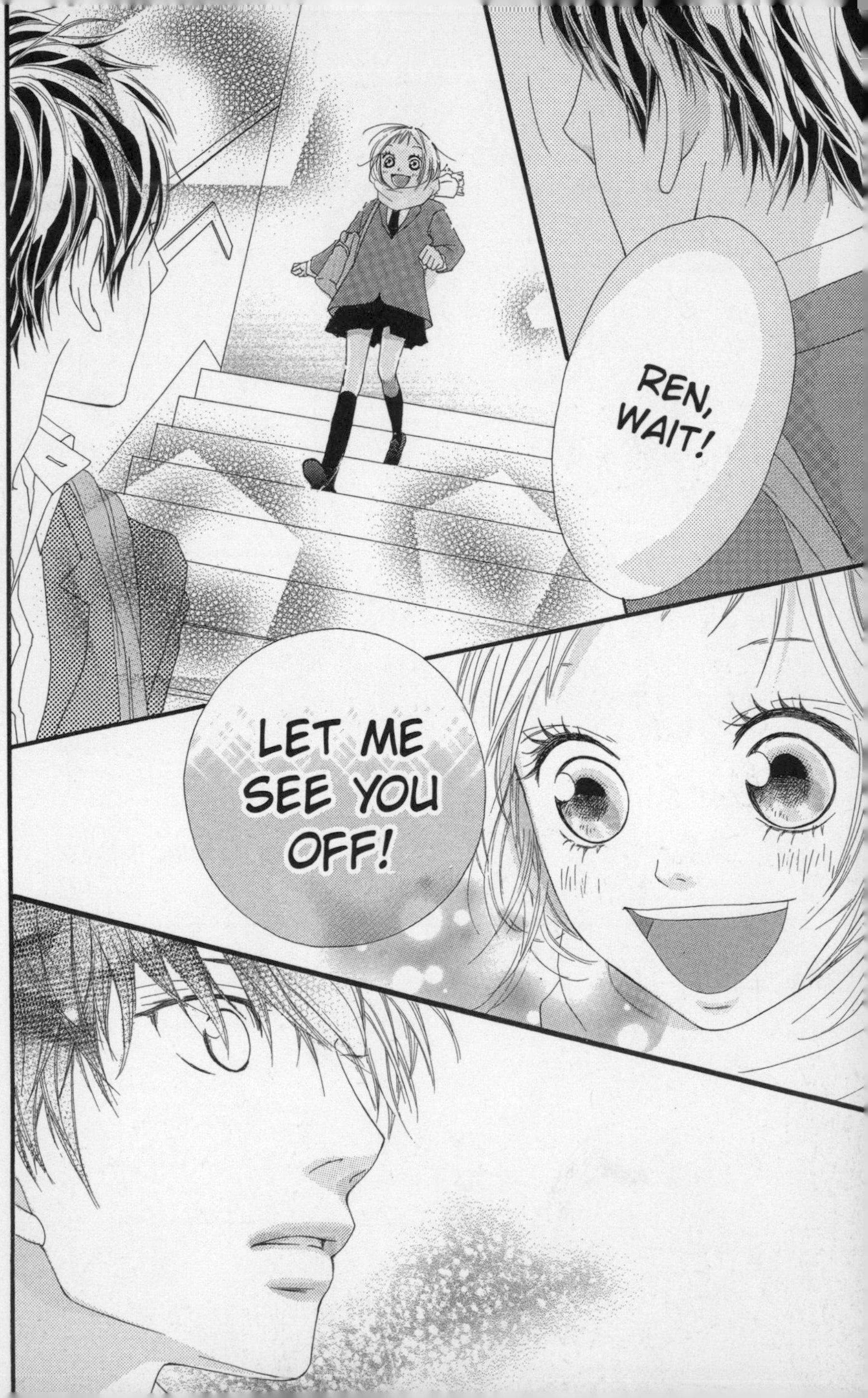
REN, WAIT!
LET ME SEE YOU OFF!

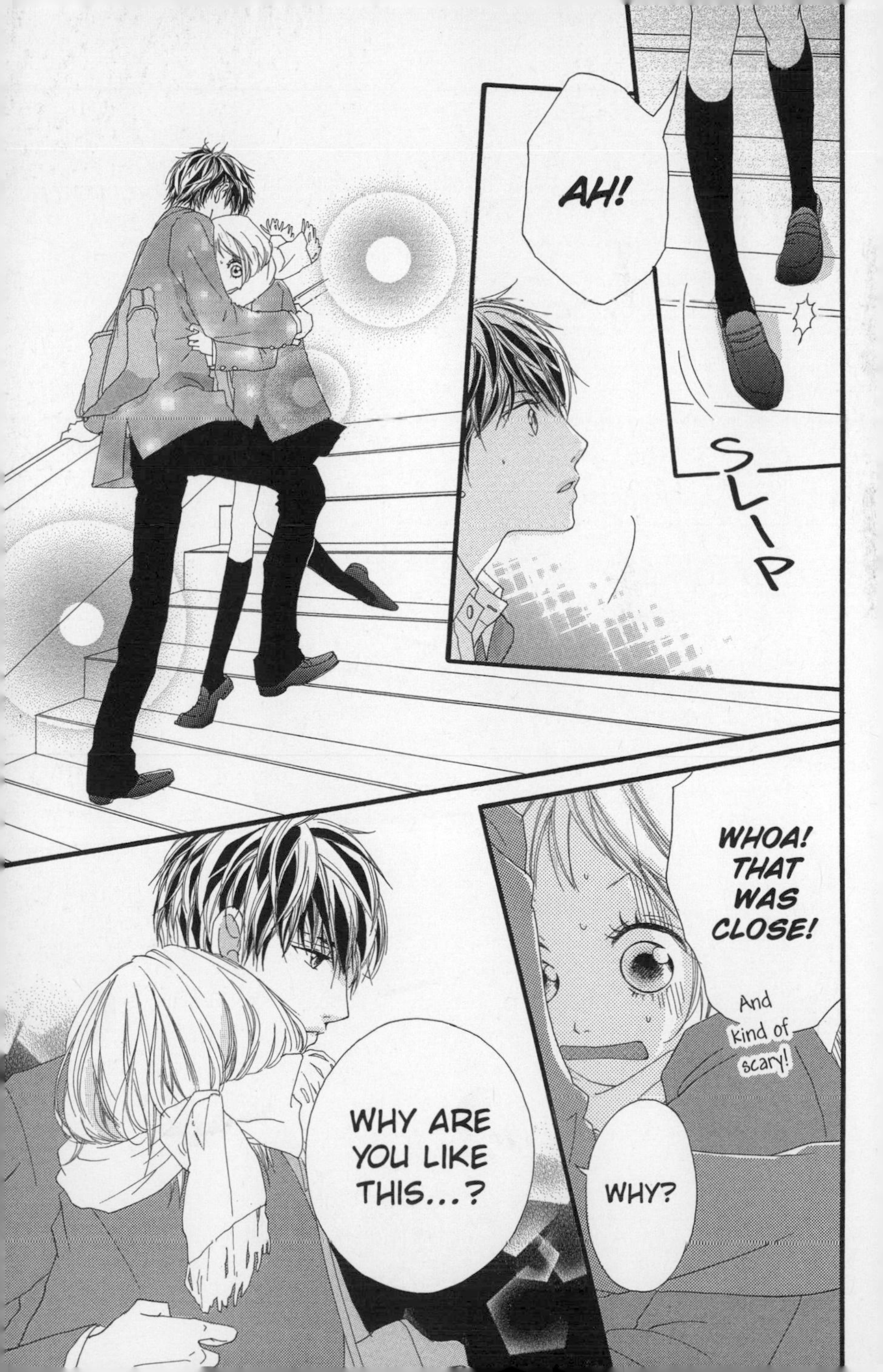
SLIP
AH!
WHOA! THAT WAS CLOSE!
And kind of scary!
WHY?
WHY ARE YOU LIKE THIS...?

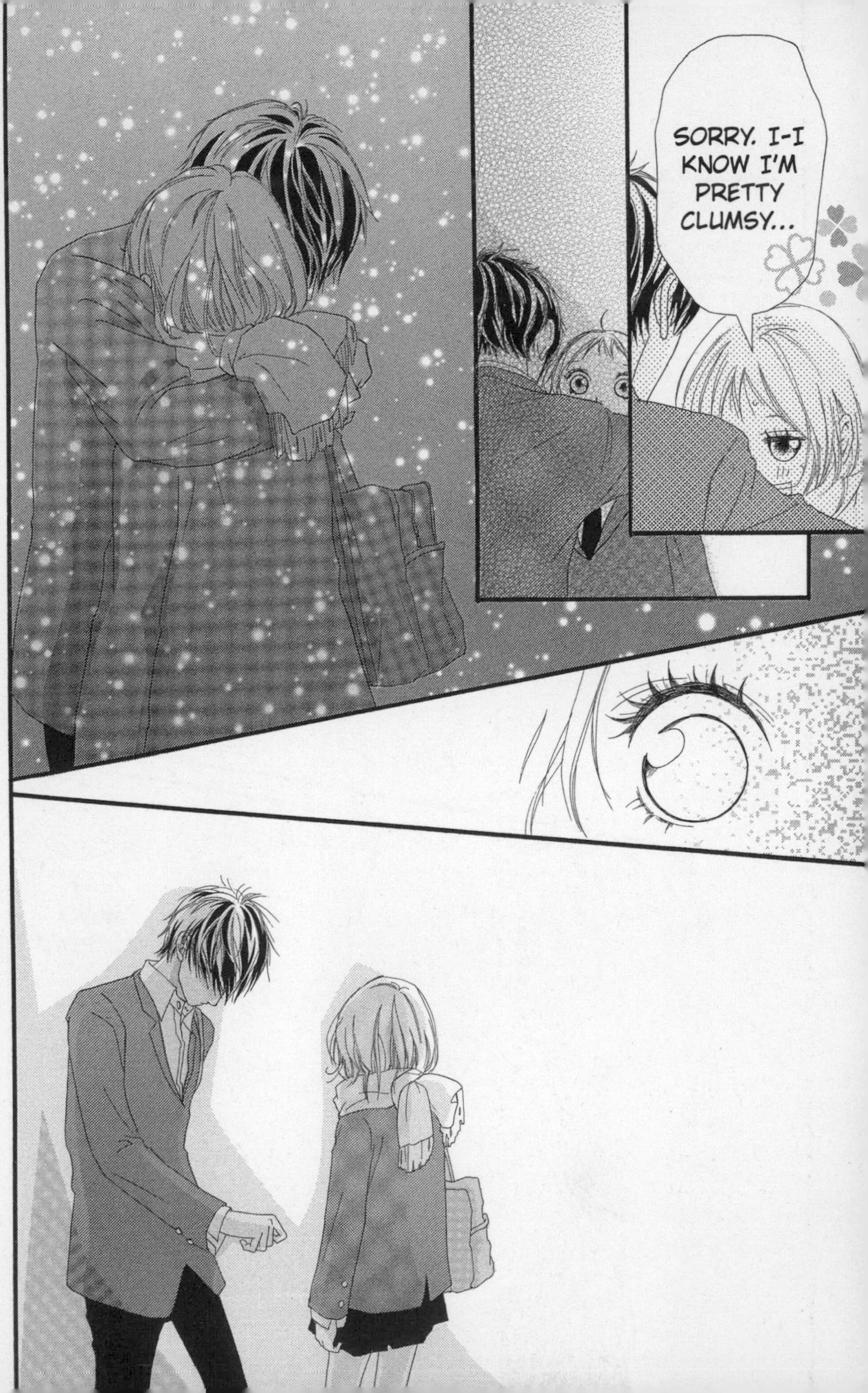
SORRY. I-I KNOW I'M PRETTY CLUMSY...

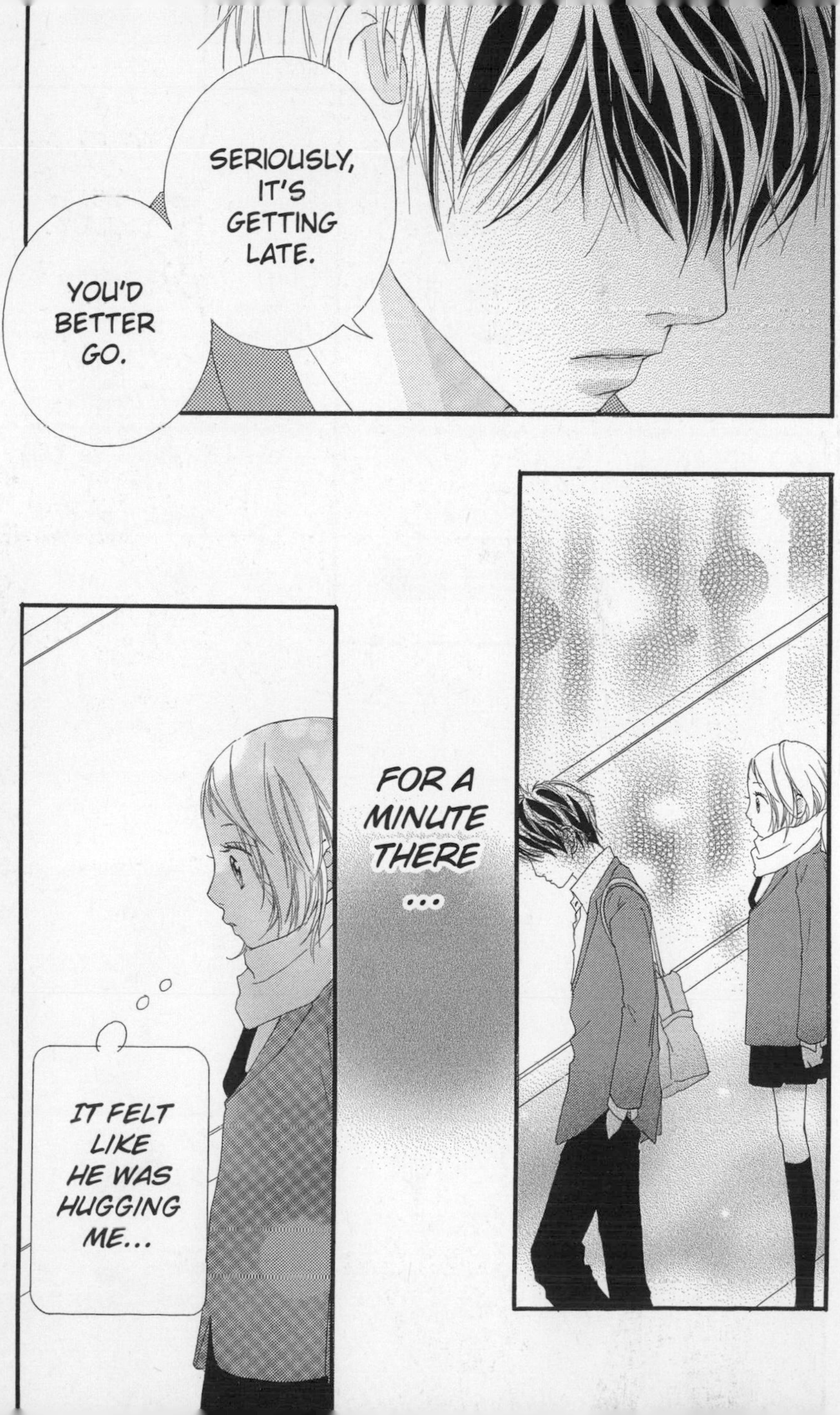
SERIOUSLY, IT'S GETTING LATE.
YOU'D BETTER GO.
FOR A MINUTE THERE...
IT FELT LIKE HE WAS HUGGING ME...

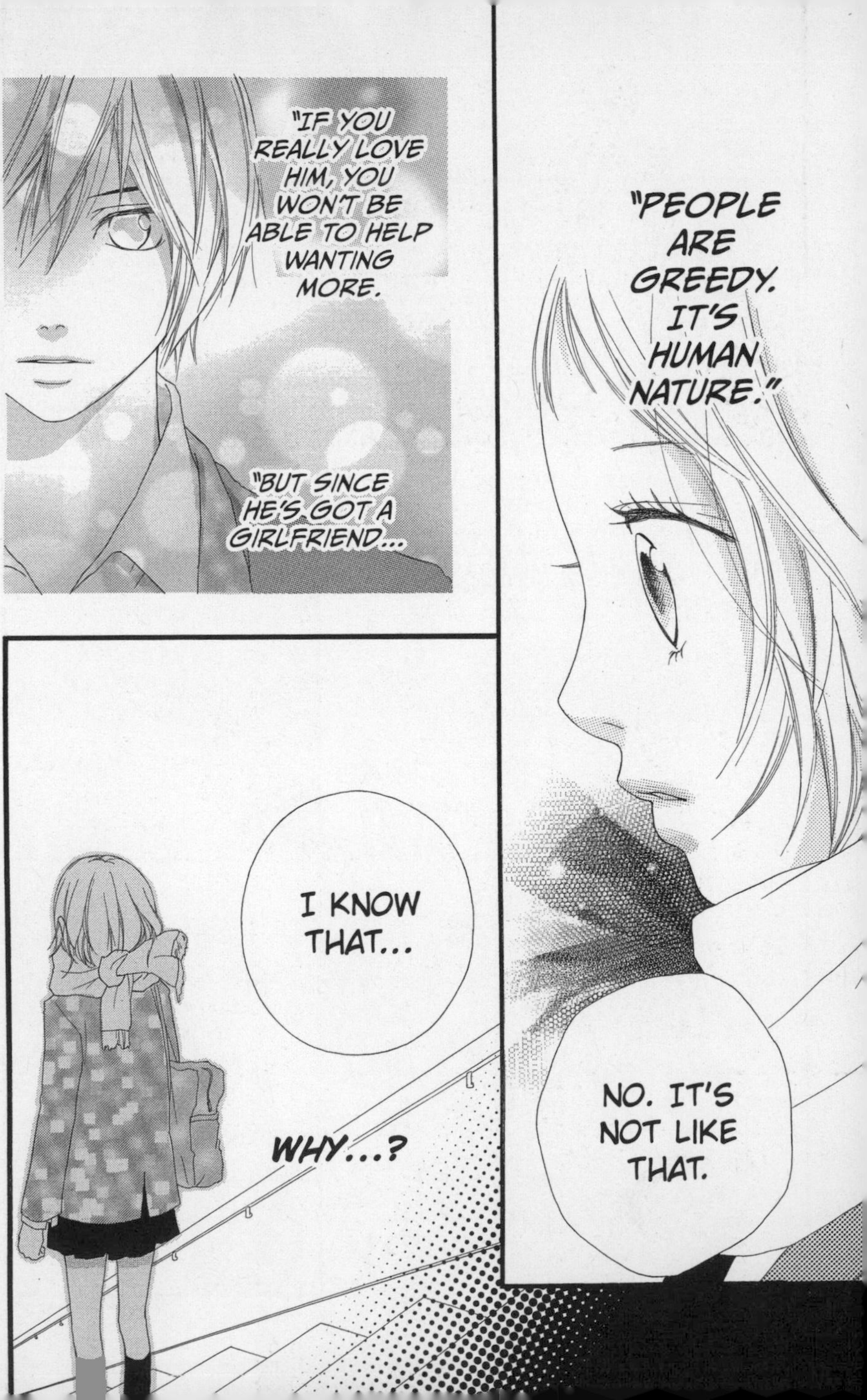
"PEOPLE ARE GREEDY. IT'S HUMAN NATURE."
NO. IT'S NOT LIKE THAT.
"IF YOU REALLY LOVE HIM, YOU WON'T BE ABLE TO HELP WANTING MORE.
"BUT SINCE HE'S GOT A GIRLFRIEND...
I KNOW THAT...
WHY...?

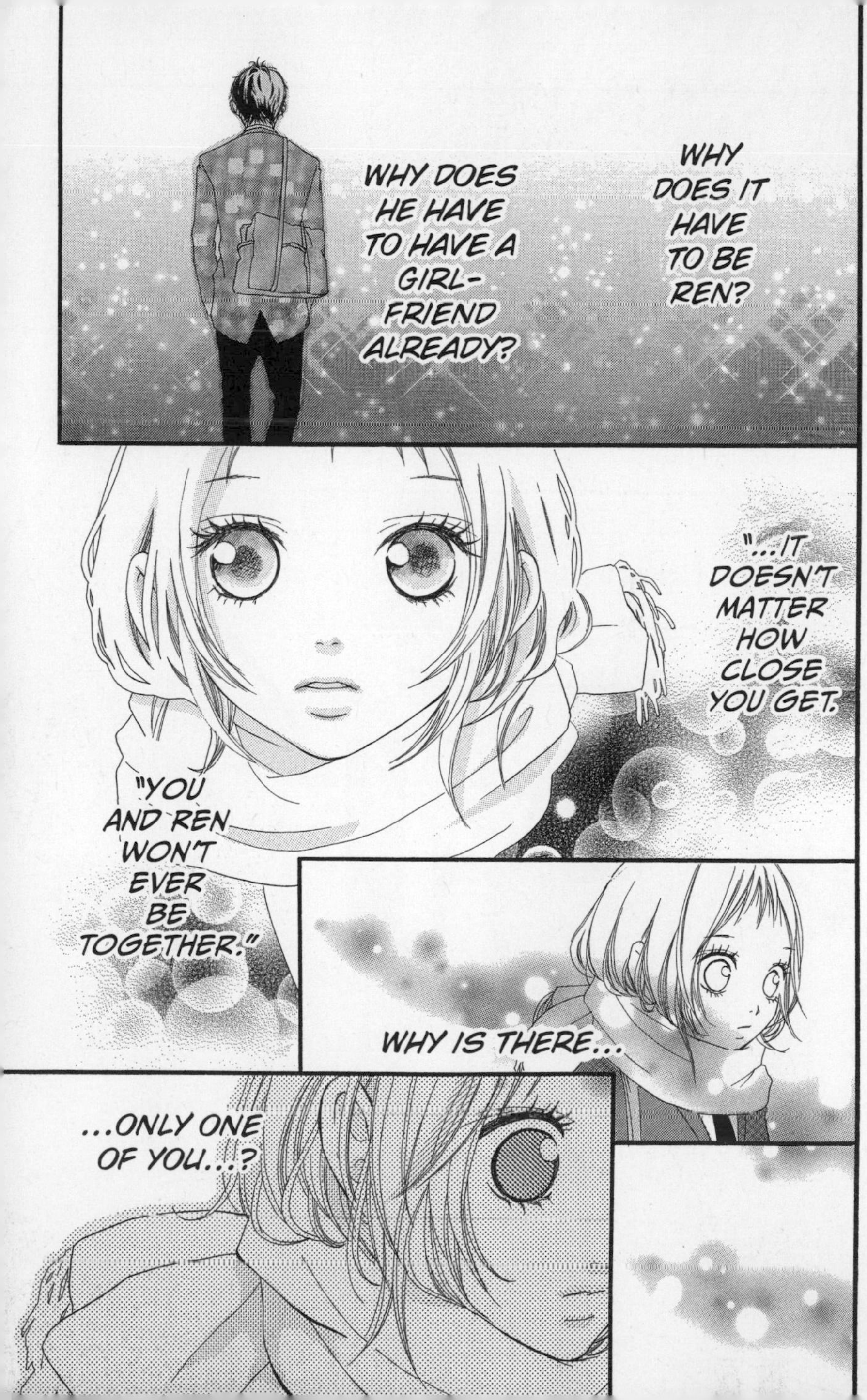
WHY DOES IT HAVE TO BE REN?
WHY DOES HE HAVE TO HAVE A GIRL-FRIEND ALREADY?
"...IT DOESN'T MATTER HOW CLOSE YOU GET.
"YOU AND REN WON'T EVER BE TOGETHER."
WHY IS THERE...
...ONLY ONE OF YOU...?

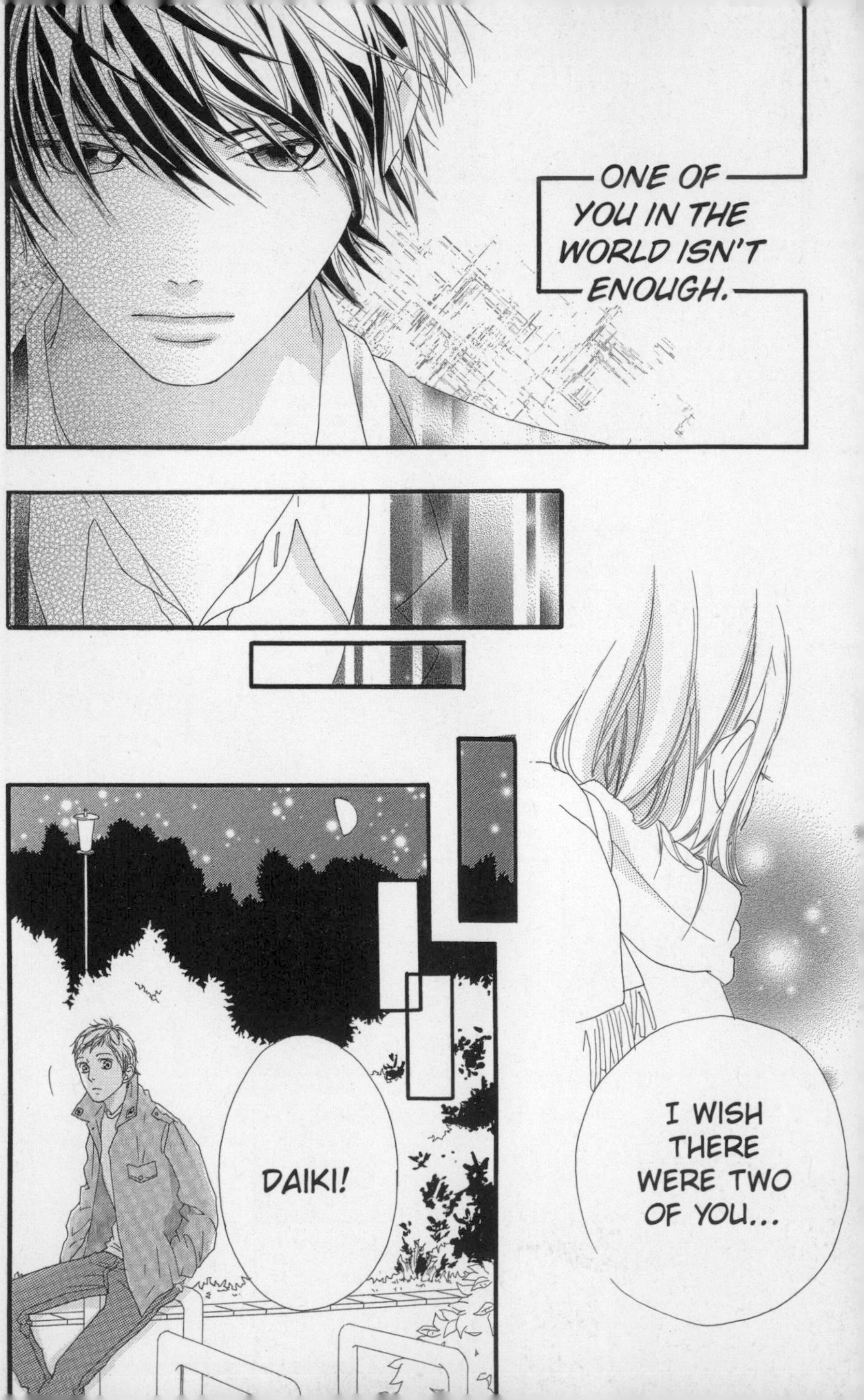
ONE OF YOU IN THE WORLD ISN'T ENOUGH.
I WISH THERE WERE TWO OF YOU...
DAIKI!

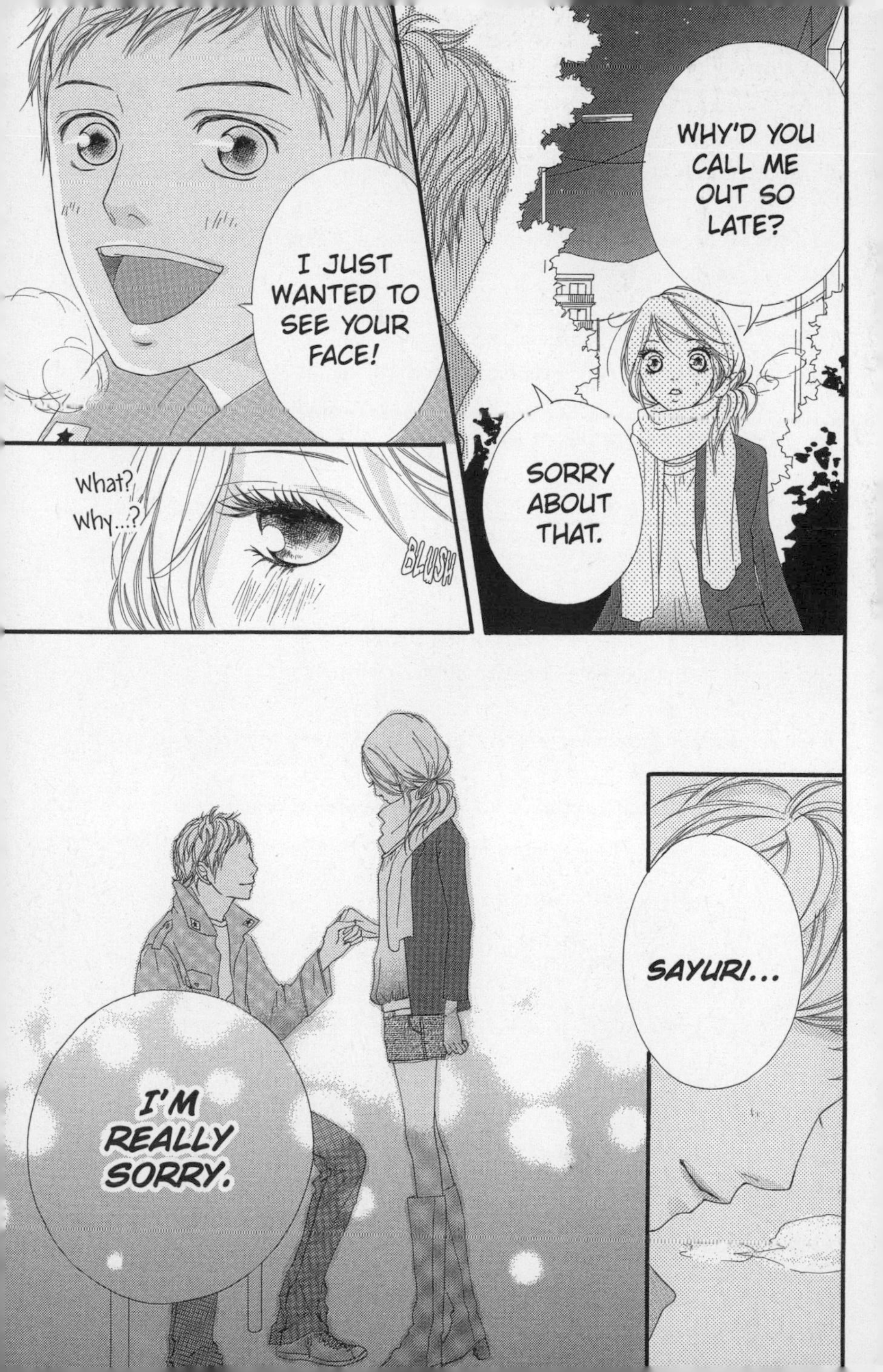
WHY'D YOU CALL ME OUT SO LATE?
SORRY ABOUT THAT.
I JUST WANTED TO SEE YOUR FACE!
What? Why...?
BLUSH
SAYURI...
I'M REALLY SORRY.

In the previous couple of volumes, I put out a call for people to join the Towel Blanket Club and the Fantasy Club. I thought maybe that was pushing it, but then I heard from several readers who said they wanted to join! I'm so happy!

So if you somehow inadvertently wrote "Sign me up!" I already consider you a member. Are you ready for it?

One person even created and submitted an application form. I cracked up as soon as I saw it. It even said "Application Enclosed" on the envelope. I love it when someone responds to my bad joke with another bad joke! So naturally I immediately inducted that person into the club.

Both clubs promote self-directed training and activities. There are no club or membership fees!

Rules:
*Don't bother other people while conducting activities.
*Act in ways that encourage peace, even outside of the club.

If you can observe these rules, you're welcome to join. Let's be friends!

Examples of my activities as a member of the:

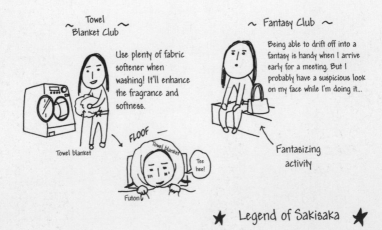

~ Towel Blanket Club ~

Use plenty of fabric softener when washing! It'll enhance the fragrance and softness.

Towel blanket

FLOOF

Towel blanket

Tee hee!

Futon

~ Fantasy Club ~

Being able to drift off into a fantasy is handy when I arrive early for a meeting. But I probably have a suspicious look on my face while I'm doing it...

Fantasizing activity

★ Legend of Sakisaka ★

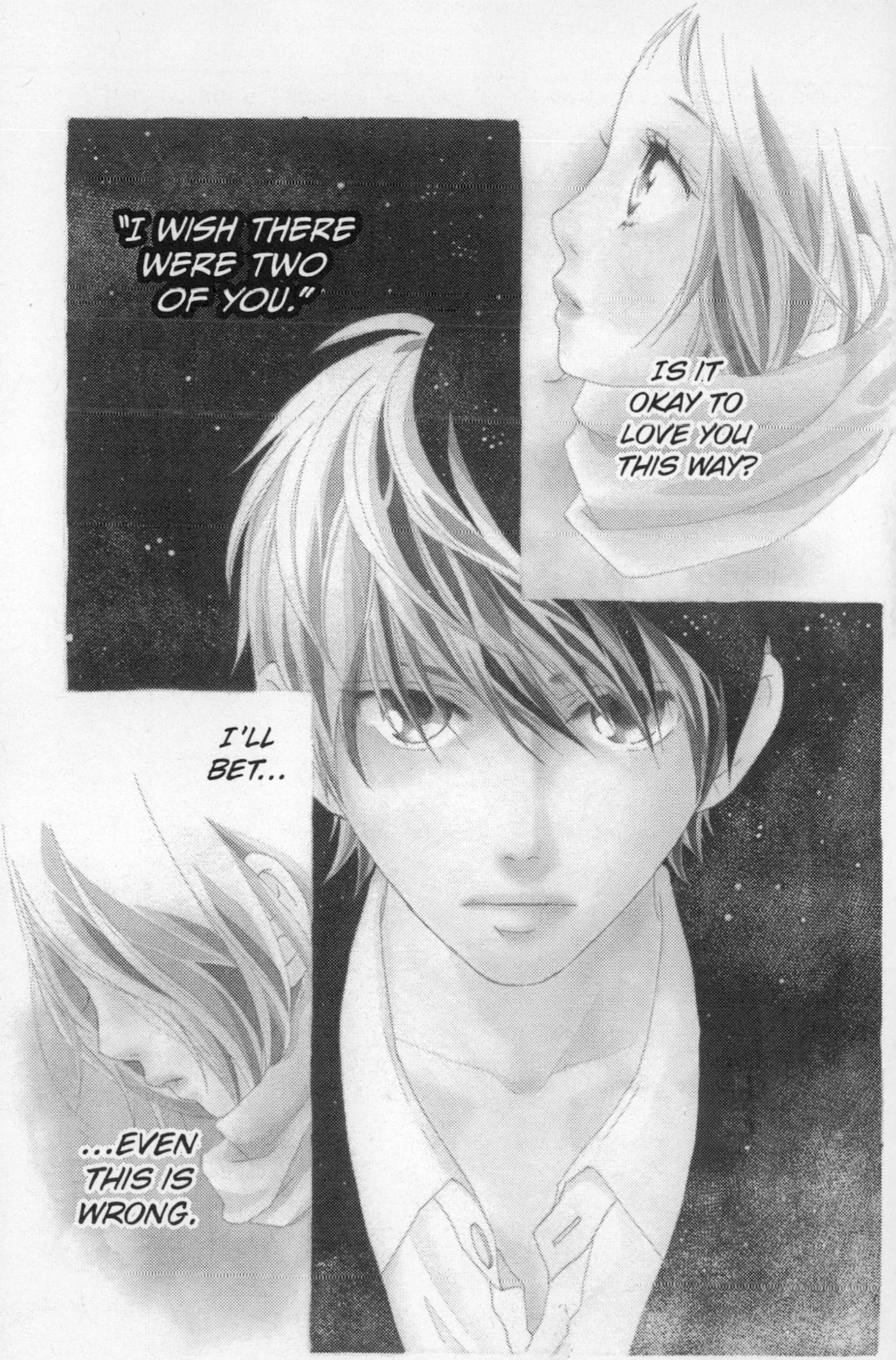
IS IT OKAY TO LOVE YOU THIS WAY?
"I WISH THERE WERE TWO OF YOU."
I'LL BET...
...EVEN THIS IS WRONG.

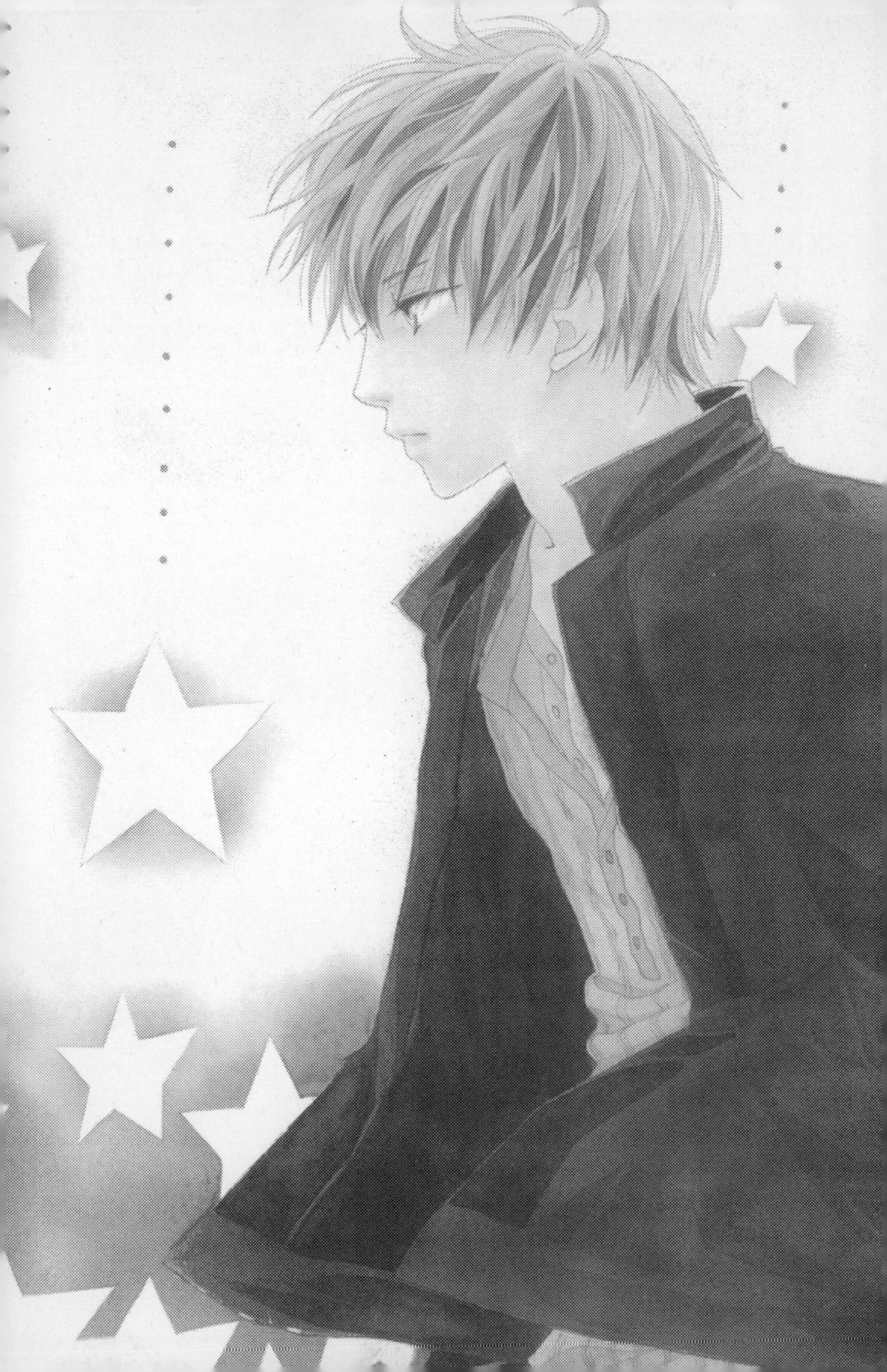

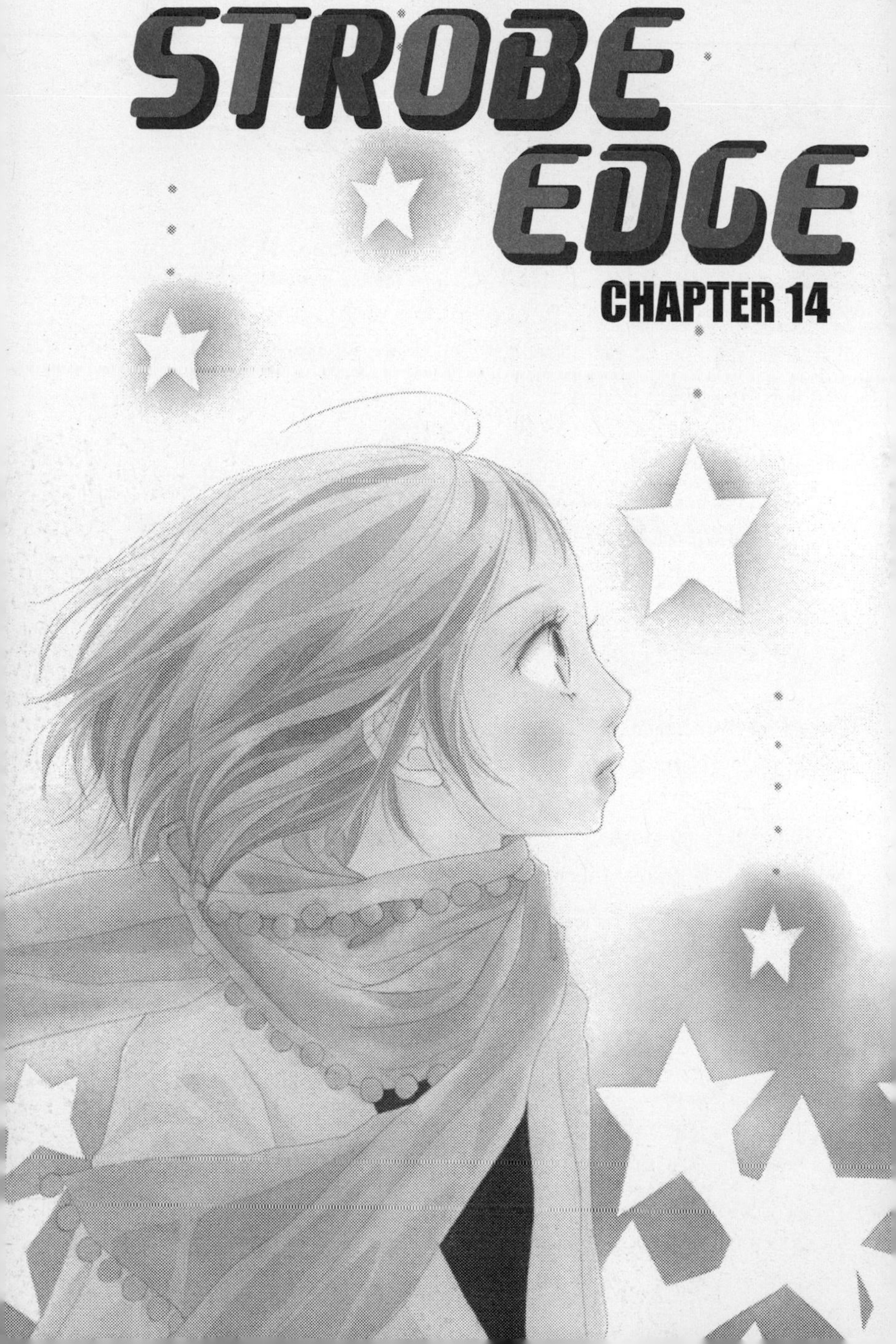
STROBE EDGE
CHAPTER 14

I never listen to music when I'm thinking about the plot or rough outline of a story because it makes me lose focus. Trying to work at a coffee shop (which I dream of) is entirely out of the question—I'd be distracted not only by the noise, but also by the presence of all the people there around me.

And when I'm in a daze, on a roll with a good story, I probably look like this. ⟶ It's practically a crime.

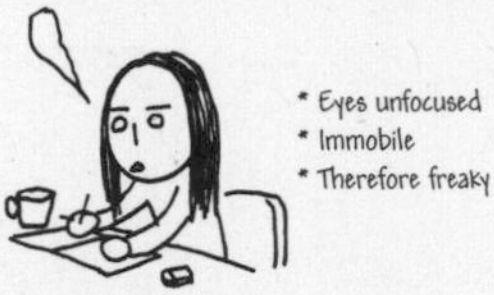

* Eyes unfocused
* Immobile
* Therefore freaky

Back in the day I tried to do work at a coffee shop. Sadly, it was way too distracting and I got nothing done. I think I basically lack focus.

Once I start sketching my rough draft, I do turn on the music. But again, the problem is that I begin to focus more on the music than the work at hand. Next thing you know, there's a recital starting up in my head! Unfortunately, I love these internal recitals—once one gets going, it takes me a long time to tear myself away and return to reality. For some reason, I can totally focus on those recitals for hours on end. Imagine how wonderful it would be if I could focus on my work that way!

★ Rebel Sakisaka ★

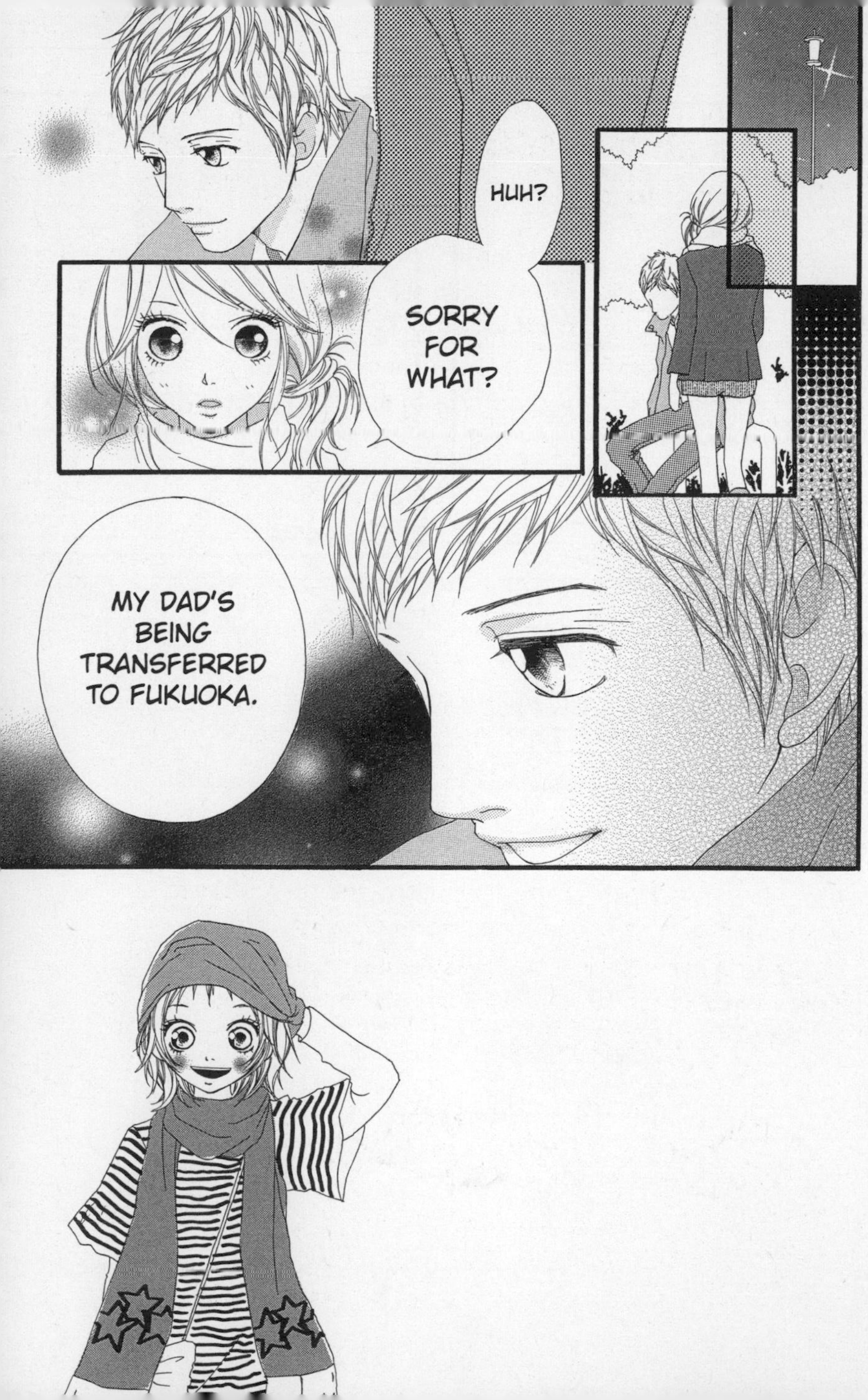
HUH?
SORRY FOR WHAT?
MY DAD'S BEING TRANSFERRED TO FUKUOKA.

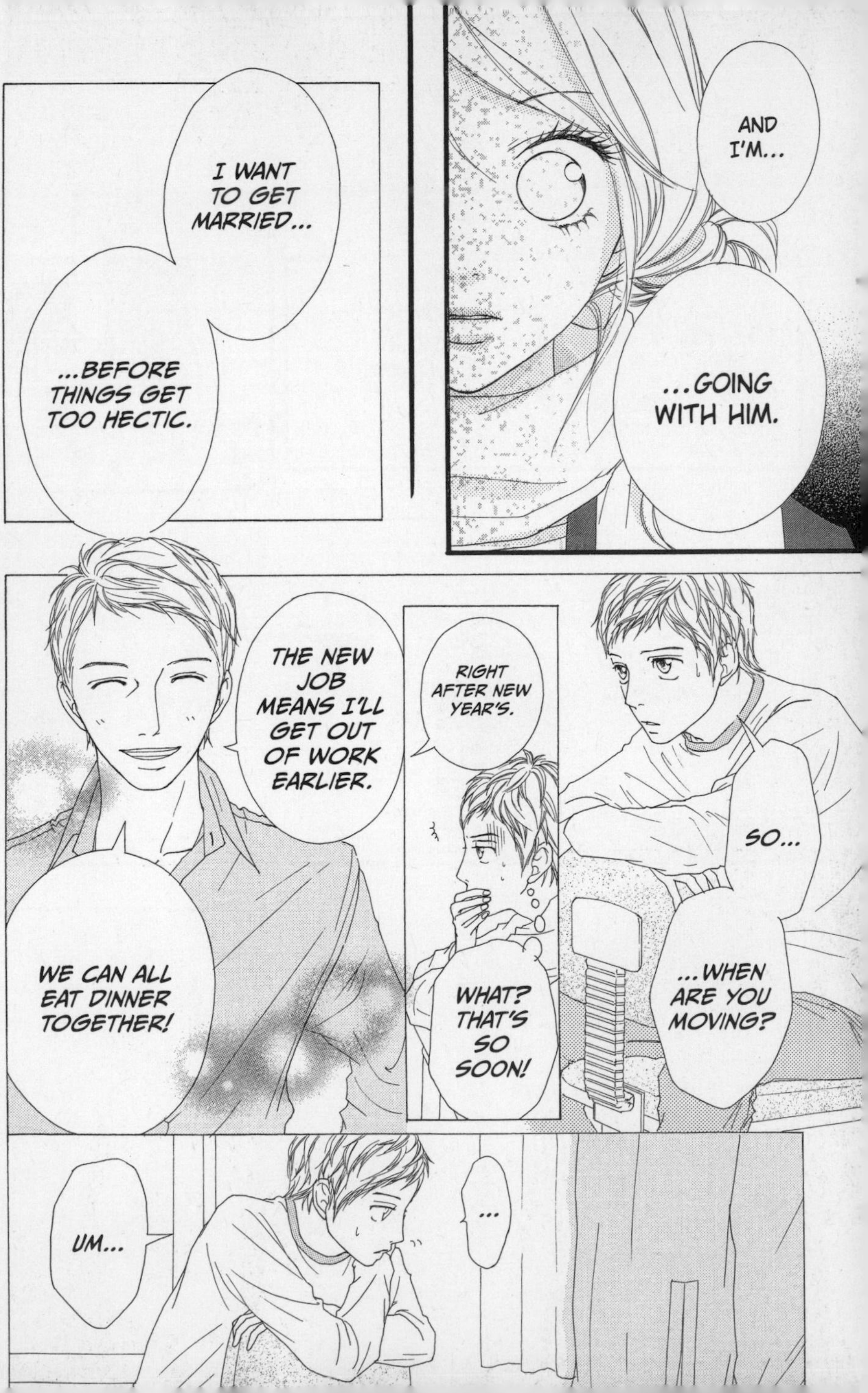
AND I'M...
...GOING WITH HIM.
I WANT TO GET MARRIED...
...BEFORE THINGS GET TOO HECTIC.
SO...
...WHEN ARE YOU MOVING?
RIGHT AFTER NEW YEAR'S.
WHAT? THAT'S SO SOON!
THE NEW JOB MEANS I'LL GET OUT OF WORK EARLIER.
WE CAN ALL EAT DINNER TOGETHER!
...
UM...

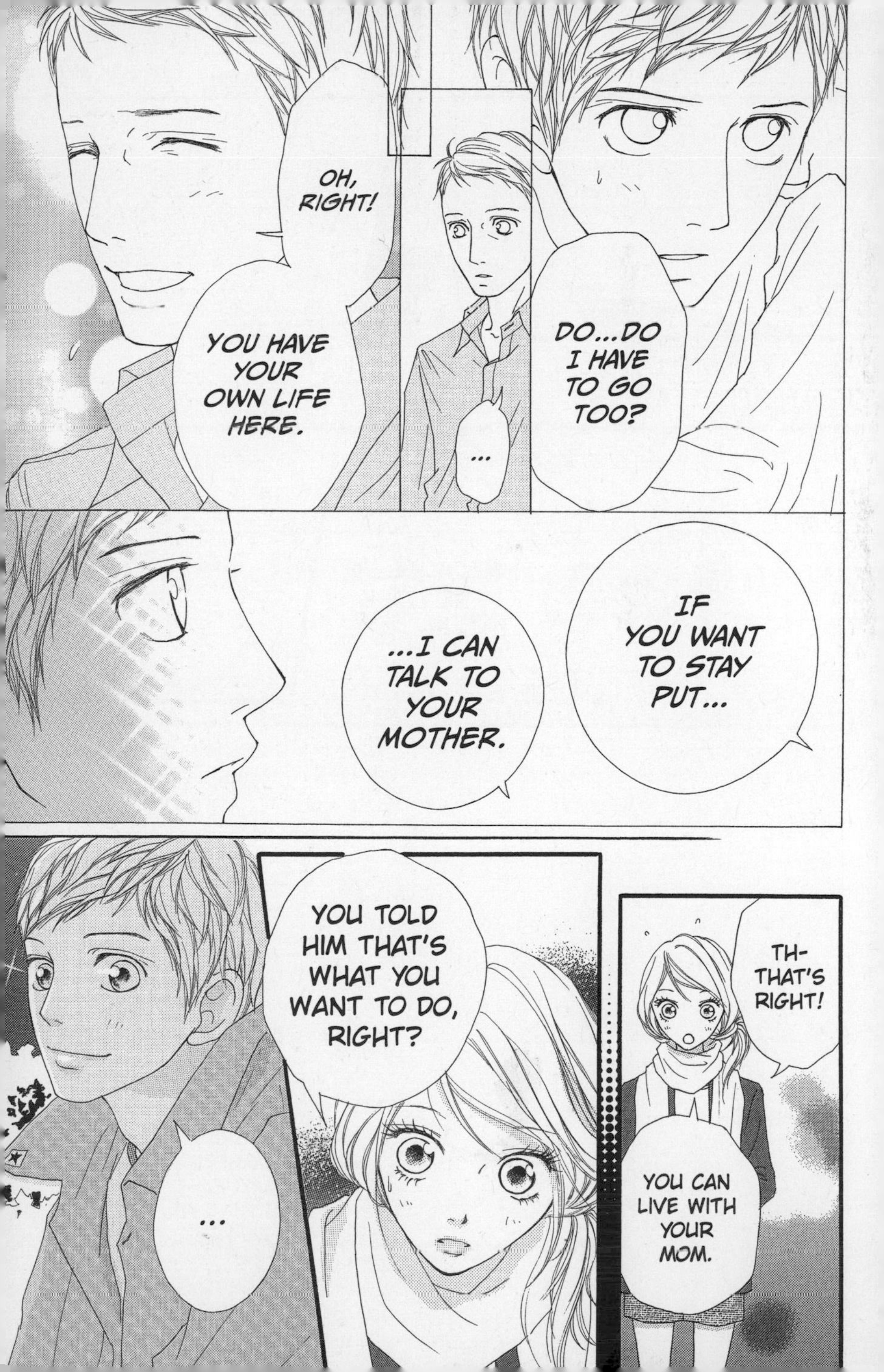
DO...DO I HAVE TO GO TOO?
...
OH, RIGHT!
YOU HAVE YOUR OWN LIFE HERE.
IF YOU WANT TO STAY PUT...
...I CAN TALK TO YOUR MOTHER.
TH-THAT'S RIGHT!
YOU CAN LIVE WITH YOUR MOM.
YOU TOLD HIM THAT'S WHAT YOU WANT TO DO, RIGHT?
...

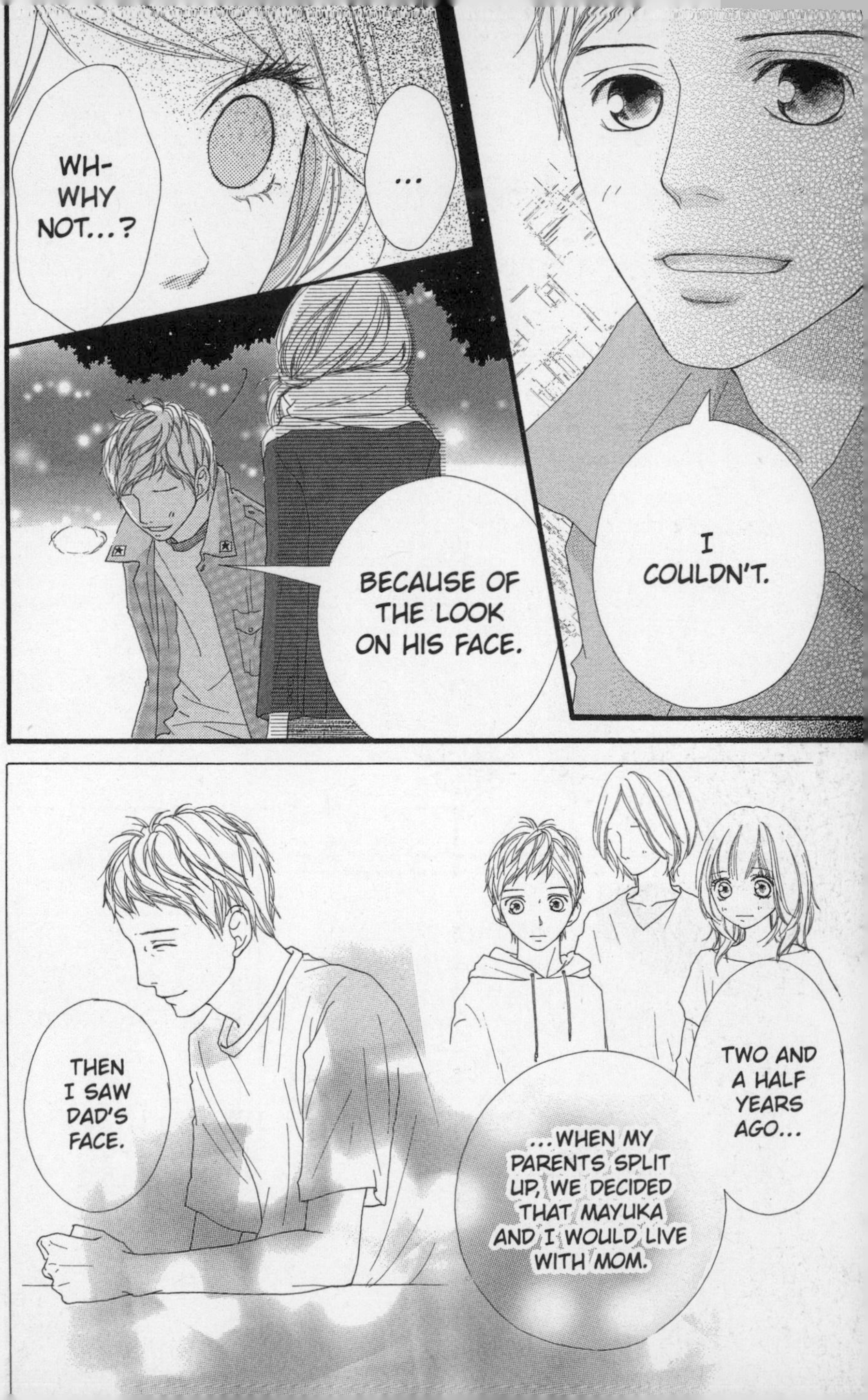
I COULDN'T.
...
WH- WHY NOT...?
BECAUSE OF THE LOOK ON HIS FACE.
TWO AND A HALF YEARS AGO...
...WHEN MY PARENTS SPLIT UP, WE DECIDED THAT MAYUKA AND I WOULD LIVE WITH MOM.
THEN I SAW DAD'S FACE.

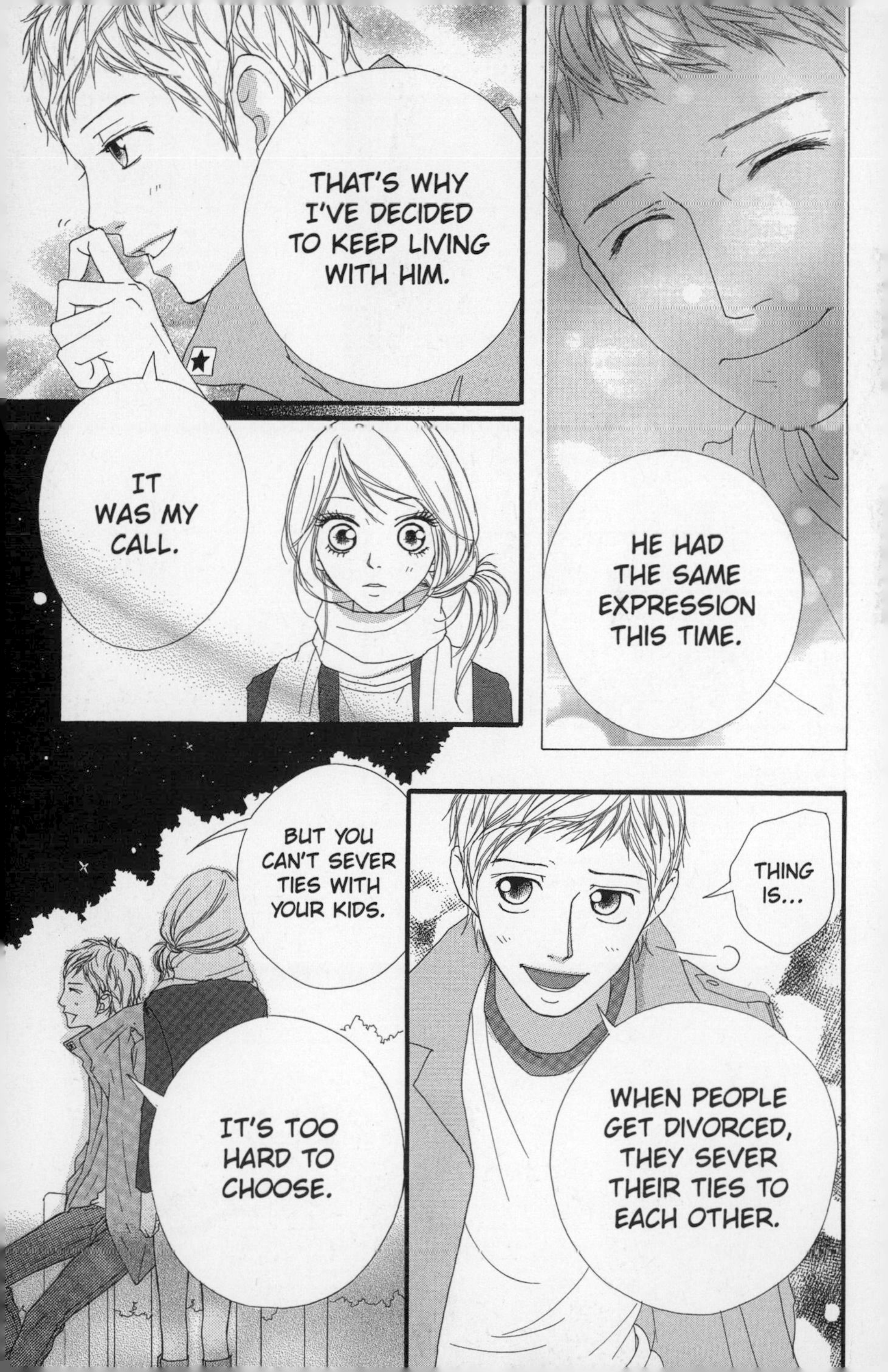
HE HAD THE SAME EXPRESSION THIS TIME.
THAT'S WHY I'VE DECIDED TO KEEP LIVING WITH HIM.
IT WAS MY CALL.
THING IS...
WHEN PEOPLE GET DIVORCED, THEY SEVER THEIR TIES TO EACH OTHER.
BUT YOU CAN'T SEVER TIES WITH YOUR KIDS.
IT'S TOO HARD TO CHOOSE.

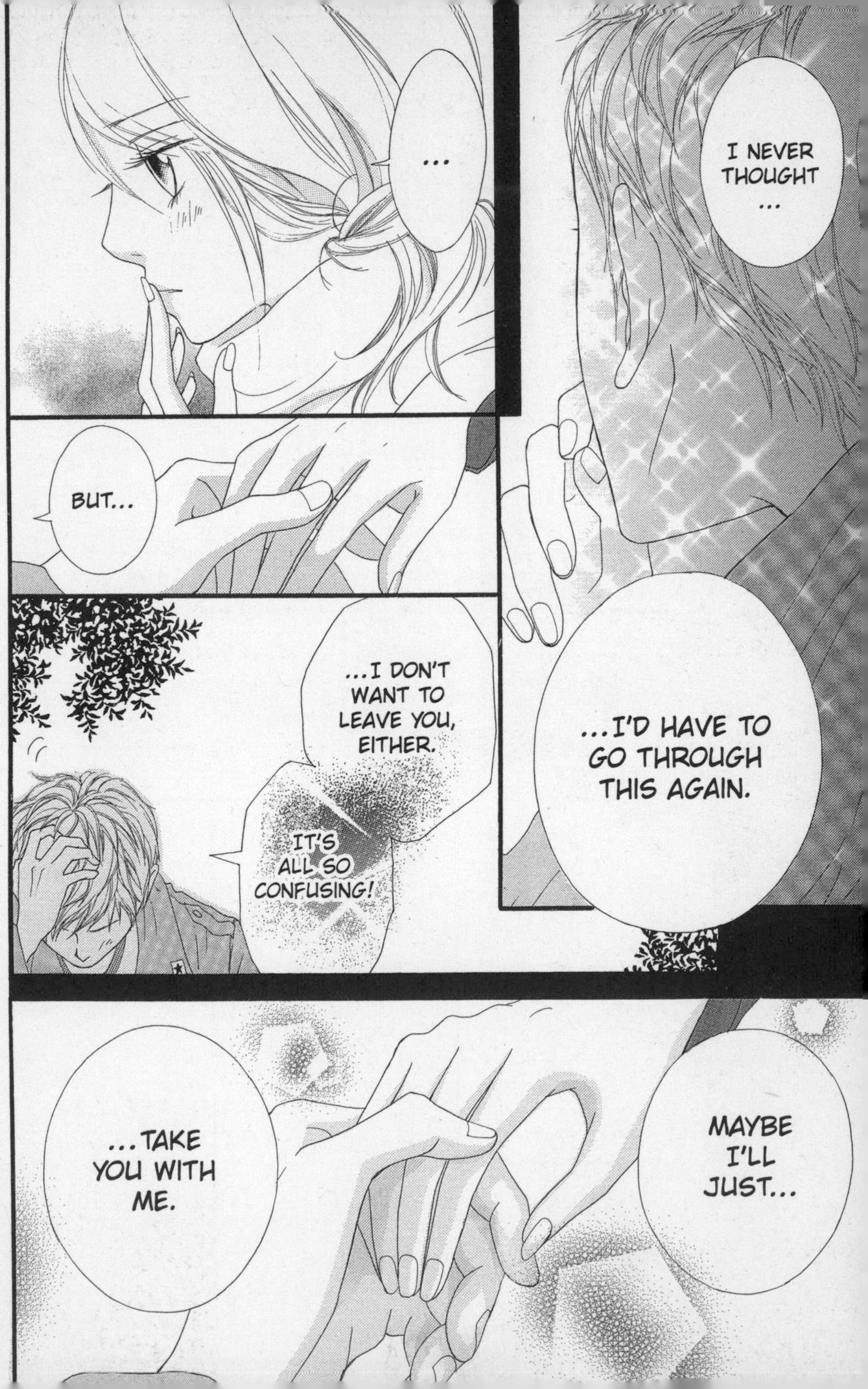
I NEVER THOUGHT ...
...I'D HAVE TO GO THROUGH THIS AGAIN.
...
BUT...
...I DON'T WANT TO LEAVE YOU, EITHER.
IT'S ALL SO CONFUSING!
MAYBE I'LL JUST...
...TAKE YOU WITH ME.

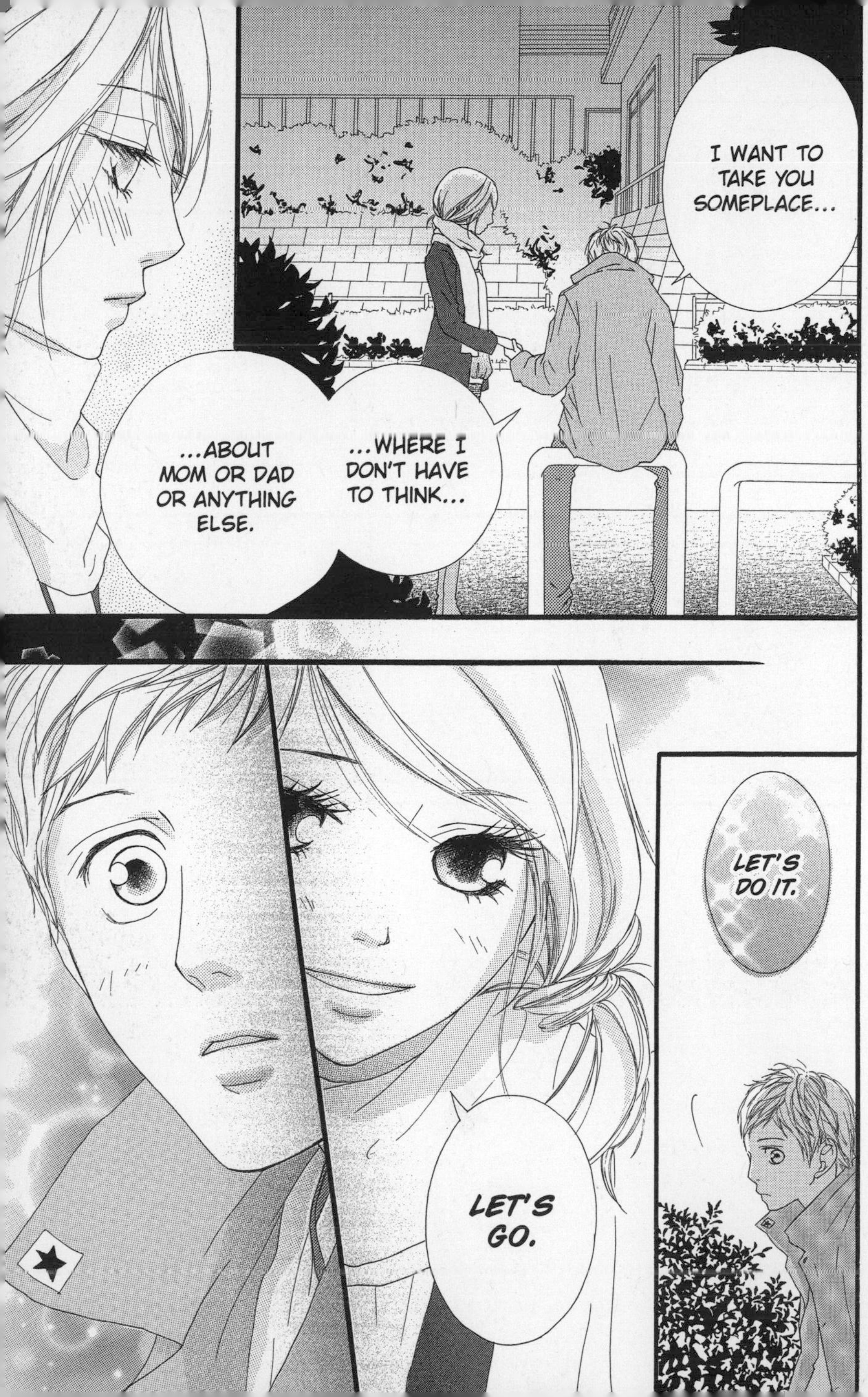
I WANT TO TAKE YOU SOMEPLACE...
...WHERE I DON'T HAVE TO THINK...
...ABOUT MOM OR DAD OR ANYTHING ELSE.
LET'S DO IT.
LET'S GO.

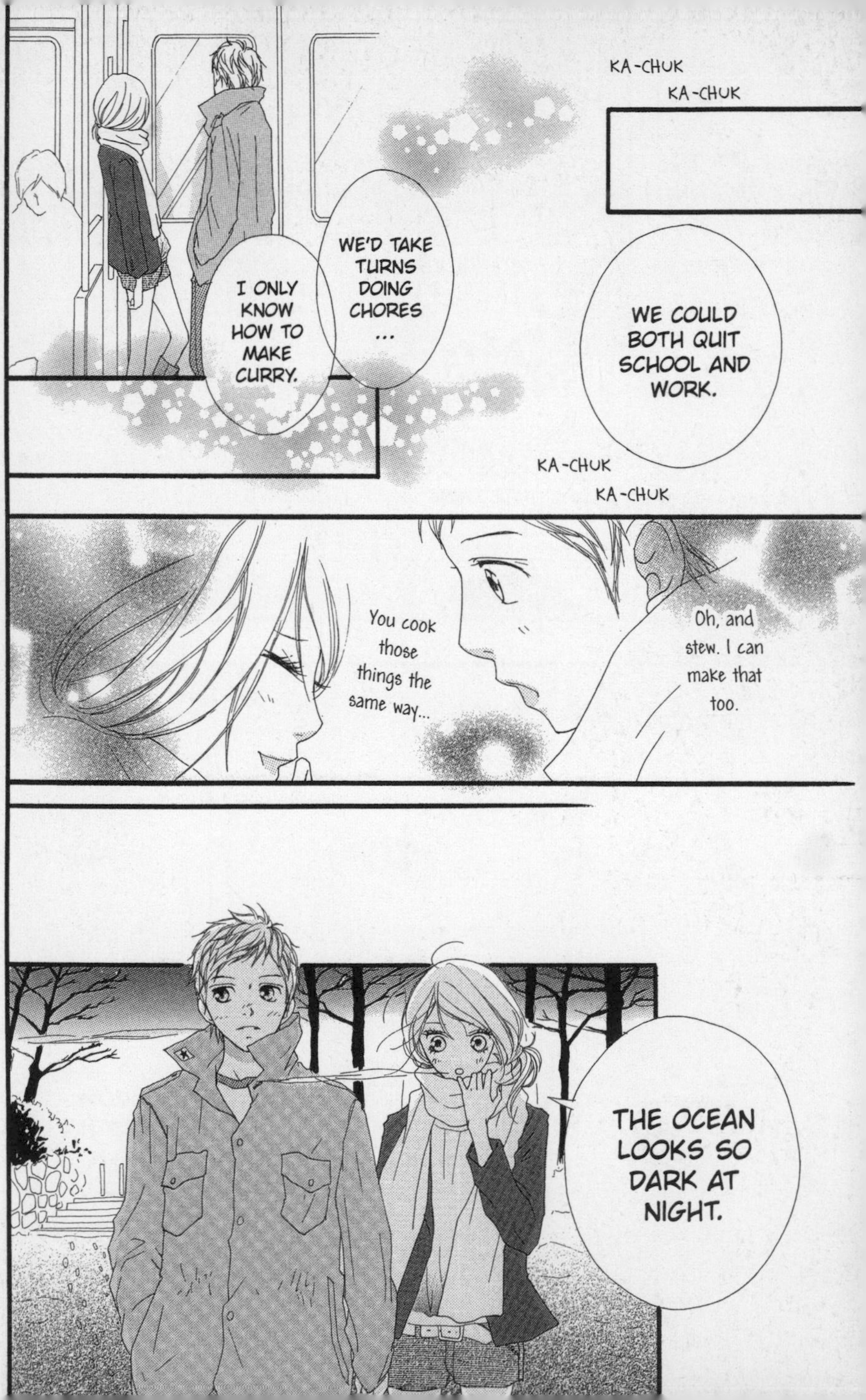
KA-CHUK
KA-CHUK
WE COULD BOTH QUIT SCHOOL AND WORK.
WE'D TAKE TURNS DOING CHORES ...
I ONLY KNOW HOW TO MAKE CURRY.
KA-CHUK
KA-CHUK
Oh, and stew. I can make that too.
You cook those things the same way...
THE OCEAN LOOKS SO DARK AT NIGHT.

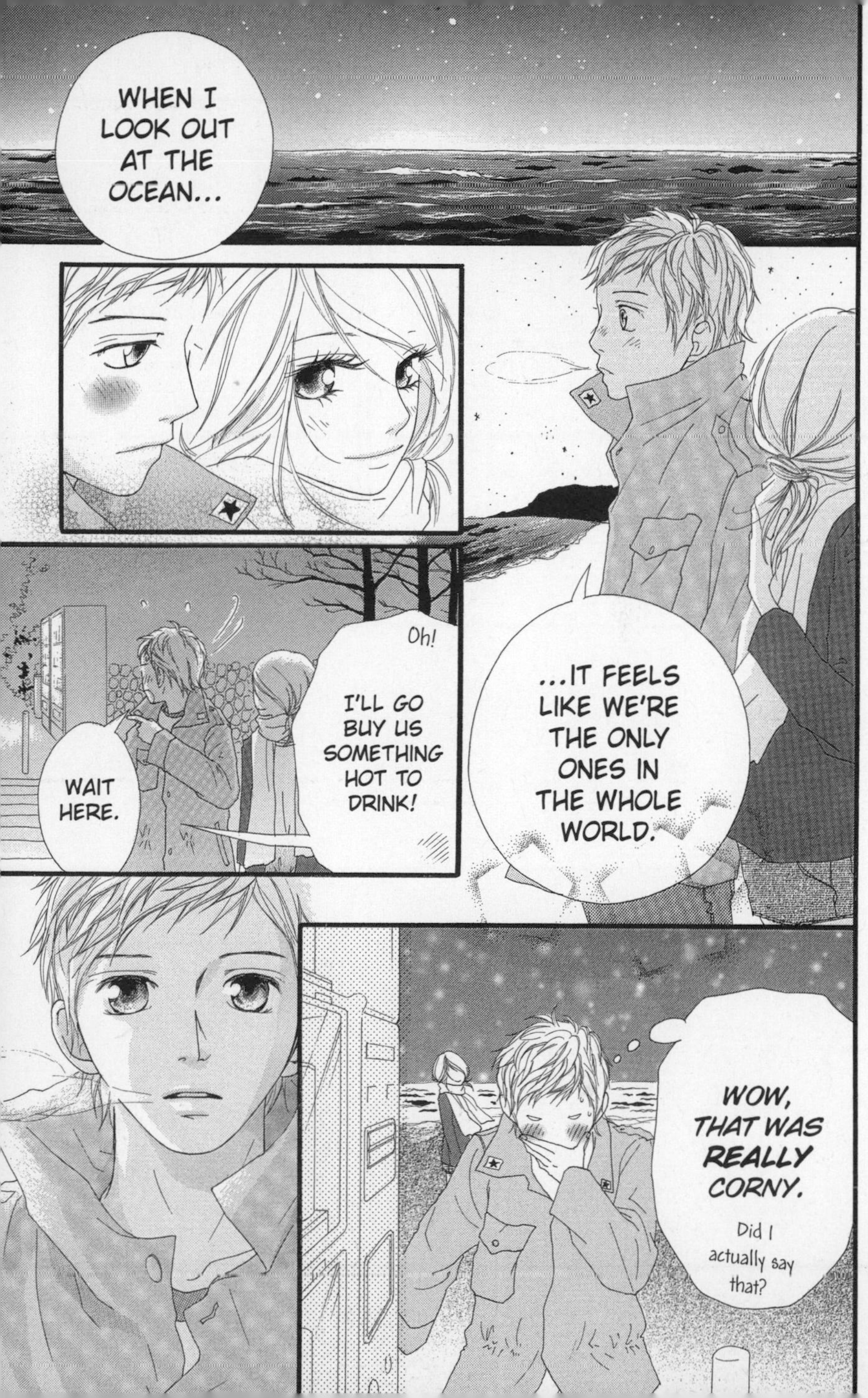
WHEN I LOOK OUT AT THE OCEAN...
...IT FEELS LIKE WE'RE THE ONLY ONES IN THE WHOLE WORLD.
Oh!
I'LL GO BUY US SOMETHING HOT TO DRINK!
WAIT HERE.
WOW, THAT WAS REALLY CORNY.
Did I actually say that?

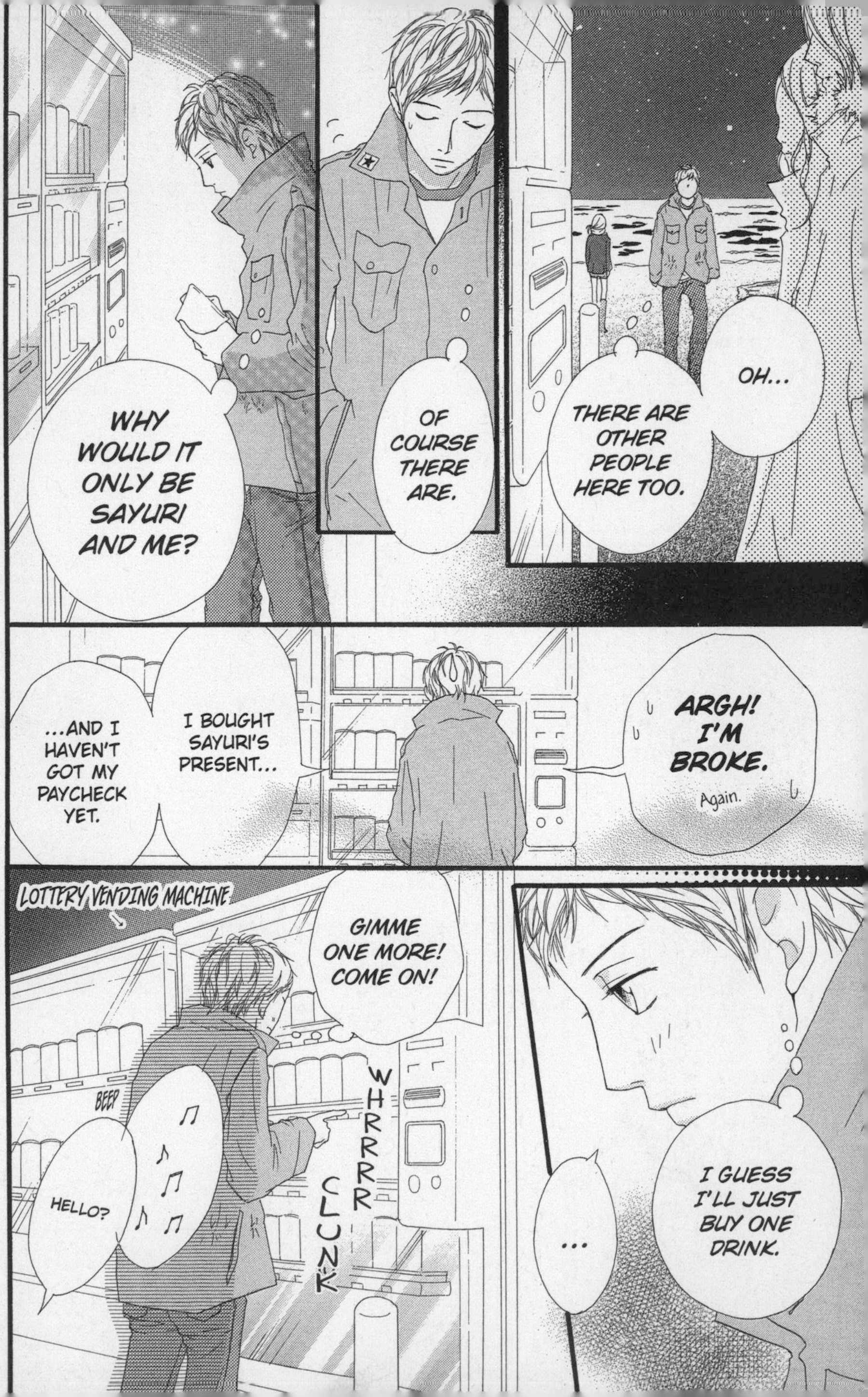
OH...
THERE ARE OTHER PEOPLE HERE TOO.
OF COURSE THERE ARE.
WHY WOULD IT ONLY BE SAYURI AND ME?
ARGH! I'M BROKE.
Again.
I BOUGHT SAYURI'S PRESENT...
...AND I HAVEN'T GOT MY PAYCHECK YET.
I GUESS I'LL JUST BUY ONE DRINK.
...
GIMME ONE MORE! COME ON!
LOTTERY VENDING MACHINE
WHRRRR
CLUNK
BEEP
HELLO?

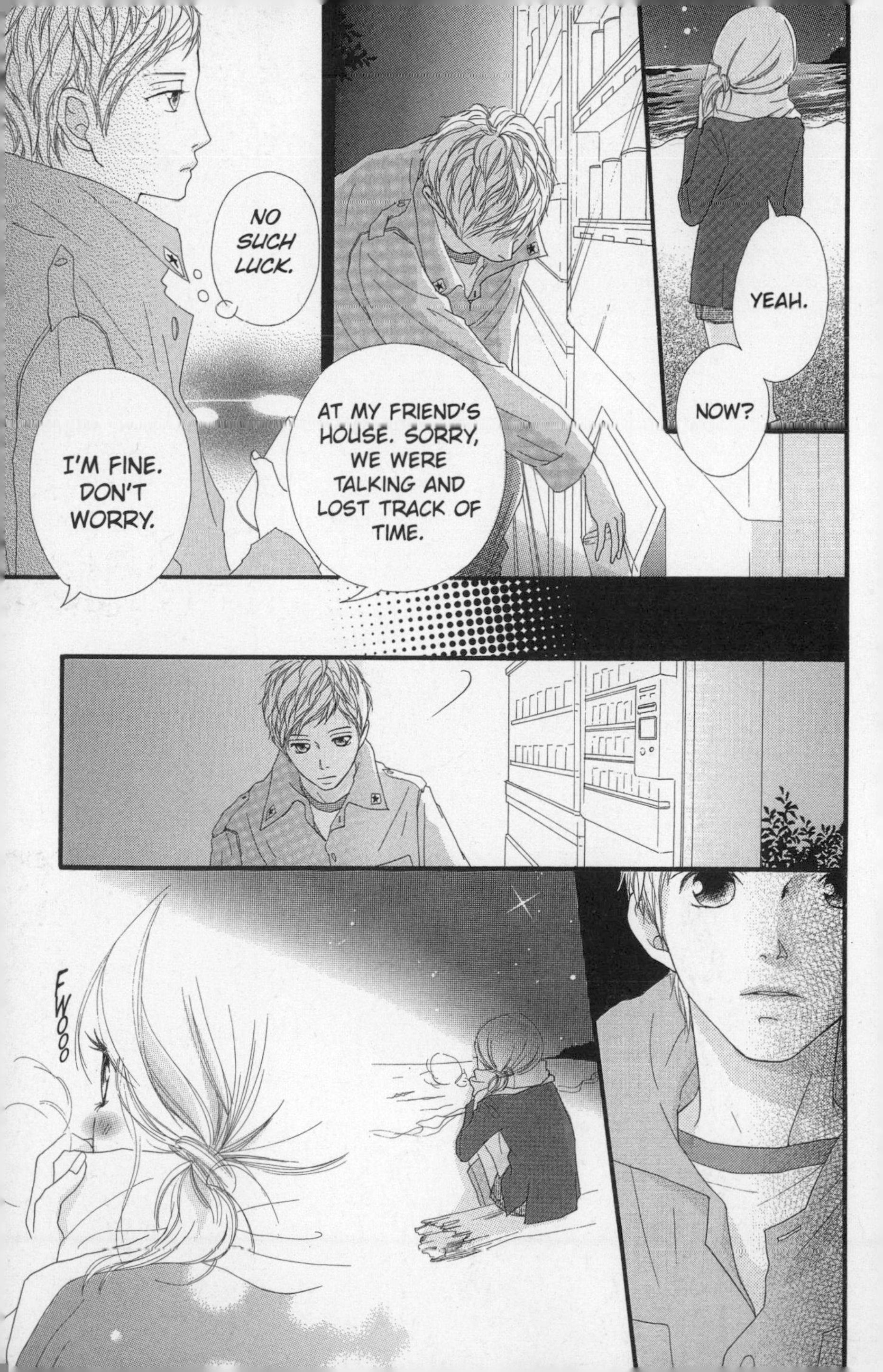
YEAH.
NOW?
AT MY FRIEND'S HOUSE. SORRY, WE WERE TALKING AND LOST TRACK OF TIME.
NO SUCH LUCK.
I'M FINE. DON'T WORRY.
FWOOO

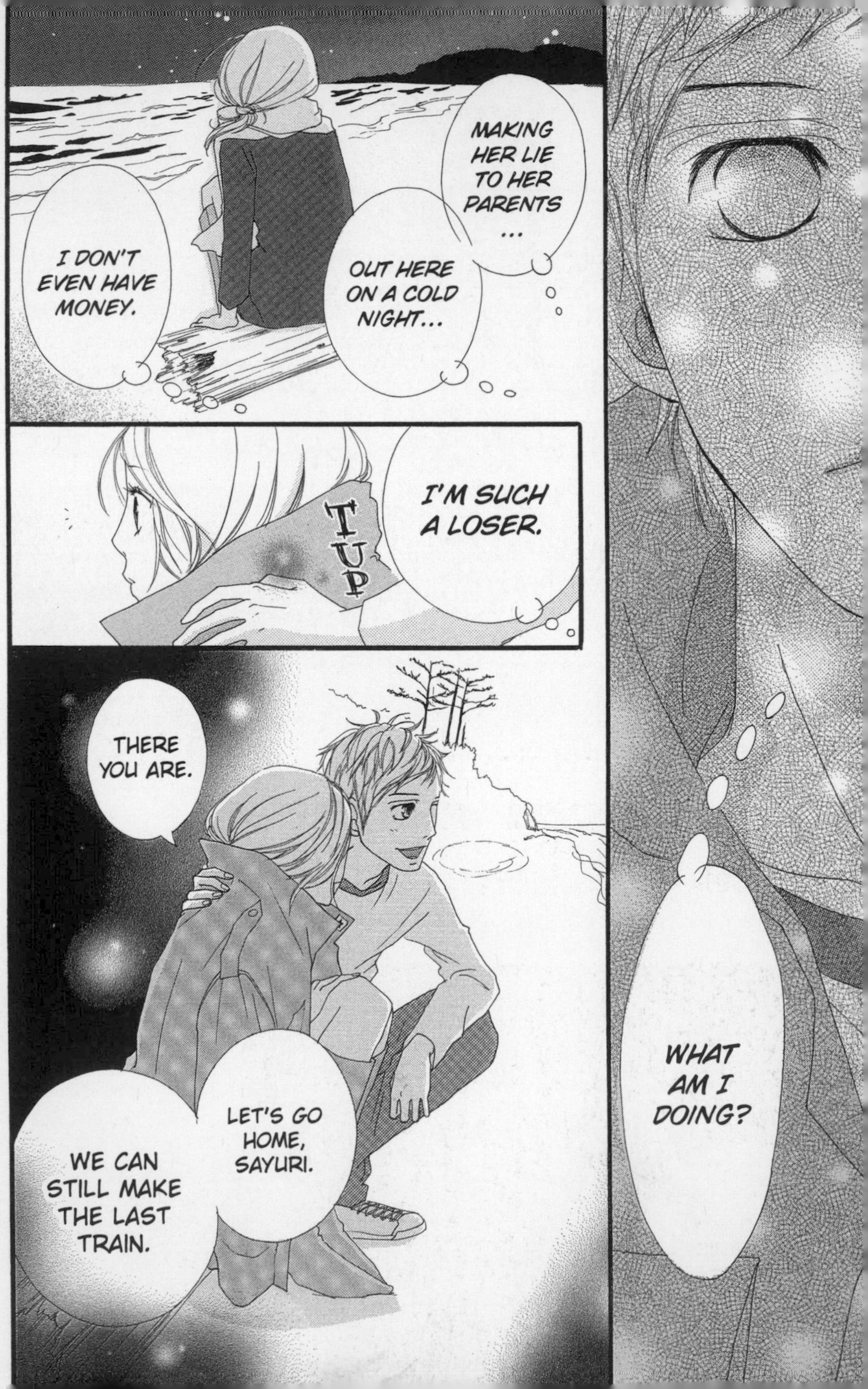
WHAT AM I DOING?
MAKING HER LIE TO HER PARENTS...
OUT HERE ON A COLD NIGHT...
I DON'T EVEN HAVE MONEY.
I'M SUCH A LOSER.
TUP
THERE YOU ARE.
LET'S GO HOME, SAYURI.
WE CAN STILL MAKE THE LAST TRAIN.

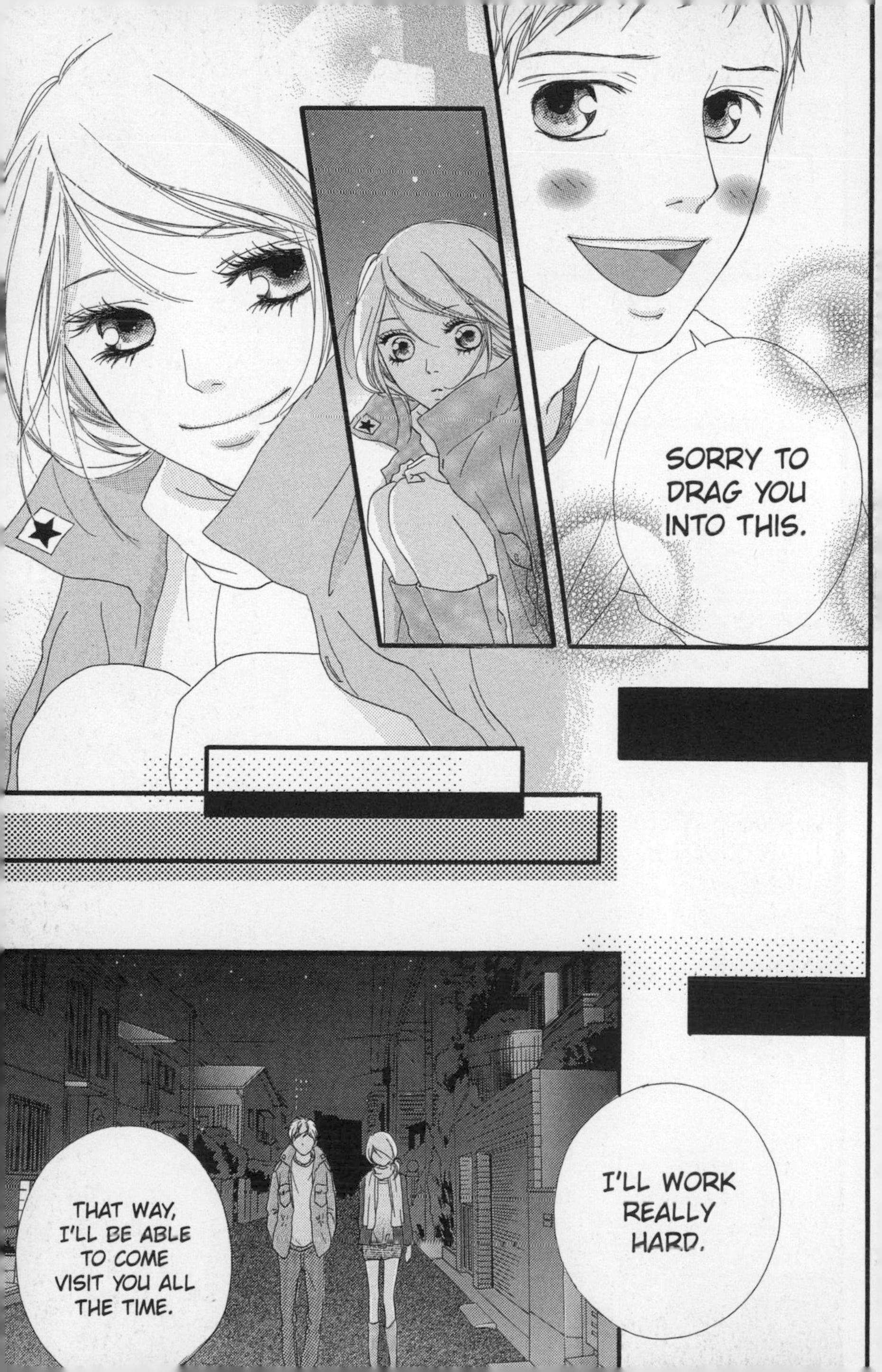
SORRY TO DRAG YOU INTO THIS.
I'LL WORK REALLY HARD.
THAT WAY, I'LL BE ABLE TO COME VISIT YOU ALL THE TIME.

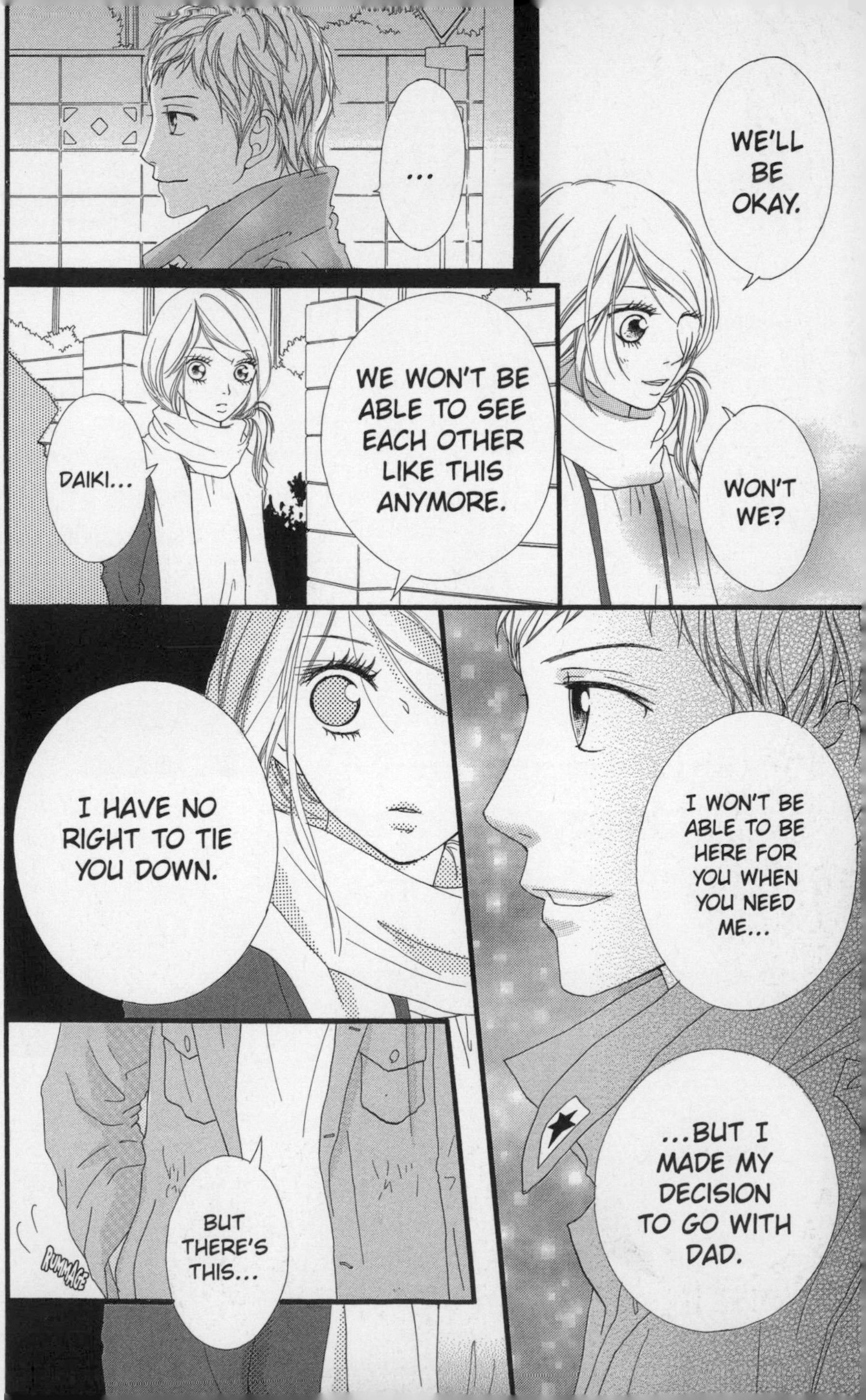
WE'LL BE OKAY.
WON'T WE?
...
WE WON'T BE ABLE TO SEE EACH OTHER LIKE THIS ANYMORE.
DAIKI...
I WON'T BE ABLE TO BE HERE FOR YOU WHEN YOU NEED ME...
...BUT I MADE MY DECISION TO GO WITH DAD.
I HAVE NO RIGHT TO TIE YOU DOWN.
BUT THERE'S THIS...
RUMMAGE

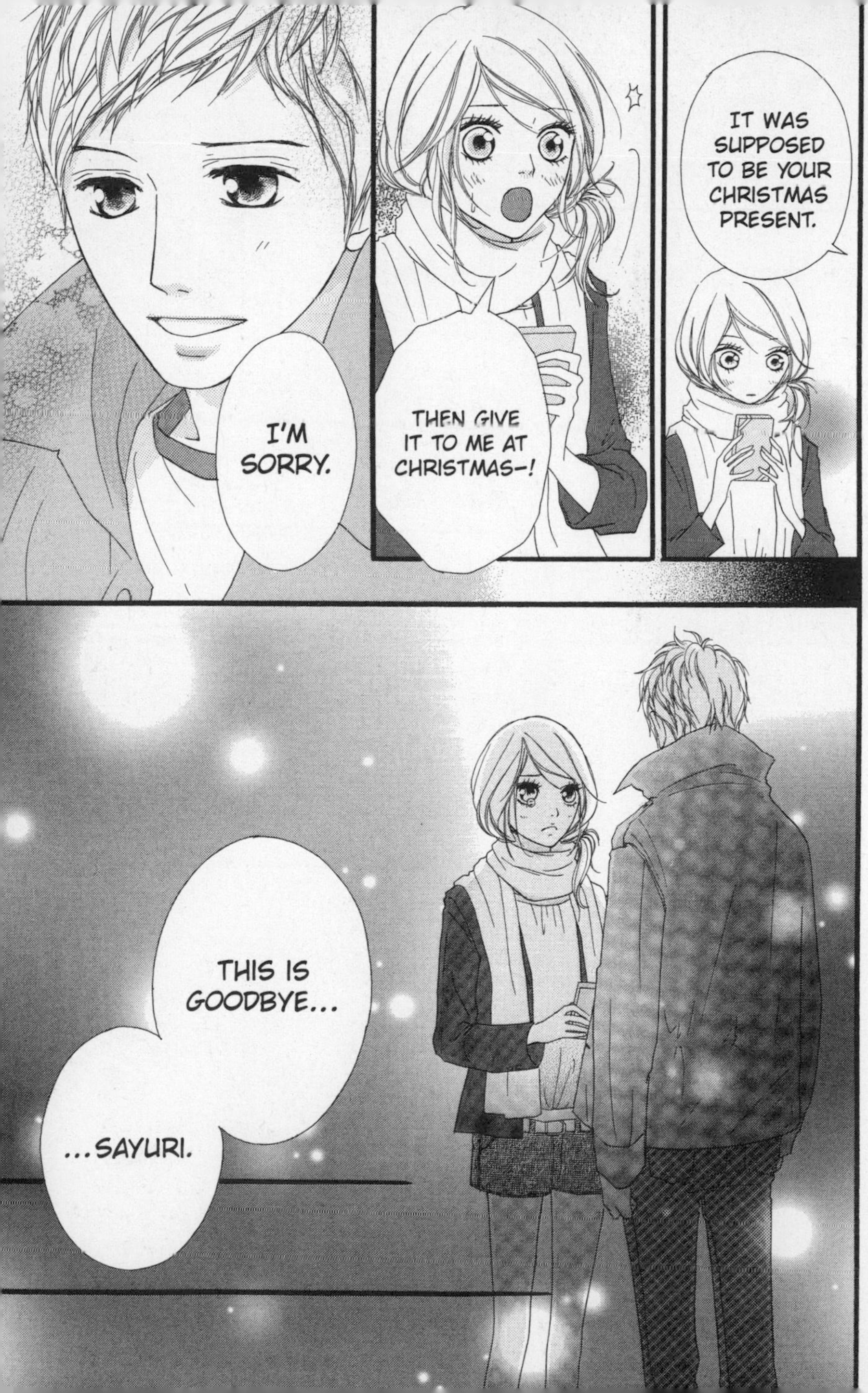
IT WAS SUPPOSED TO BE YOUR CHRISTMAS PRESENT.
THEN GIVE IT TO ME AT CHRISTMAS-!
I'M SORRY.
THIS IS GOODBYE...
...SAYURI.

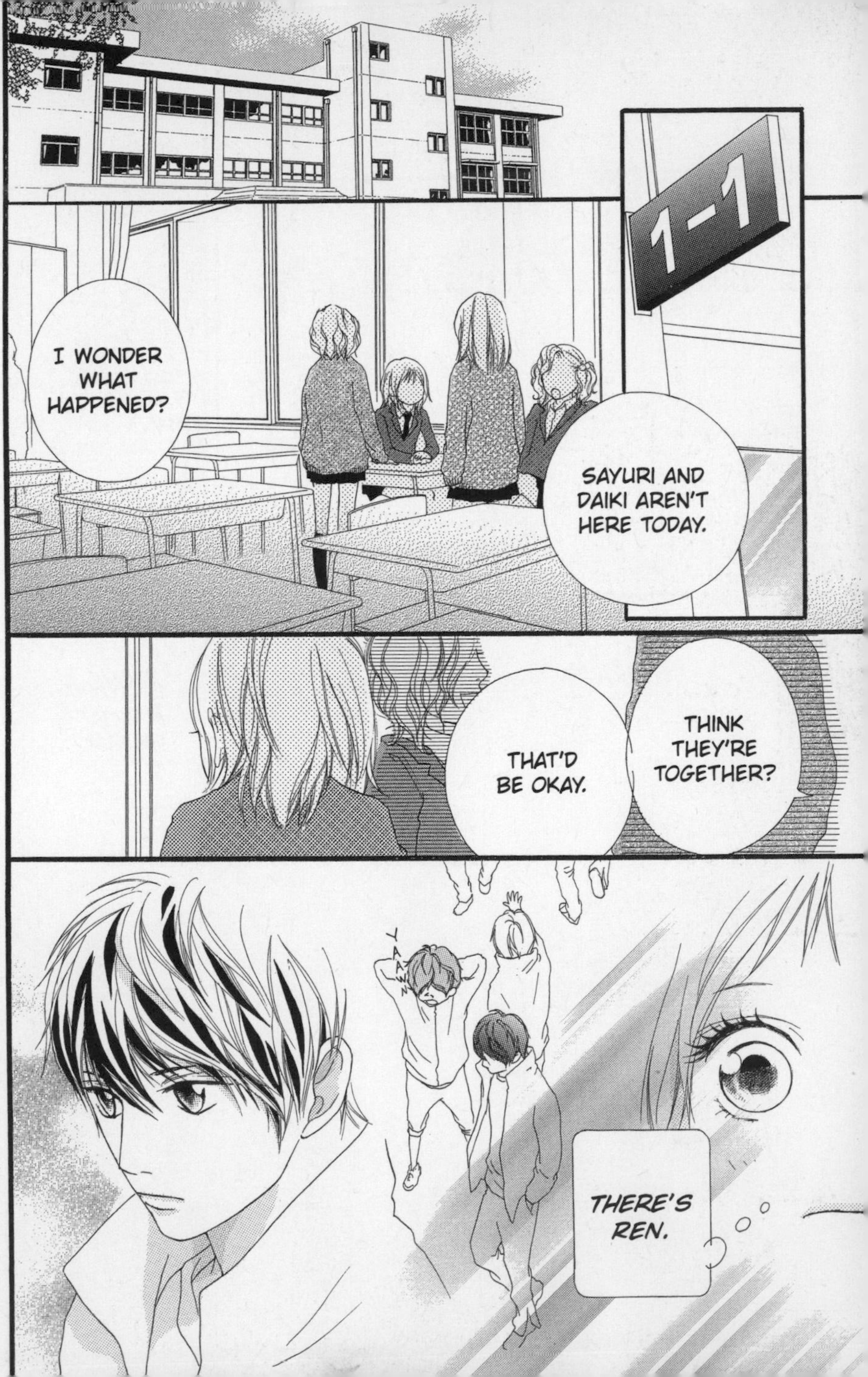
1-1
SAYURI AND DAIKI AREN'T HERE TODAY.
I WONDER WHAT HAPPENED?
THINK THEY'RE TOGETHER?
THAT'D BE OKAY.
THERE'S REN.
YAAAWN

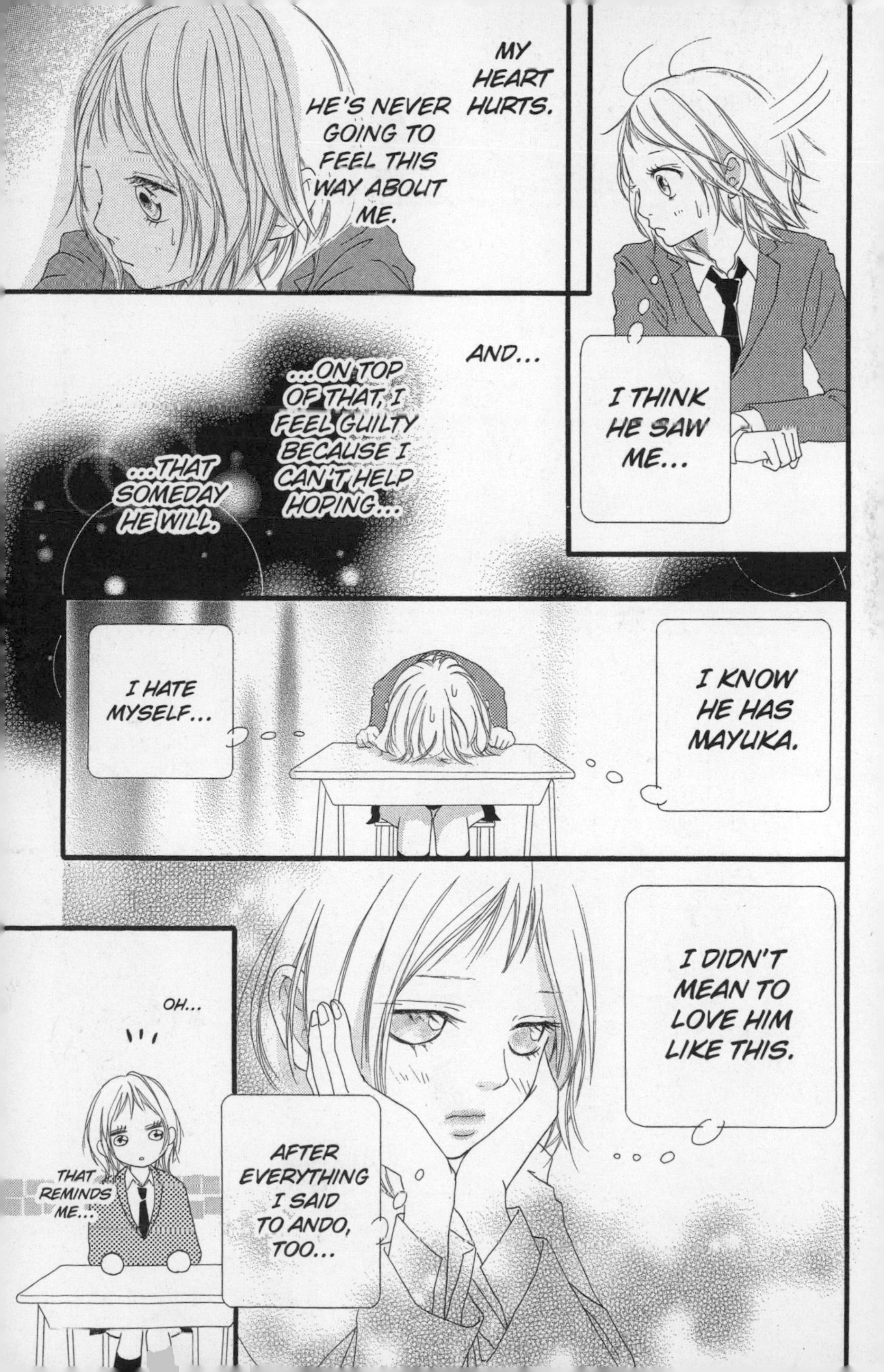
MY HEART HURTS.
HE'S NEVER GOING TO FEEL THIS WAY ABOUT ME.
I THINK HE SAW ME...
AND...
...ON TOP OF THAT, I FEEL GUILTY BECAUSE I CAN'T HELP HOPING...
...THAT SOMEDAY HE WILL.
I KNOW HE HAS MAYUKA.
I HATE MYSELF...
I DIDN'T MEAN TO LOVE HIM LIKE THIS.
AFTER EVERYTHING I SAID TO ANDO, TOO...
OH...
THAT REMINDS ME...

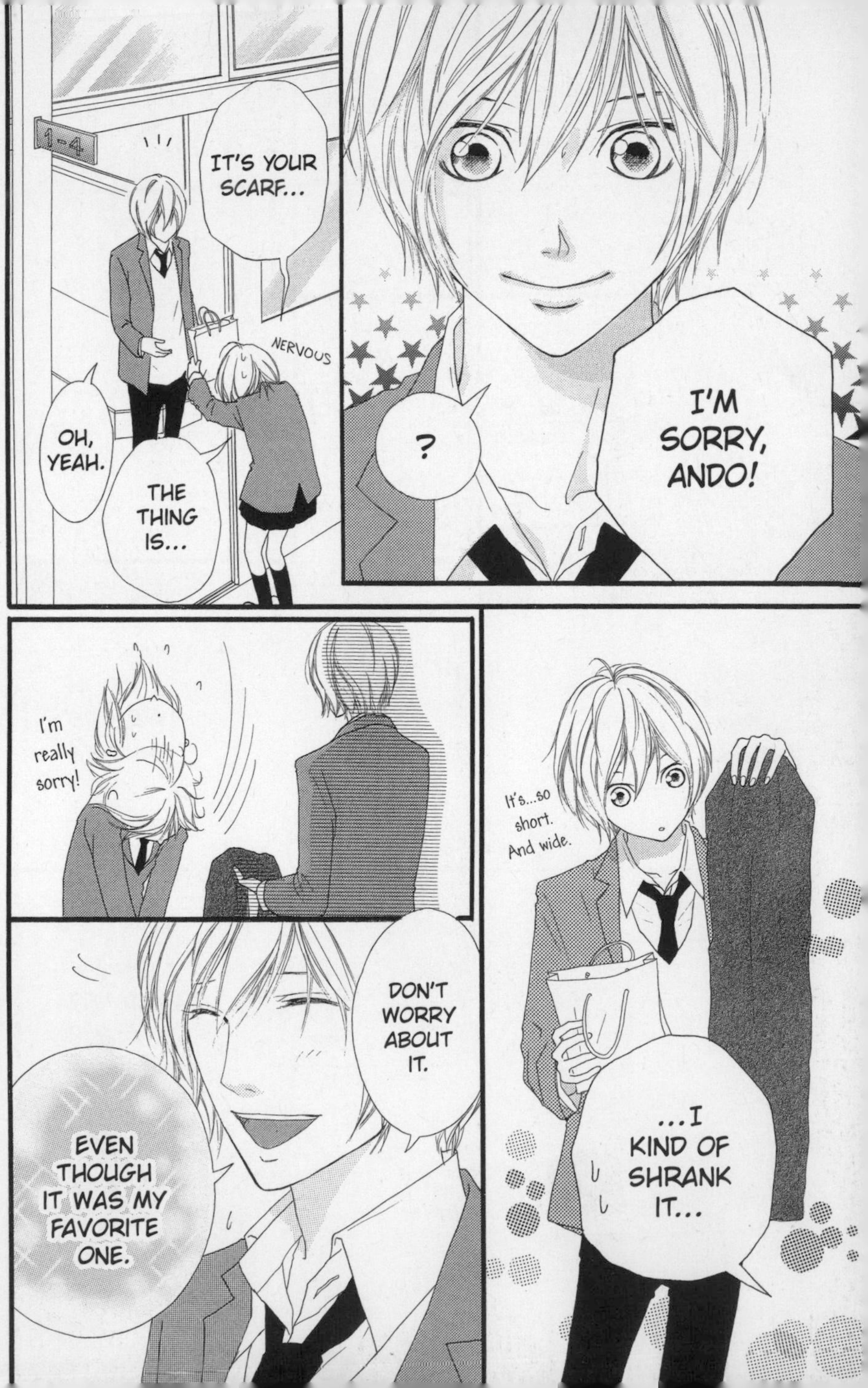
I'M SORRY, ANDO!
?
IT'S YOUR SCARF...
NERVOUS
OH, YEAH.
THE THING IS...
It's...so short. And wide.
...I KIND OF SHRANK IT...
I'm really sorry!
DON'T WORRY ABOUT IT.
EVEN THOUGH IT WAS MY FAVORITE ONE.

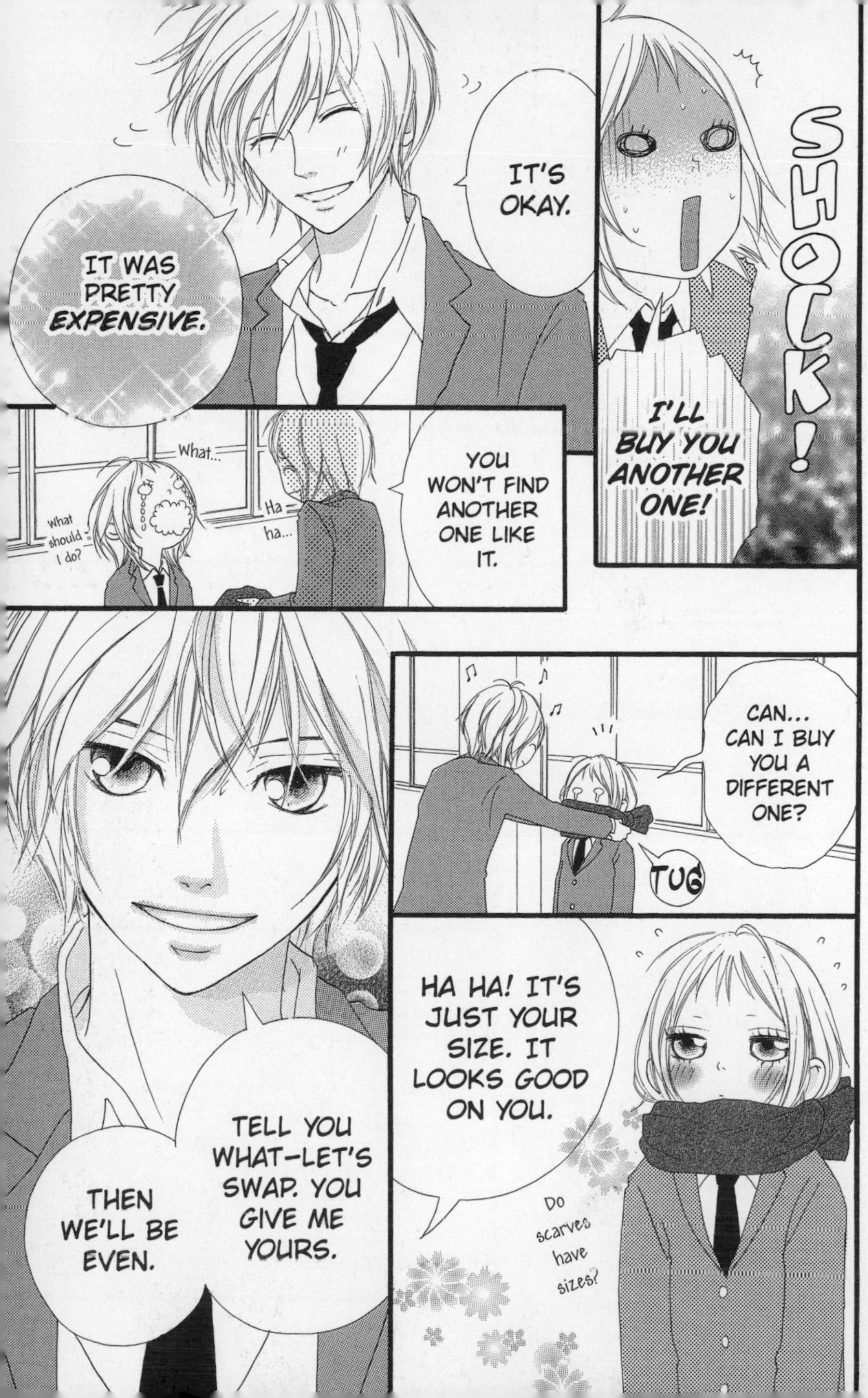
SHOCK!
I'LL BUY YOU ANOTHER ONE!
IT'S OKAY.
IT WAS PRETTY EXPENSIVE.
YOU WON'T FIND ANOTHER ONE LIKE IT.
Ha ha...
What...
What should I do?
CAN... CAN I BUY YOU A DIFFERENT ONE?
TUG
HA HA! IT'S JUST YOUR SIZE. IT LOOKS GOOD ON YOU.
Do scarves have sizes?
TELL YOU WHAT—LET'S SWAP. YOU GIVE ME YOURS.
THEN WE'LL BE EVEN.

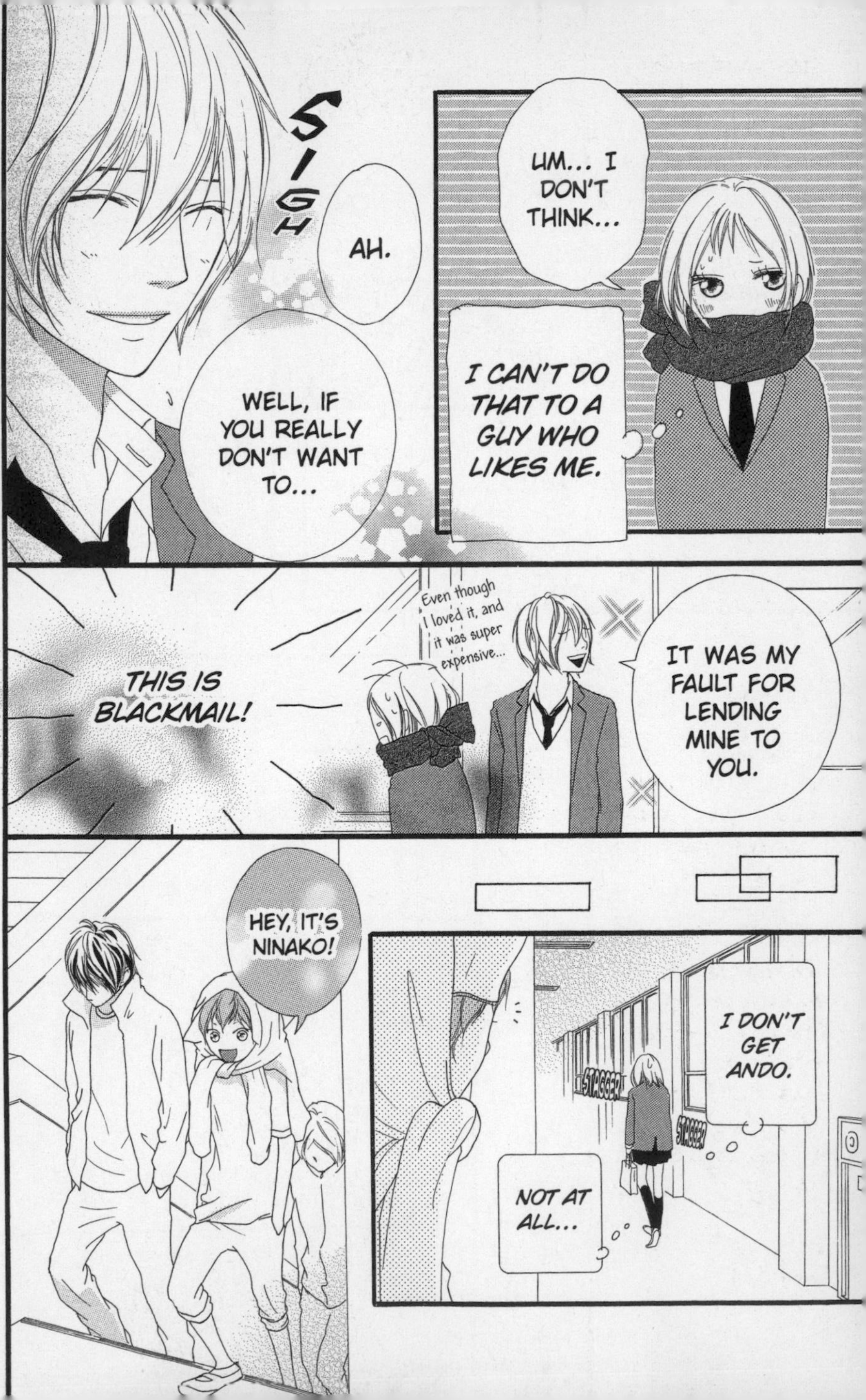
UM... I DON'T THINK...
I CAN'T DO THAT TO A GUY WHO LIKES ME.
SIGH
AH.
WELL, IF YOU REALLY DON'T WANT TO...
IT WAS MY FAULT FOR LENDING MINE TO YOU.
Even though I loved it, and it was super expensive...
THIS IS BLACKMAIL!
I DON'T GET ANDO.
STAGGER
STAGGER
NOT AT ALL...
HEY, IT'S NINAKO!

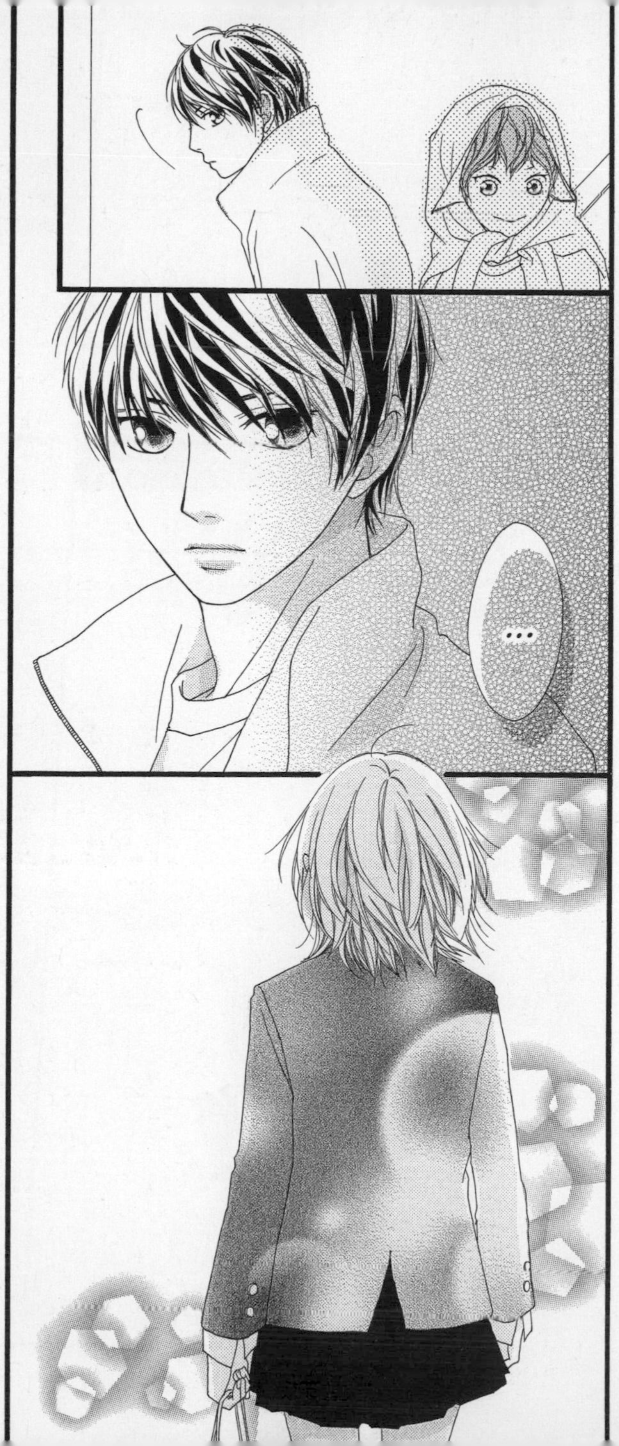
...

There's a coffee shop I use for meetings, but the drinks there are huge. A cup of coffee is easily three times bigger than normal. But that's nothing compared to the cups of juice! They're served in enormous glasses that look like vases, or maybe even fishbowls. Huge!

Their pancakes are funny too. I ordered them once, and they came to the table looking like this:

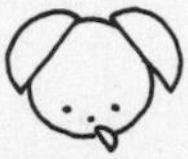

Tired doggie

I think the eyes were raisins and the tongue was a tangerine segment. The ears were pancakes cut in half.

What? What is this? I'm not a kid anymore... but I admit I was a little excited, and I had to laugh. I'm sure the server laughed while putting the pancake dog together. I know I would have!

By the way, the doggie was delicious...

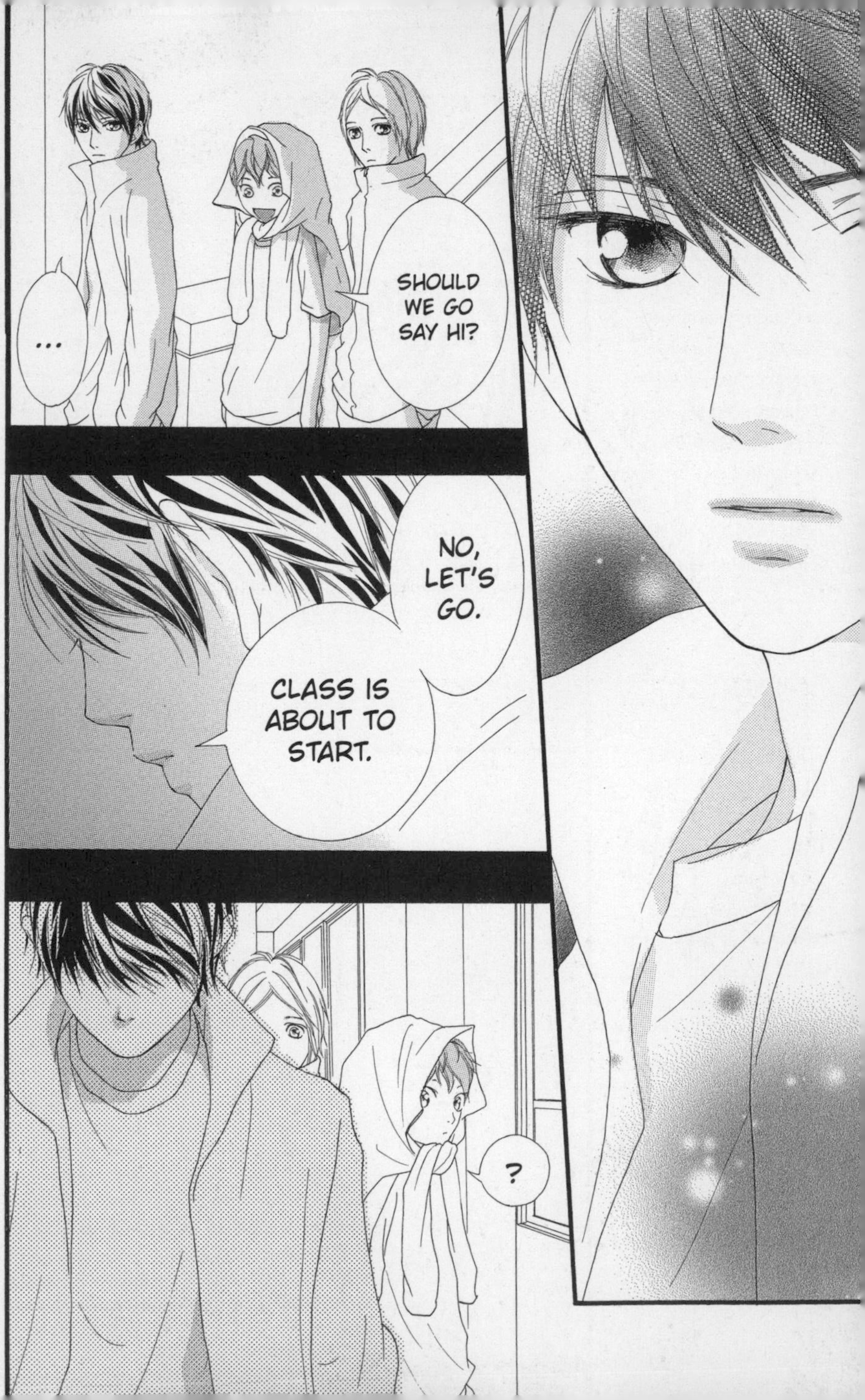
SHOULD WE GO SAY HI?
...
NO, LET'S GO.
CLASS IS ABOUT TO START.
?

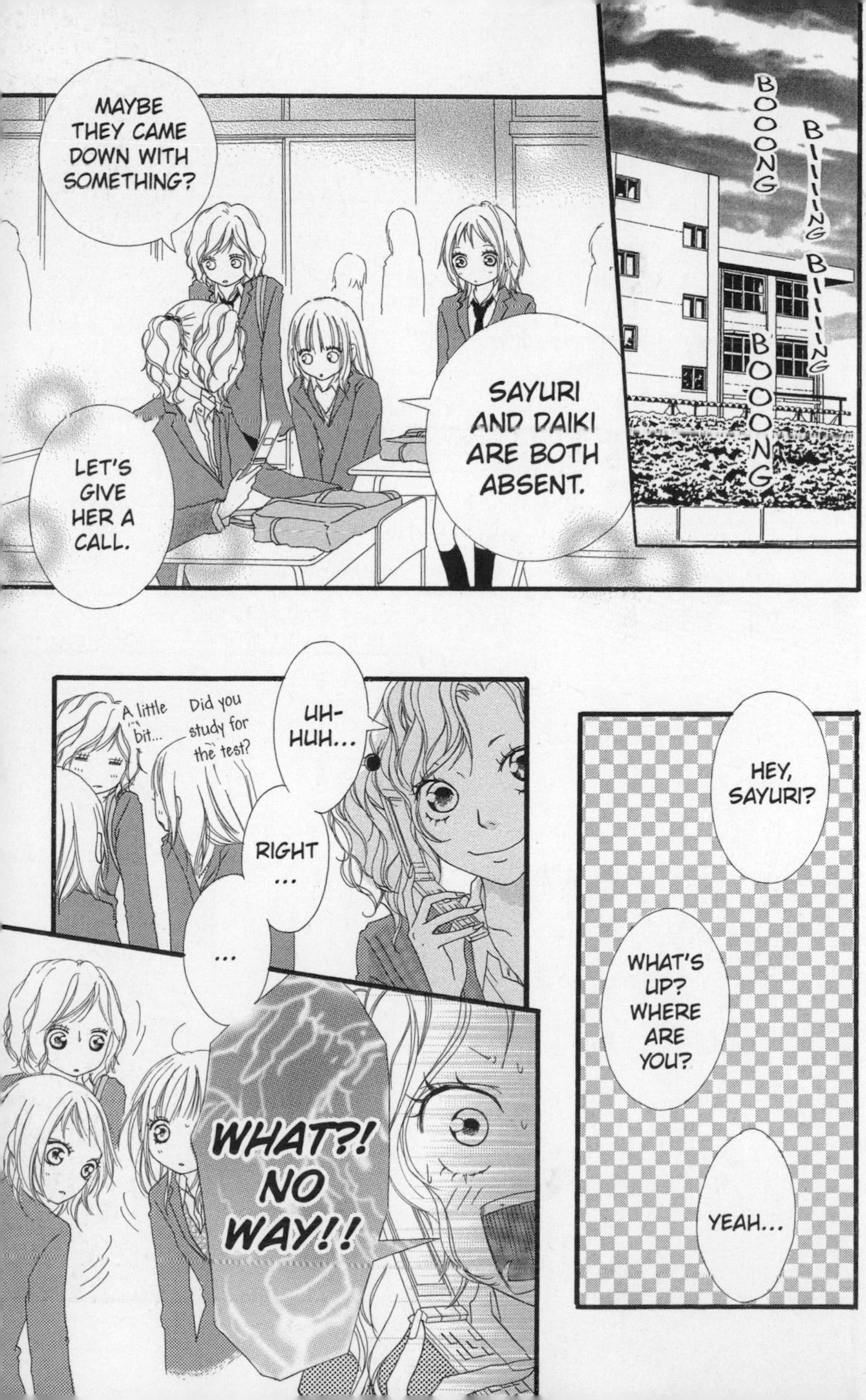
BOOONG
BIIIING
BIIIING
BOOONG
SAYURI AND DAIKI ARE BOTH ABSENT.
MAYBE THEY CAME DOWN WITH SOMETHING?
LET'S GIVE HER A CALL.
HEY, SAYURI?
WHAT'S UP? WHERE ARE YOU?
YEAH...
UH-HUH...
Did you study for the test?
A little bit...
RIGHT ...
...
WHAT?! NO WAY!!

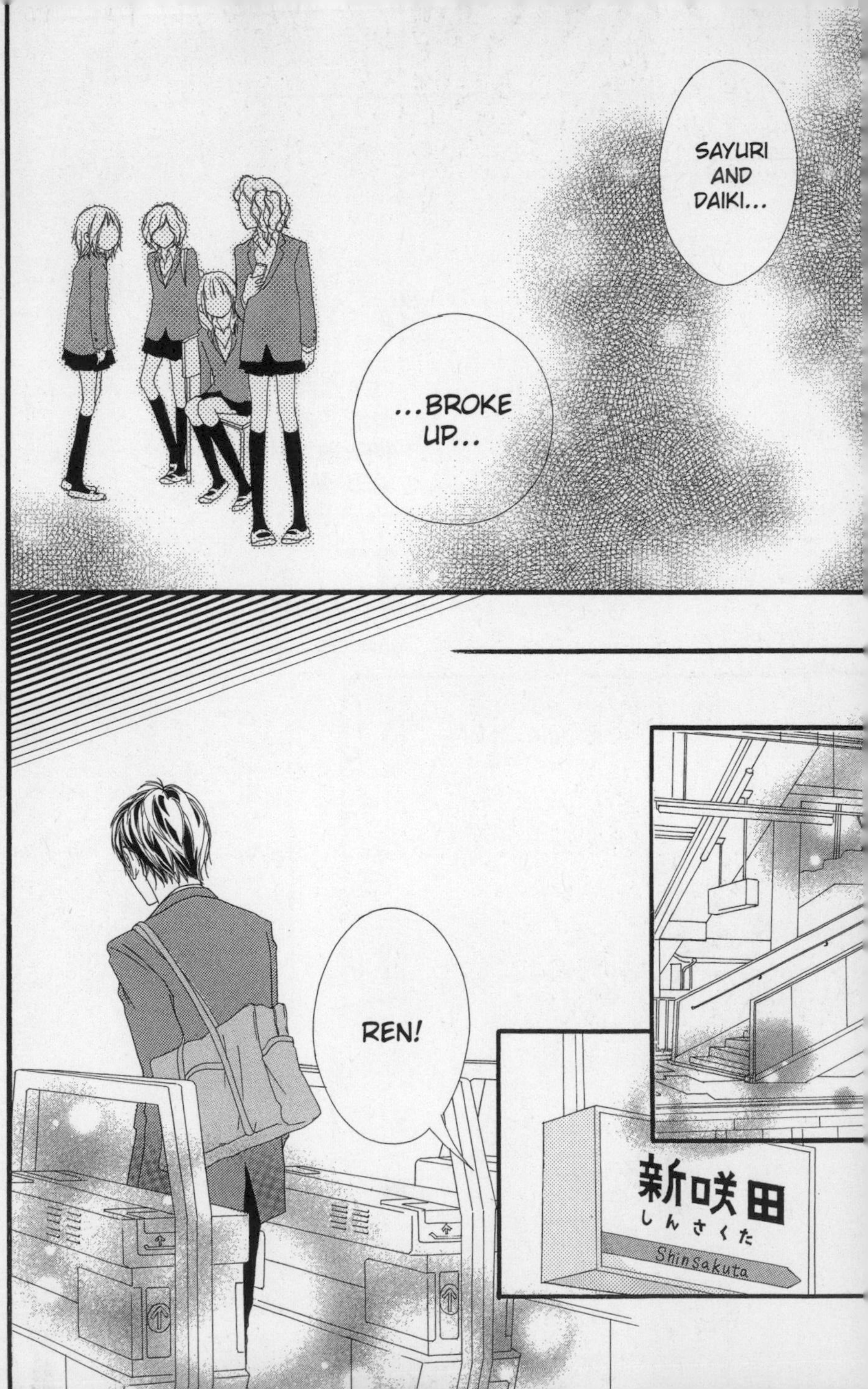
SAYURI AND DAIKI...
...BROKE UP...
新咲田
しんさくた
Shinsakuta
REN!

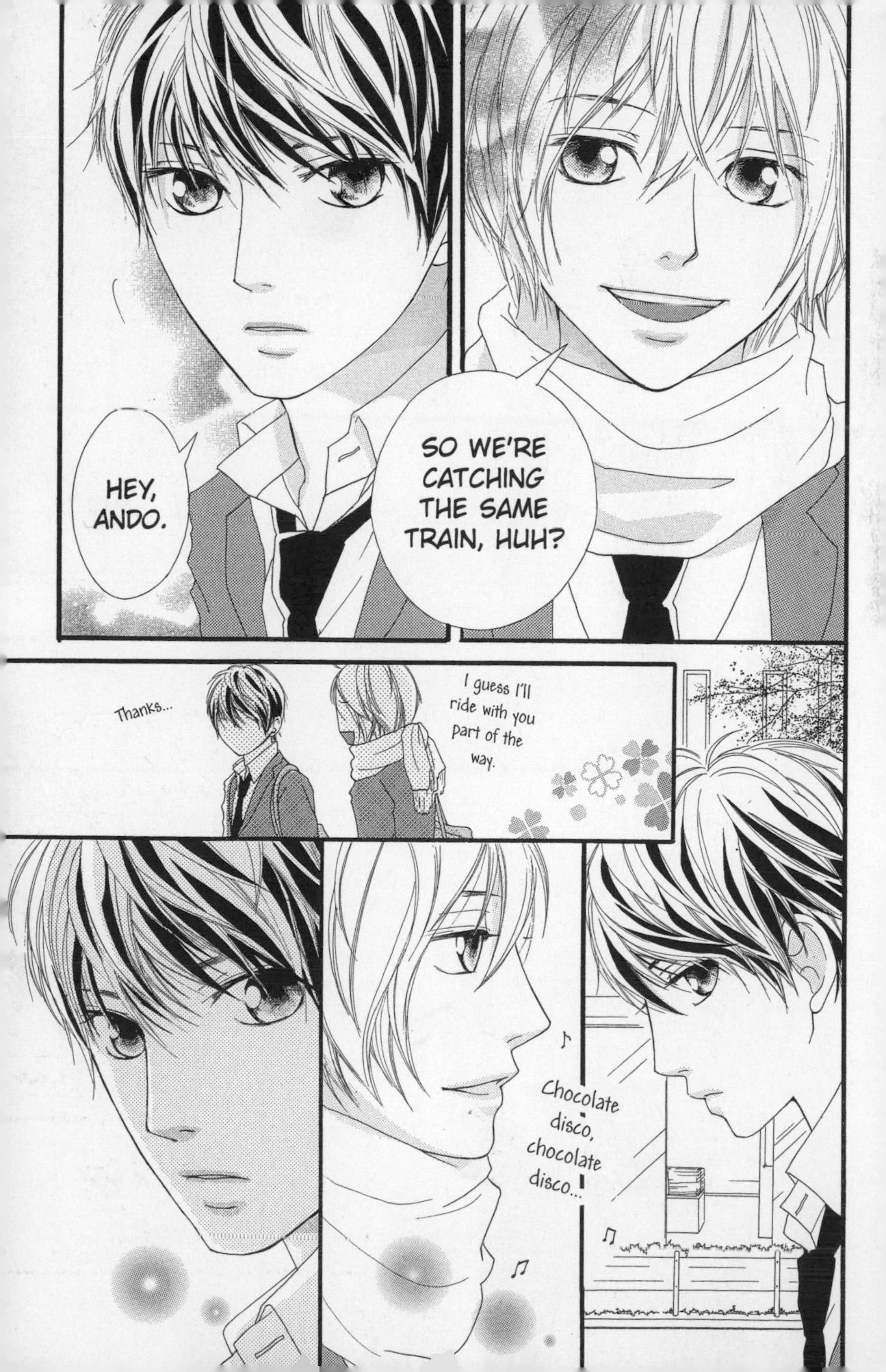
SO WE'RE CATCHING THE SAME TRAIN, HUH?
HEY, ANDO.
I guess I'll ride with you part of the way.
Thanks...
Chocolate disco, chocolate disco...

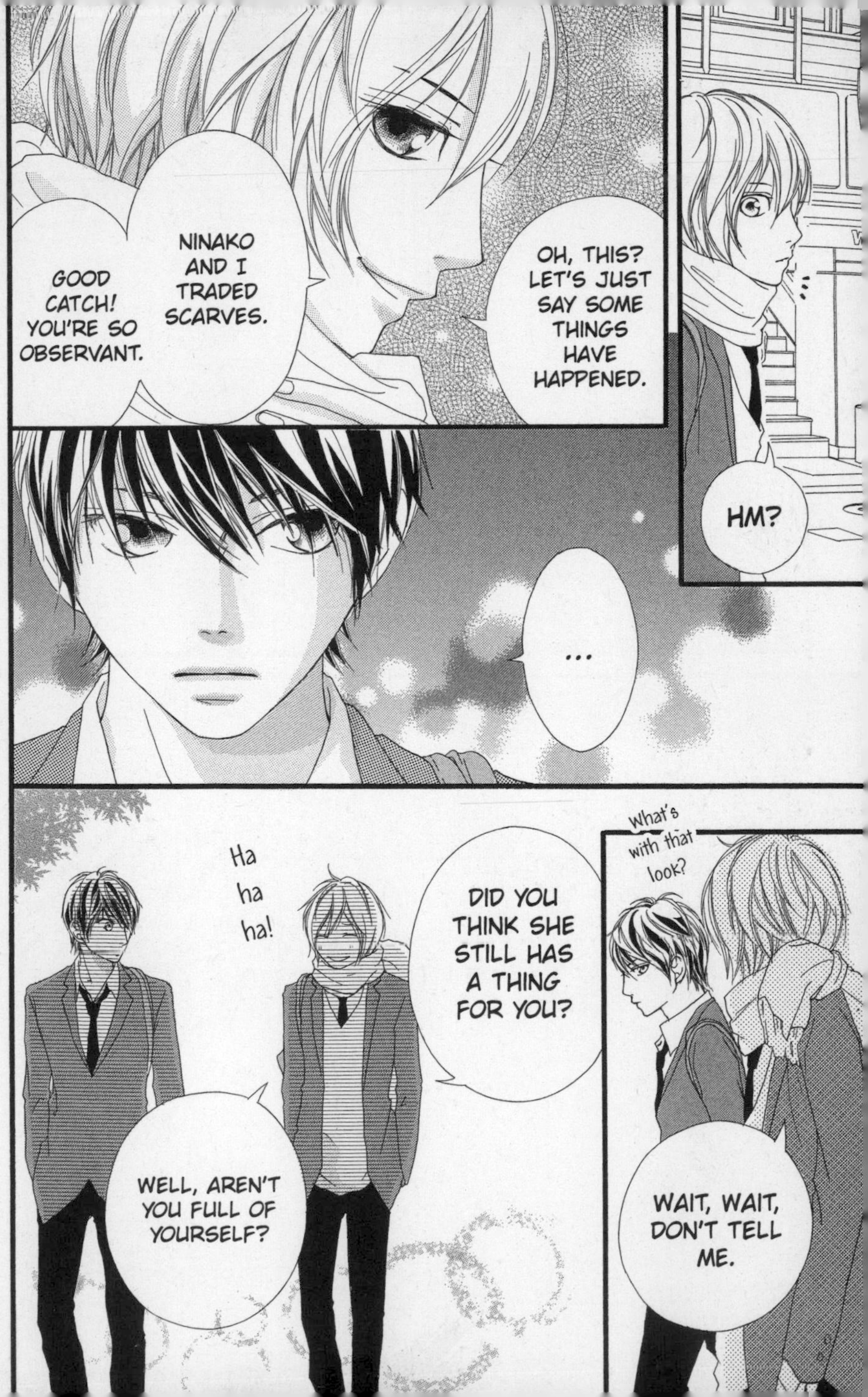
HM?
OH, THIS? LET'S JUST SAY SOME THINGS HAVE HAPPENED.
NINAKO AND I TRADED SCARVES.
GOOD CATCH! YOU'RE SO OBSERVANT.
...
What's with that look?
WAIT, WAIT, DON'T TELL ME.
DID YOU THINK SHE STILL HAS A THING FOR YOU?
Ha ha ha!
WELL, AREN'T YOU FULL OF YOURSELF?

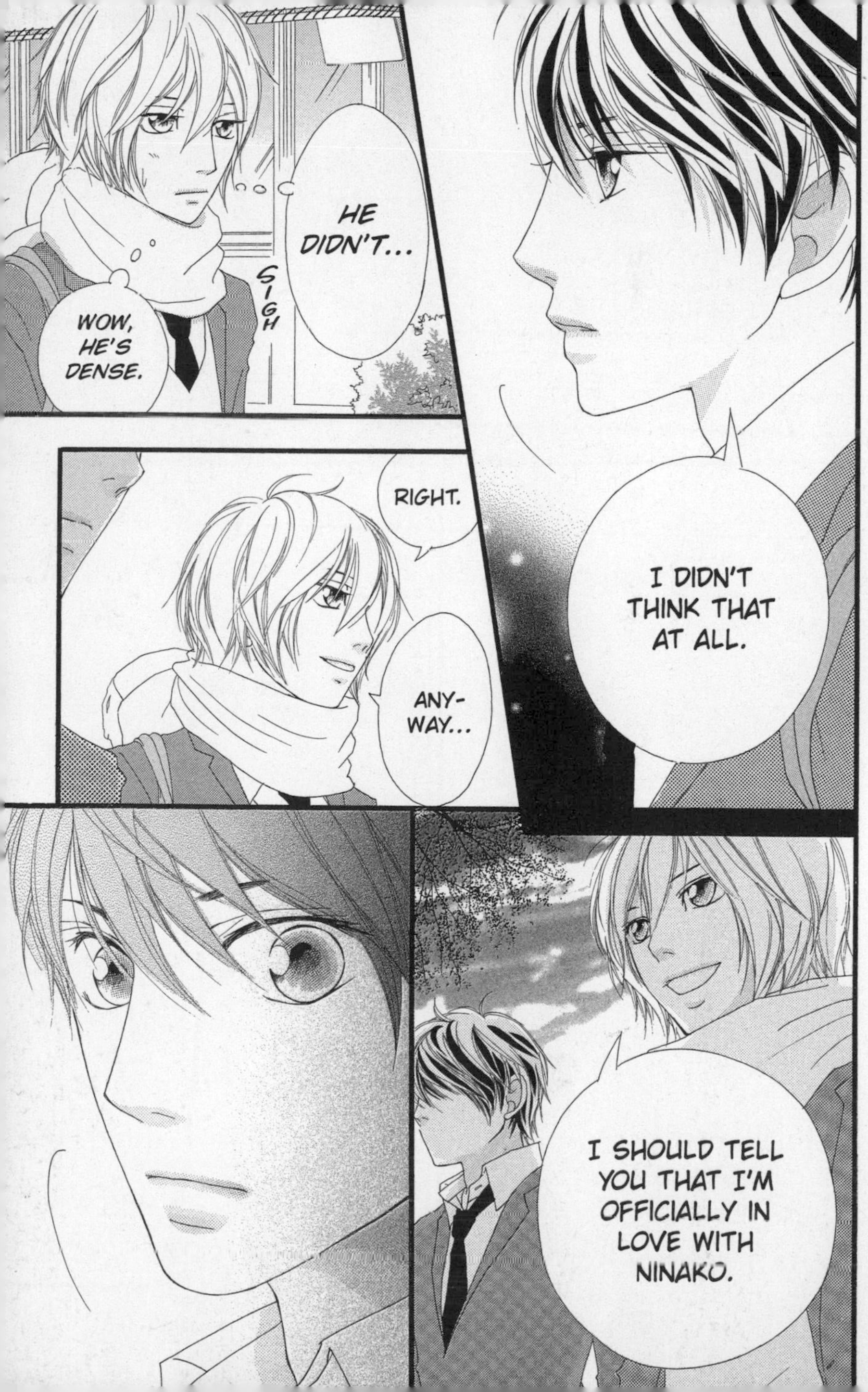
I DIDN'T THINK THAT AT ALL.
HE DIDN'T...
SIGH
WOW, HE'S DENSE.
RIGHT.
ANY-WAY...
I SHOULD TELL YOU THAT I'M OFFICIALLY IN LOVE WITH NINAKO.

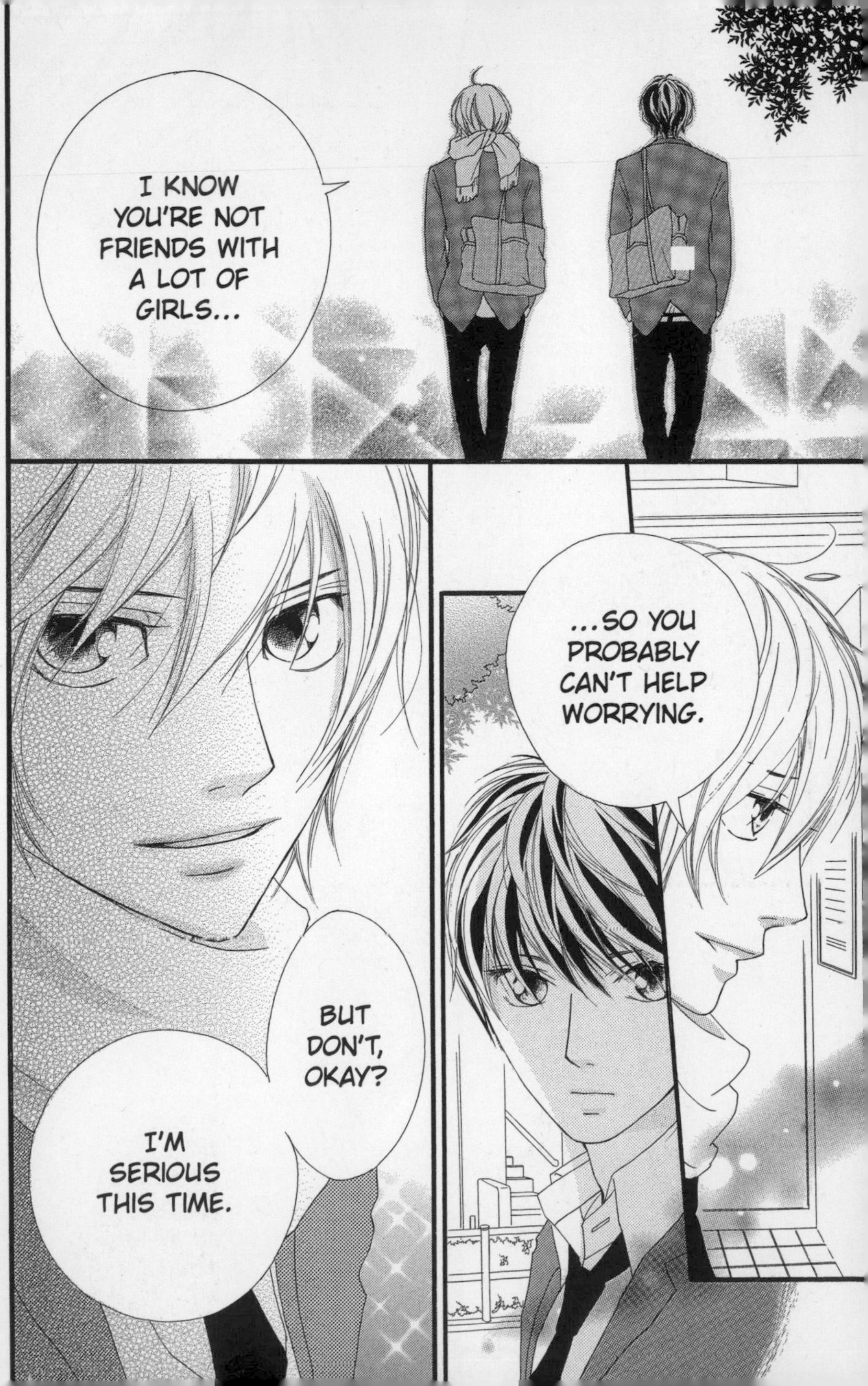
I KNOW YOU'RE NOT FRIENDS WITH A LOT OF GIRLS...
...SO YOU PROBABLY CAN'T HELP WORRYING.
BUT DON'T, OKAY?
I'M SERIOUS THIS TIME.

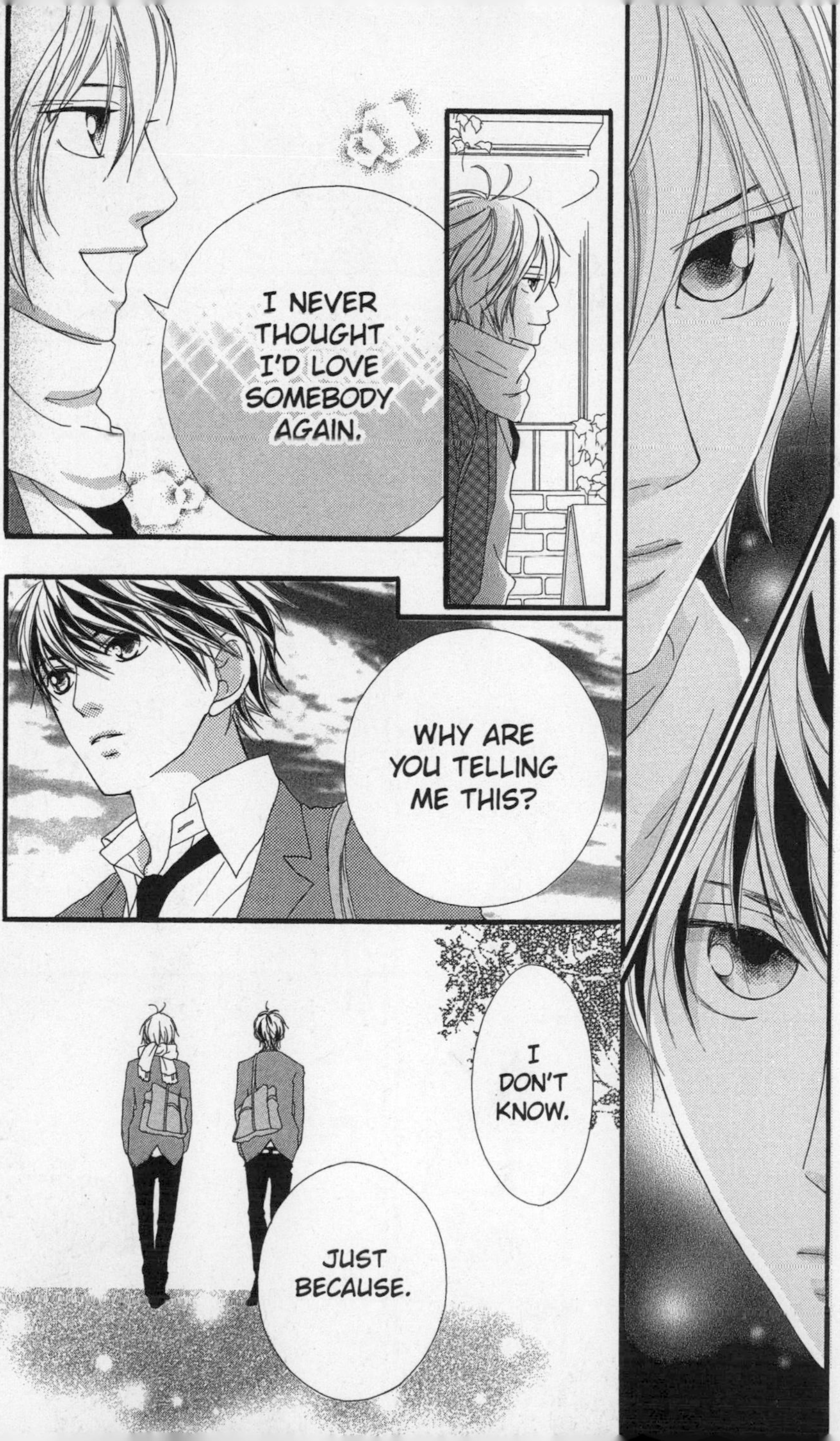
I NEVER THOUGHT I'D LOVE SOMEBODY AGAIN.
WHY ARE YOU TELLING ME THIS?
I DON'T KNOW.
JUST BECAUSE.

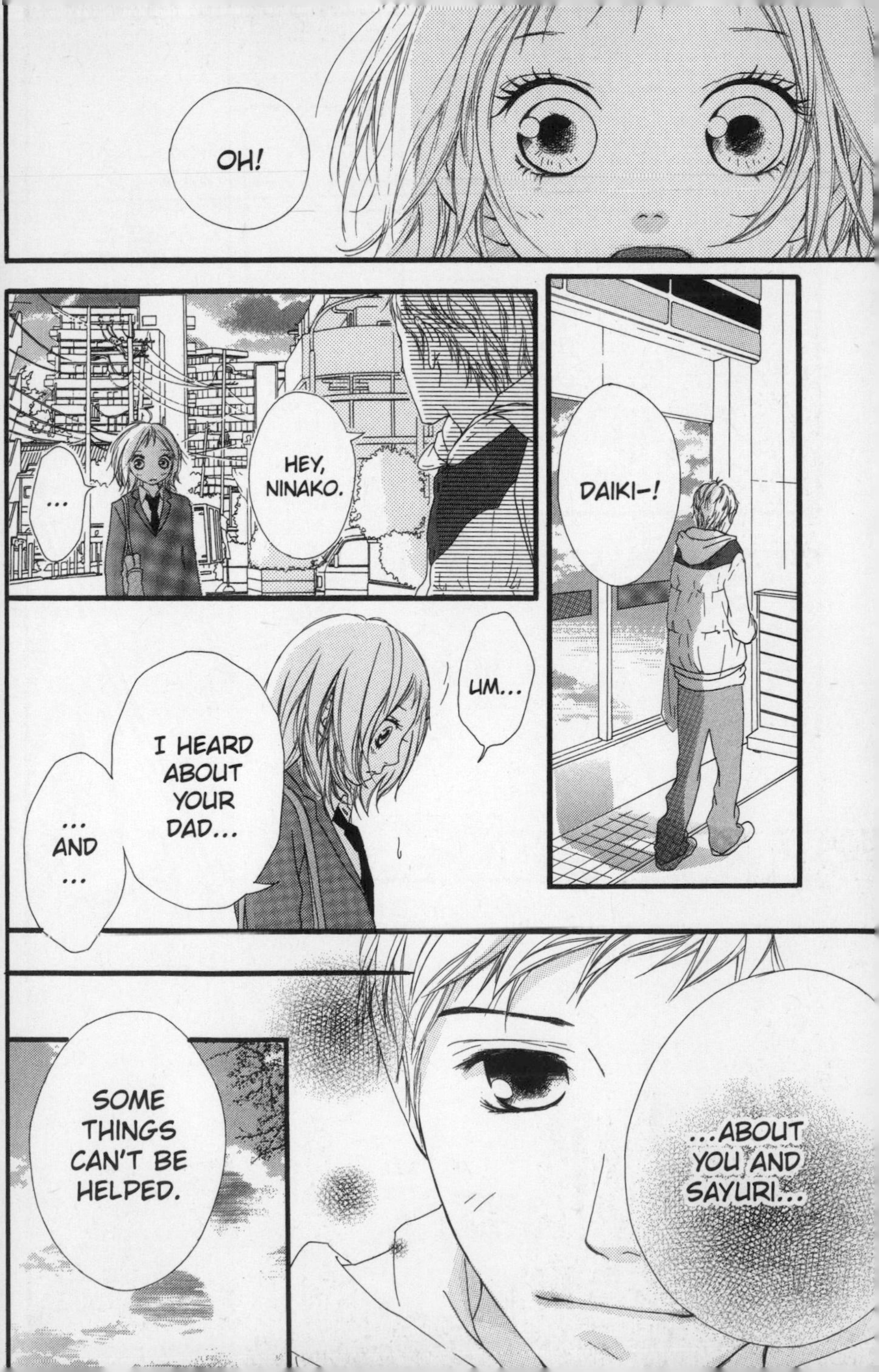
OH!
DAIKI-!
HEY, NINAKO.
...
UM...
I HEARD ABOUT YOUR DAD...
... AND ...
...ABOUT YOU AND SAYURI...
SOME THINGS CAN'T BE HELPED.

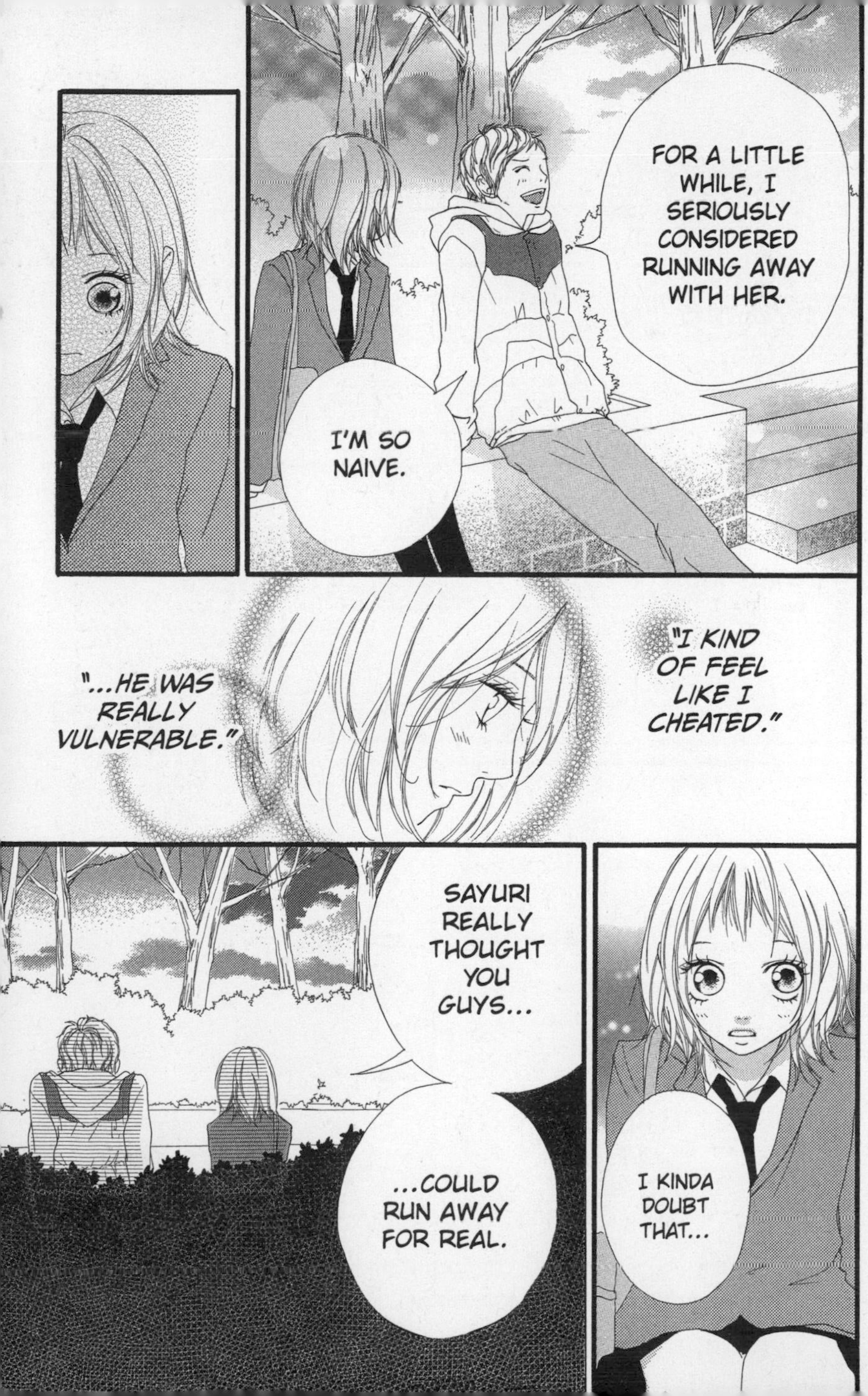
FOR A LITTLE WHILE, I SERIOUSLY CONSIDERED RUNNING AWAY WITH HER.
I'M SO NAIVE.
"I KIND OF FEEL LIKE I CHEATED."
"...HE WAS REALLY VULNERABLE."
I KINDA DOUBT THAT...
SAYURI REALLY THOUGHT YOU GUYS...
...COULD RUN AWAY FOR REAL.

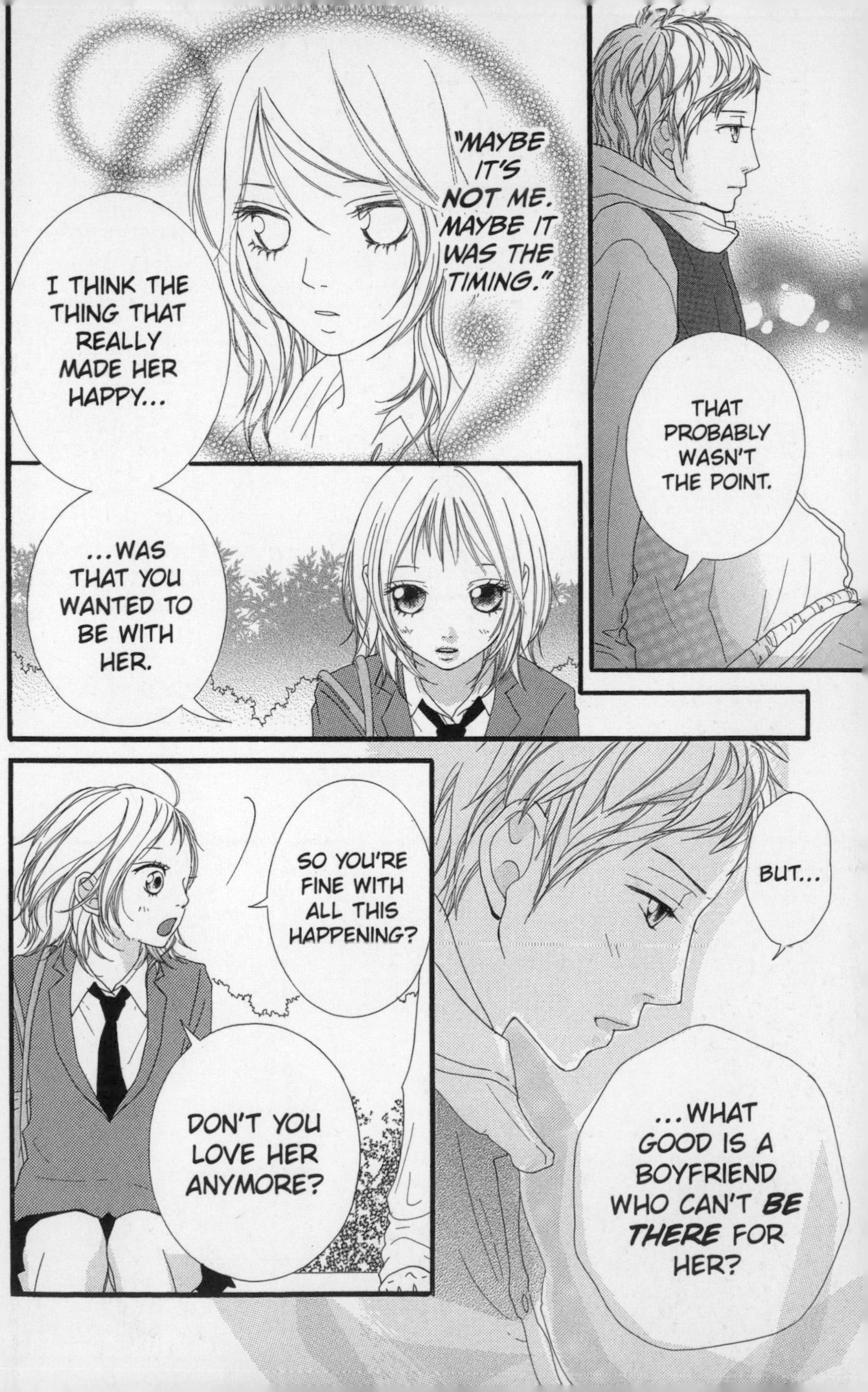
THAT PROBABLY WASN'T THE POINT.
"MAYBE IT'S NOT ME. MAYBE IT WAS THE TIMING."
I THINK THE THING THAT REALLY MADE HER HAPPY...
...WAS THAT YOU WANTED TO BE WITH HER.
BUT...
...WHAT GOOD IS A BOYFRIEND WHO CAN'T ***BE THERE*** FOR HER?
SO YOU'RE FINE WITH ALL THIS HAPPENING?
DON'T YOU LOVE HER ANYMORE?

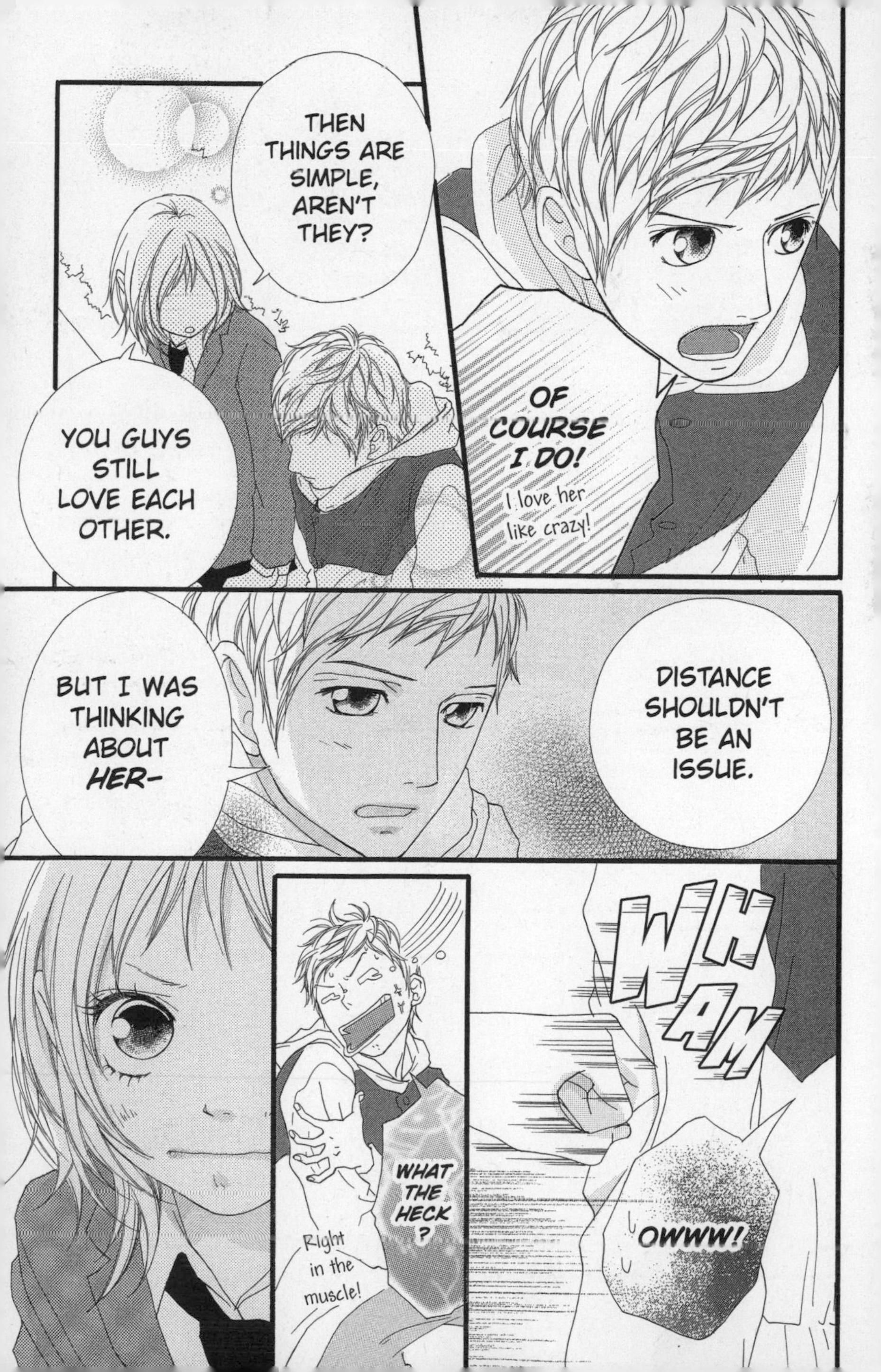
OF COURSE I DO!
I love her like crazy!
THEN THINGS ARE SIMPLE, AREN'T THEY?
YOU GUYS STILL LOVE EACH OTHER.
DISTANCE SHOULDN'T BE AN ISSUE.
BUT I WAS THINKING ABOUT HER-
WHAM
OWWW!
WHAT THE HECK?
Right in the muscle!

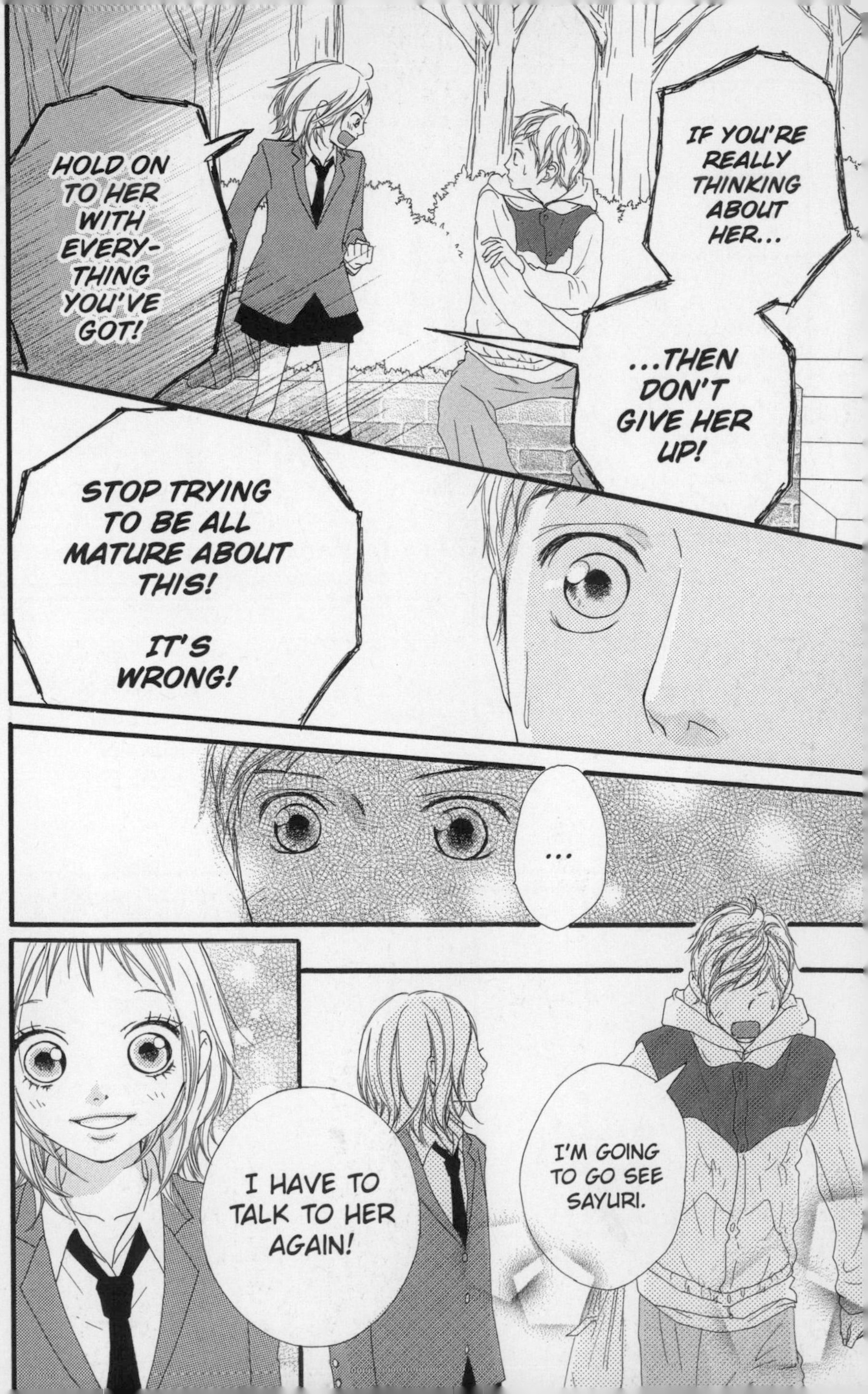
IF YOU'RE REALLY THINKING ABOUT HER...
...THEN DON'T GIVE HER UP!
HOLD ON TO HER WITH EVERY-THING YOU'VE GOT!
STOP TRYING TO BE ALL MATURE ABOUT THIS!
IT'S WRONG!
...
I'M GOING TO GO SEE SAYURI.
I HAVE TO TALK TO HER AGAIN!

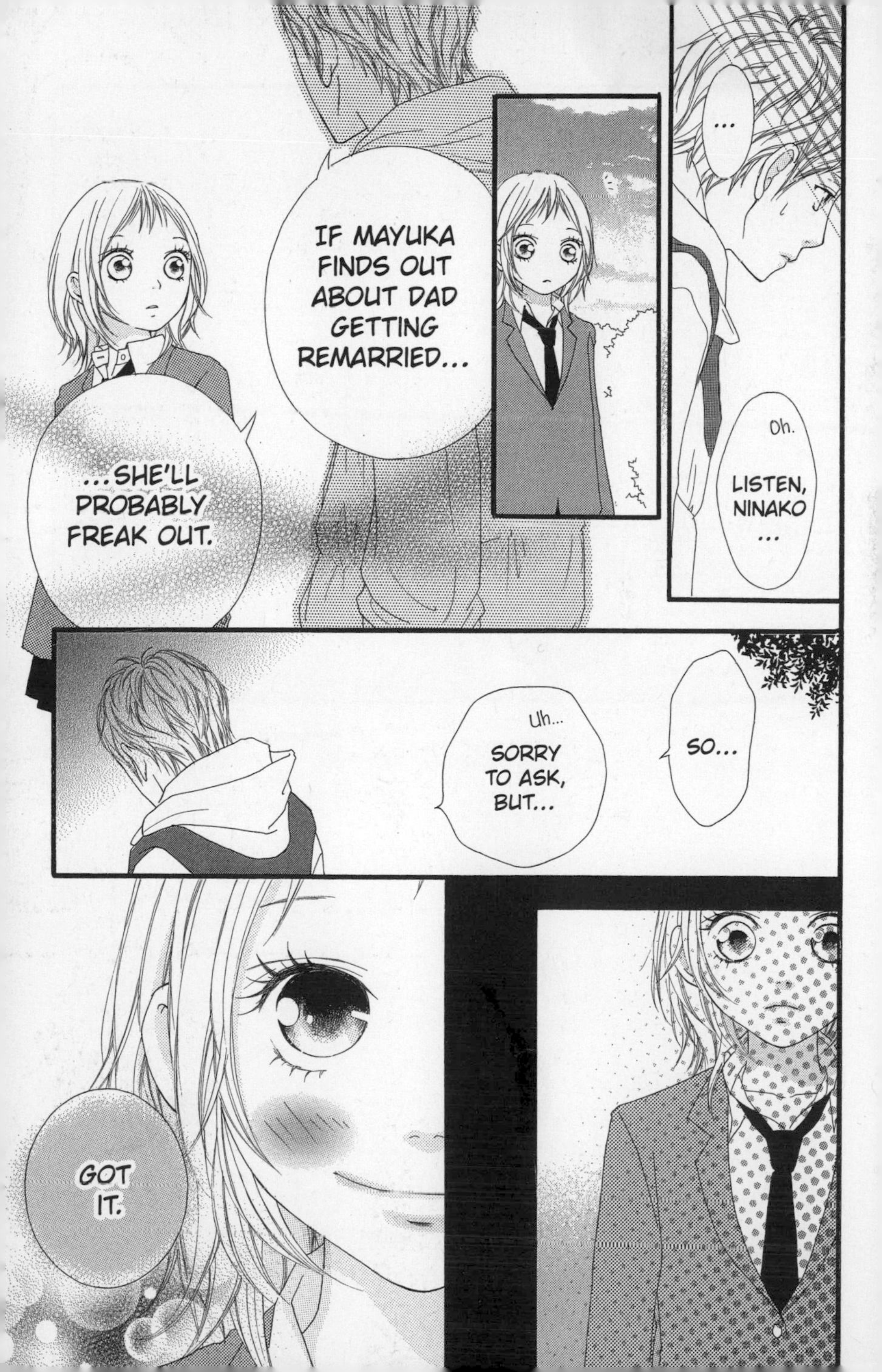
...
Oh.
LISTEN, NINAKO ...
IF MAYUKA FINDS OUT ABOUT DAD GETTING REMARRIED...
...SHE'LL PROBABLY FREAK OUT.
SO...
Uh...
SORRY TO ASK, BUT...
GOT IT.

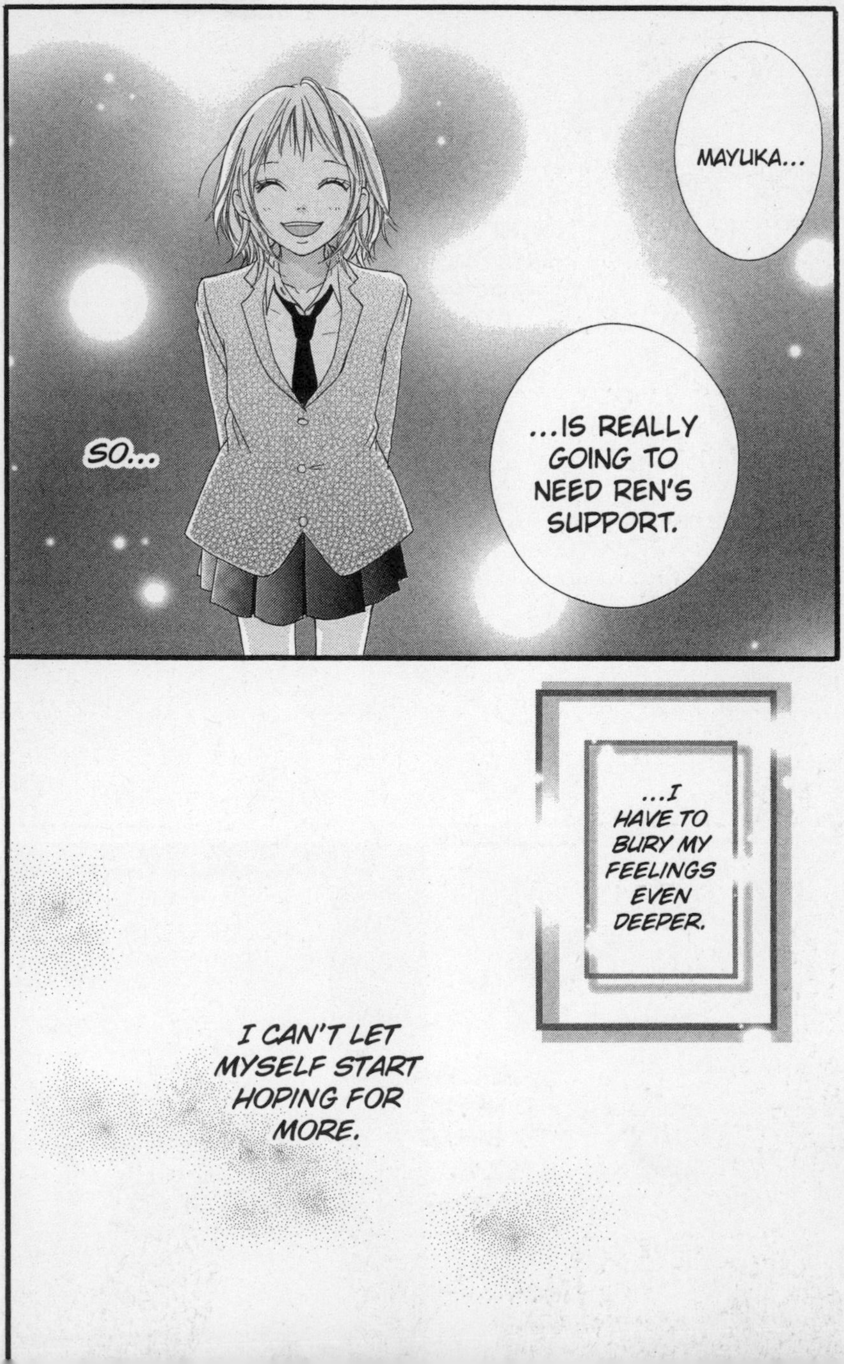
MAYUKA...
...IS REALLY GOING TO NEED REN'S SUPPORT.
SO...
...I HAVE TO BURY MY FEELINGS EVEN DEEPER.
I CAN'T LET MYSELF START HOPING FOR MORE.

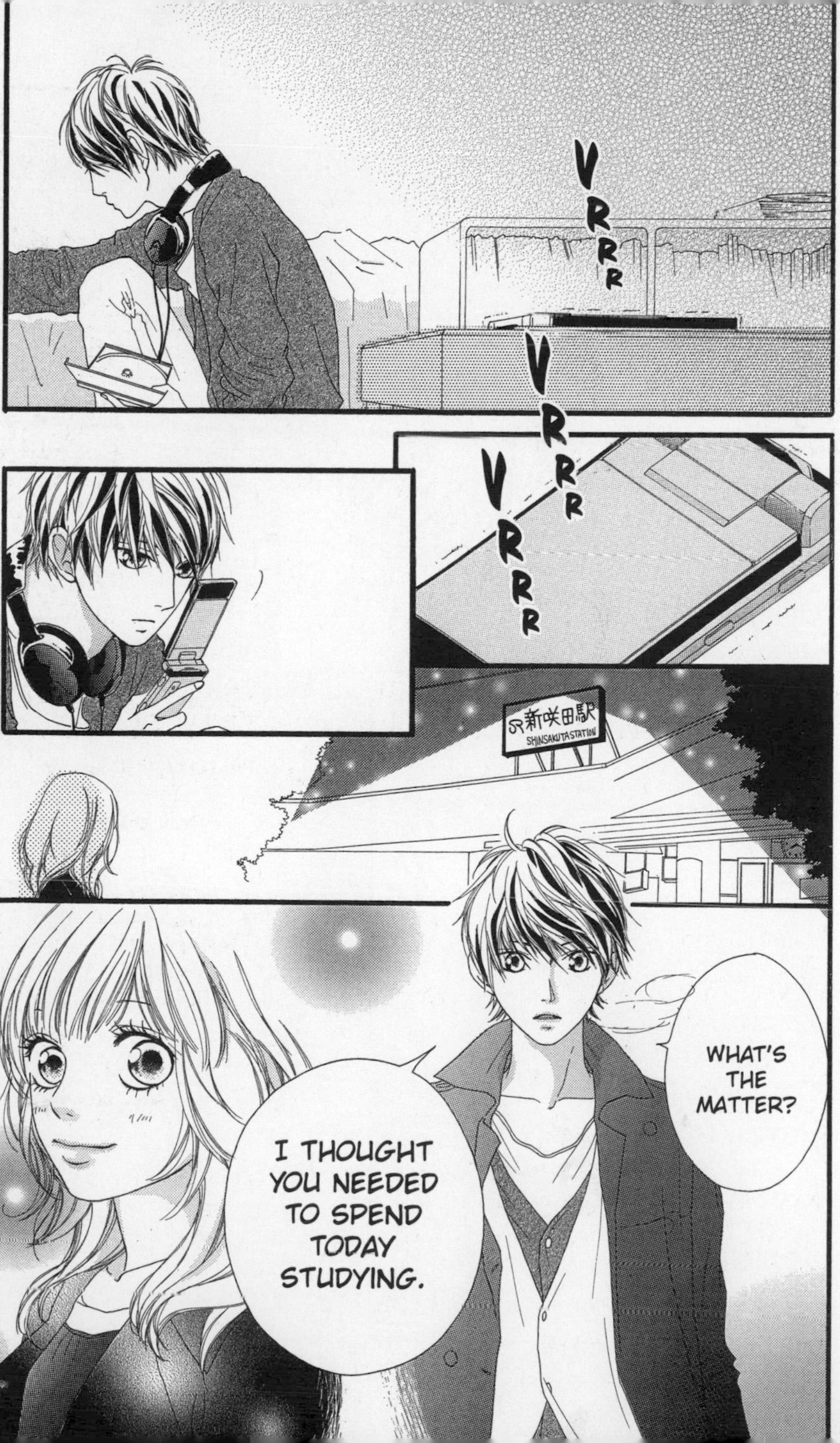
VRRR
VRRR
VRRR
新咲田駅
SHINSAKUTA STATION
WHAT'S THE MATTER?
I THOUGHT YOU NEEDED TO SPEND TODAY STUDYING.

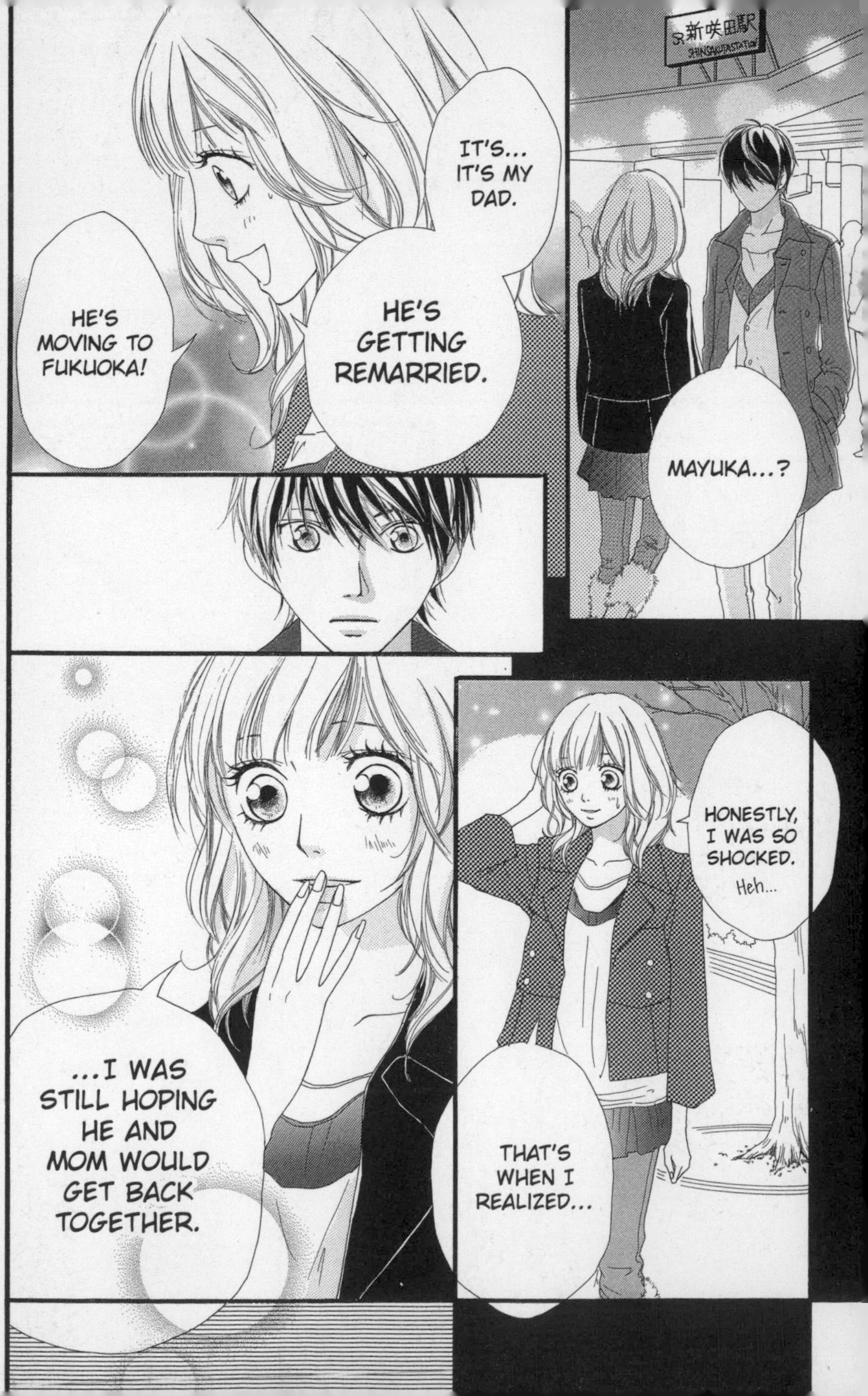
新咲田駅
MAYUKA...?
IT'S... IT'S MY DAD.
HE'S GETTING REMARRIED.
HE'S MOVING TO FUKUOKA!
HONESTLY, I WAS SO SHOCKED.
Heh...
THAT'S WHEN I REALIZED...
...I WAS STILL HOPING HE AND MOM WOULD GET BACK TOGETHER.

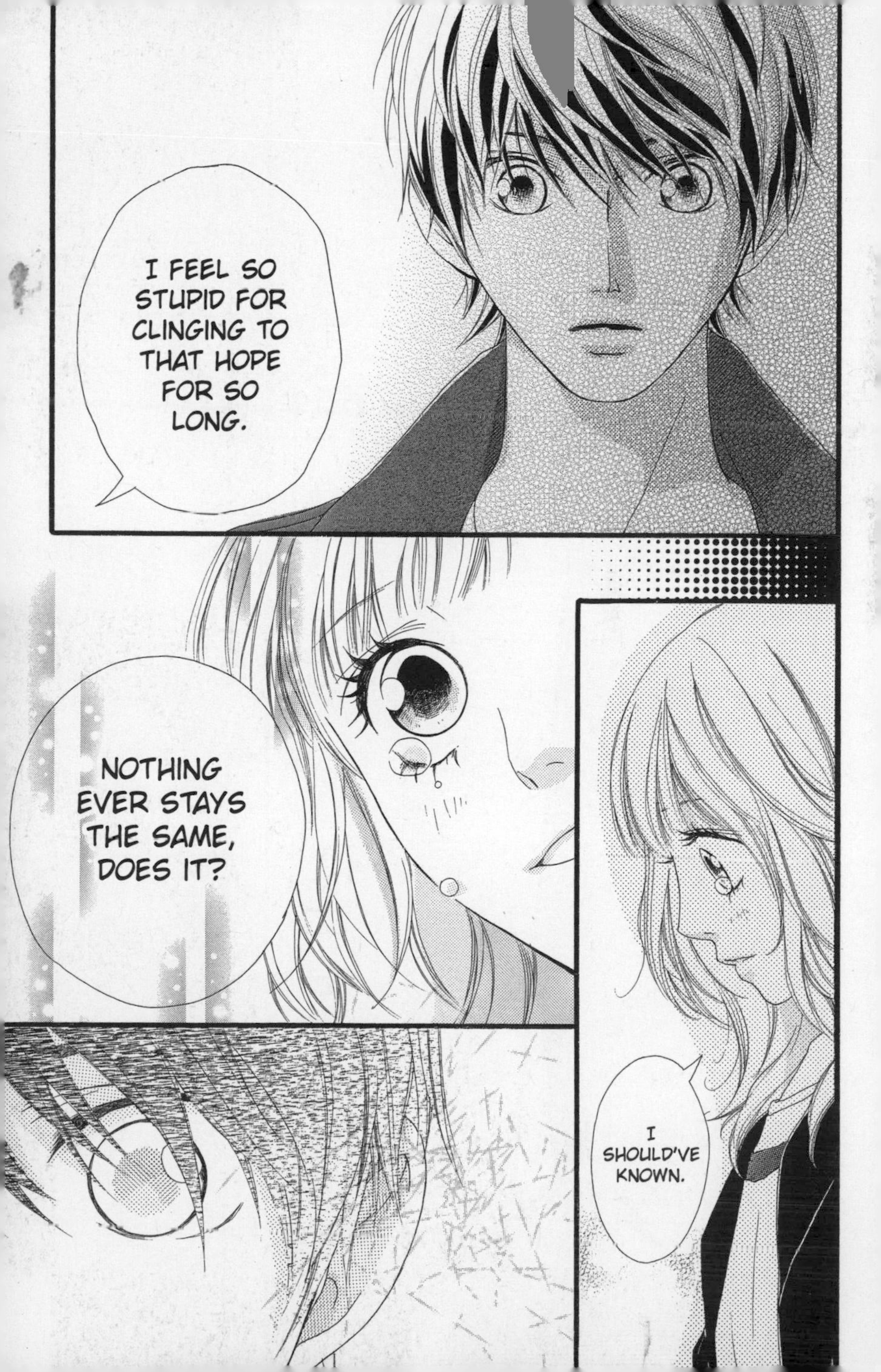
I FEEL SO STUPID FOR CLINGING TO THAT HOPE FOR SO LONG.
I SHOULD'VE KNOWN.
NOTHING EVER STAYS THE SAME, DOES IT?

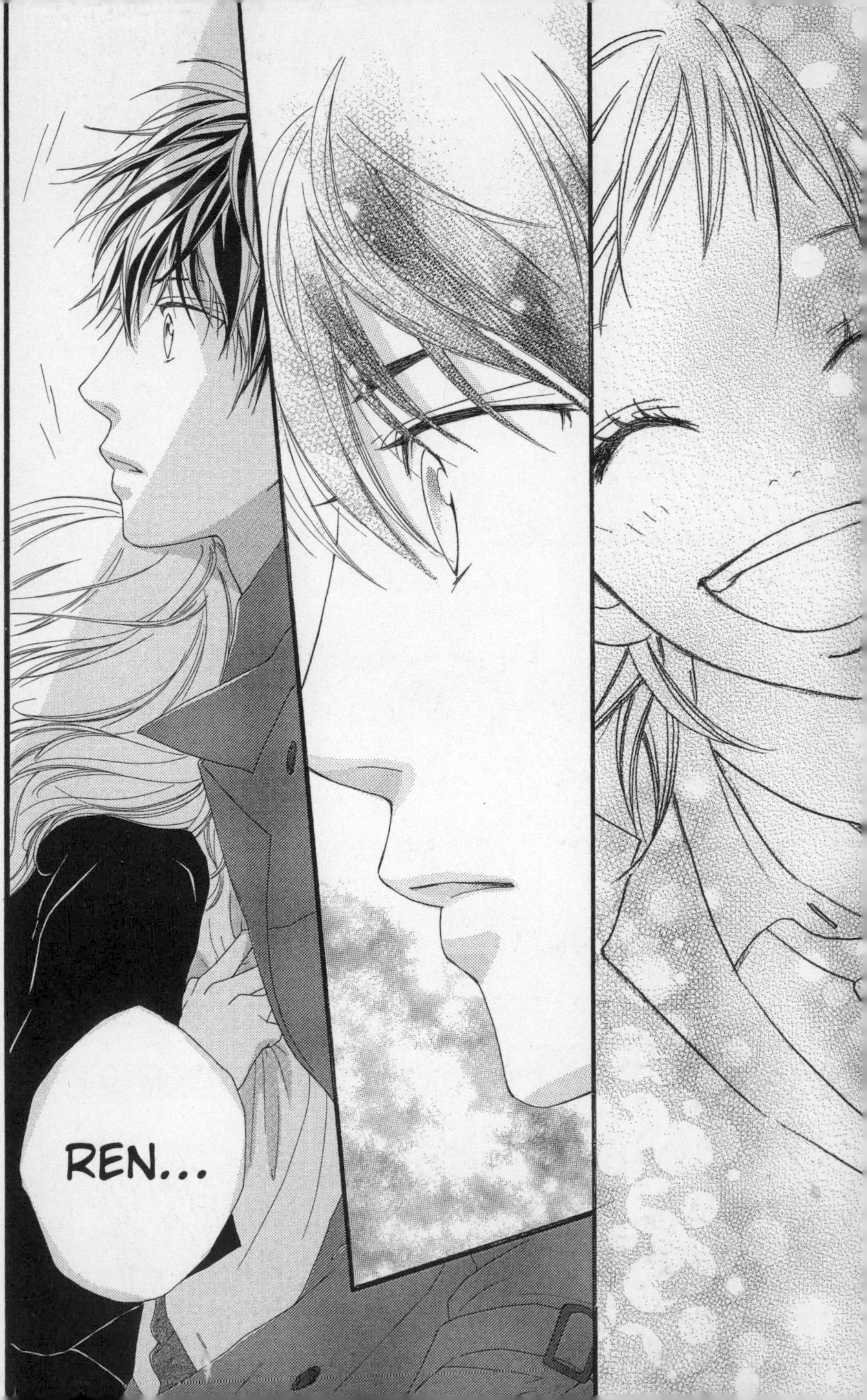
REN...

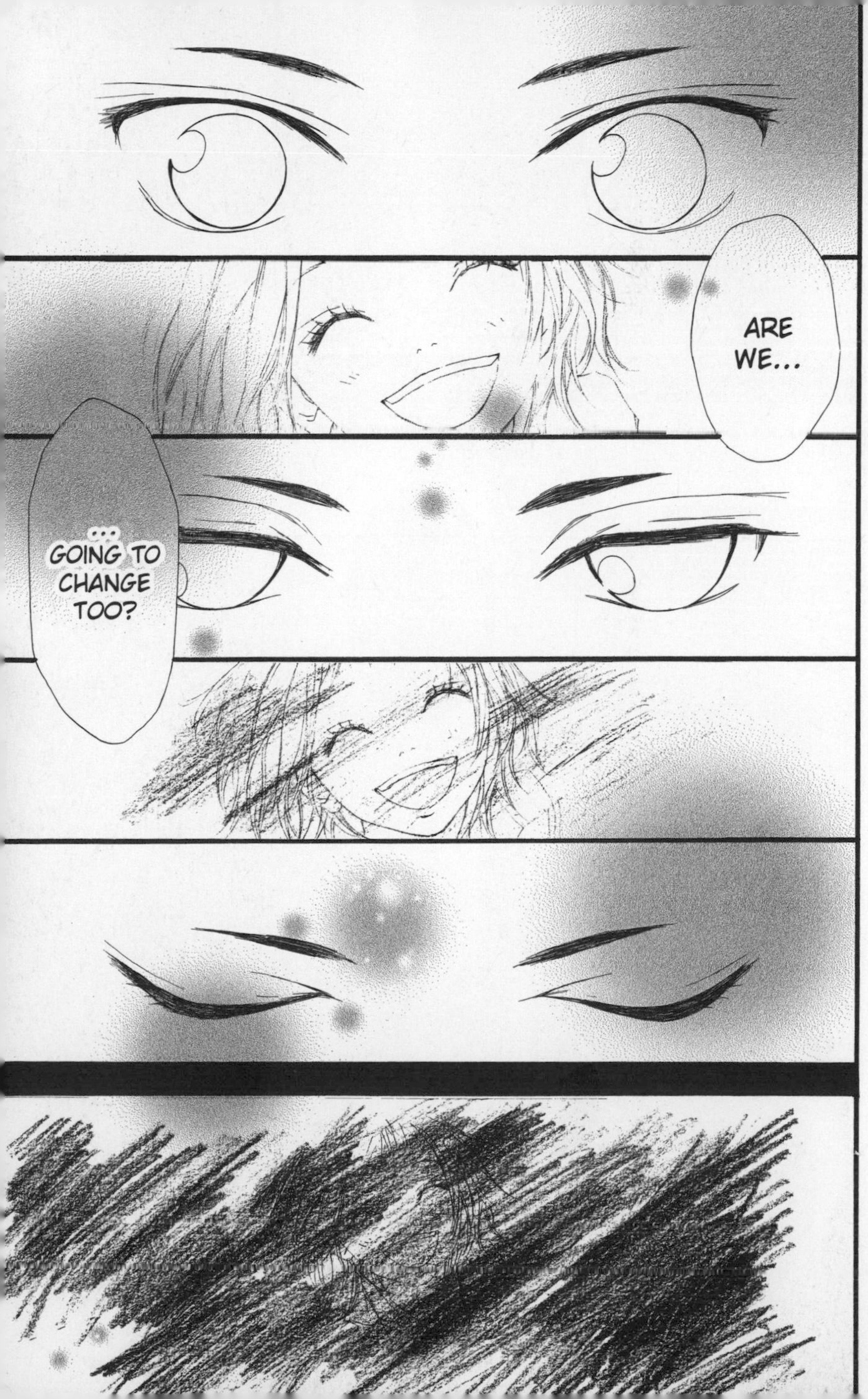
ARE WE...
...GOING TO CHANGE TOO?

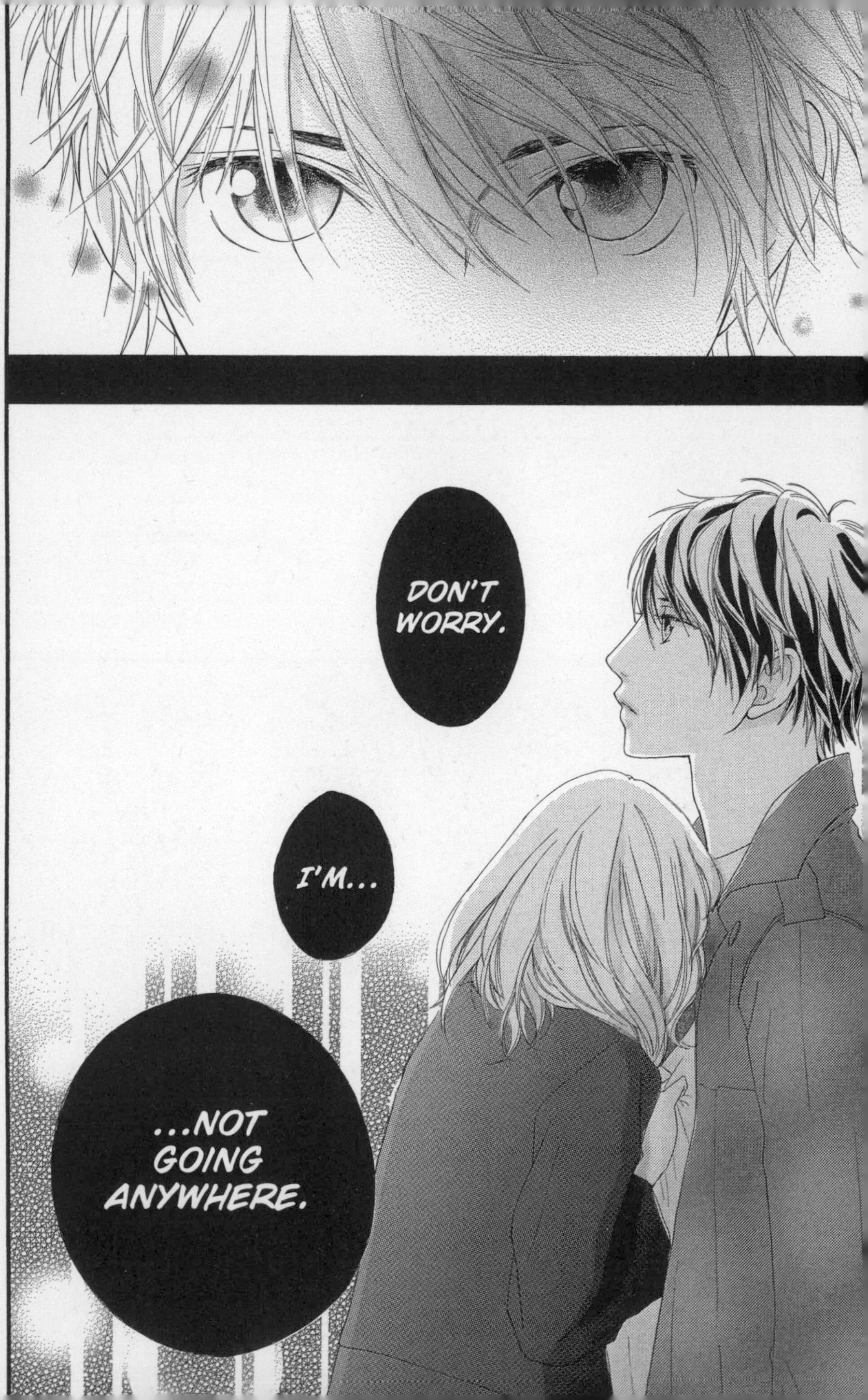
DON'T WORRY.
I'M...
...NOT GOING ANYWHERE.

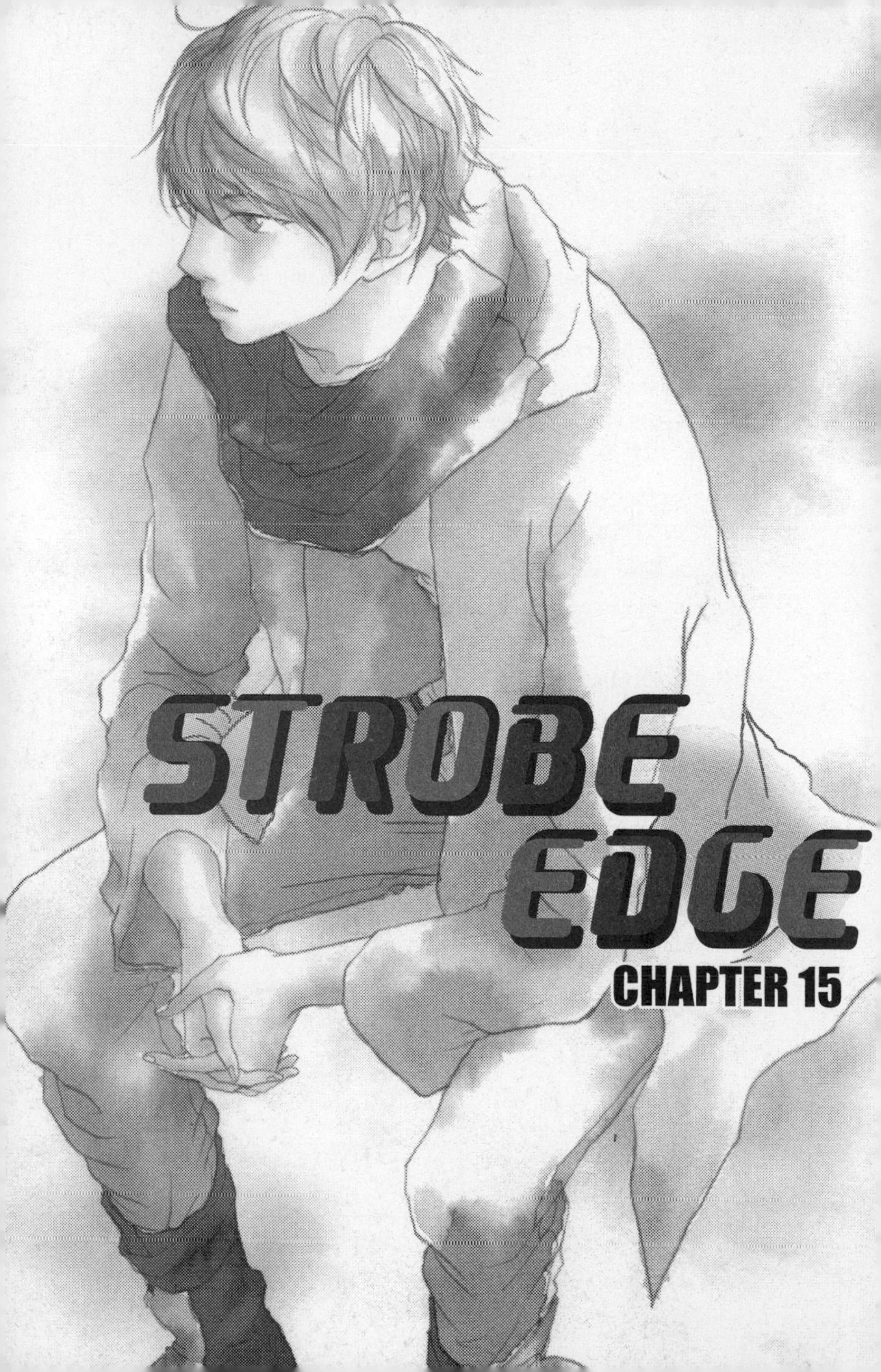
STROBE EDGE
CHAPTER 15

You can basically put human emotions into categories: joy, anger, pathos and humor. But sometimes an emotion springs up that defies categorization! Maybe I'm not identifying the truth behind that emotion clearly, or maybe it's a blend of two or more (which would make it hard to classify).

I don't mind that unsettling feeling that comes when one of those emotions wells up. It's a sense of wonder that defies being put into words, but it still exists.

My hope is that someday I'll be able to portray that sense of wonder. It won't be easy, but I won't give up! So please keep supporting me as I work toward it!

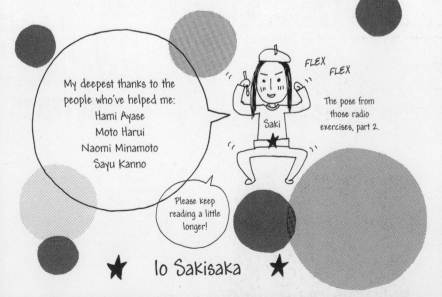

My deepest thanks to the people who've helped me:
Hami Ayase
Moto Harui
Naomi Minamoto
Sayu Kanno

FLEX
FLEX
Saki

The pose from those radio exercises, part 2.

Please keep reading a little longer!

★ Io Sakisaka ★

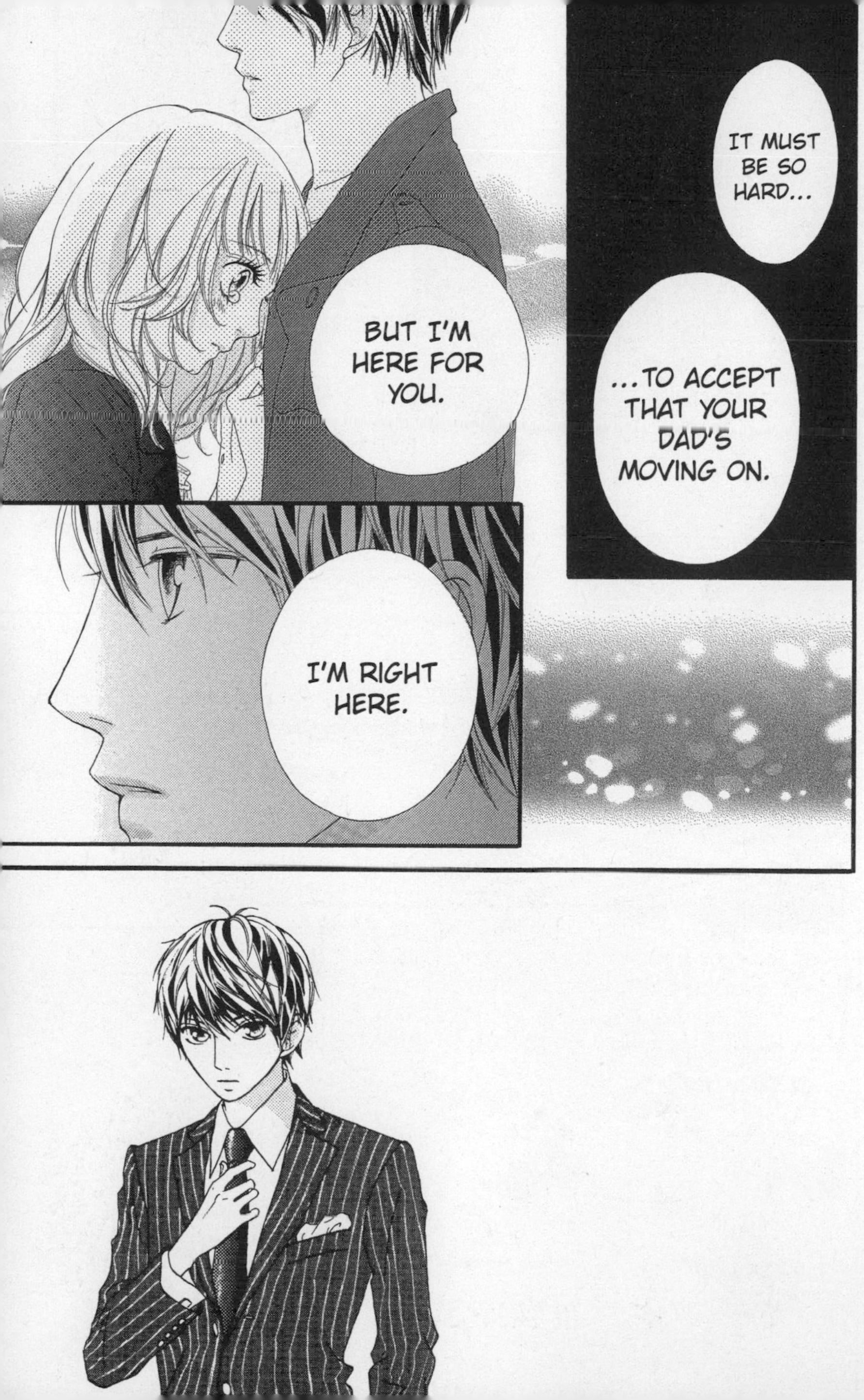
IT MUST BE SO HARD...
...TO ACCEPT THAT YOUR DAD'S MOVING ON.
BUT I'M HERE FOR YOU.
I'M RIGHT HERE.

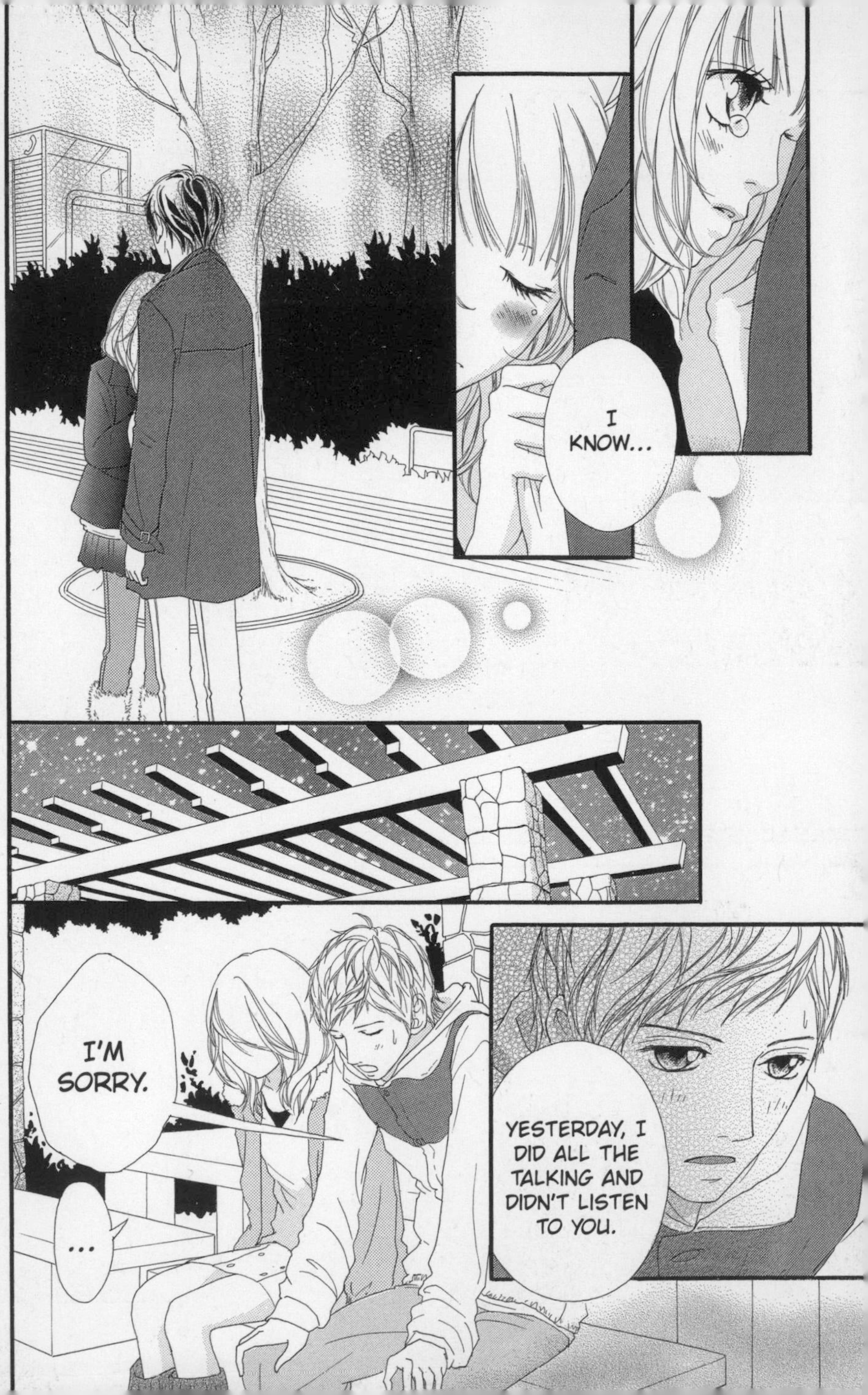
I KNOW...
YESTERDAY, I DID ALL THE TALKING AND DIDN'T LISTEN TO YOU.
I'M SORRY.
...

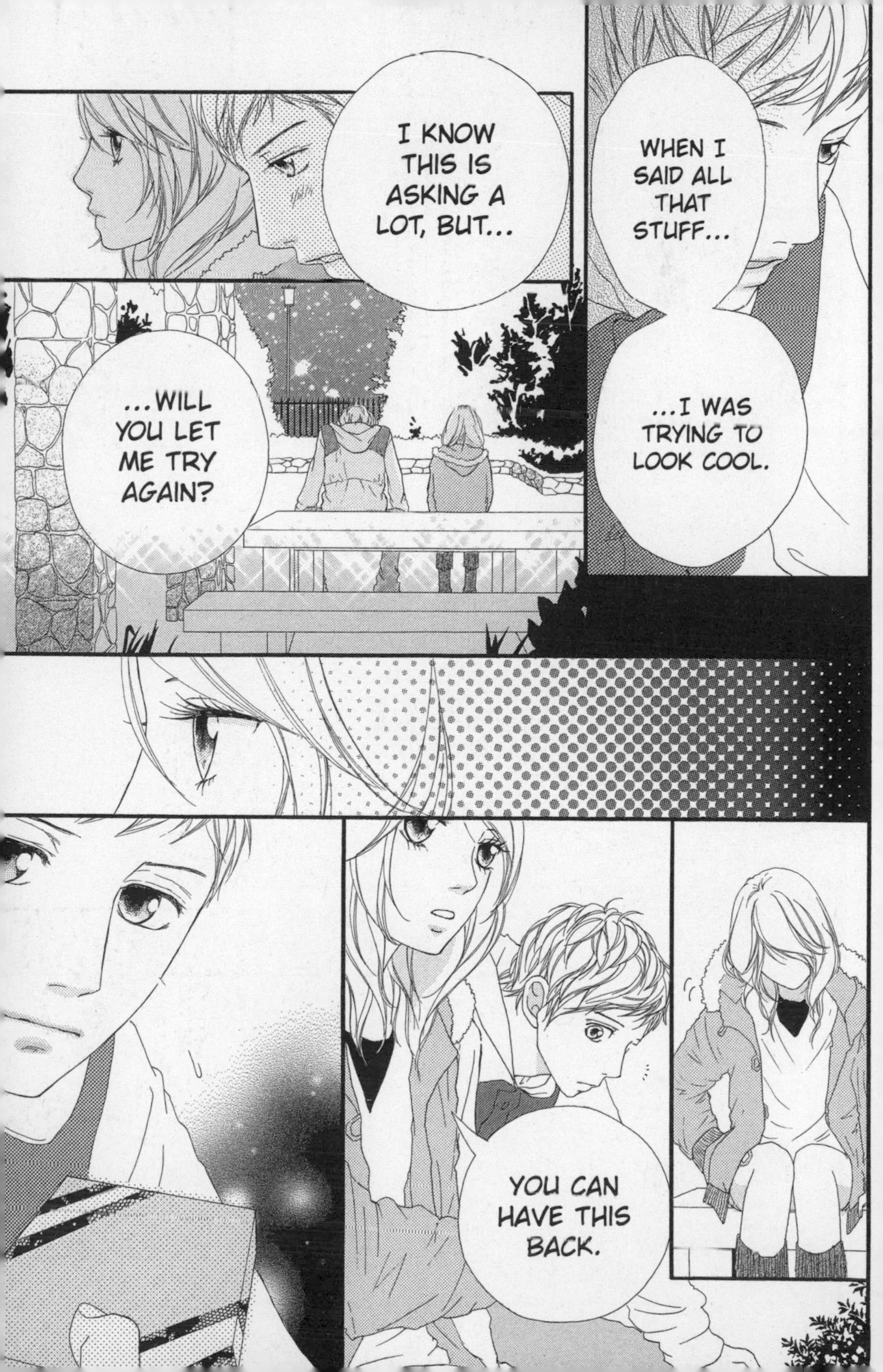
WHEN I SAID ALL THAT STUFF...
...I WAS TRYING TO LOOK COOL.
I KNOW THIS IS ASKING A LOT, BUT...
...WILL YOU LET ME TRY AGAIN?
YOU CAN HAVE THIS BACK.

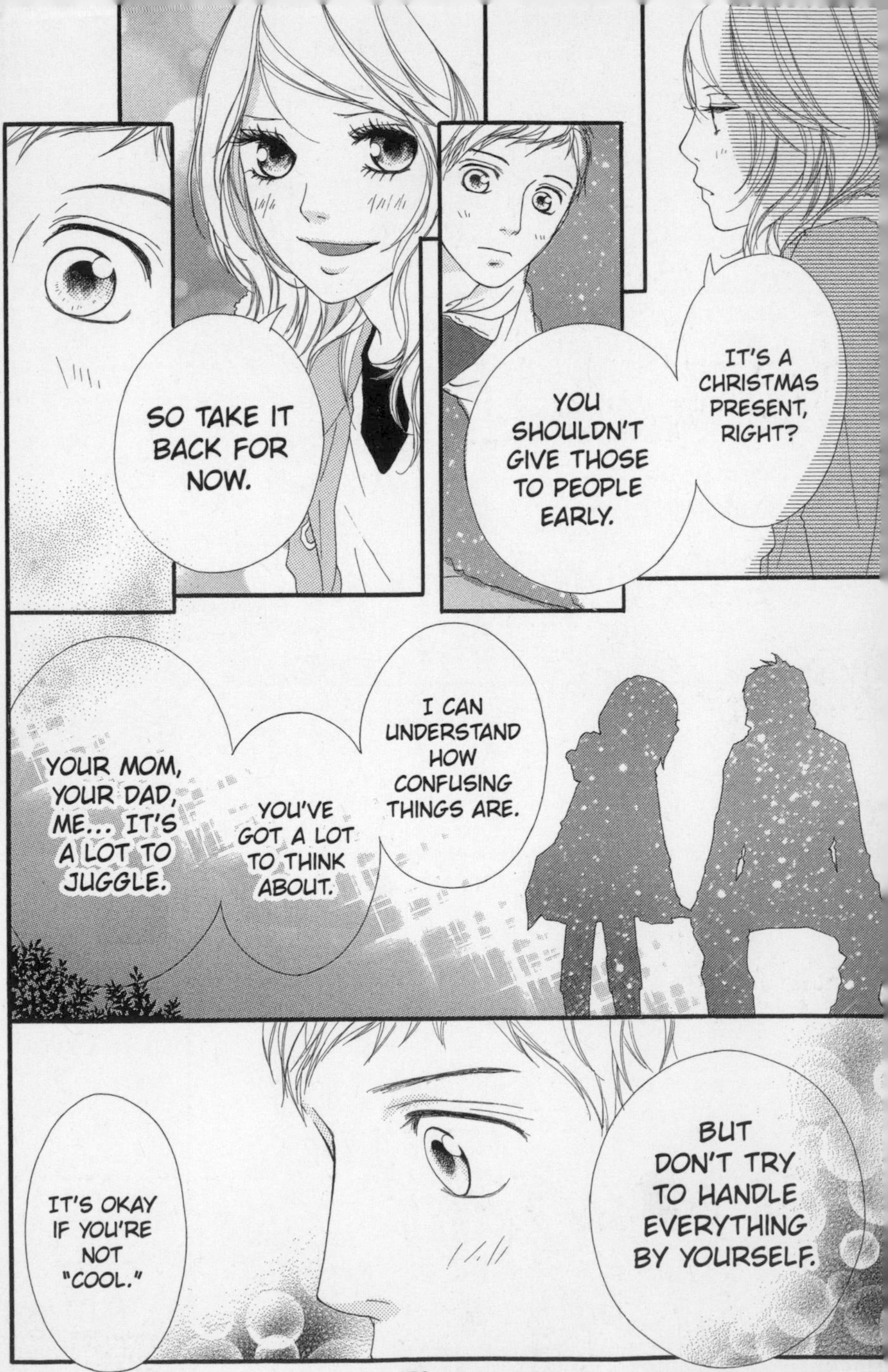
IT'S A CHRISTMAS PRESENT, RIGHT?
YOU SHOULDN'T GIVE THOSE TO PEOPLE EARLY.
SO TAKE IT BACK FOR NOW.
I CAN UNDERSTAND HOW CONFUSING THINGS ARE.
YOU'VE GOT A LOT TO THINK ABOUT.
YOUR MOM, YOUR DAD, ME... IT'S A LOT TO JUGGLE.
BUT DON'T TRY TO HANDLE EVERYTHING BY YOURSELF.
IT'S OKAY IF YOU'RE NOT "COOL."

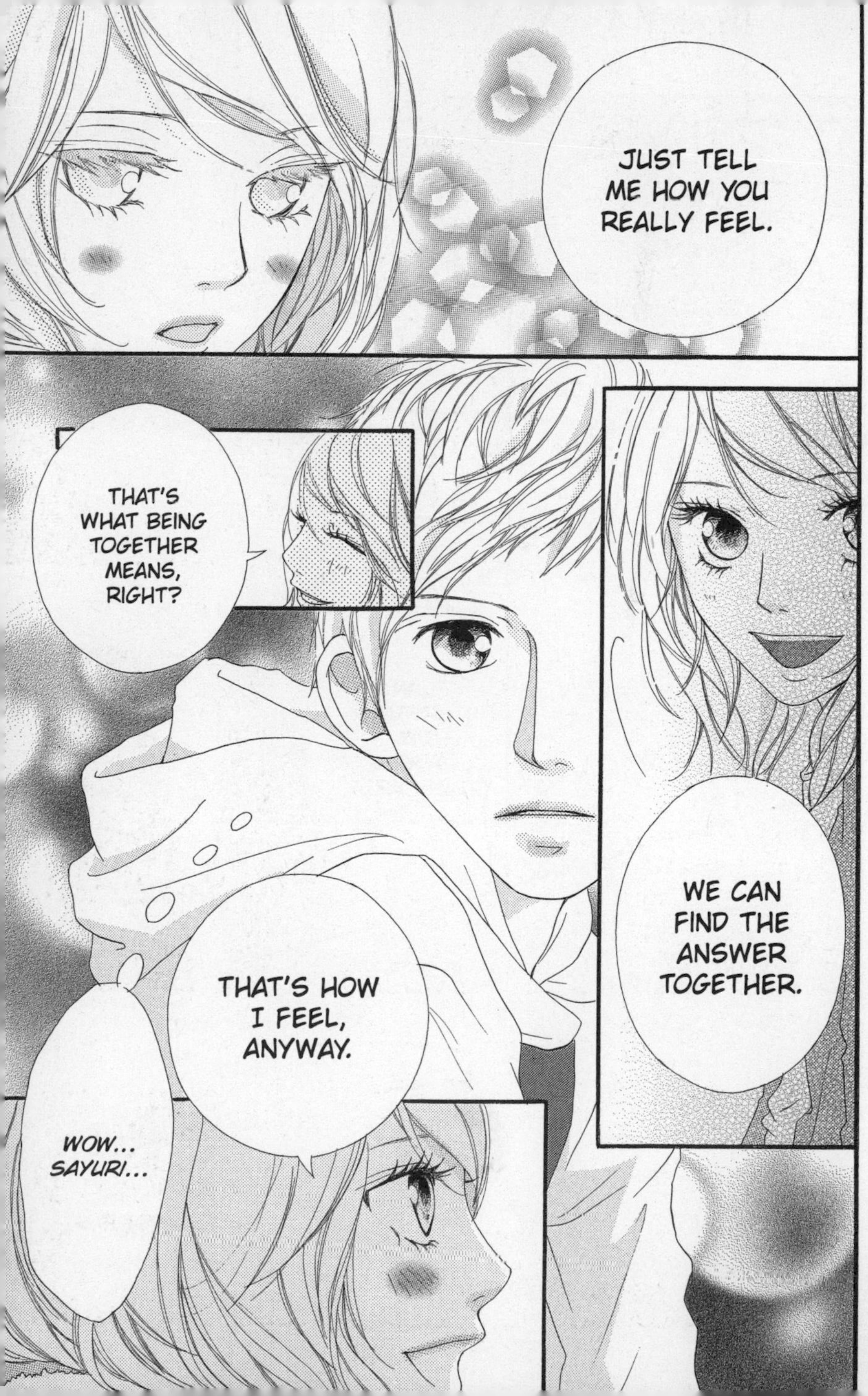
JUST TELL ME HOW YOU REALLY FEEL.
WE CAN FIND THE ANSWER TOGETHER.
THAT'S WHAT BEING TOGETHER MEANS, RIGHT?
THAT'S HOW I FEEL, ANYWAY.
WOW... SAYURI...

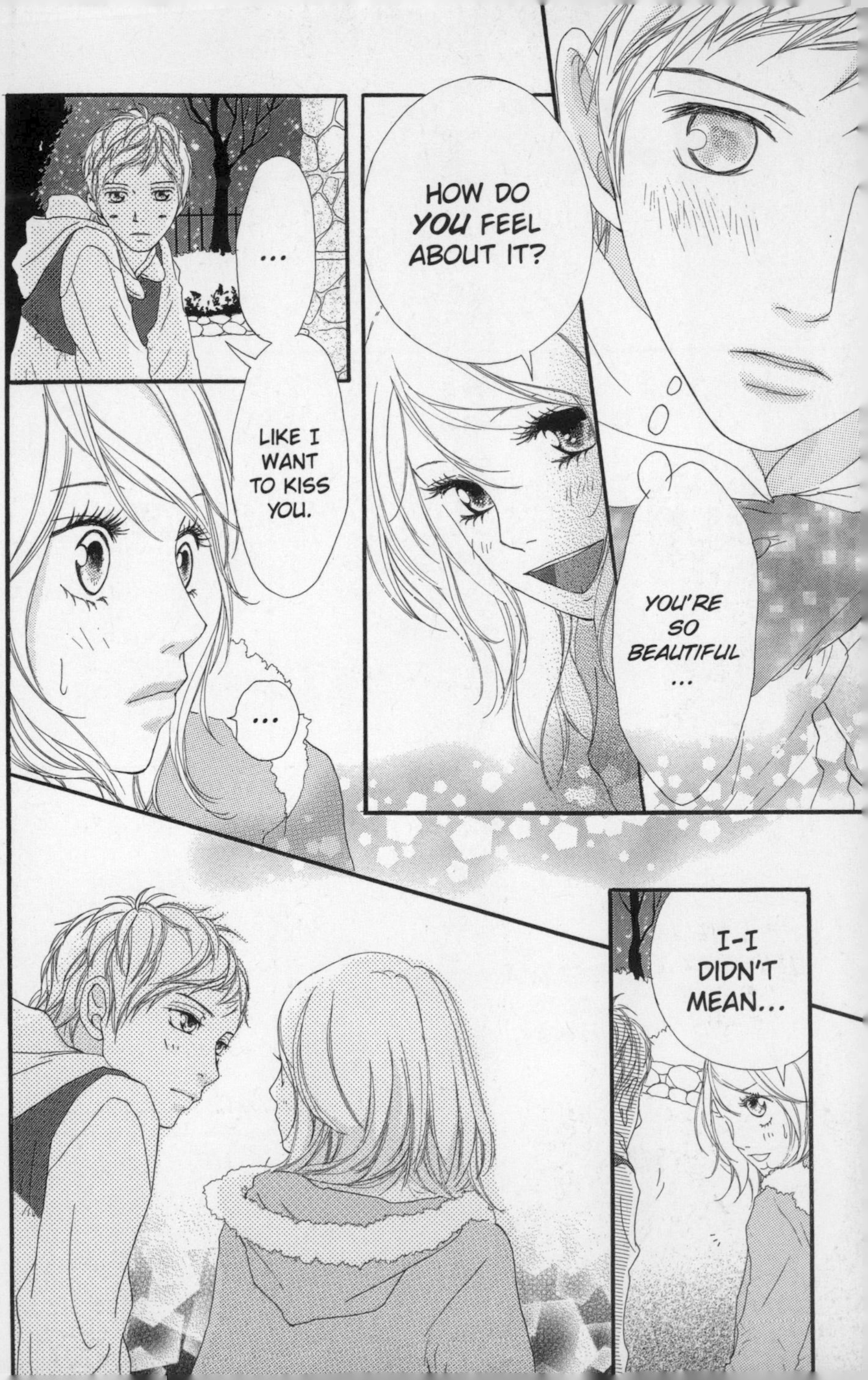
HOW DO *YOU* FEEL ABOUT IT?
YOU'RE SO BEAUTIFUL...
...
LIKE I WANT TO KISS YOU.
...
I-I DIDN'T MEAN...

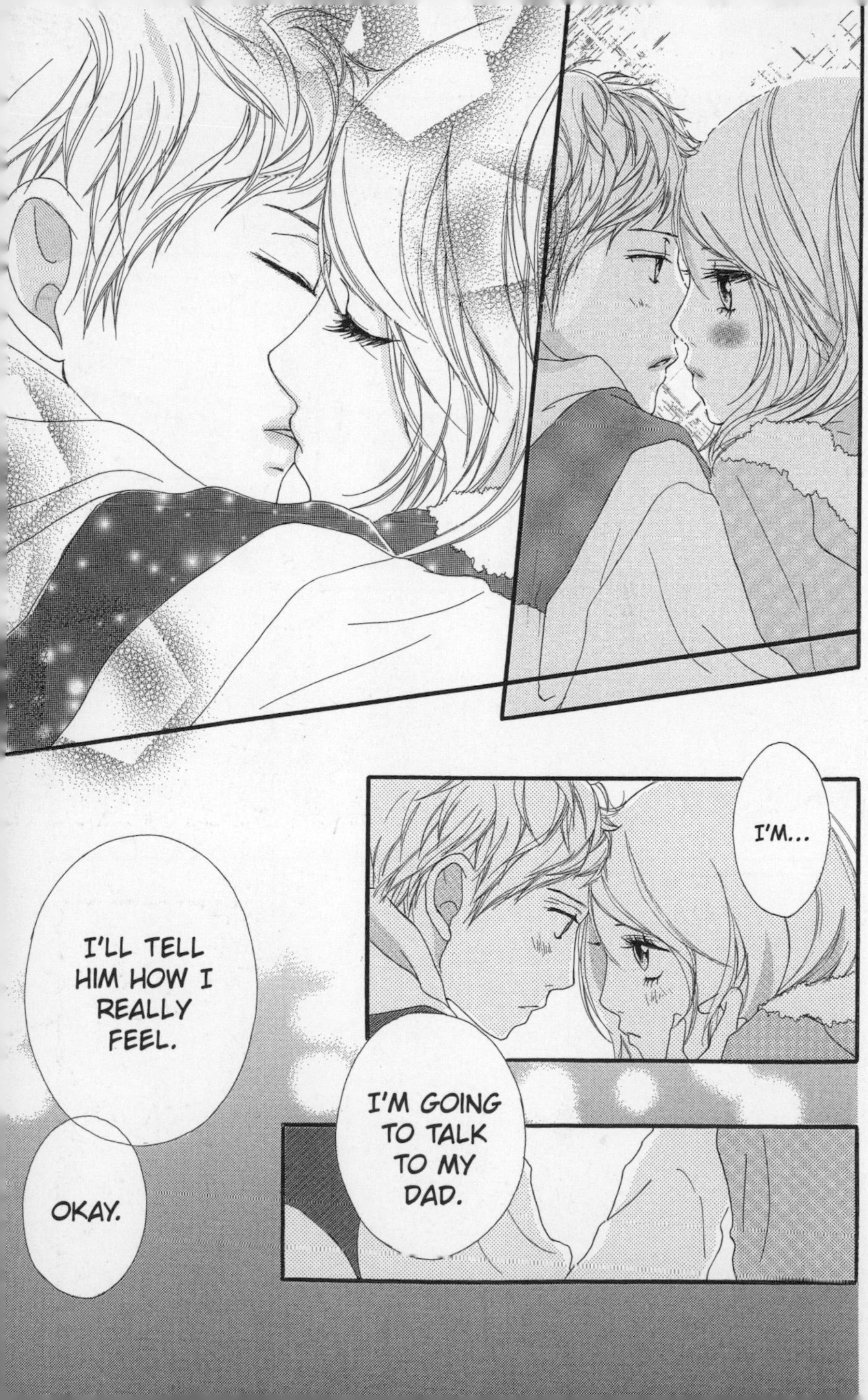
I'M...
I'M GOING TO TALK TO MY DAD.
I'LL TELL HIM HOW I REALLY FEEL.
OKAY.

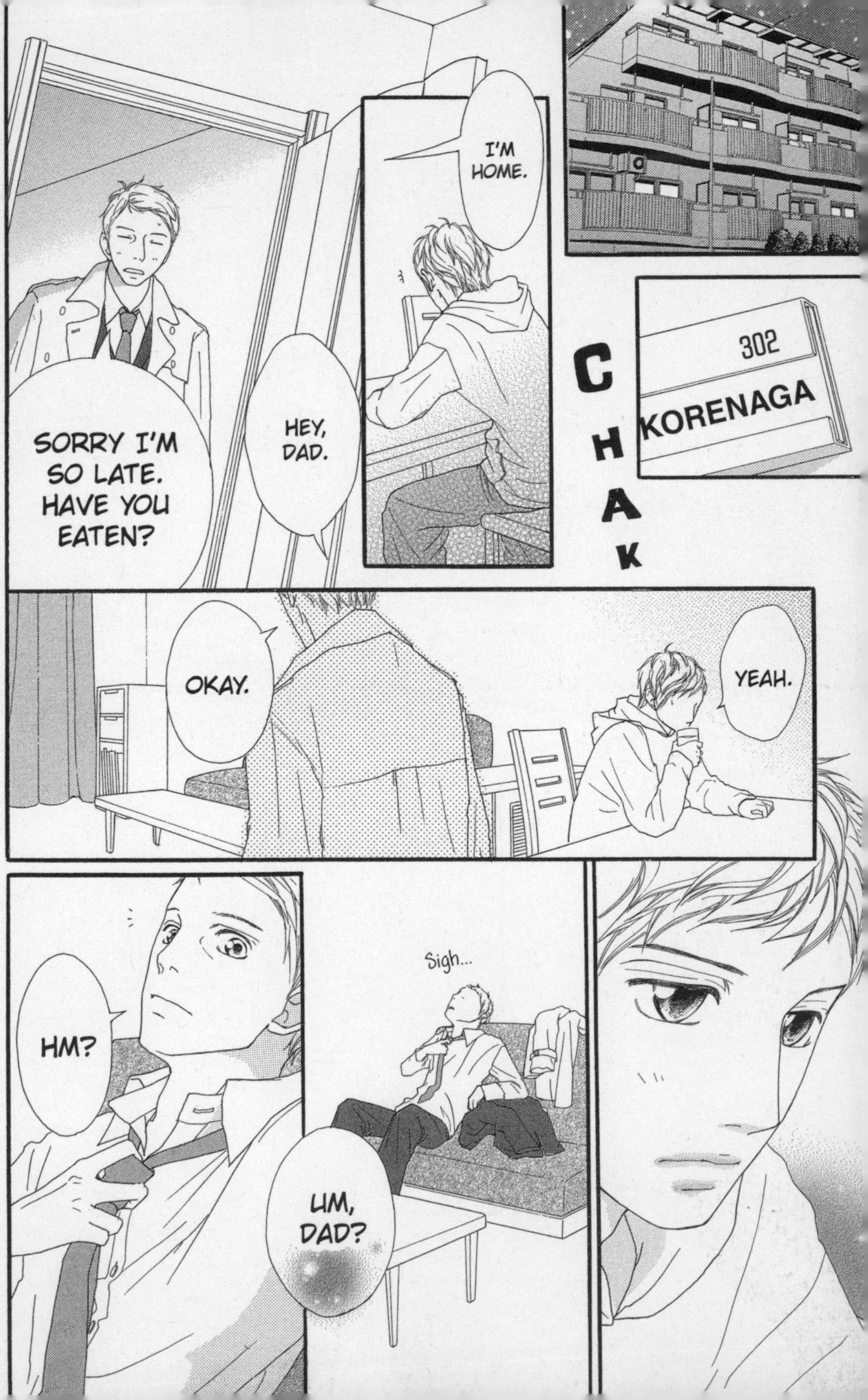
302
KORENAGA
CHAK
I'M HOME.
HEY, DAD.
SORRY I'M SO LATE. HAVE YOU EATEN?
YEAH.
OKAY.
Sigh...
UM, DAD?
HM?

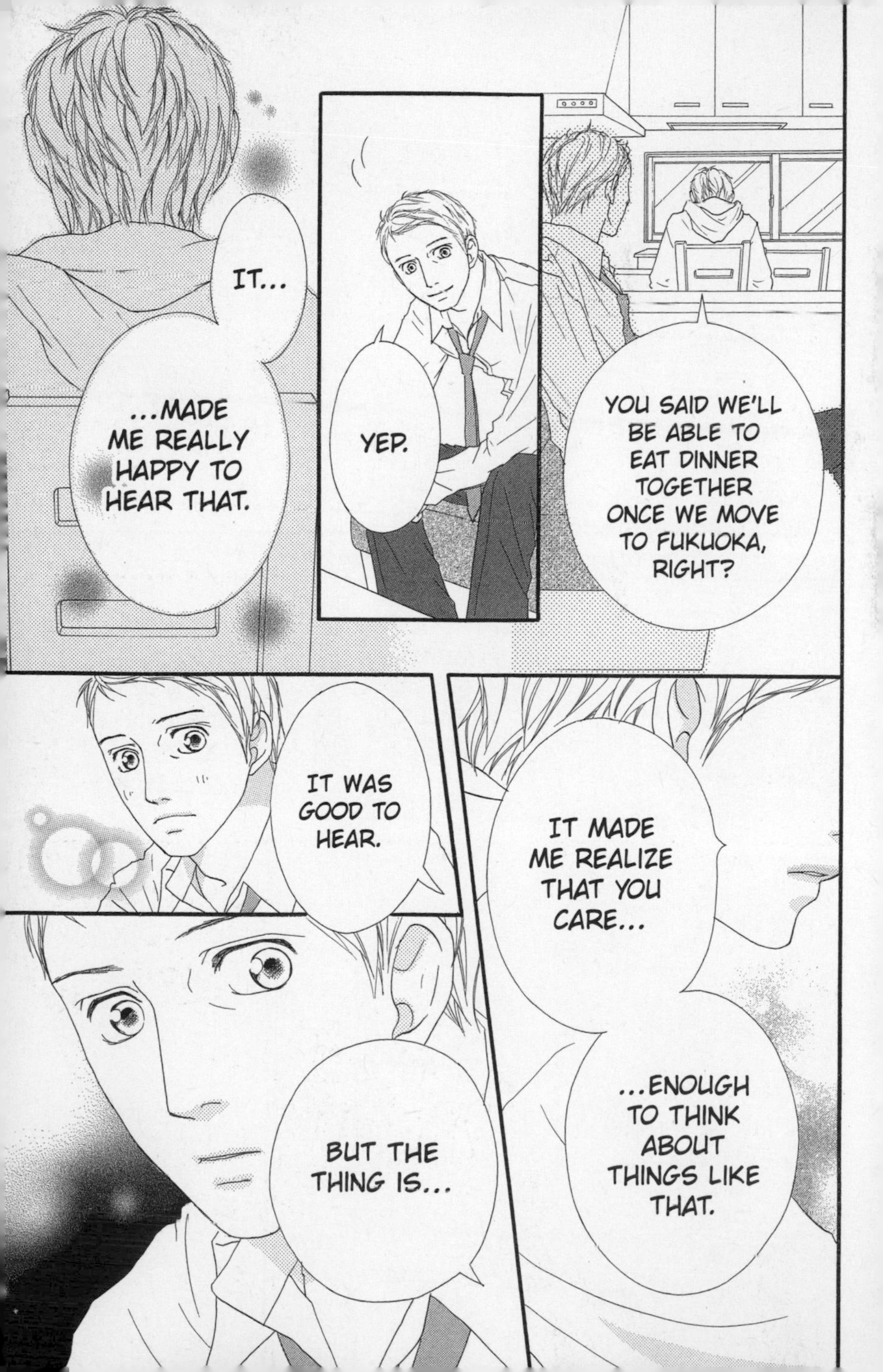
YOU SAID WE'LL BE ABLE TO EAT DINNER TOGETHER ONCE WE MOVE TO FUKUOKA, RIGHT?
YEP.
IT...
...MADE ME REALLY HAPPY TO HEAR THAT.
IT MADE ME REALIZE THAT YOU CARE...
...ENOUGH TO THINK ABOUT THINGS LIKE THAT.
IT WAS GOOD TO HEAR.
BUT THE THING IS...

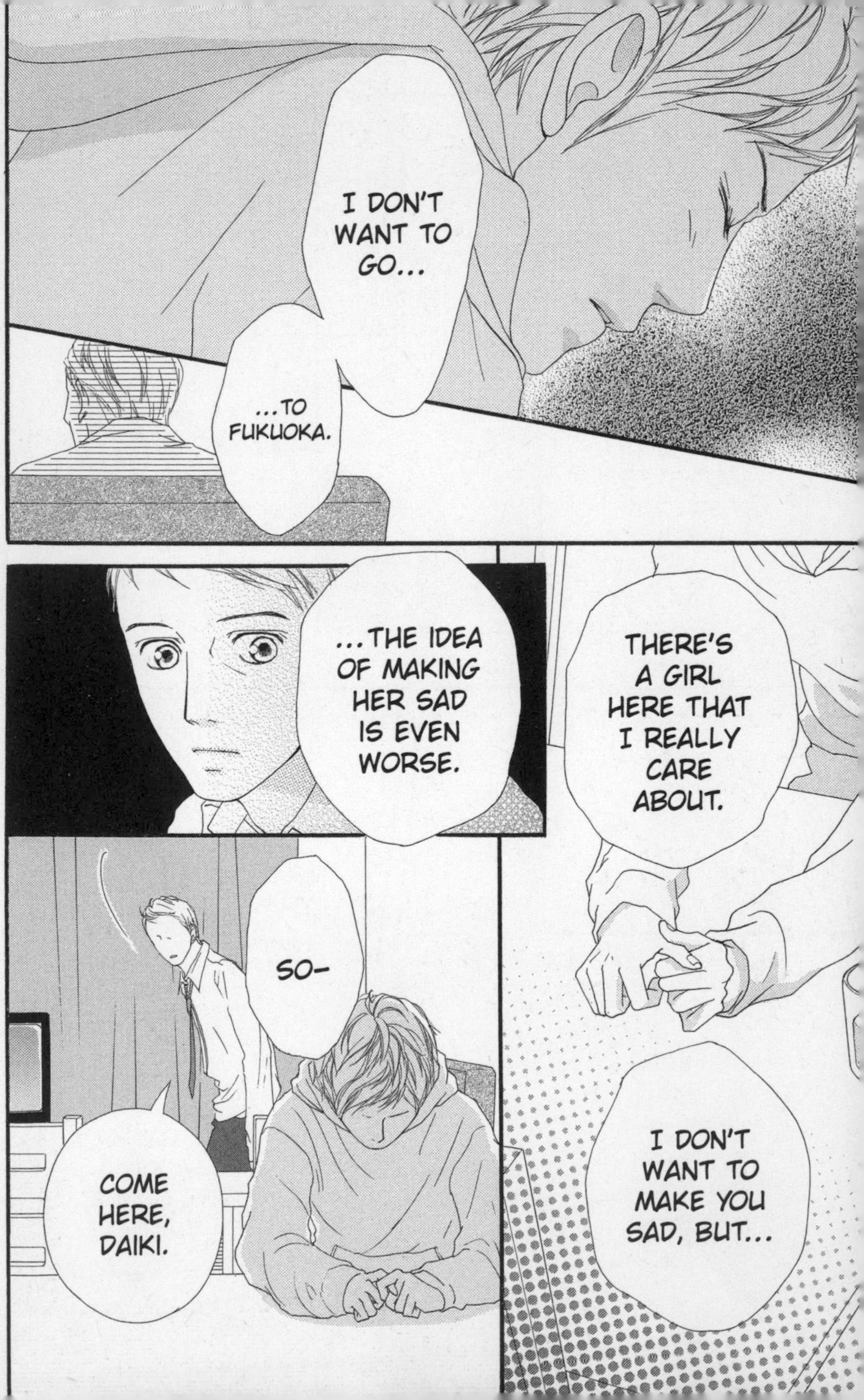
I DON'T WANT TO GO...
...TO FUKUOKA.
THERE'S A GIRL HERE THAT I REALLY CARE ABOUT.
I DON'T WANT TO MAKE YOU SAD, BUT...
...THE IDEA OF MAKING HER SAD IS EVEN WORSE.
SO-
COME HERE, DAIKI.

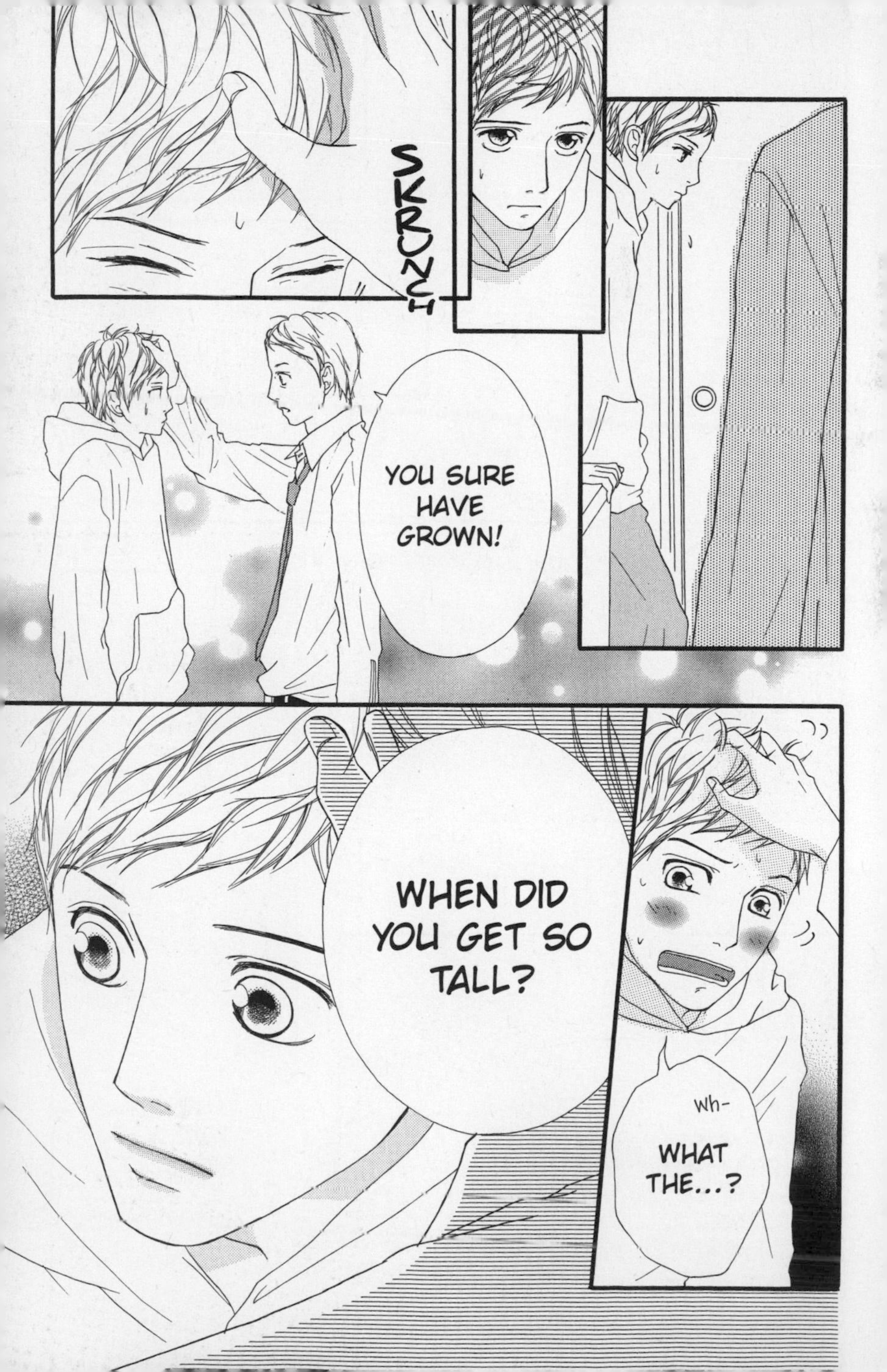
SKRUNCH
YOU SURE HAVE GROWN!
Wh-
WHAT THE...?
WHEN DID YOU GET SO TALL?

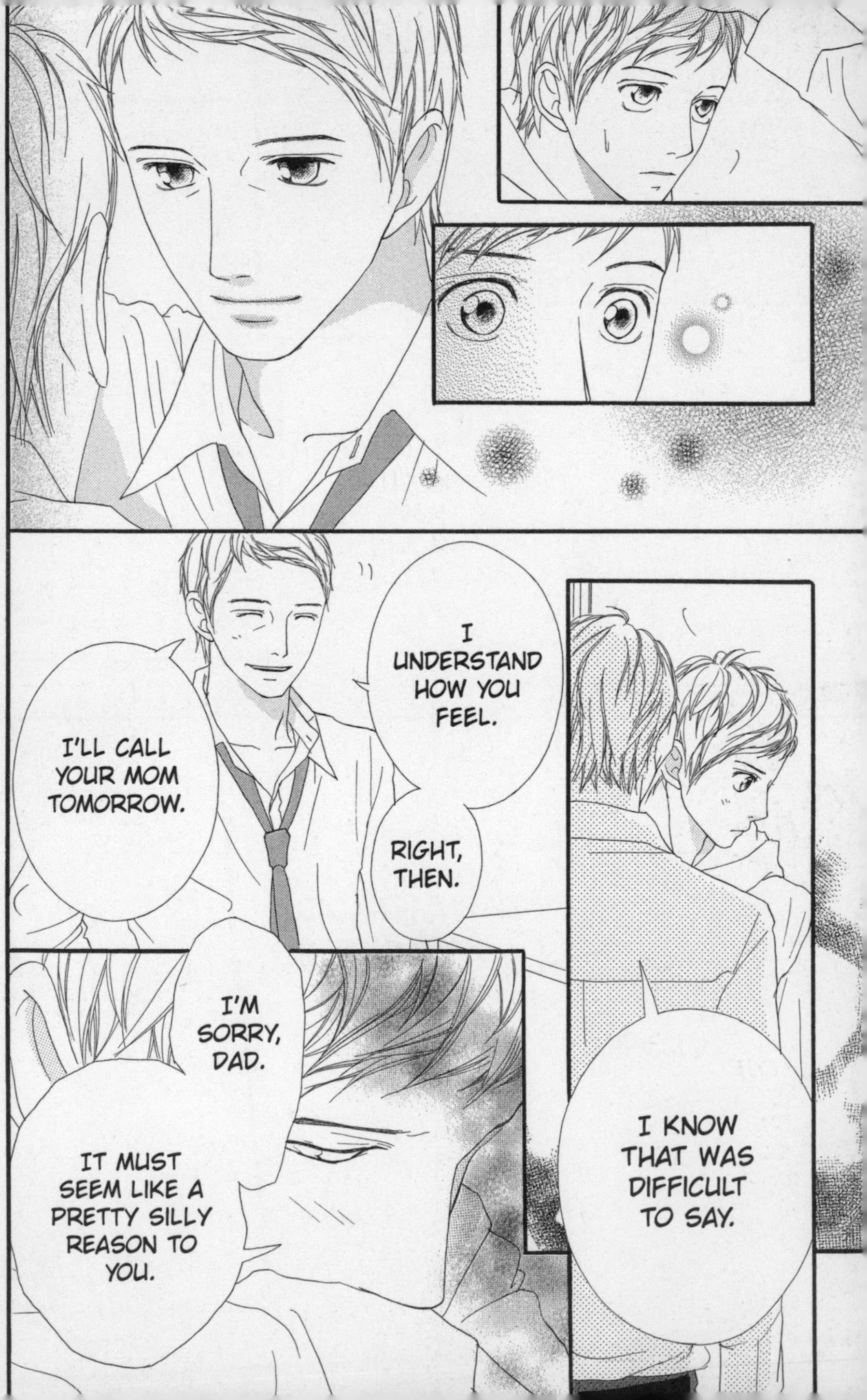
I KNOW THAT WAS DIFFICULT TO SAY.
I UNDERSTAND HOW YOU FEEL.
RIGHT, THEN.
I'LL CALL YOUR MOM TOMORROW.
I'M SORRY, DAD.
IT MUST SEEM LIKE A PRETTY SILLY REASON TO YOU.

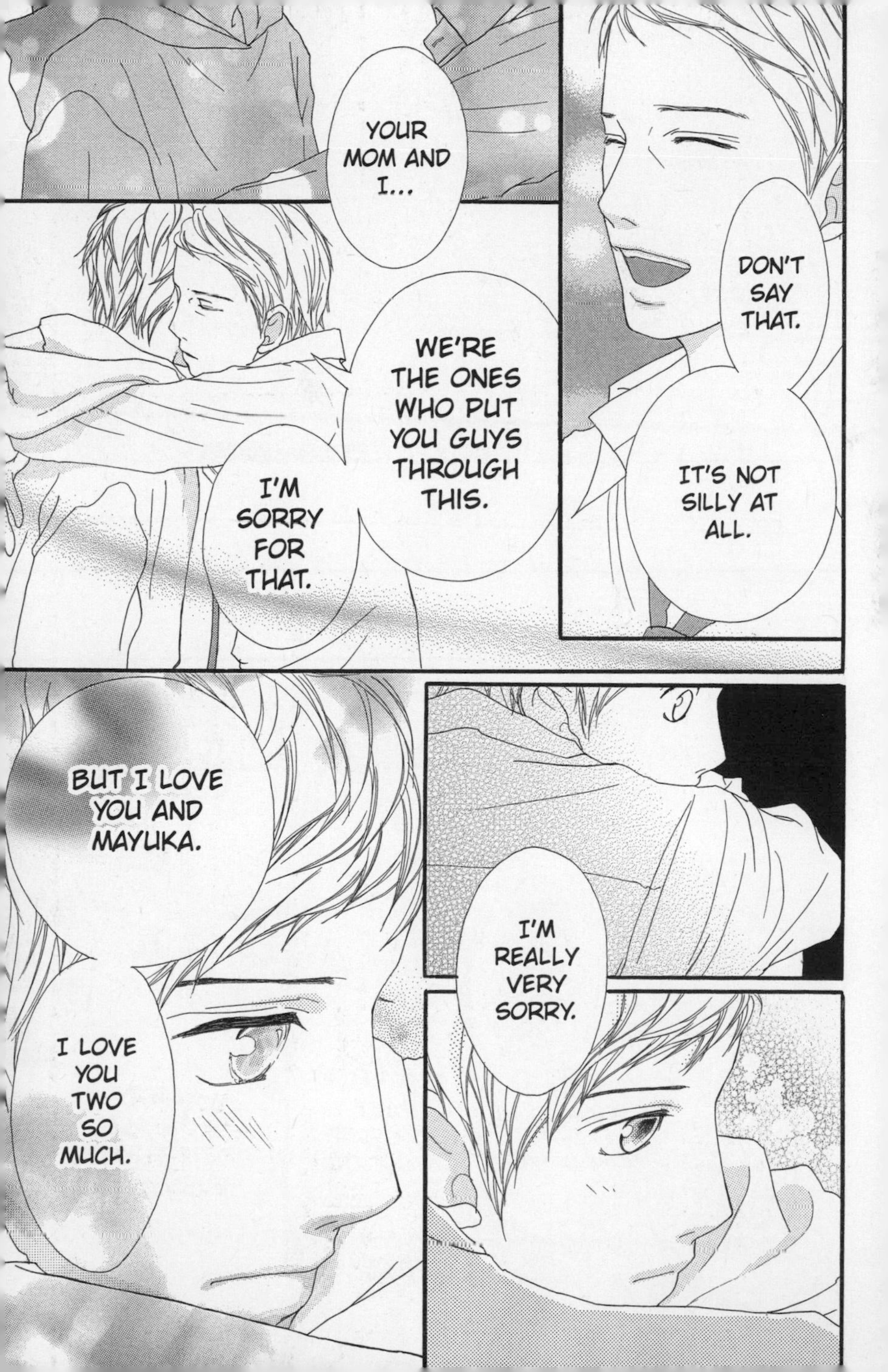
DON'T SAY THAT.
IT'S NOT SILLY AT ALL.
YOUR MOM AND I...
WE'RE THE ONES WHO PUT YOU GUYS THROUGH THIS.
I'M SORRY FOR THAT.
I'M REALLY VERY SORRY.
BUT I LOVE YOU AND MAYUKA.
I LOVE YOU TWO SO MUCH.

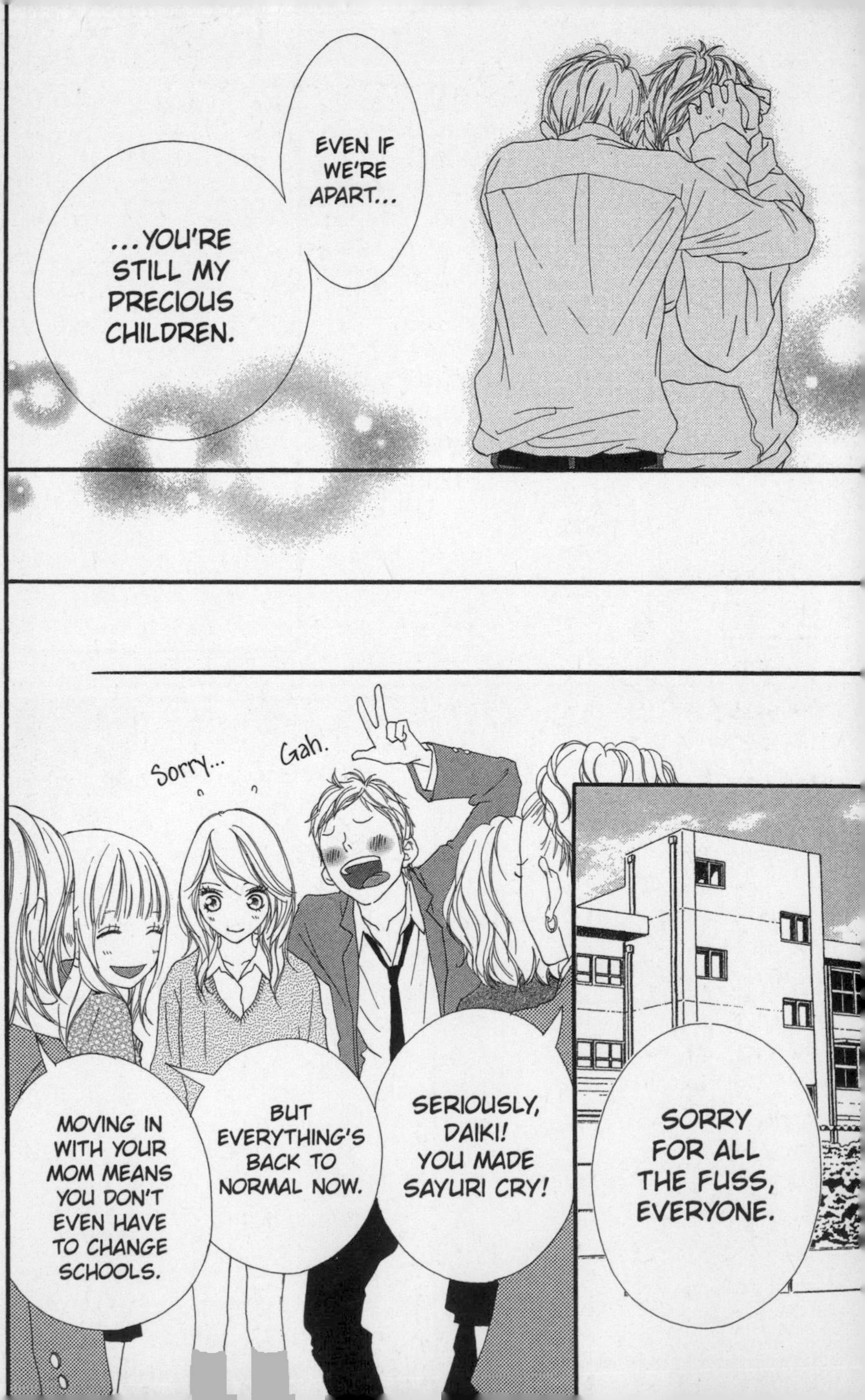
EVEN IF WE'RE APART...
...YOU'RE STILL MY PRECIOUS CHILDREN.
SORRY FOR ALL THE FUSS, EVERYONE.
Gah.
Sorry...
SERIOUSLY, DAIKI! YOU MADE SAYURI CRY!
BUT EVERYTHING'S BACK TO NORMAL NOW.
MOVING IN WITH YOUR MOM MEANS YOU DON'T EVEN HAVE TO CHANGE SCHOOLS.

I love incense. Right now, I'm hooked on an incense called "Smile" that's sold at gift shops. I'd describe the scent as "like the jungle after it rains," but I've never been to the jungle when it was raining. Actually, I've never been to a jungle, period, so I'm just guessing.

When I smell that incense, I'm overwhelmed by a sensation—it's like a memory, but just out of reach. It's kind of poignant. Maybe there was a similar smell in the air at a time when my heart was broken, but I can't bring it to mind. Or maybe it's a similar scent but not exactly the same, and that's why I can't remember it. Who knows? But it's a perfect scent for a rainy Sunday morning...although at that point I'm usually still asleep! (Get up!)

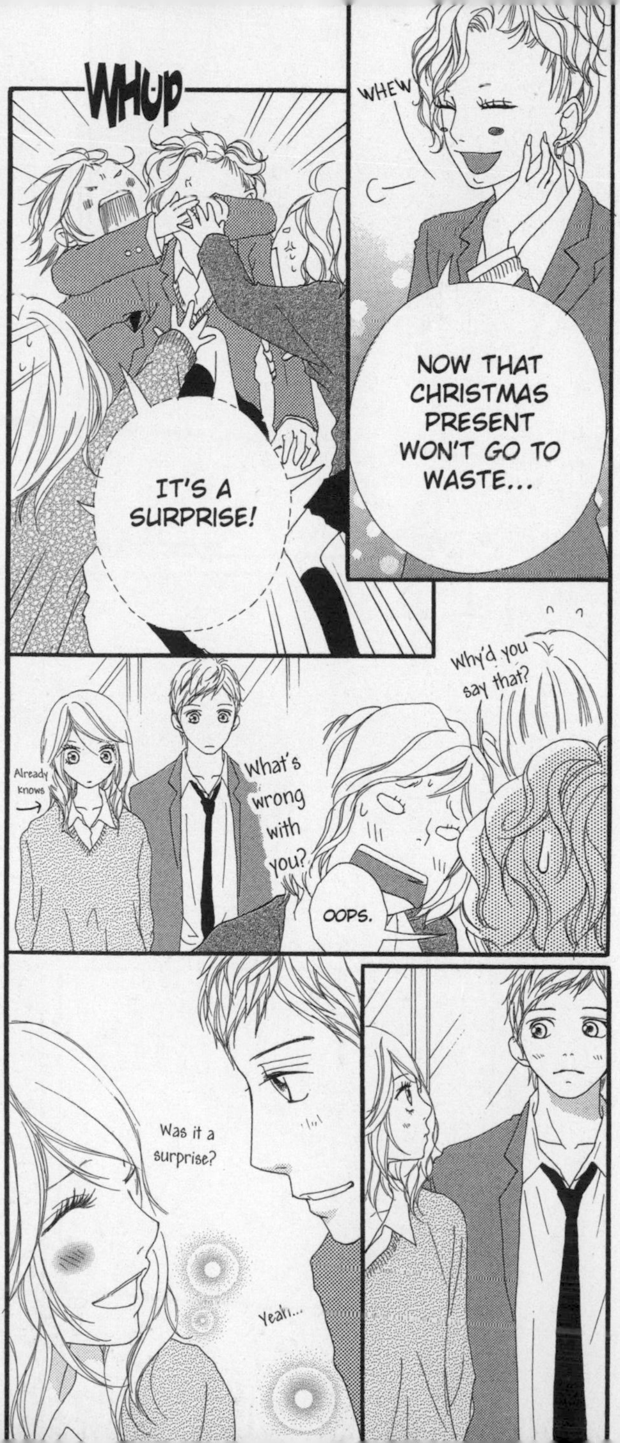
WHEW
NOW THAT CHRISTMAS PRESENT WON'T GO TO WASTE...
WHUP
IT'S A SURPRISE!
Why'd you say that?
What's wrong with you?
OOPS.
Already knows
Was it a surprise?
Yeah...

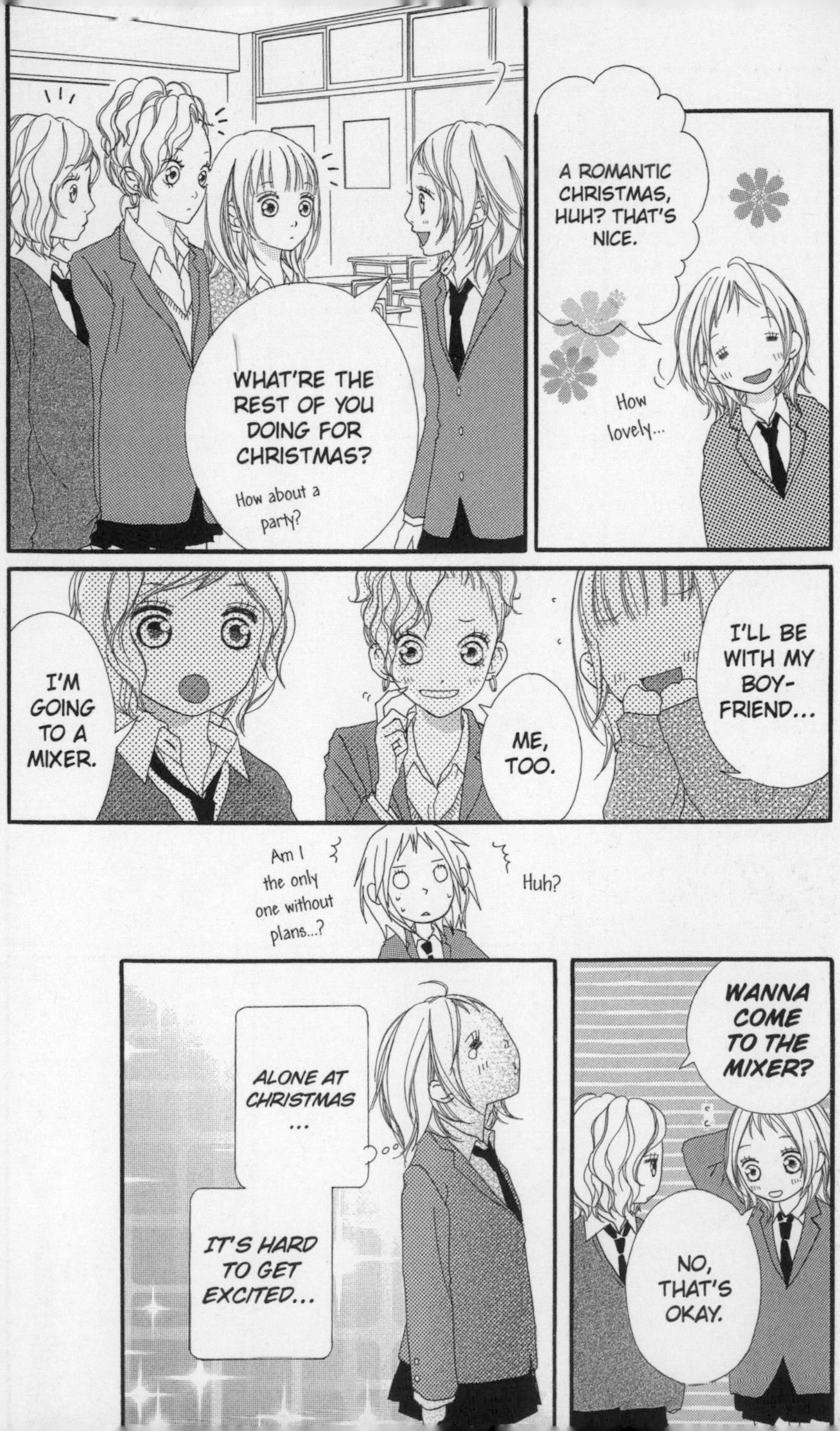
A ROMANTIC CHRISTMAS, HUH? THAT'S NICE.
How lovely...
WHAT'RE THE REST OF YOU DOING FOR CHRISTMAS?
How about a party?
I'LL BE WITH MY BOY-FRIEND...
ME, TOO.
I'M GOING TO A MIXER.
Huh?
Am I the only one without plans...?
WANNA COME TO THE MIXER?
NO, THAT'S OKAY.
ALONE AT CHRISTMAS...
IT'S HARD TO GET EXCITED...

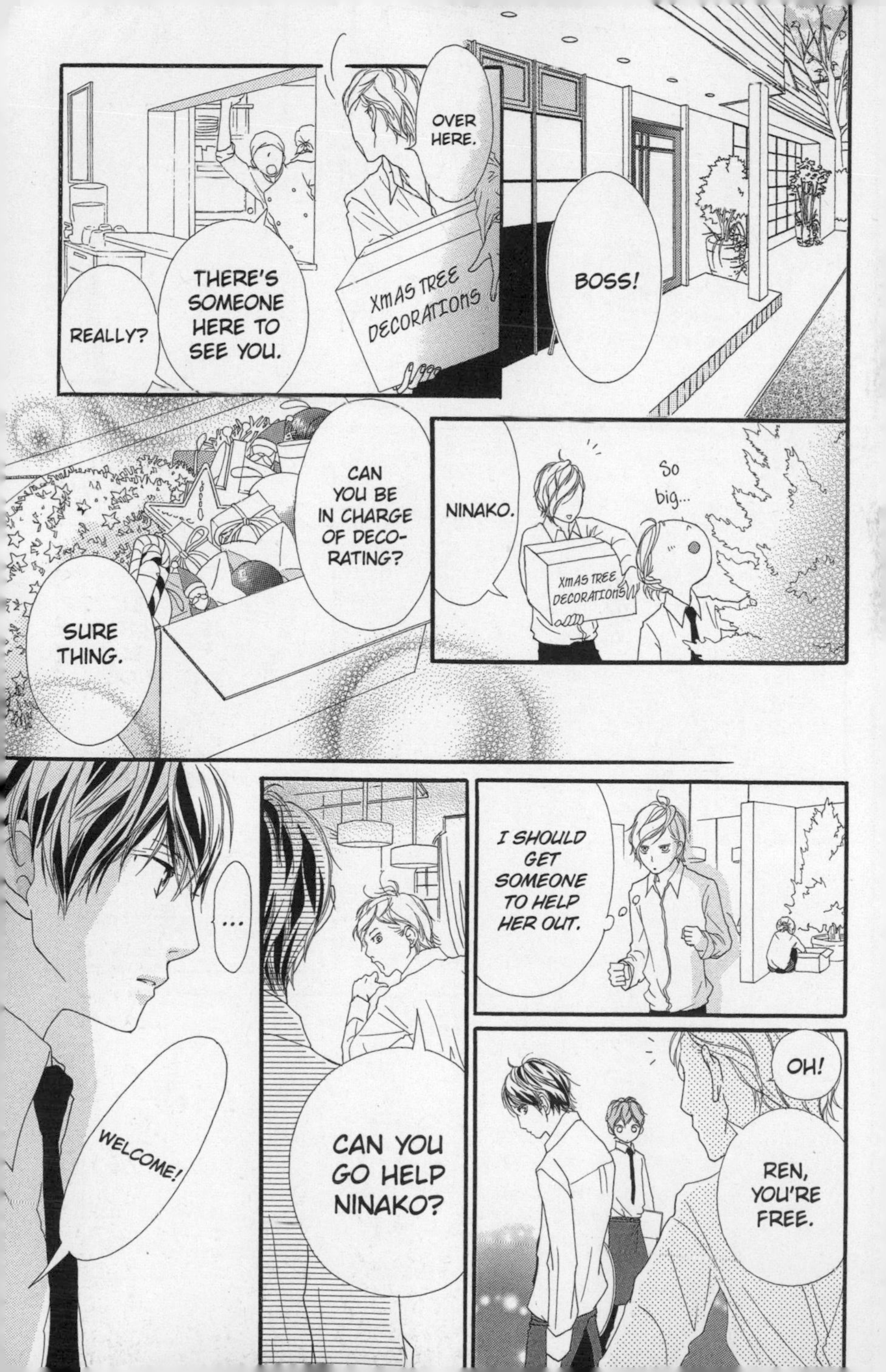
BOSS!
OVER HERE.
XmAS TREE DECORATIONS
THERE'S SOMEONE HERE TO SEE YOU.
REALLY?
So big...
NINAKO.
XmAS TREE DECORATIONS
CAN YOU BE IN CHARGE OF DECO-RATING?
SURE THING.
I SHOULD GET SOMEONE TO HELP HER OUT.
OH!
REN, YOU'RE FREE.
CAN YOU GO HELP NINAKO?
...
WELCOME!

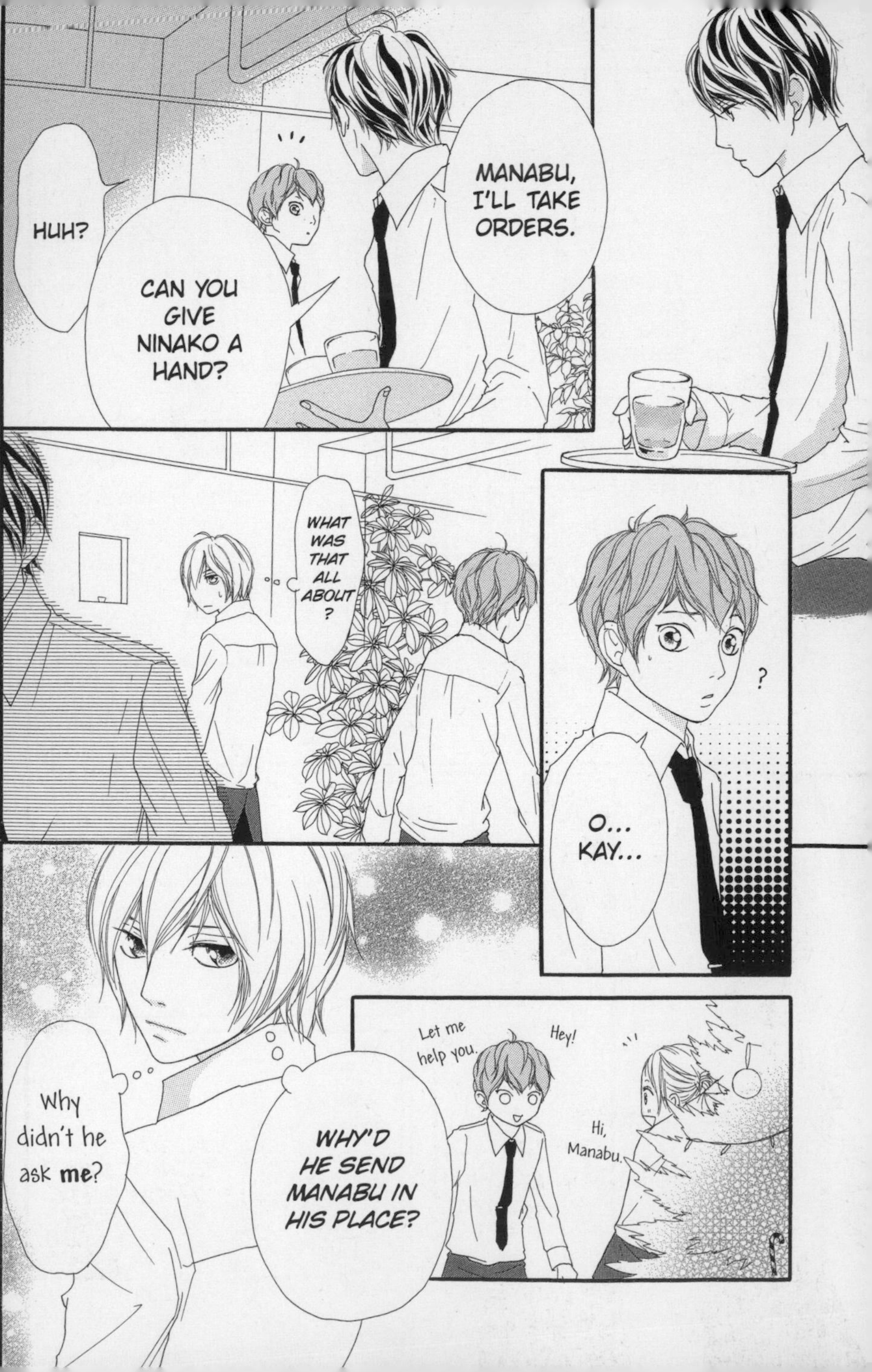
MANABU, I'LL TAKE ORDERS.
CAN YOU GIVE NINAKO A HAND?
HUH?
?
O... KAY...
WHAT WAS THAT ALL ABOUT?
Hey!
Let me help you.
Hi, Manabu.
WHY'D HE SEND MANABU IN HIS PLACE?
Why didn't he ask **me**?

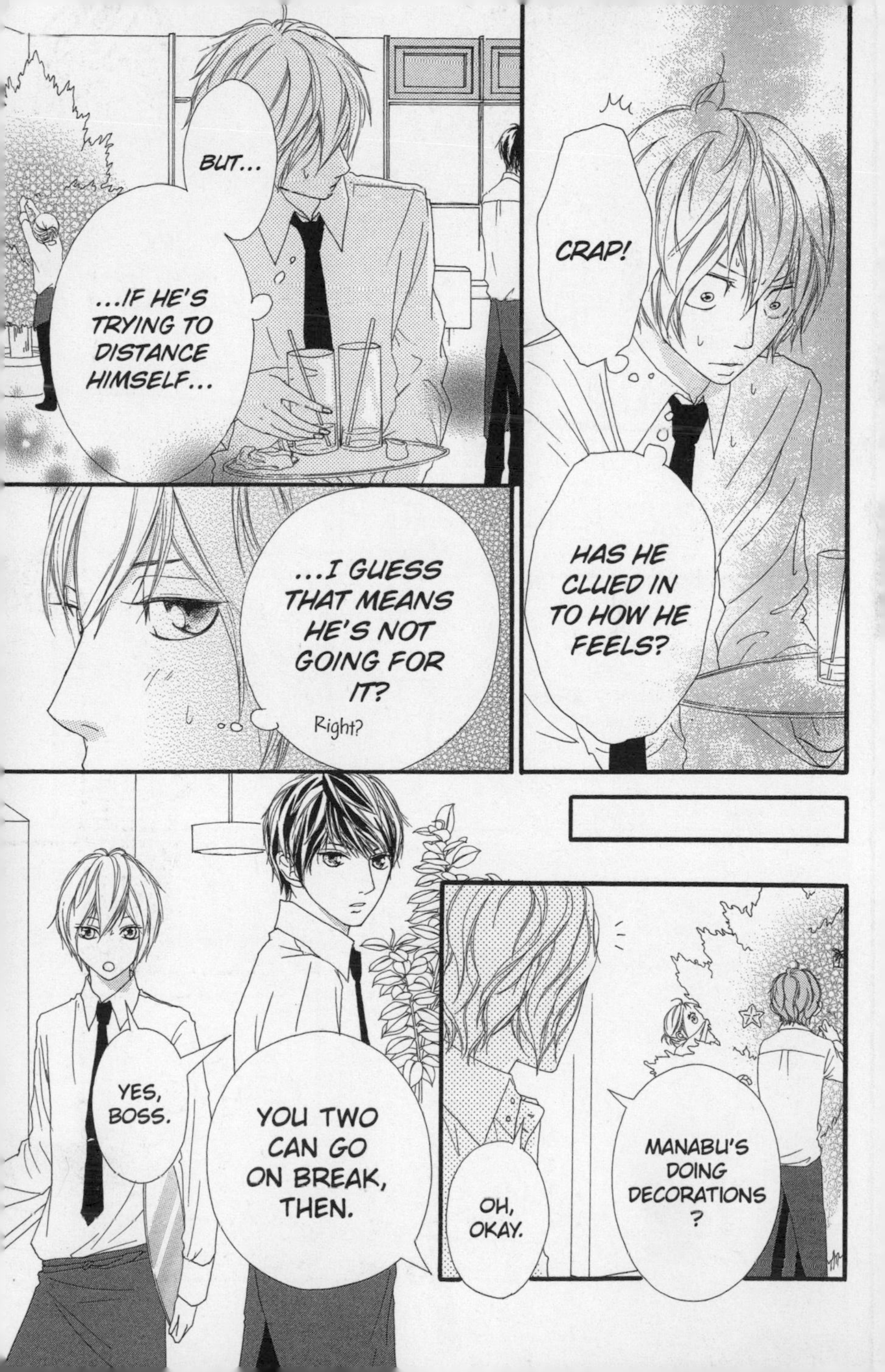
CRAP!
HAS HE CLUED IN TO HOW HE FEELS?
BUT...
...IF HE'S TRYING TO DISTANCE HIMSELF...
...I GUESS THAT MEANS HE'S NOT GOING FOR IT?
Right?
MANABU'S DOING DECORATIONS?
OH, OKAY.
YOU TWO CAN GO ON BREAK, THEN.
YES, BOSS.

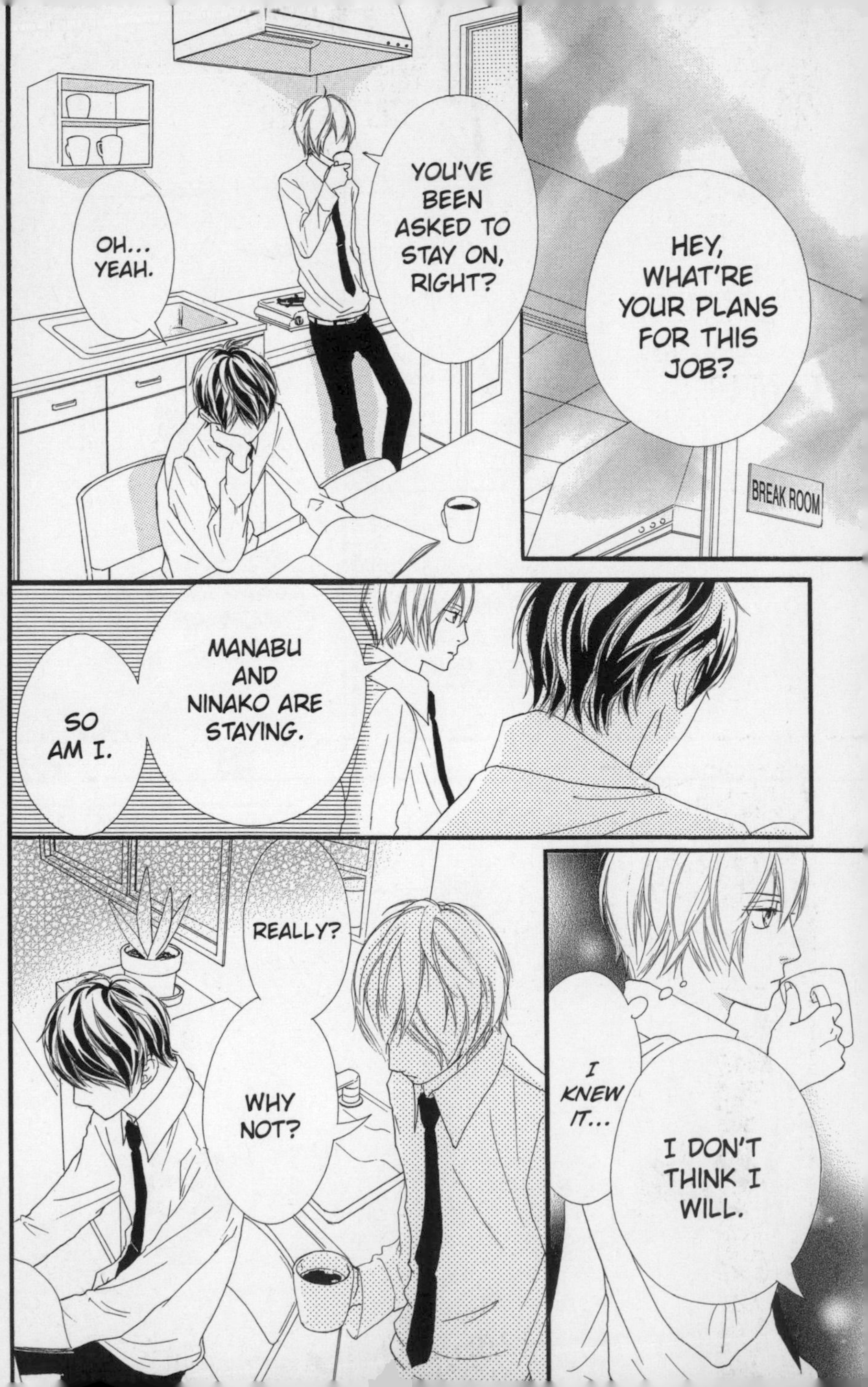
HEY, WHAT'RE YOUR PLANS FOR THIS JOB?
BREAK ROOM
YOU'VE BEEN ASKED TO STAY ON, RIGHT?
OH... YEAH.
MANABU AND NINAKO ARE STAYING.
SO AM I.
I KNEW IT...
I DON'T THINK I WILL.
REALLY?
WHY NOT?

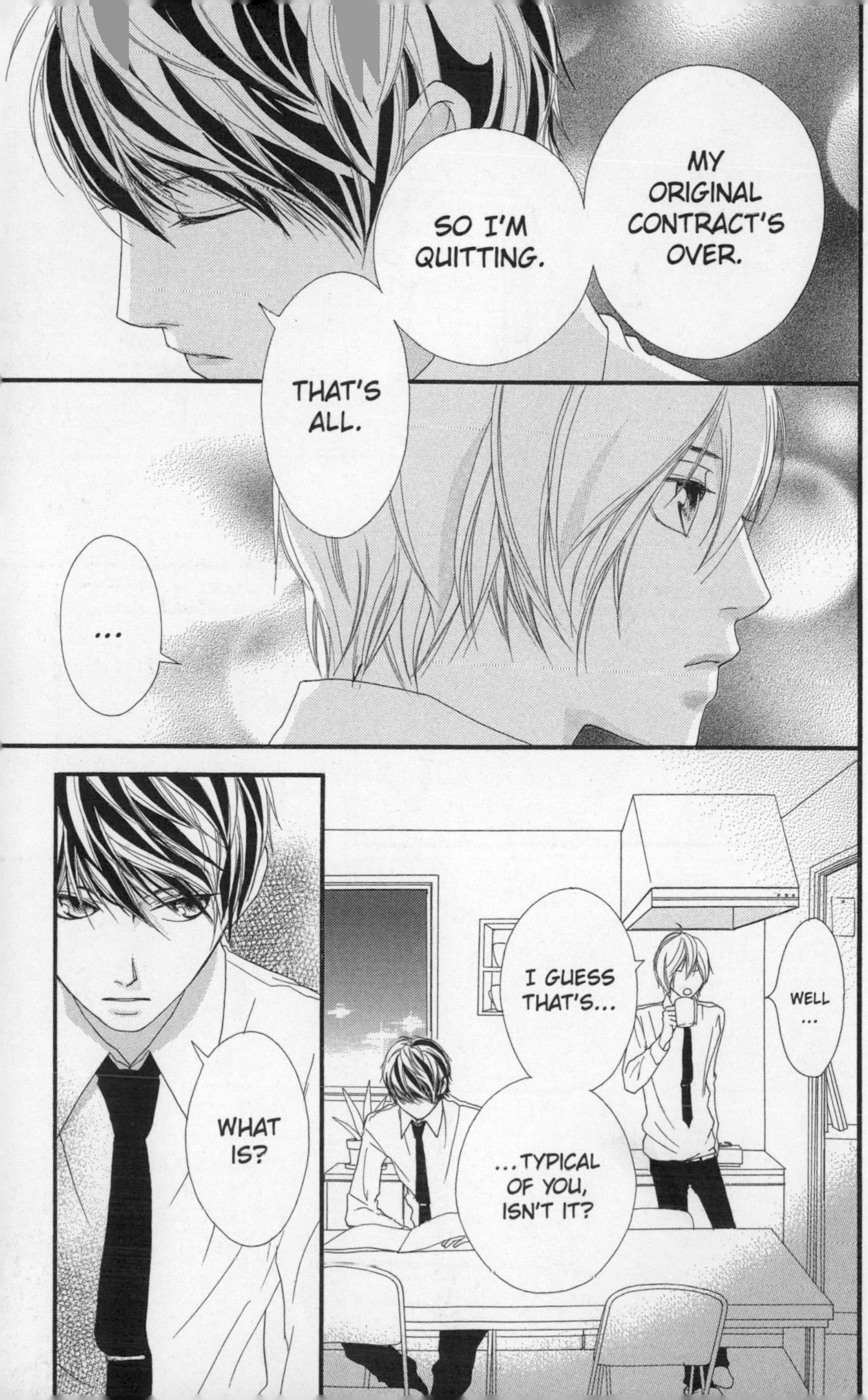
MY ORIGINAL CONTRACT'S OVER.
SO I'M QUITTING.
THAT'S ALL.
...
WELL...
I GUESS THAT'S...
...TYPICAL OF YOU, ISN'T IT?
WHAT IS?

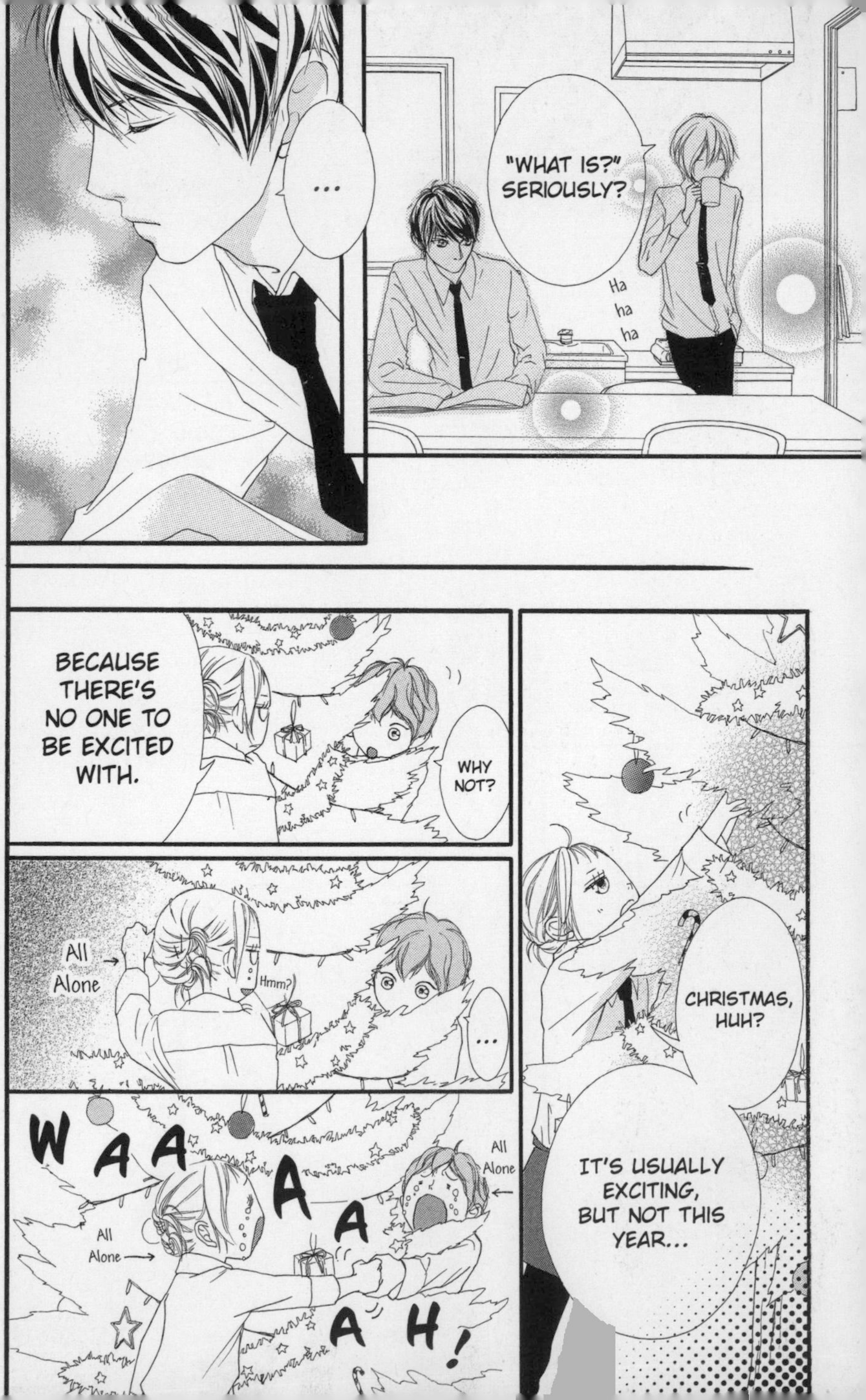
"WHAT IS?" SERIOUSLY?
Ha ha ha
...
CHRISTMAS, HUH?
IT'S USUALLY EXCITING, BUT NOT THIS YEAR...
WHY NOT?
BECAUSE THERE'S NO ONE TO BE EXCITED WITH.
...
Hmm?
All Alone
WAAAAAH!
All Alone
All Alone

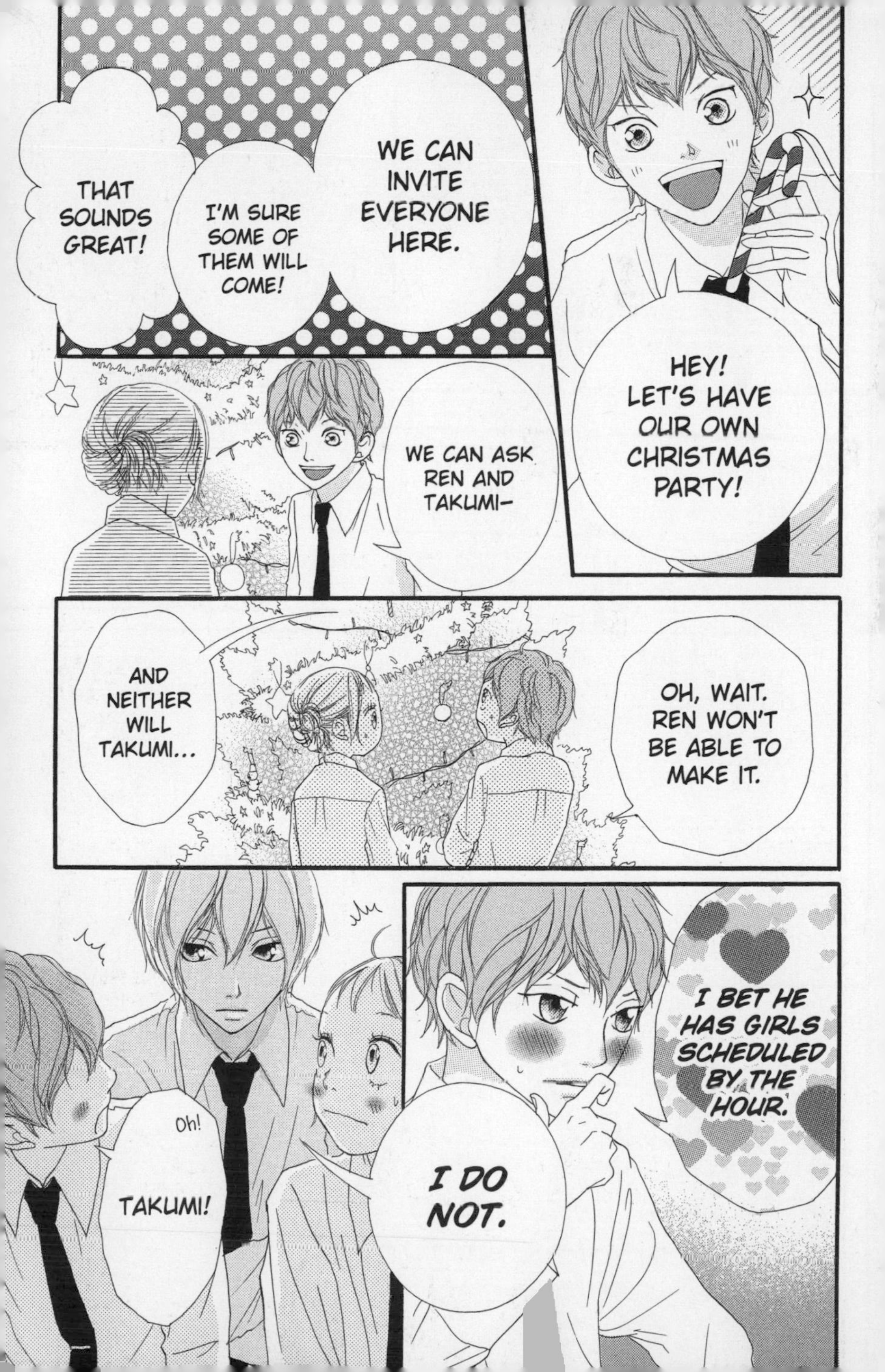
HEY! LET'S HAVE OUR OWN CHRISTMAS PARTY!
WE CAN INVITE EVERYONE HERE.
I'M SURE SOME OF THEM WILL COME!
THAT SOUNDS GREAT!
WE CAN ASK REN AND TAKUMI—
OH, WAIT. REN WON'T BE ABLE TO MAKE IT.
AND NEITHER WILL TAKUMI...
I BET HE HAS GIRLS SCHEDULED BY THE HOUR.
I DO NOT.
Oh!
TAKUMI!

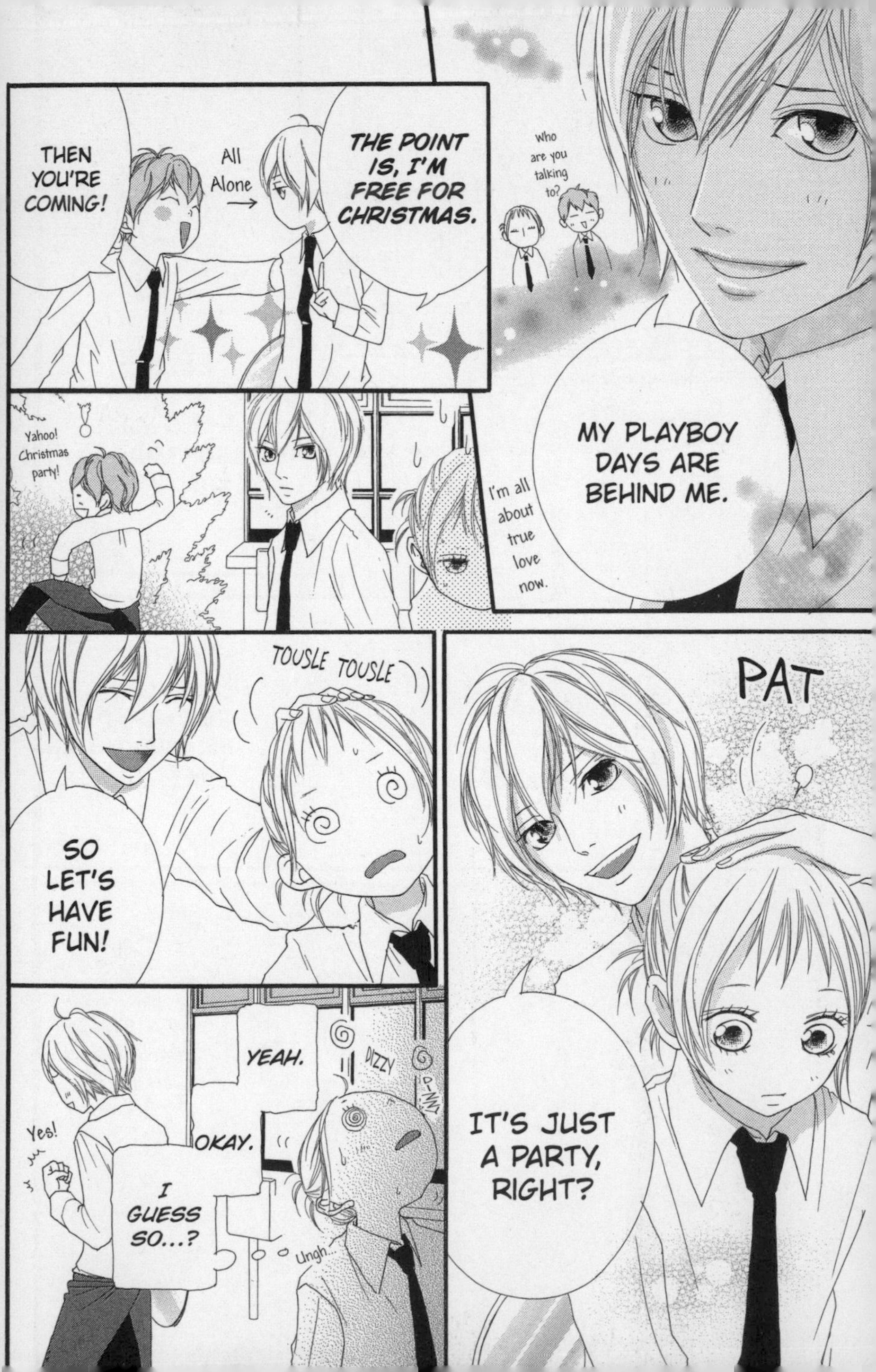
Who are you talking to?
MY PLAYBOY DAYS ARE BEHIND ME.
I'm all about true love now.
THE POINT IS, I'M FREE FOR CHRISTMAS.
All Alone →
THEN YOU'RE COMING!
Yahoo! Christmas party!
PAT
IT'S JUST A PARTY, RIGHT?
TOUSLE TOUSLE
SO LET'S HAVE FUN!
DIZZY
DIZZY
YEAH.
OKAY.
I GUESS SO...?
Unngh...
Yes!

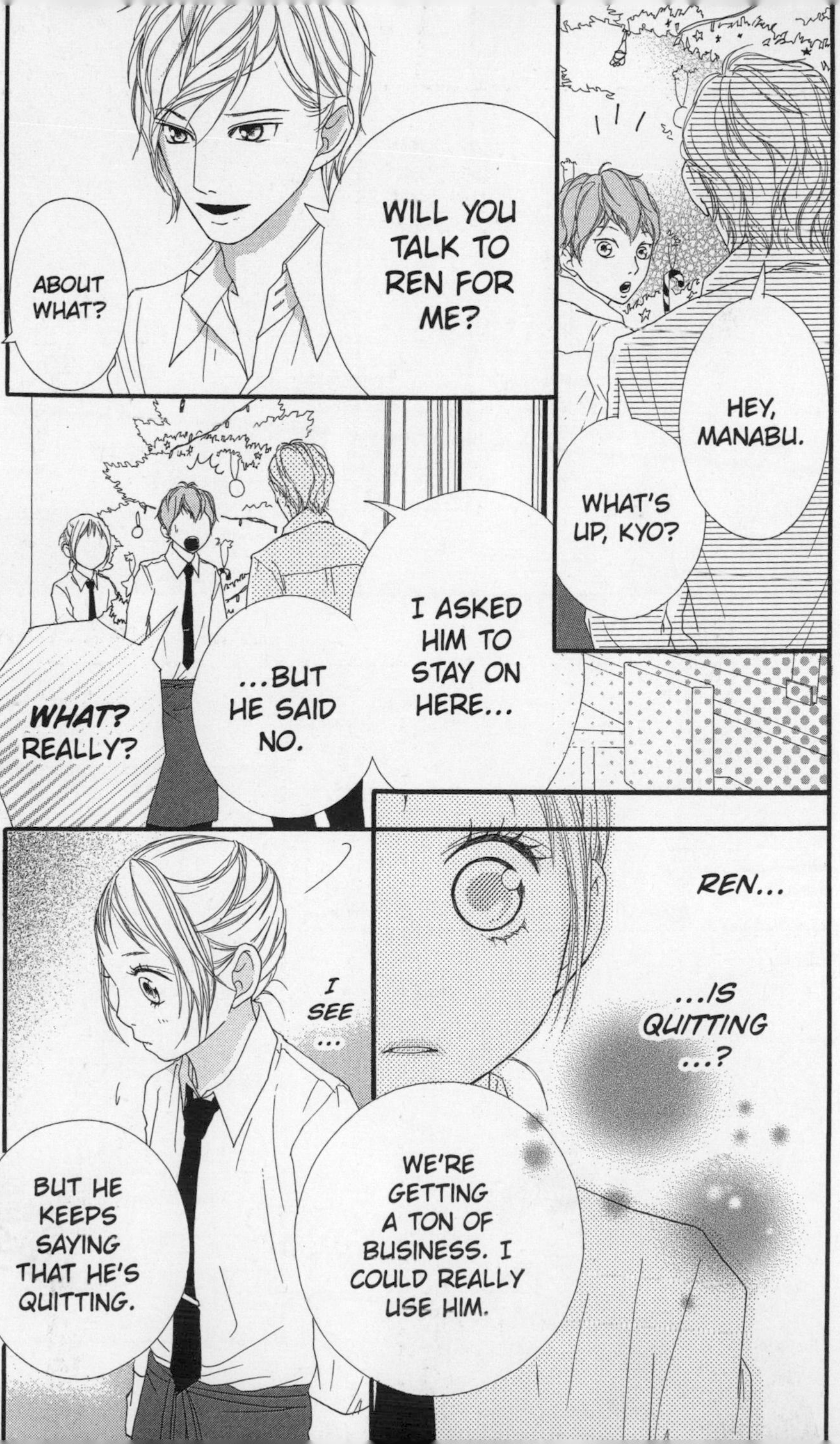
HEY, MANABU.
WHAT'S UP, KYO?
WILL YOU TALK TO REN FOR ME?
ABOUT WHAT?
I ASKED HIM TO STAY ON HERE...
...BUT HE SAID NO.
WHAT? REALLY?
REN...
...IS QUITTING...?
WE'RE GETTING A TON OF BUSINESS. I COULD REALLY USE HIM.
I SEE...
BUT HE KEEPS SAYING THAT HE'S QUITTING.

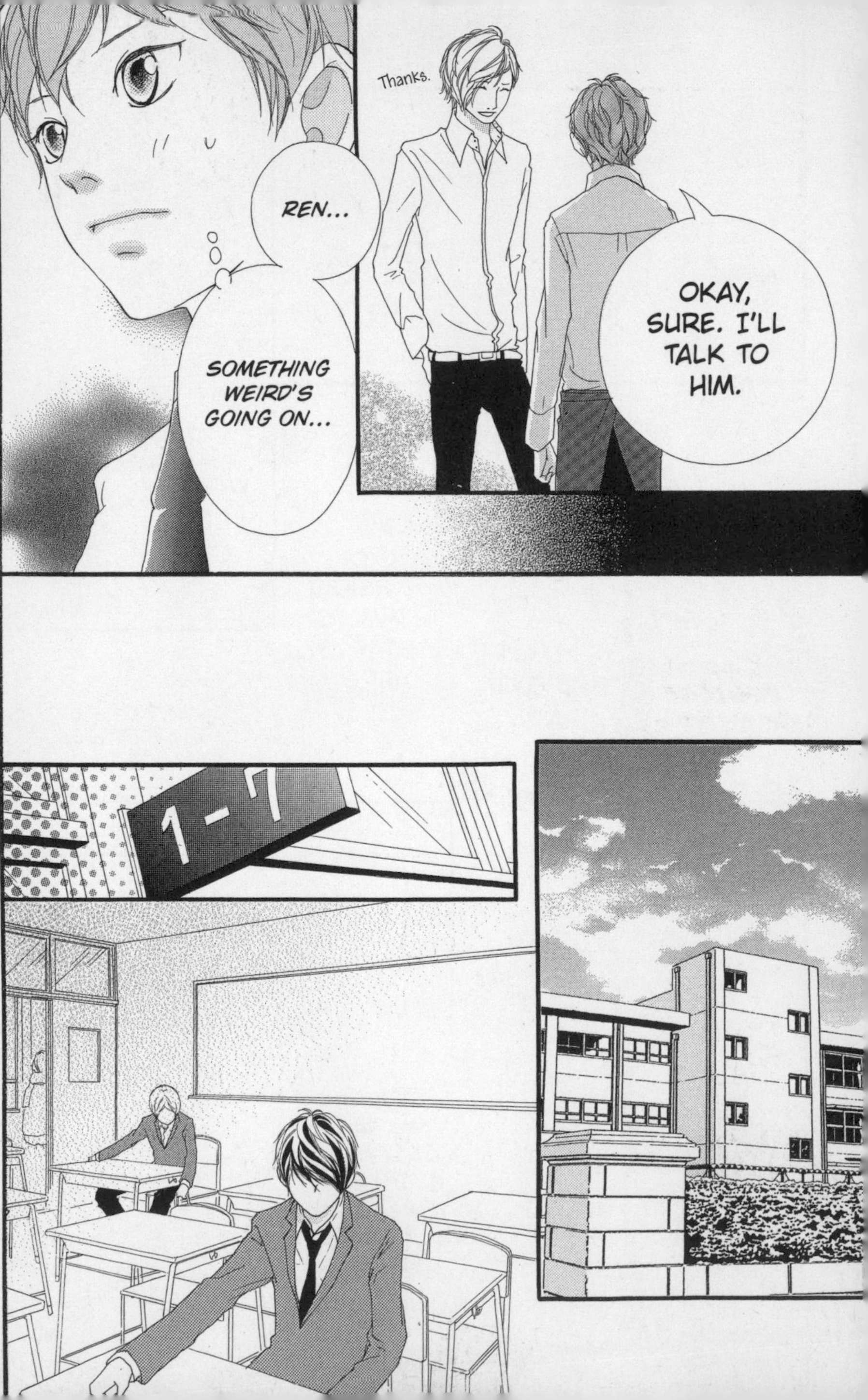
OKAY, SURE. I'LL TALK TO HIM.
Thanks.
REN...
SOMETHING WEIRD'S GOING ON...
1-7

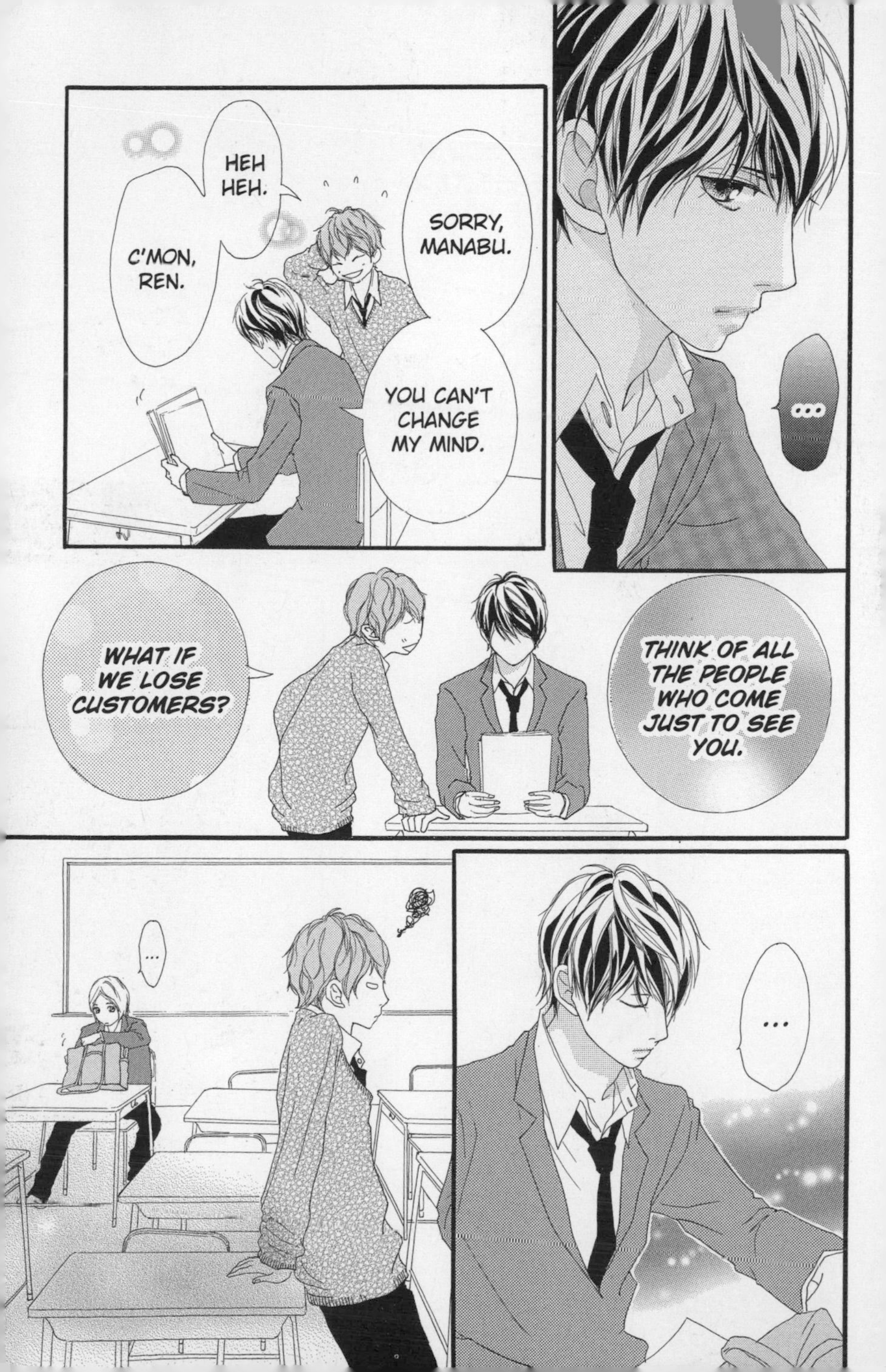
...
SORRY, MANABU.
HEH HEH.
C'MON, REN.
YOU CAN'T CHANGE MY MIND.
THINK OF ALL THE PEOPLE WHO COME JUST TO SEE YOU.
WHAT IF WE LOSE CUSTOMERS?
...
...

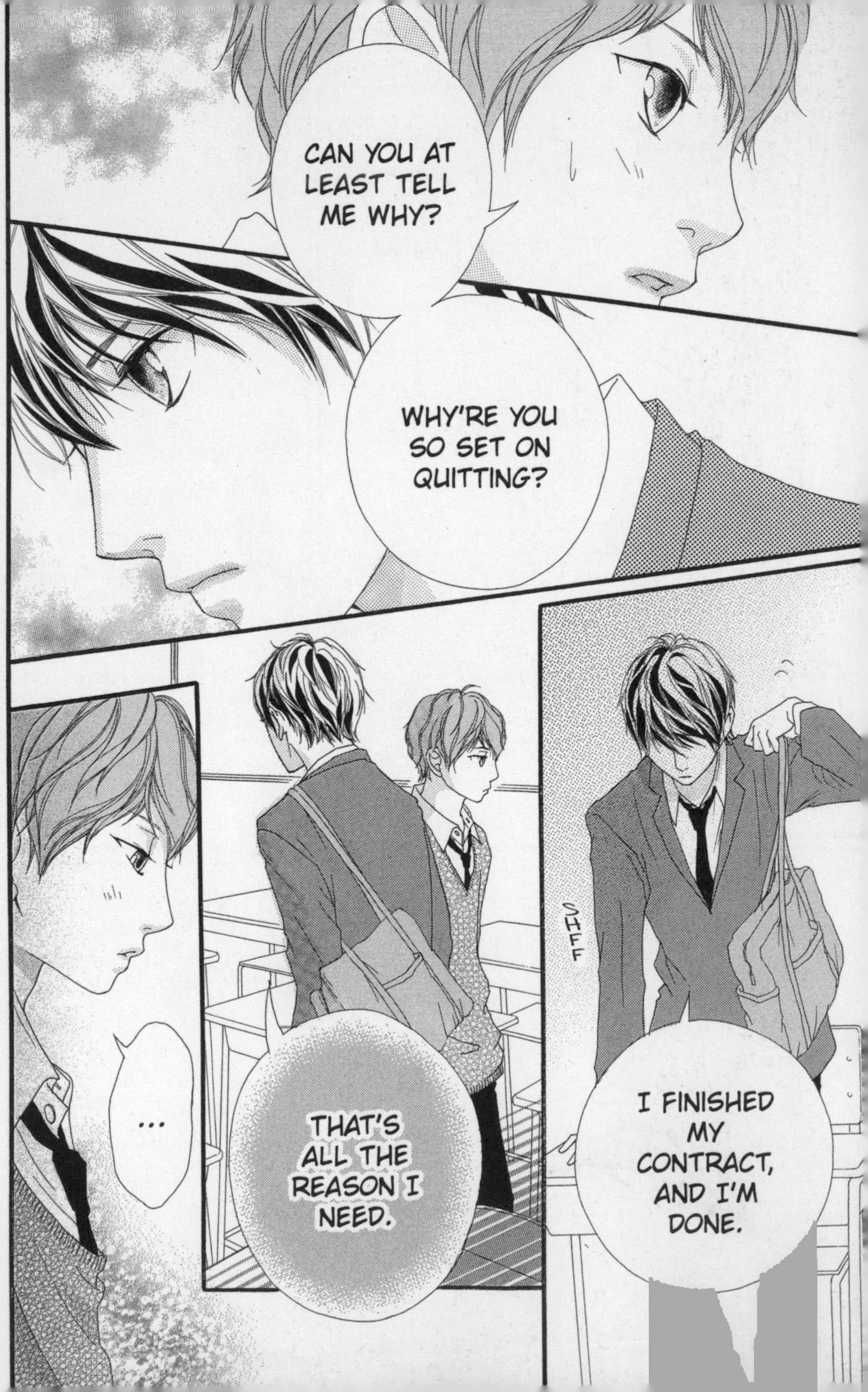
CAN YOU AT LEAST TELL ME WHY?
WHY'RE YOU SO SET ON QUITTING?
SHFF
I FINISHED MY CONTRACT, AND I'M DONE.
THAT'S ALL THE REASON I NEED.
...

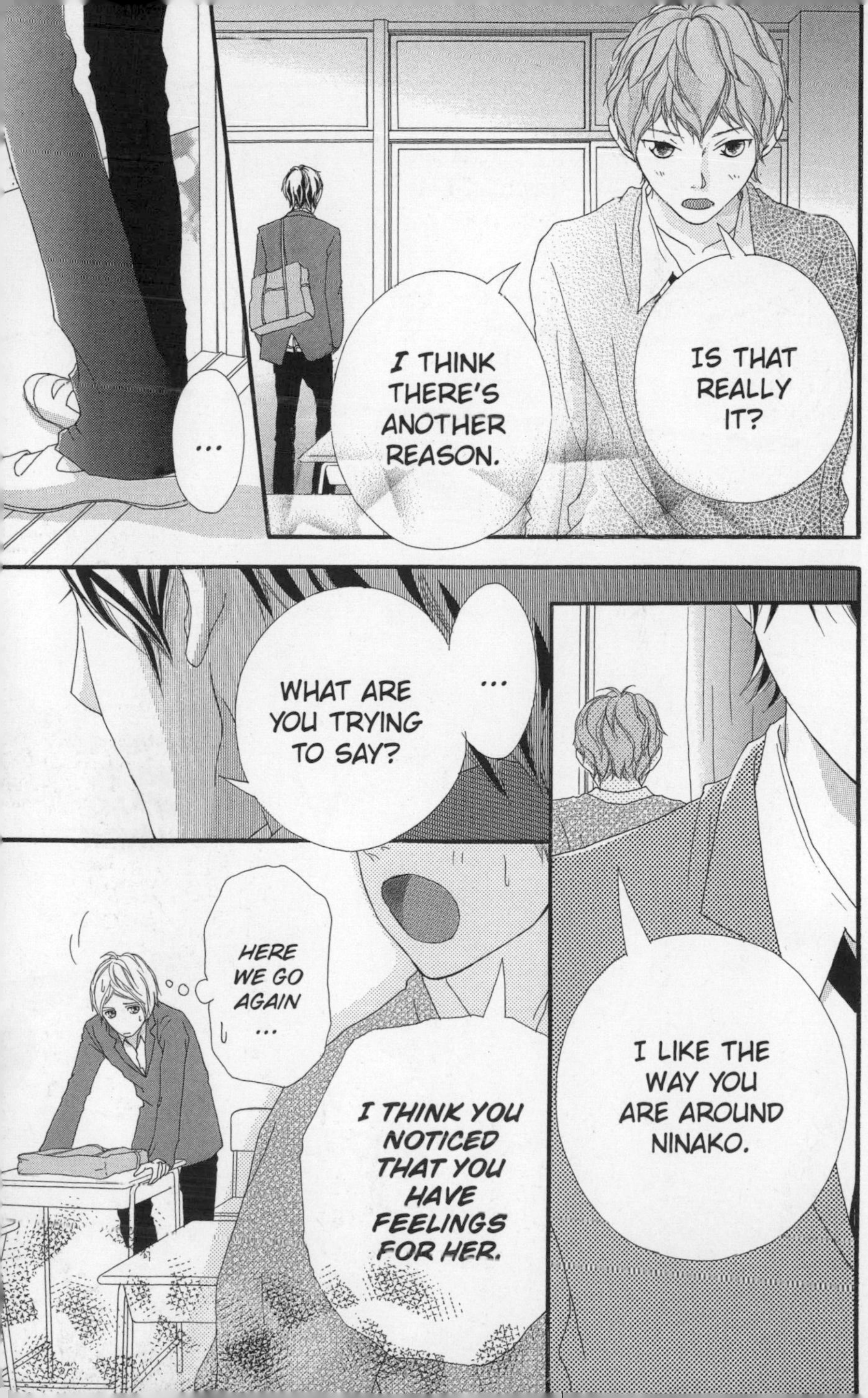
IS THAT REALLY IT?
I THINK THERE'S ANOTHER REASON.
...
I LIKE THE WAY YOU ARE AROUND NINAKO.
...
WHAT ARE YOU TRYING TO SAY?
I THINK YOU NOTICED THAT YOU HAVE FEELINGS FOR HER.
HERE WE GO AGAIN ...

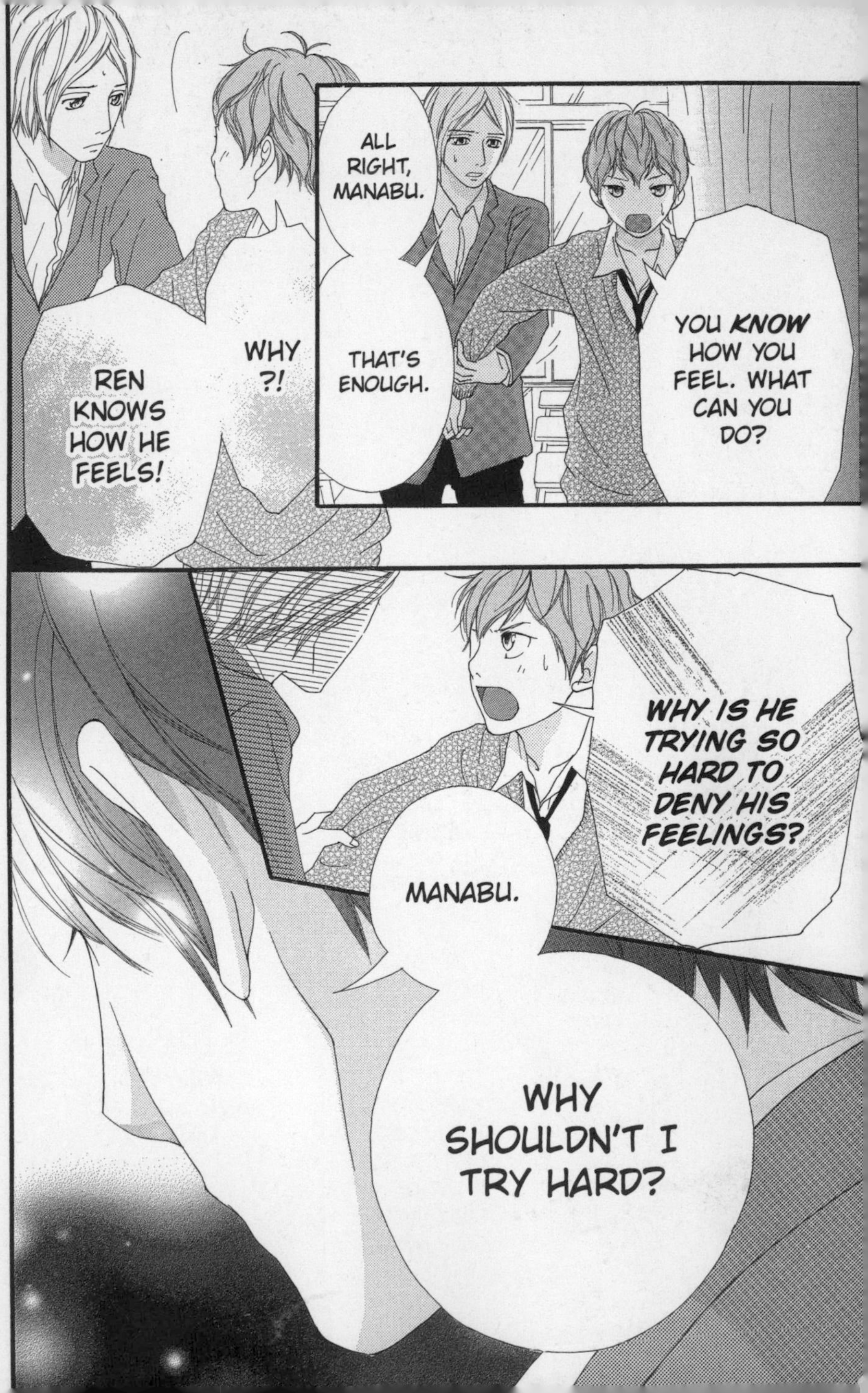
YOU KNOW HOW YOU FEEL. WHAT CAN YOU DO?
ALL RIGHT, MANABU.
THAT'S ENOUGH.
WHY ?!
REN KNOWS HOW HE FEELS!
WHY IS HE TRYING SO HARD TO DENY HIS FEELINGS?
MANABU.
WHY SHOULDN'T I TRY HARD?

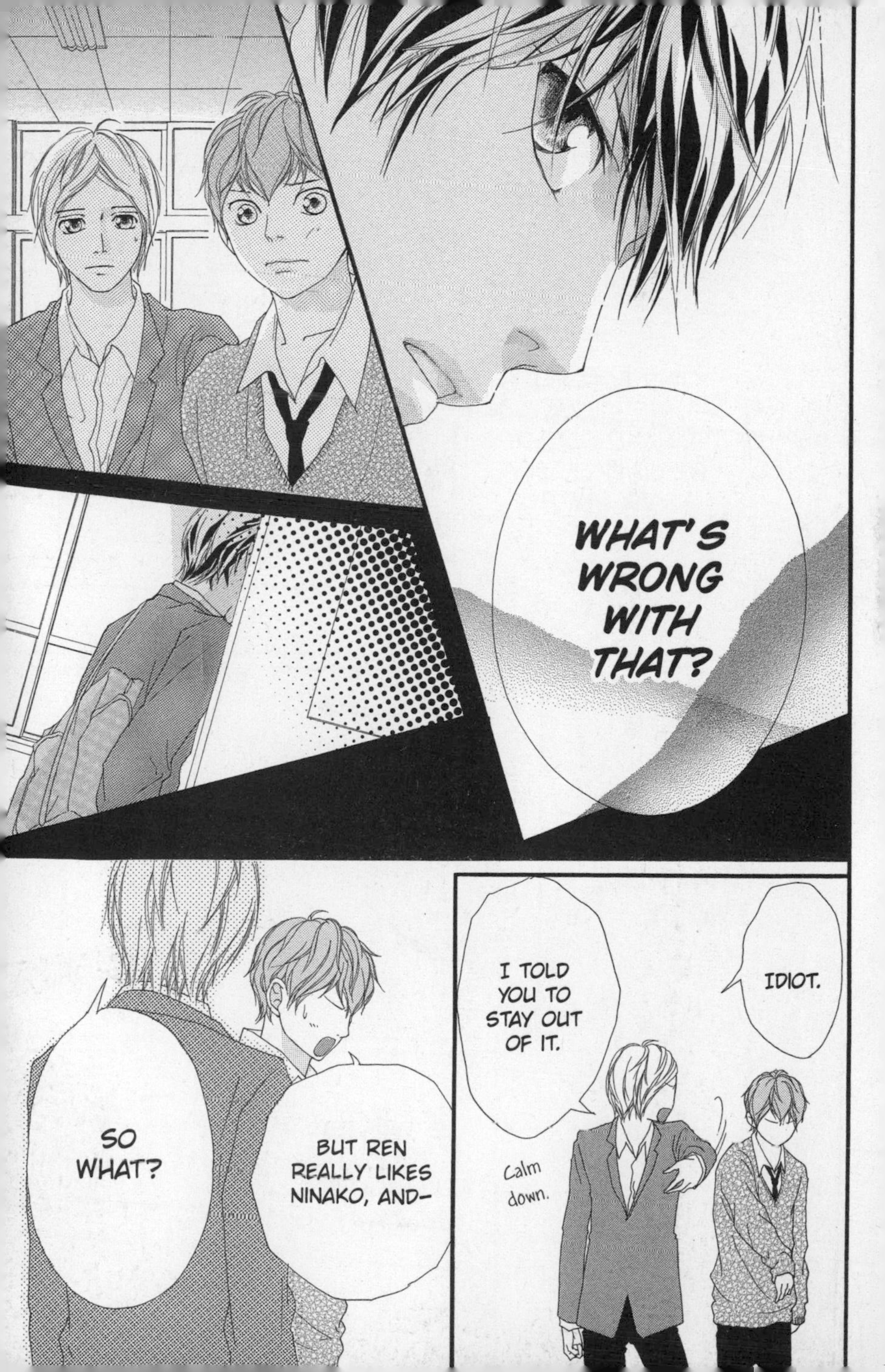
WHAT'S WRONG WITH THAT?
IDIOT.
I TOLD YOU TO STAY OUT OF IT.
Calm down.
BUT REN REALLY LIKES NINAKO, AND–
SO WHAT?

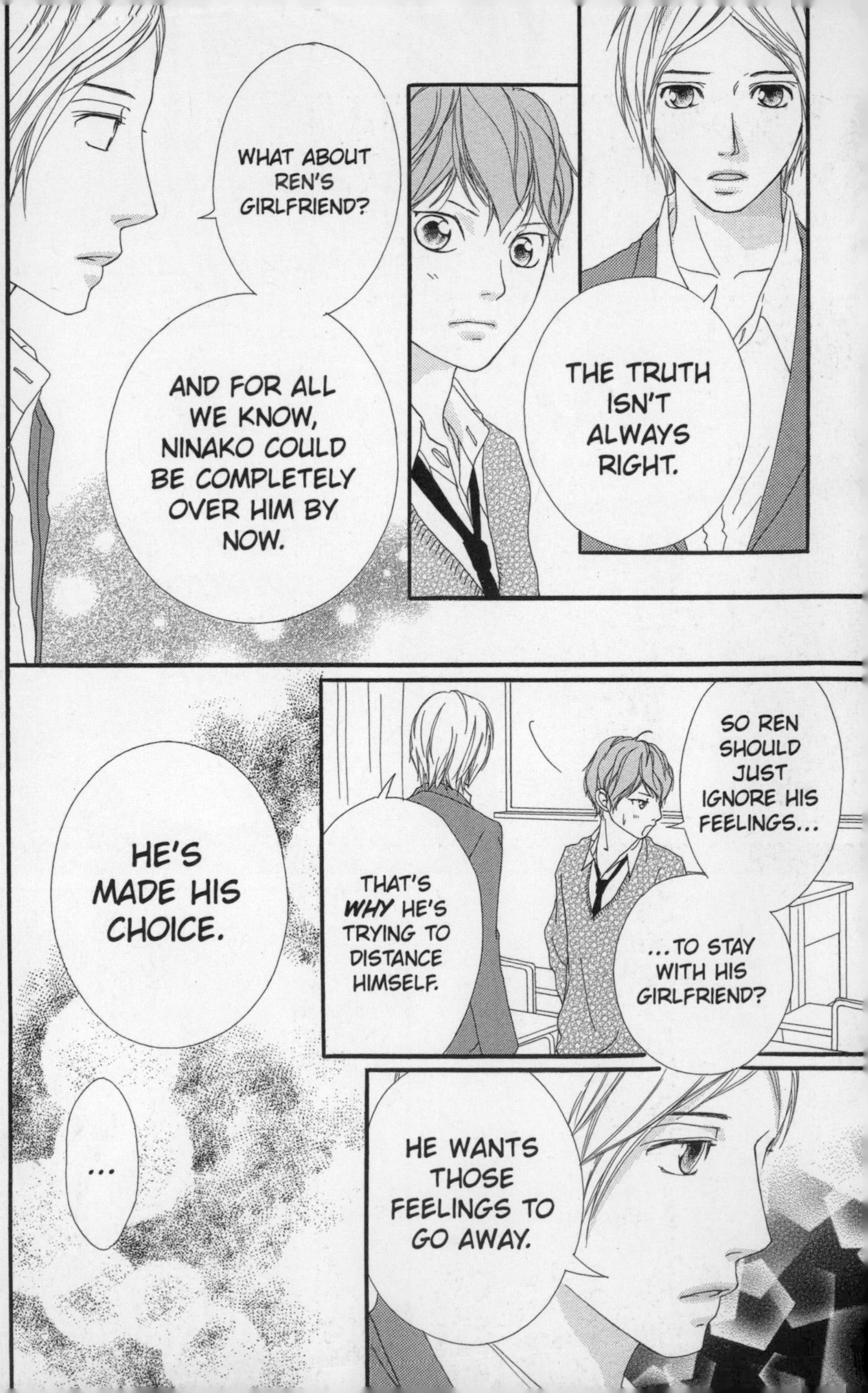
THE TRUTH ISN'T ALWAYS RIGHT.
WHAT ABOUT REN'S GIRLFRIEND?
AND FOR ALL WE KNOW, NINAKO COULD BE COMPLETELY OVER HIM BY NOW.
SO REN SHOULD JUST IGNORE HIS FEELINGS...
...TO STAY WITH HIS GIRLFRIEND?
THAT'S *WHY* HE'S TRYING TO DISTANCE HIMSELF.
HE WANTS THOSE FEELINGS TO GO AWAY.
HE'S MADE HIS CHOICE.
...

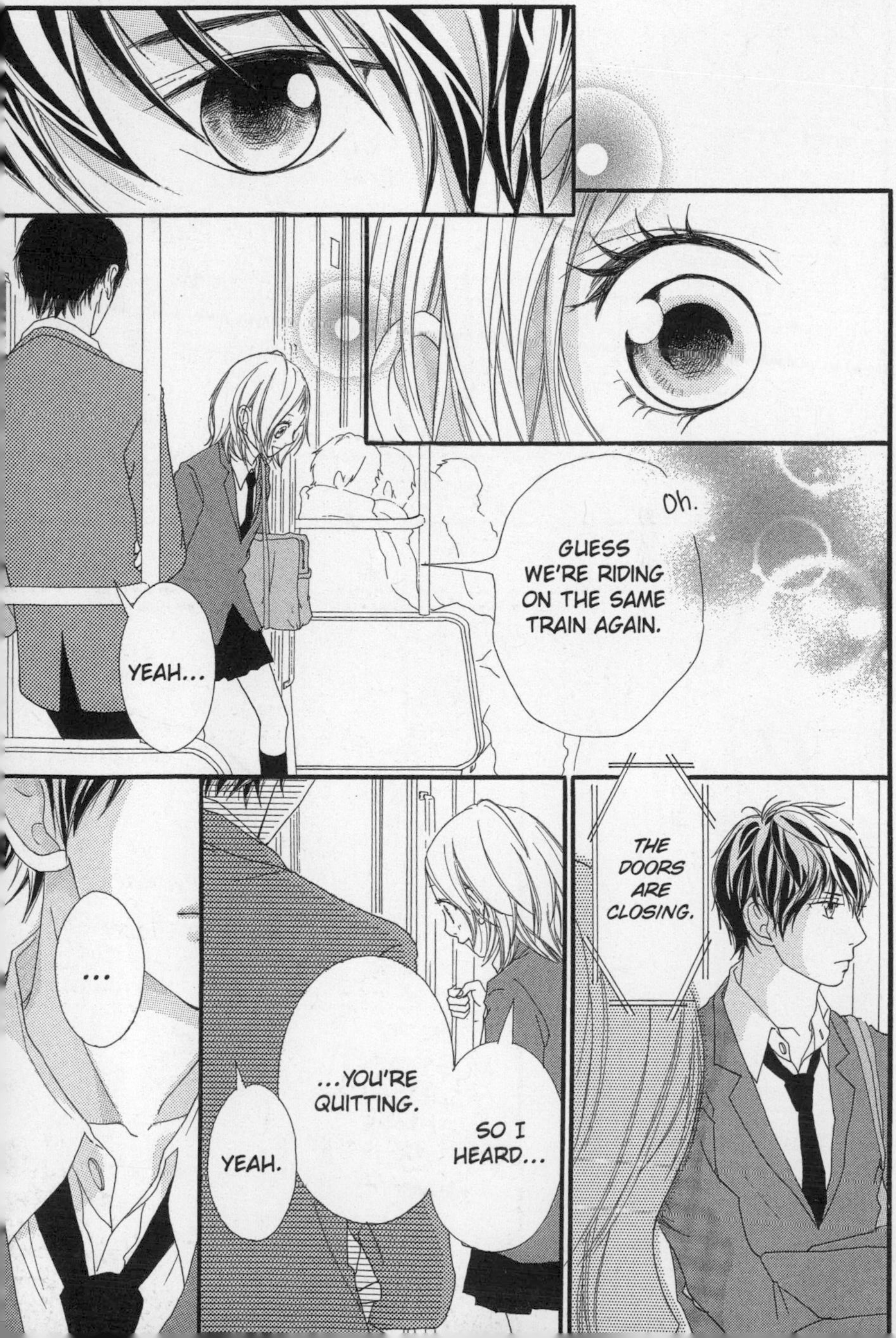
Oh.
GUESS WE'RE RIDING ON THE SAME TRAIN AGAIN.
YEAH...
THE DOORS ARE CLOSING.
SO I HEARD...
...YOU'RE QUITTING.
YEAH.
...

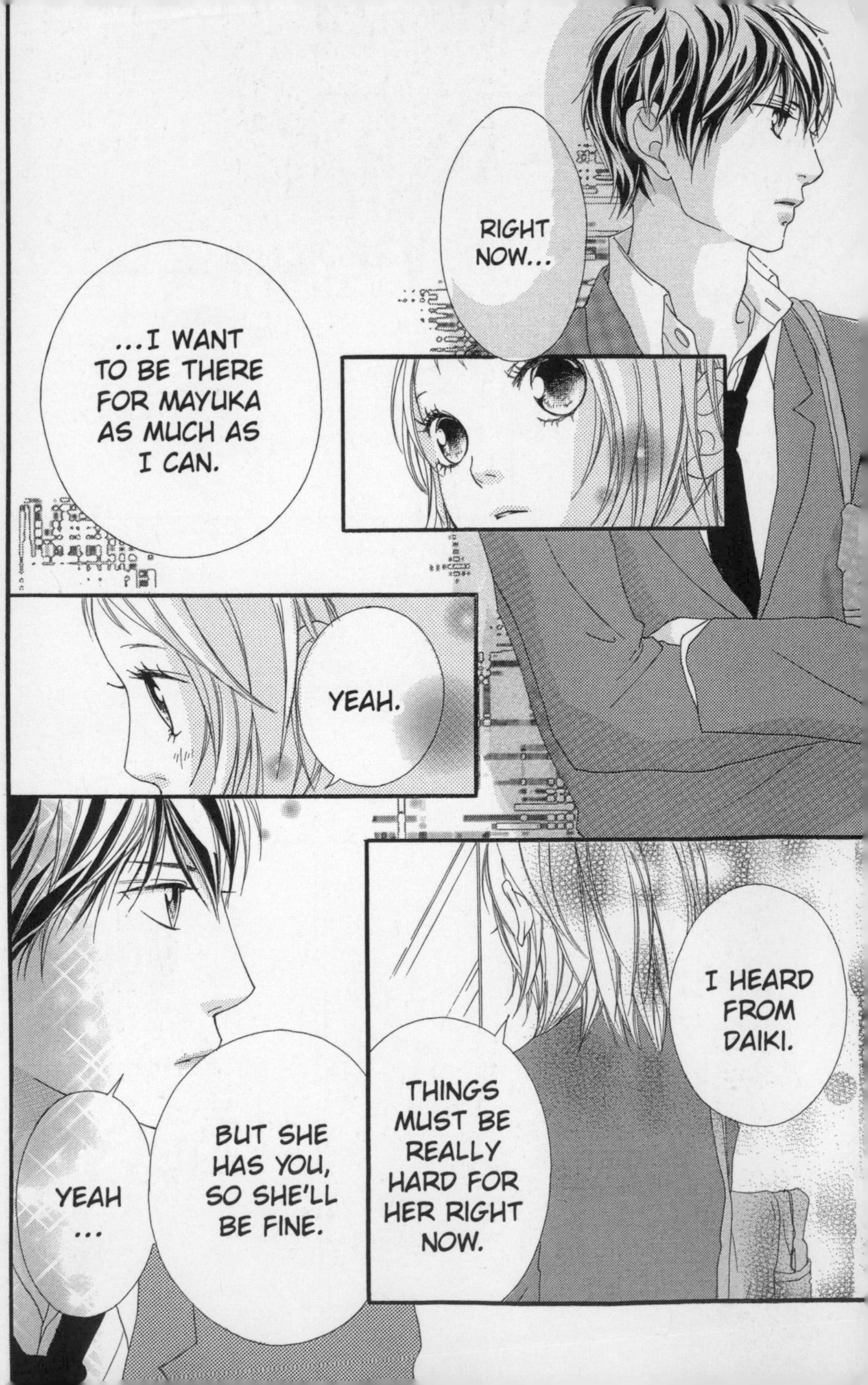
RIGHT NOW...
...I WANT TO BE THERE FOR MAYUKA AS MUCH AS I CAN.
YEAH.
I HEARD FROM DAIKI.
THINGS MUST BE REALLY HARD FOR HER RIGHT NOW.
BUT SHE HAS YOU, SO SHE'LL BE FINE.
YEAH ...

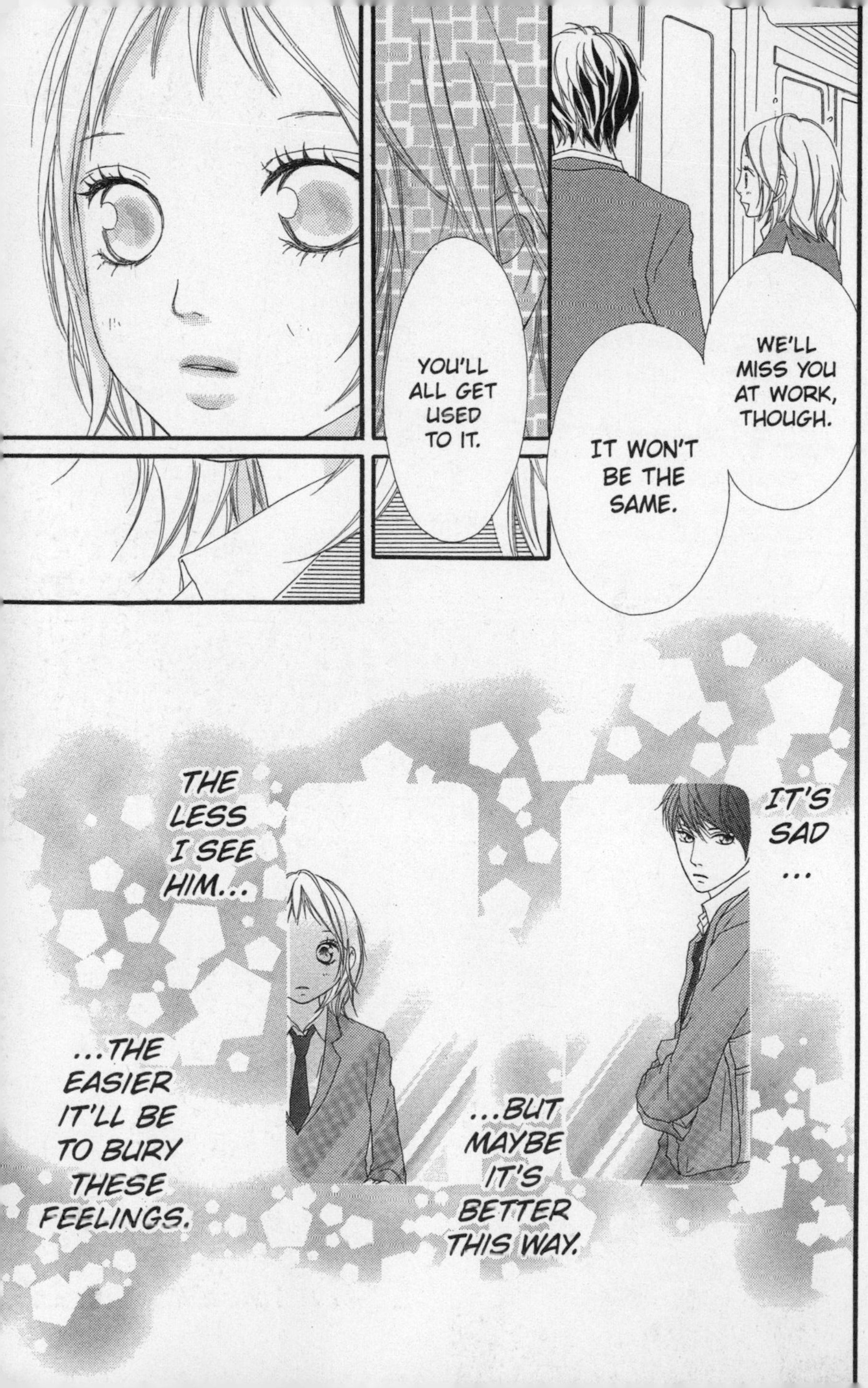
WE'LL MISS YOU AT WORK, THOUGH.
IT WON'T BE THE SAME.
YOU'LL ALL GET USED TO IT.
IT'S SAD...
...BUT MAYBE IT'S BETTER THIS WAY.
THE LESS I SEE HIM...
...THE EASIER IT'LL BE TO BURY THESE FEELINGS.

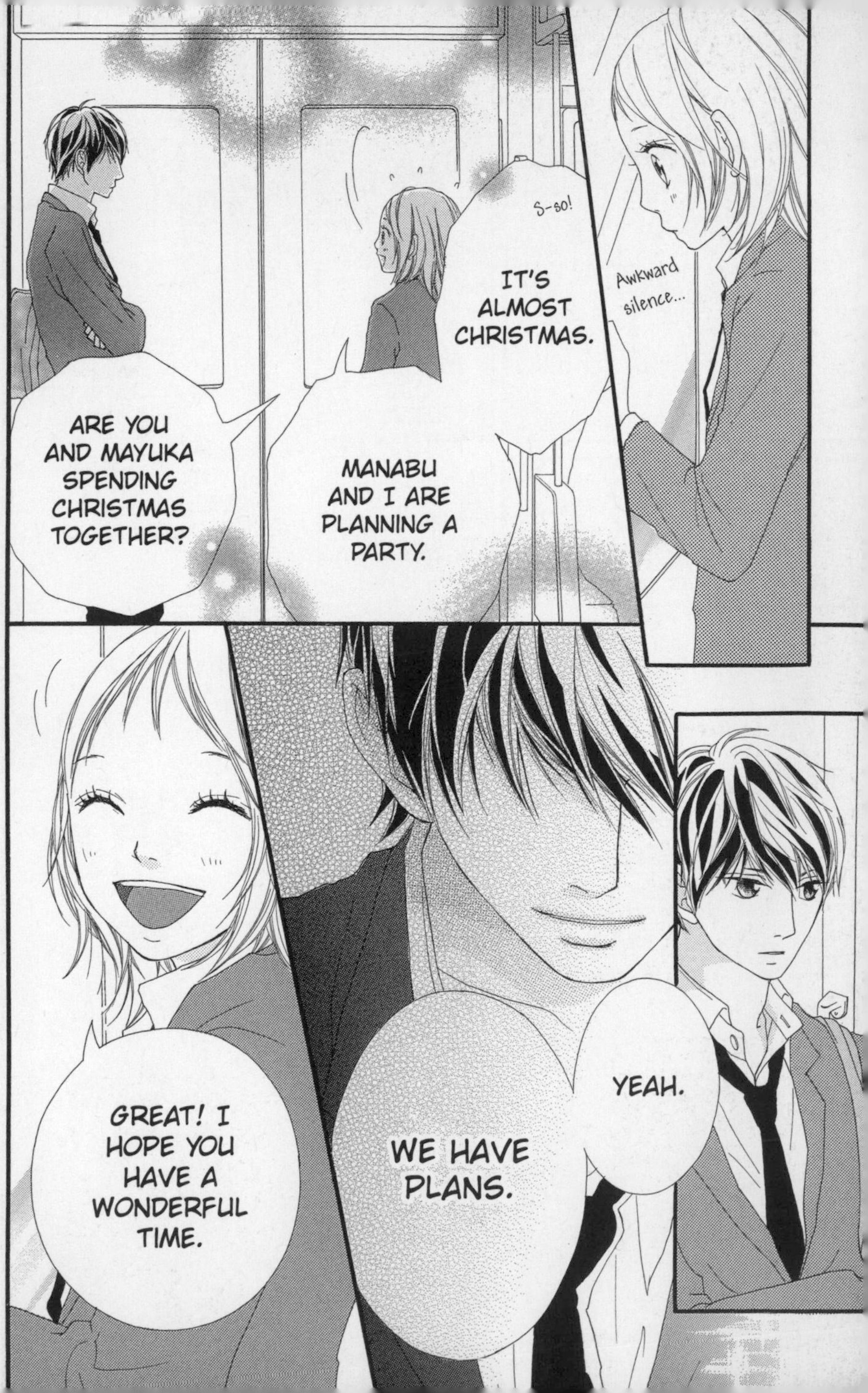
Awkward silence...
S-so!
IT'S ALMOST CHRISTMAS.
MANABU AND I ARE PLANNING A PARTY.
ARE YOU AND MAYUKA SPENDING CHRISTMAS TOGETHER?
YEAH.
WE HAVE PLANS.
GREAT! I HOPE YOU HAVE A WONDERFUL TIME.

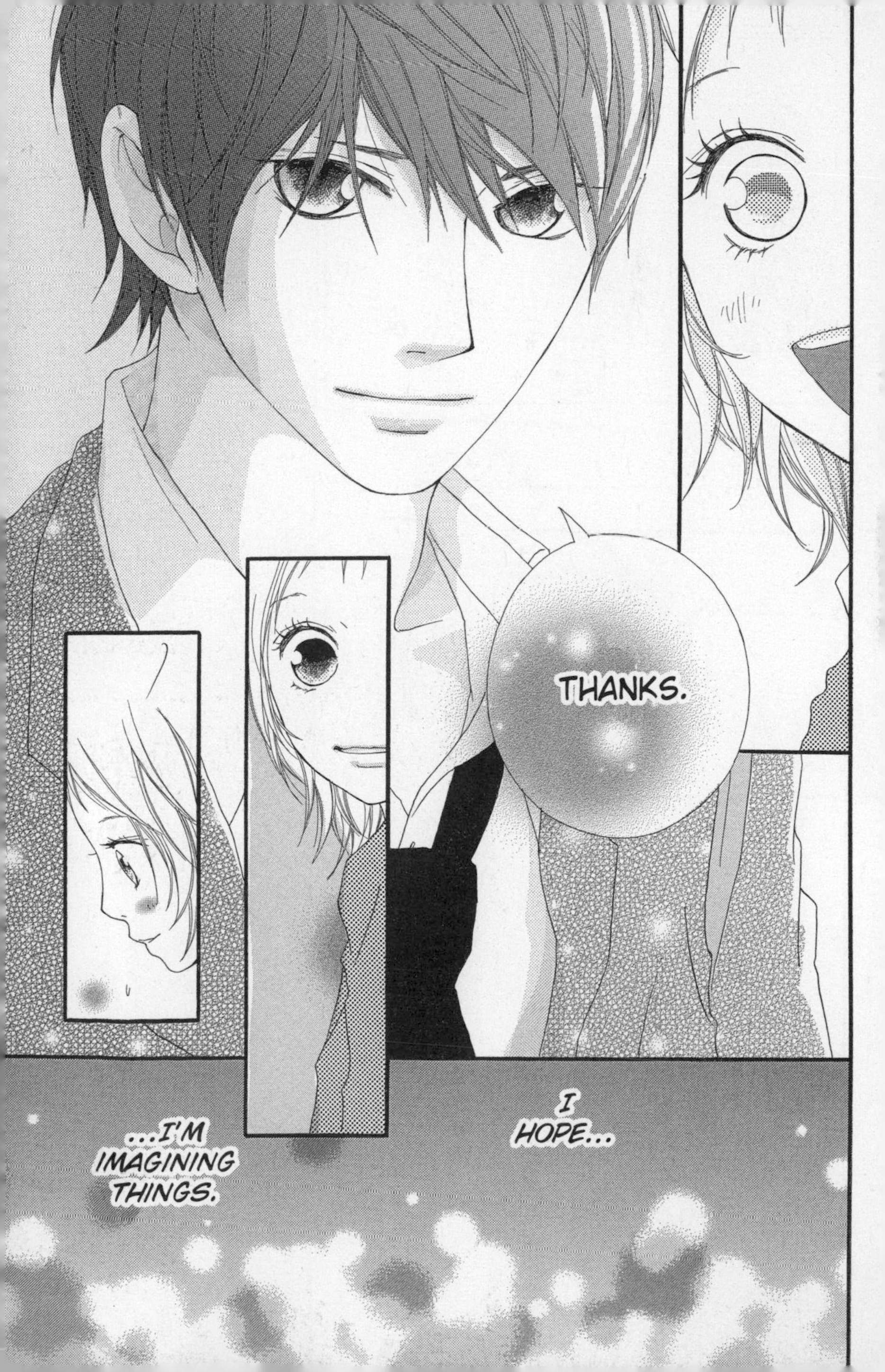
THANKS.
I HOPE...
...I'M IMAGINING THINGS.

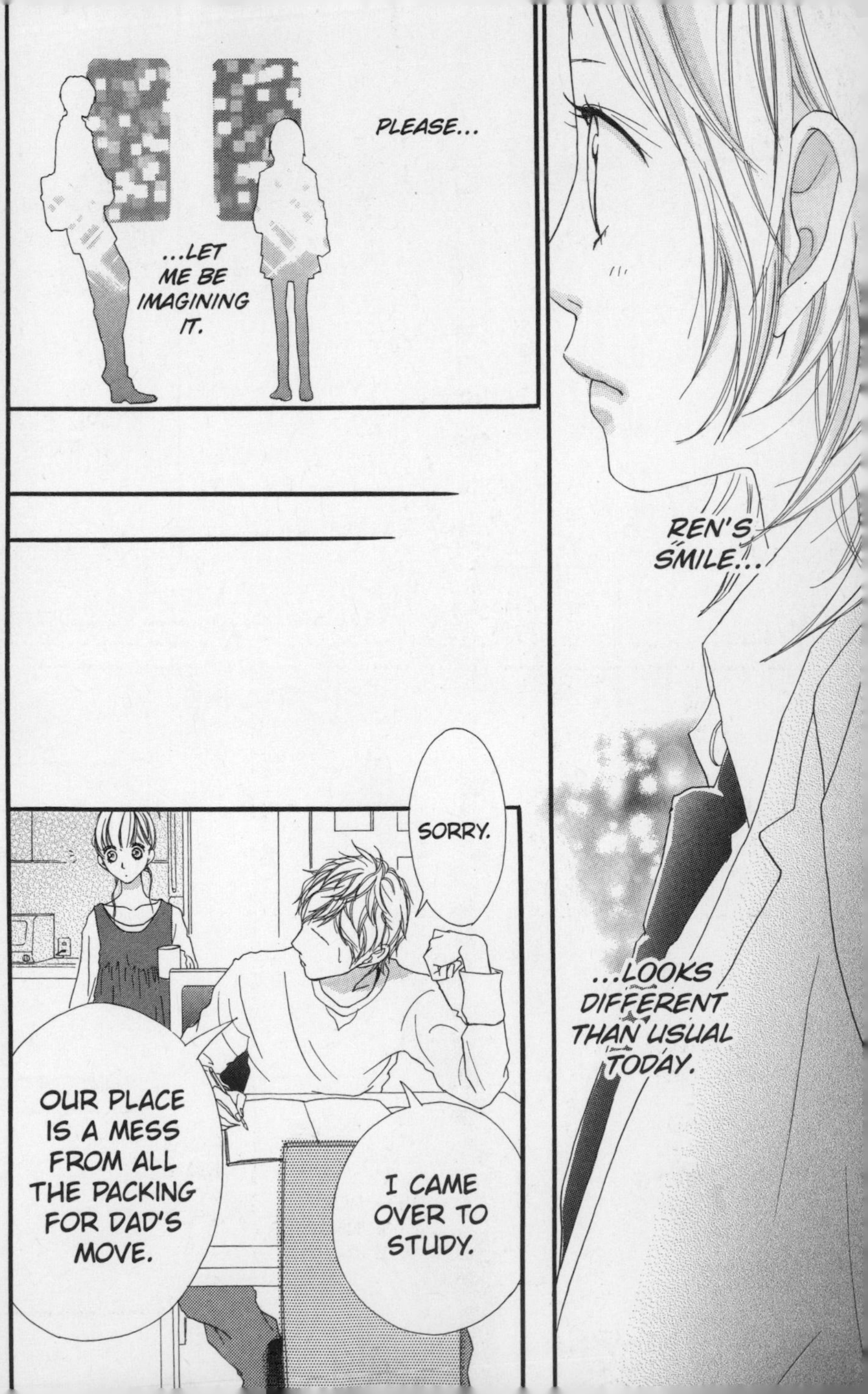
REN'S SMILE...
...LOOKS DIFFERENT THAN USUAL TODAY.
PLEASE...
...LET ME BE IMAGINING IT.
SORRY.
I CAME OVER TO STUDY.
OUR PLACE IS A MESS FROM ALL THE PACKING FOR DAD'S MOVE.

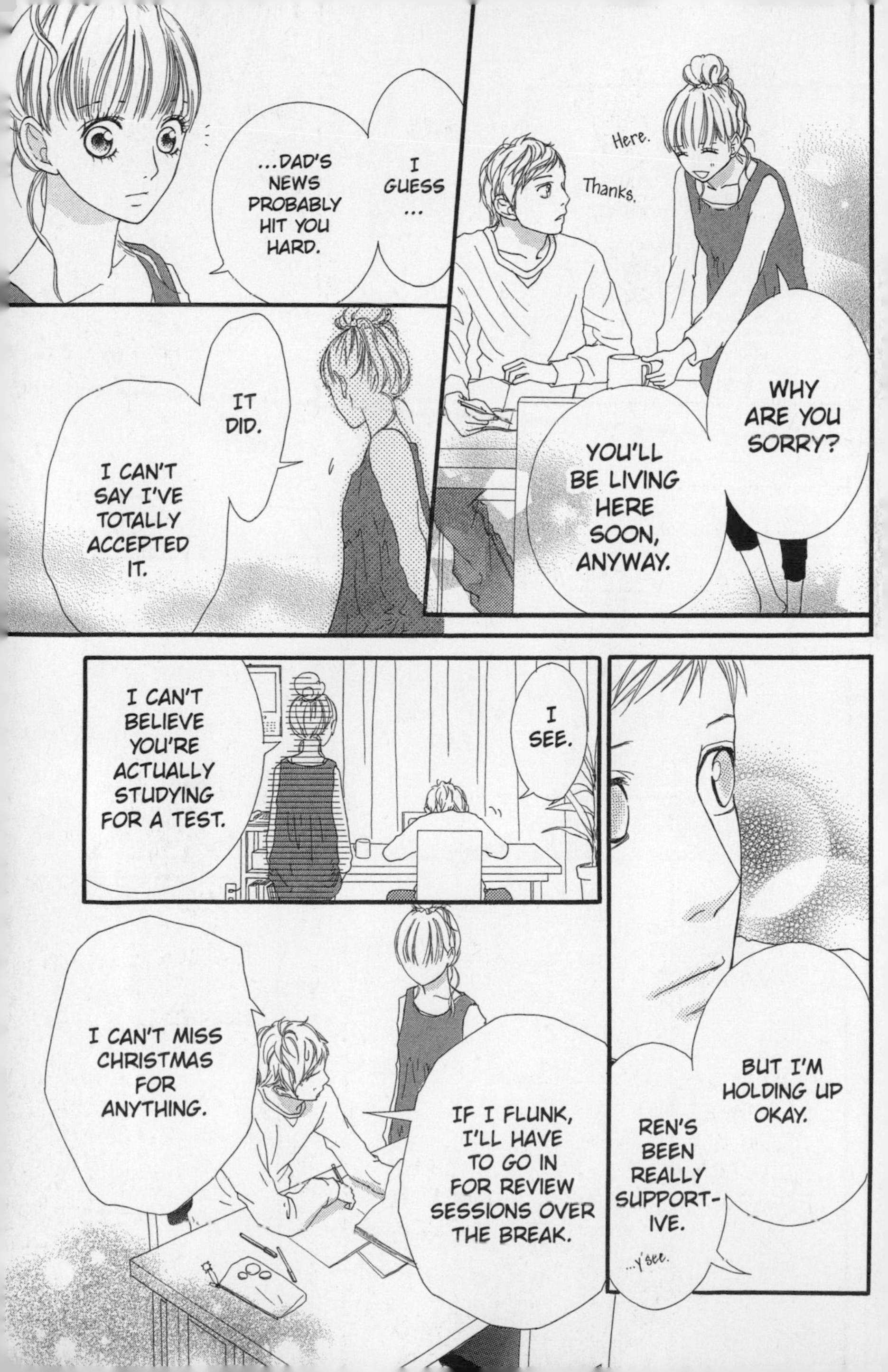
Here.
Thanks.
WHY ARE YOU SORRY?
YOU'LL BE LIVING HERE SOON, ANYWAY.
I GUESS ...
...DAD'S NEWS PROBABLY HIT YOU HARD.
IT DID.
I CAN'T SAY I'VE TOTALLY ACCEPTED IT.
BUT I'M HOLDING UP OKAY.
REN'S BEEN REALLY SUPPORT-IVE.
...y'see.
I SEE.
I CAN'T BELIEVE YOU'RE ACTUALLY STUDYING FOR A TEST.
IF I FLUNK, I'LL HAVE TO GO IN FOR REVIEW SESSIONS OVER THE BREAK.
I CAN'T MISS CHRISTMAS FOR ANYTHING.

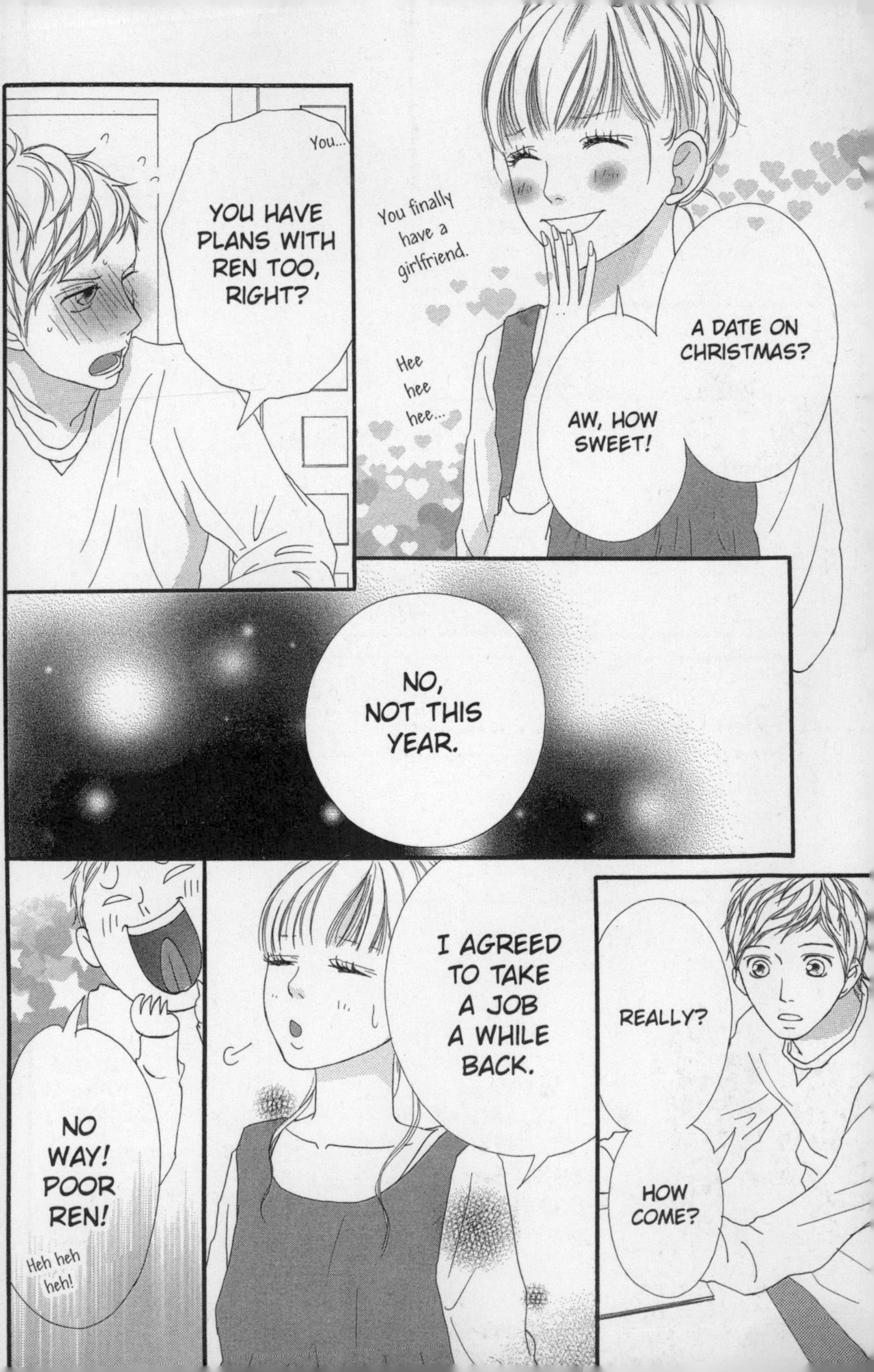
A DATE ON CHRISTMAS?
AW, HOW SWEET!
You finally have a girlfriend.
Hee hee hee...
You...
YOU HAVE PLANS WITH REN TOO, RIGHT?
NO, NOT THIS YEAR.
REALLY?
HOW COME?
I AGREED TO TAKE A JOB A WHILE BACK.
NO WAY! POOR REN!
Heh heh heh!

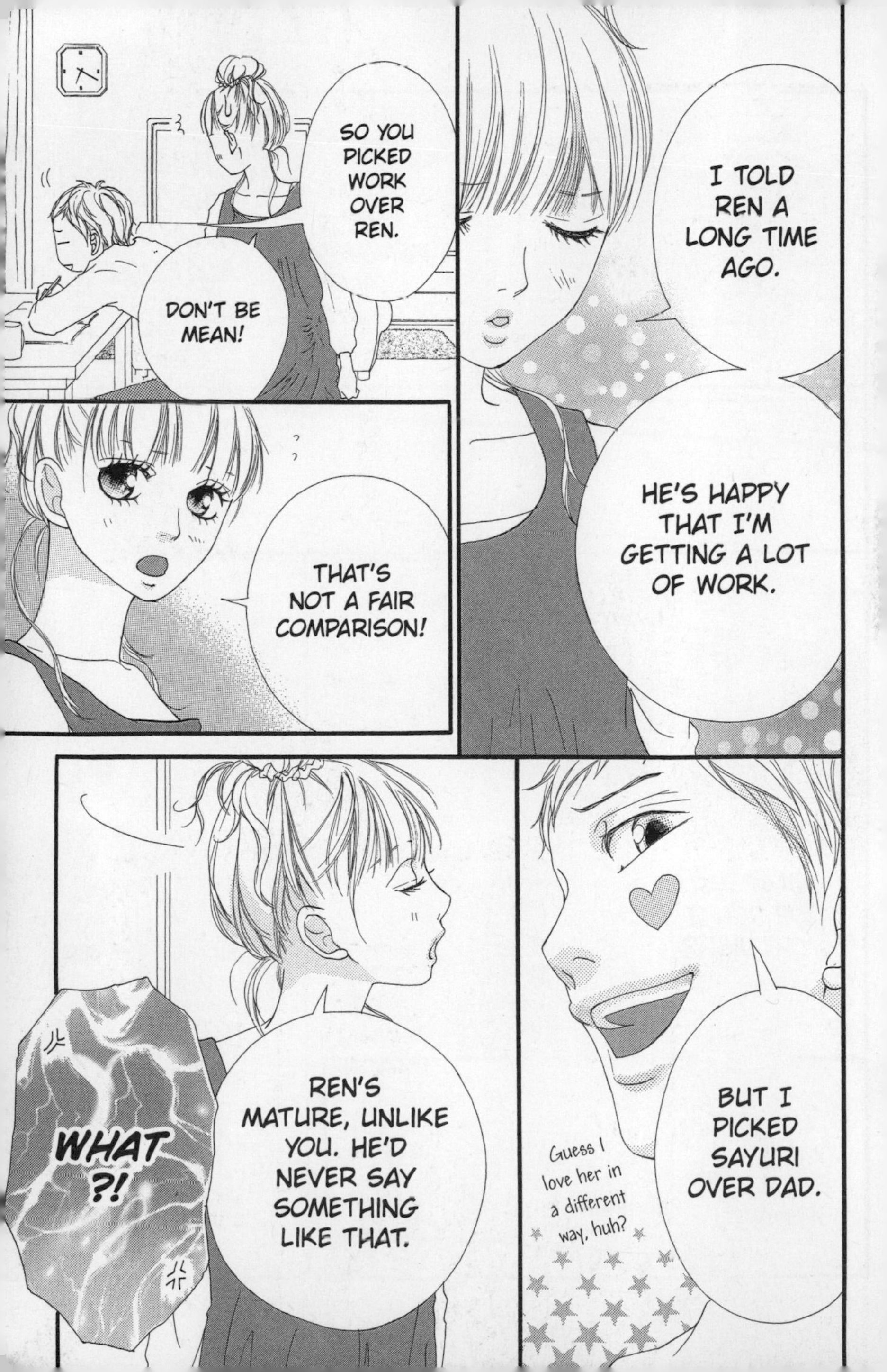
I TOLD REN A LONG TIME AGO.
HE'S HAPPY THAT I'M GETTING A LOT OF WORK.
SO YOU PICKED WORK OVER REN.
DON'T BE MEAN!
THAT'S NOT A FAIR COMPARISON!
BUT I PICKED SAYURI OVER DAD.
Guess I love her in a different way, huh?
REN'S MATURE, UNLIKE YOU. HE'D NEVER SAY SOMETHING LIKE THAT.
WHAT?!

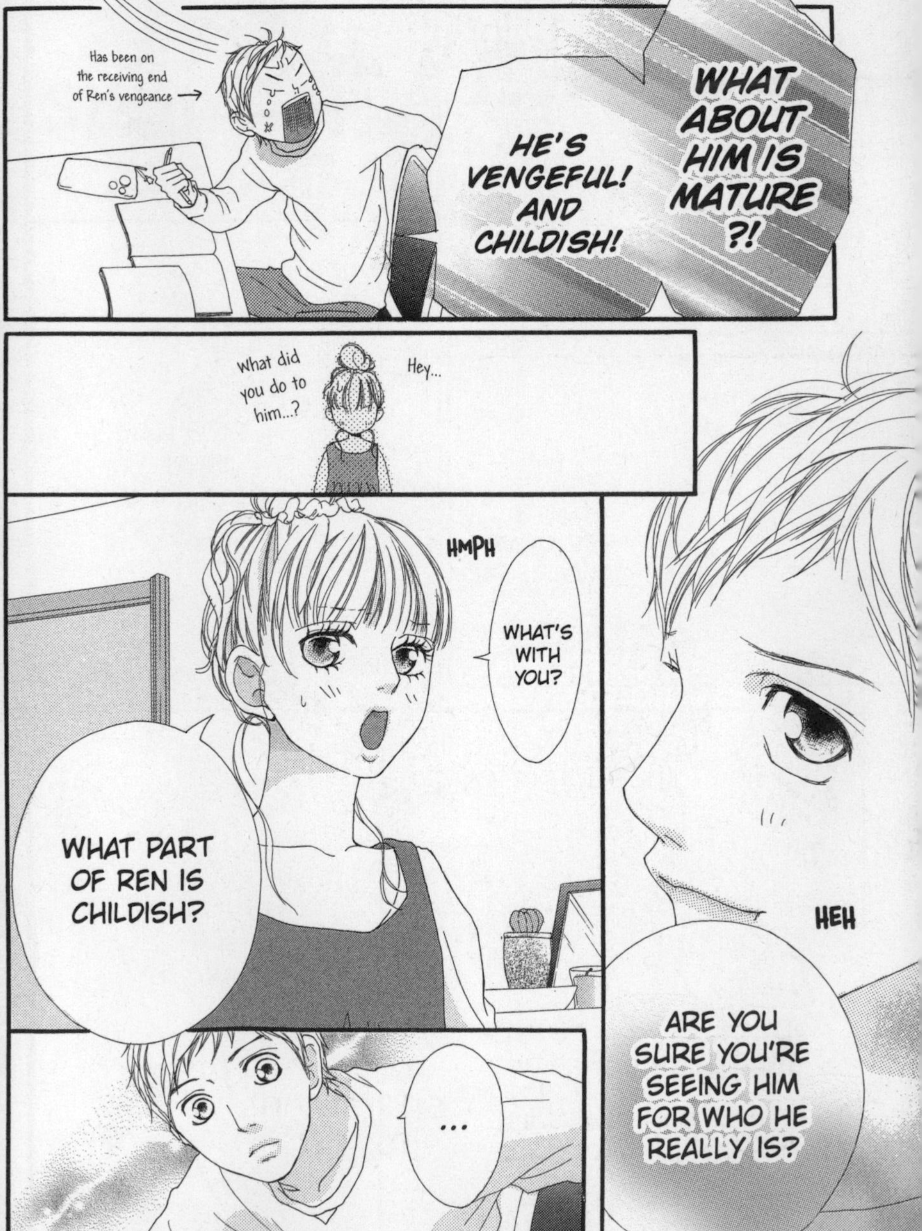
WHAT ABOUT HIM IS MATURE ?!
HE'S VENGEFUL! AND CHILDISH!
Has been on the receiving end of Ren's vengeance →
Hey...
What did you do to him...?
WHAT PART OF REN IS CHILDISH?
HMPH
WHAT'S WITH YOU?
HEH
ARE YOU SURE YOU'RE SEEING HIM FOR WHO HE REALLY IS?
...

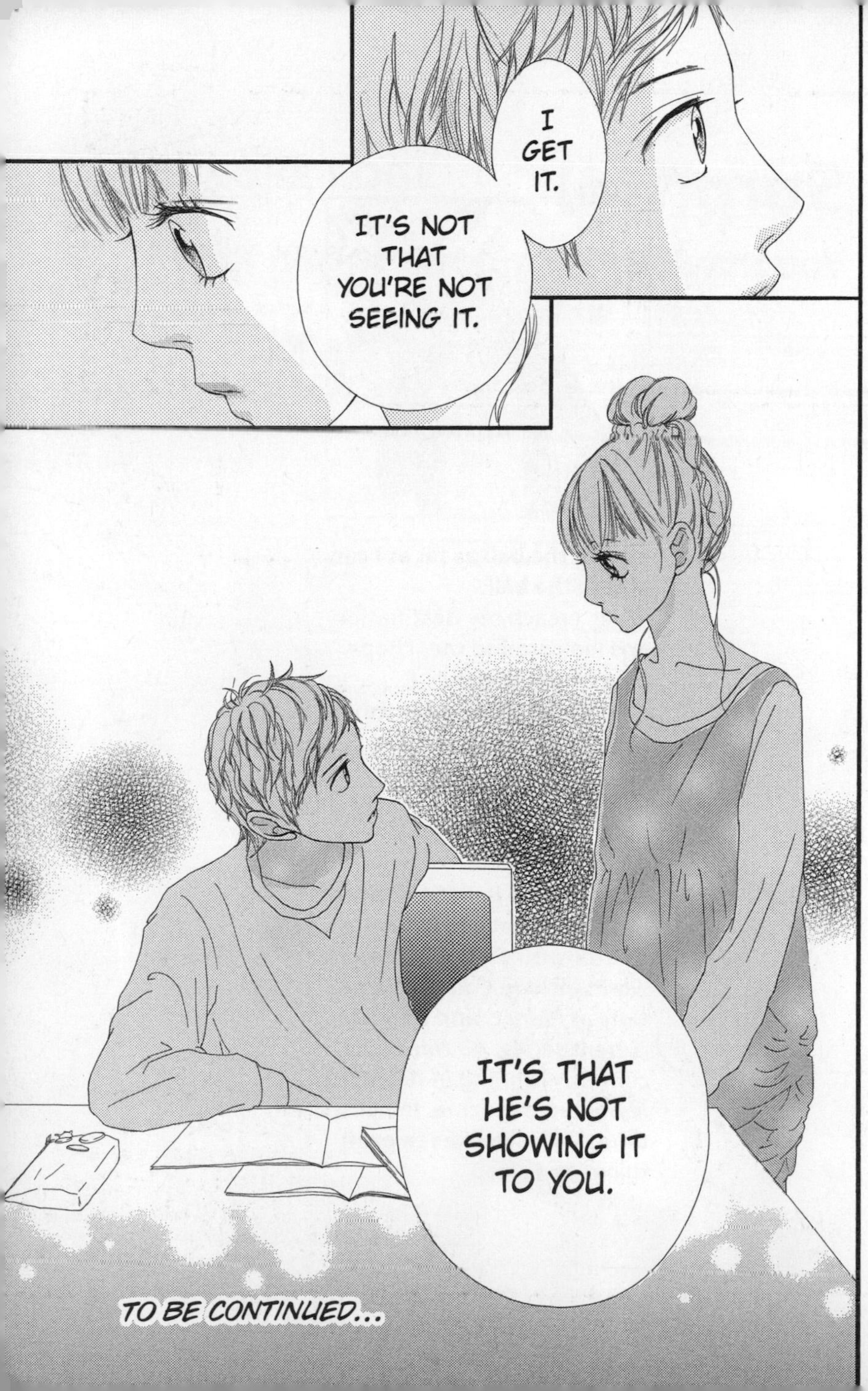
I GET IT.
IT'S NOT THAT YOU'RE NOT SEEING IT.
IT'S THAT HE'S NOT SHOWING IT TO YOU.
TO BE CONTINUED...

To be
continued...

...in
volume 5 ♪

I throw the ball as far as I can.
I chase the ball.
When I reach my destination
and look around me, I hope
that I'm smiling.
That's how I feel as I write
this story.

— Io Sakisaka

Born on June 8, Io Sakisaka
made her debut as a manga
creator with *Sakura, Chiru*. Her
works include *Call My Name*,
Gate of Planet, and *Blue*. Her
current series, *Ao Haru Ride*, is
currently running in *Bessatsu
Margaret* magazine. In her spare
time, Sakisaka likes to paint
things and sleep.

STROBE EDGE
Vol. 4
Shojo Beat Edition

STORY AND ART BY
IO SAKISAKA

English Adaptation/Ysabet MacFarlane
Translation/JN Productions
Touch-up Art & Lettering/John Hunt
Design/Shawn Carrico
Editor/Amy Yu

A CIP catalogue record for this book is available from the British Library.

Printed in the U.S.A.

Published by VIZ Media, LLC
P.O. Box 77010
San Francisco, CA 94107

10 9 8 7 6 5 4 3 2 1
First printing, May 2013

www.viz.com www.shojobeat.com

PARENTAL ADVISORY
STROBE EDGE is rated T for Teen and is recommended for ages 13 and up. This volume contains suggestive themes.
ratings.viz.com

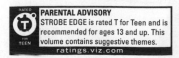

Surprise!

You may be reading the wrong way!

It's true: In keeping with the original Japanese comic format, this book reads from right to left—so action, sound effects, and word balloons are completely reversed. This preserves the orientation of the original artwork—plus, it's fun! Check out the diagram shown here to get the hang of things, and then turn to the other side of the book to get started!

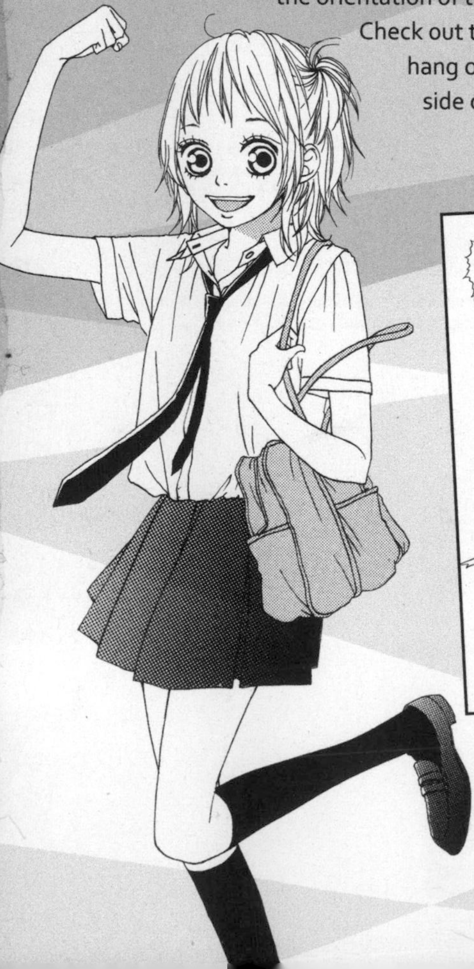

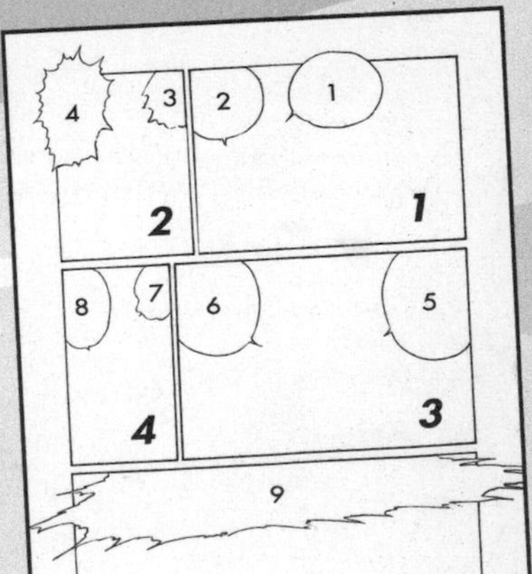
1
2
3
4
1
2
5
6
7
8
3
4
9
5
142

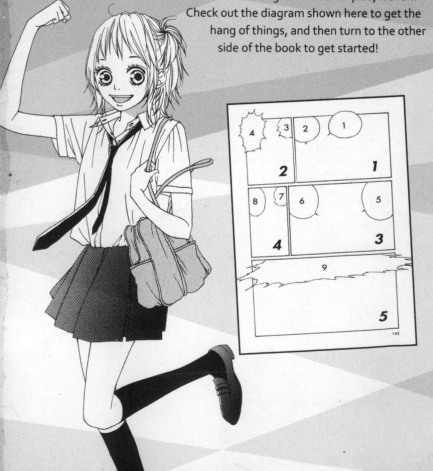